PRAXIS

SOCIAL STUDIES 0081, 5081

By: Sharon Wynne, M.S.

XAMonline, INC.
Boston

XAMonline, Inc.
21 Orient Avenue
Melrose, MA 02176
Toll Free 1-800-301-4647
Email: info@xamonline.com
Web: www.xamonline.com
Fax: 1-617-583-5552

Library of Congress Cataloging-in-Publication Data

Wynne, Sharon A.
PRAXIS Social Studies 0081, 5081 / Sharon A. Wynne
ISBN 978-1-60787-404-1
1. Social Studies 0081, 5081
2. Study Guides
3. PRAXIS
4. Teachers' Certification & Licensure
5. Careers

Disclaimer:
The opinions expressed in this publication are the sole works of XAMonline and were created independently from the National Education Association, Educational Testing Service, or any State Department of Education, National Evaluation Systems or other testing affiliates.

Between the time of publication and printing, state specific standards as well as testing formats and Web site information may change and therefore would not be included in part or in whole within this product. Sample test questions are developed by XAMonline and reflect content similar to that on real tests; however, they are not former test questions. XAMonline assembles content that aligns with state standards but makes no claims nor guarantees teacher candidates a passing score. Numerical scores are determined by testing companies such as NES or ETS and then are compared with individual state standards. A passing score varies from state to state.

Printed in the United States of America œ-1

PRAXIS Social Studies 0081, 5081
ISBN: 978-1-60787-404-1

Table of Contents

DOMAIN I

DOMAIN II

DOMAIN III

GOVERNMENT/CIVICS/POLITICAL SCIENCE 183

DOMAIN IV

GEOGRAPHY 201

DOMAIN V

ECONOMICS 225

DOMAIN VI

SAMPLE TEST 1

PRAXIS
SOCIAL STUDIES 0081, 5081

Three full Practice Tests

Now with Adaptive Assessments!

Adaptive learning is an educational method which uses computers as interactive teaching devices. Computers adapt the presentation of educational material according to students' learning needs, as indicated by their responses to questions. The technology encompasses aspects derived from various fields of study including computer science, education, and psychology.

In Computer Adaptive Testing (CAT), the test subject is presented with questions that are selected based on their level of difficulty in relation to the presumed skill level of the subject. As the test proceeds, the computer adjusts the subject's score based on their answers, continuously fine-tuning the score by selecting questions from a narrower range of difficulty.

The results are available immediately, the amount of time students spend taking tests decreases, and the tests provided more reliable information about what students know—especially those at the very low and high ends of the spectrum. With Adaptive Assessments, the skills that need more study are immediately pinpointed and reported to the student.

Adaptive assessments provide a unique way to assess your preparation for high stakes exams. The questions are asked at the mid-level of difficulty and then, based on the response, the level of difficulty is either increased or decreased. Thus, the test adapts to the competency level of the learner. This is proven method which is also used by examinations such as SAT and GRE. The Adaptive Assessment Engine used for your online self-assessment is based on a robust adaptive assessment algorithm and has been validated by a large pool of test takers. Use this robust and precise assessment to prepare for your exams.

Our Adaptive Assessments can be accessed here: **xamonline.4dlspace.com/AAE**
You will be presented with a short form to complete for your account registration.
You will need an active email address to register.

SECTION 1
ABOUT XAMONLINE

XAMonline—A Specialty Teacher Certification Company

Created in 1996, XAMonline was the first company to publish study guides for state-specific teacher certification examinations. Founder Sharon Wynne found it frustrating that materials were not available for teacher certification preparation and decided to create the first single, state-specific guide. XAMonline has grown into a company of over 1,800 contributors and writers and offers over 300 titles for the entire PRAXIS series and every state examination. No matter what state you plan on teaching in, XAMonline has a unique teacher certification study guide just for you.

XAMonline—Value and Innovation

We are committed to providing value and innovation. Our print-on-demand technology allows us to be the first in the market to reflect changes in test standards and user feedback as they occur. Our guides are written by experienced teachers who are experts in their fields. And our content reflects the highest standards of quality. Comprehensive practice tests with varied levels of rigor means that your study experience will closely match the actual in-test experience.

To date, XAMonline has helped nearly 600,000 teachers pass their certification or licensing exams. Our commitment to preparation exceeds simply providing the proper material for study—it extends to helping teachers **gain mastery** of the subject matter, giving them the **tools** to become the most effective classroom leaders possible, and ushering today's students toward a **successful future**.

SECTION 2
ABOUT THIS STUDY GUIDE

Purpose of This Guide

Is there a little voice inside of you saying, "Am I ready?" Our goal is to replace that little voice and remove all doubt with a new voice that says, "I AM READY. **Bring it on!**" by offering the highest quality of teacher certification study guides.

Organization of Content

You will see that while every test may start with overlapping general topics, each is very unique in the skills they wish to test. Only XAMonline presents custom content that analyzes deeper than a title, a subarea, or an objective. Only XAMonline presents content and sample test assessments along with **focus statements**, the deepest-level rationale and interpretation of the skills that are unique to the exam.

Title and field number of test
→Each exam has its own name and number. XAMonline's guides are written to give you the content you need to know for the specific exam you are taking. You can be confident when you buy our guide that it contains the information you need to study for the specific test you are taking.

Subareas
→These are the major content categories found on the exam. XAMonline's guides are written to cover all of the subareas found in the test frameworks developed for the exam.

Objectives
→These are standards that are unique to the exam and represent the main subcategories of the subareas/content categories. XAMonline's guides are written to address every specific objective required to pass the exam.

Focus statements
→These are examples and interpretations of the objectives. You find them in parenthesis directly following the objective. They provide detailed examples of the range, type, and level of content that appear on the test questions. **Only XAMonline's guides drill down to this level.**

How Do We Compare with Our Competitors?

XAMonline—drills down to the focus statement level.
CliffsNotes and REA—organized at the objective level
Kaplan—provides only links to content
MoMedia—content not specific to the state test

Each subarea is divided into manageable sections that cover the specific skill areas. Explanations are easy to understand and thorough. You'll find that every test answer contains a rejoinder so if you need a refresher or further review after taking the test, you'll know exactly to which section you must return.

How to Use This Book

Our informal polls show that most people begin studying up to eight weeks prior to the test date, so start early. Then ask yourself some questions: How much do you really know? Are you coming to the test straight from your teacher-education program or are you having to review subjects you haven't considered in ten years? Either way, take a **diagnostic or assessment test** first. Also, spend time on sample tests so that you become accustomed to the way the actual test will appear.

This guide comes with an online diagnostic test of 30 questions found online at *www.XAMonline.com*. It is a little boot camp to get you up for the task and reveal things about your compendium of knowledge in general. Although this guide is structured to follow the order of the test, you are not required to study in that order. By finding a time-management and study plan that fits your life you will be more effective. The results of your diagnostic or self-assessment test can be a guide for how to manage your time and point you toward an area that needs more attention.

After taking the diagnostic exam, fill out the **Personalized Study Plan** page at the beginning of each chapter. Review the competencies and skills covered in that chapter and check the boxes that apply to your study needs. If there are sections you already know you can skip, check the "skip it" box. Taking this step will give you a study plan for each chapter.

Week	Activity
8 weeks prior to test	Take a diagnostic test found at www.XAMonline.com
7 weeks prior to test	Build your Personalized Study Plan for each chapter. Check the "skip it" box for sections you feel you are already strong in. SKIP IT ☐
6-3 weeks prior to test	For each of these four weeks, choose a content area to study. You don't have to go in the order of the book. It may be that you start with the content that needs the most review. Alternately, you may want to ease yourself into plan by starting with the most familiar material.
2 weeks prior to test	Take the sample test, score it, and create a review plan for the final week before the test.
1 week prior to test	Following your plan (which will likely be aligned with the areas that need the most review) go back and study the sections that align with the questions you may have gotten wrong. Then go back and study the sections related to the questions you answered correctly. If need be, create flashcards and drill yourself on any area that you makes you anxious.

SECTION 3
ABOUT THE PRAXIS EXAMS

What Is PRAXIS?

PRAXIS II tests measure the knowledge of specific content areas in K-12 education. The test is a way of insuring that educators are prepared to not only teach in a particular subject area, but also have the necessary teaching skills to be effective. The Educational Testing Service administers the test in most states and has worked with the states to develop the material so that it is appropriate for state standards.

PRAXIS Points

1. The PRAXIS Series comprises more than 140 different tests in over 70 different subject areas.
2. Over 90% of the PRAXIS tests measure subject area knowledge.
3. The purpose of the test is to measure whether the teacher candidate possesses a sufficient level of knowledge and skills to perform job duties effectively and responsibly.
4. Your state sets the acceptable passing score.
5. Any candidate, whether from a traditional teaching-preparation path or an alternative route, can seek to enter the teaching profession by taking a PRAXIS test.
6. PRAXIS tests are updated regularly to ensure current content.

Often **your own state's requirements** determine whether or not you should take any particular test. The most reliable source of information regarding this is your state's Department of Education. This resource should have a complete list of testing centers and dates. Test dates vary by subject area and not all test dates necessarily include your particular test, so be sure to check carefully.

If you are in a teacher-education program, check with the Education Department or the Certification Officer for specific information for testing and testing timelines. The Certification Office should have most of the information you need.

If you choose an alternative route to certification you can either rely on our website at *www.XAMonline.com* or on the resources provided by an alternative

certification program. Many states now have specific agencies devoted to alternative certification and there are some national organizations as well, for example:
National Association for Alternative Certification
http://www.alt-teachercert.org/index.asp

Interpreting Test Results

Contrary to what you may have heard, the results of a PRAXIS test are not based on time. More accurately, you will be scored on the raw number of points you earn in relation to the raw number of points available. Each question is worth one raw point. It is likely to your benefit to complete as many questions in the time allotted, but it will not necessarily work to your advantage if you hurry through the test.

Follow the guidelines provided by ETS for interpreting your score. The web site offers a sample test score sheet and clearly explains how the scores are scaled and what to expect if you have an essay portion on your test.

Scores are usually available by phone within a month of the test date and scores will be sent to your chosen institution(s) within six weeks. Additionally, ETS now makes online, downloadable reports available for 45 days from the reporting date.

It is **critical** that you be aware of your own state's passing score. Your raw score may qualify you to teach in some states, but not all. ETS administers the test and assigns a score, but the states make their own interpretations and, in some cases, consider combined scores if you are testing in more than one area.

What's on the Test?

The Praxis Social Studies 081, 5081 exam lasts 2 hours and consists of 130 multiple-choice questions. The breakdown of the questions is as follows:

Category	Approximate Number of Questions	Approximate Percentage of the Test
I: United States History	29	22%
II: World History	29	22%
III: Government/Civics/Political Science	21	16%
IV: Geography	19	15%
V: Economics	19	15%
VI: Behavioral Sciences	13	10%

Question Types

You're probably thinking, enough already, I want to study! Indulge us a little longer while we explain that there is actually more than one type of multiple-choice question. You can thank us later after you realize how well prepared you are for your exam.

1. **Complete the Statement.** The name says it all. In this question type you'll be asked to choose the correct completion of a given statement. For example:

   The Dolch Basic Sight Words consist of a relatively short list of words that children should be able to:

   A. Sound out

   B. Know the meaning of

   C. Recognize on sight

   D. Use in a sentence

   The correct answer is C. In order to check your answer, test out the statement by adding the choices to the end of it.

2. **Which of the Following.** One way to test your answer choice for this type of question is to replace the phrase "which of the following" with your selection. Use this example:

   Which of the following words is one of the twelve most frequently used in children's reading texts:

   A. There

   B. This

   C. The

   D. An

   Don't look! Test your answer. ____ is one of the twelve most frequently used in children's reading texts. Did you guess C? Then you guessed correctly.

3. **Roman Numeral Choices.** This question type is used when there is more than one possible correct answer. For example:

Which of the following two arguments accurately supports the use of cooperative learning as an effective method of instruction?

I. Cooperative learning groups facilitate healthy competition between individuals in the group.

II. Cooperative learning groups allow academic achievers to carry or cover for academic underachievers.

III. Cooperative learning groups make each student in the group accountable for the success of the group.

IV. Cooperative learning groups make it possible for students to reward other group members for achieving.

A. I and II

B. II and III

C. I and III

D. III and IV

Notice that the question states there are **two** possible answers. It's best to read all the possibilities first before looking at the answer choices. In this case, the correct answer is D.

4. **Negative Questions.** This type of question contains words such as "not," "least," and "except." Each correct answer will be the statement that does **not** fit the situation described in the question. Such as:

Multicultural education is not

A. An idea or concept

B. A "tack-on" to the school curriculum

C. An educational reform movement

D. A process

Think to yourself that the statement could be anything but the correct answer. This question form is more open to interpretation than other types, so read carefully and don't forget that you're answering a negative statement.

5. **Questions that Include Graphs, Tables, or Reading Passages.** As always, read the question carefully. It likely asks for a very specific answer and not a broad interpretation of the visual. Here is a simple (though not statistically accurate) example of a graph question:

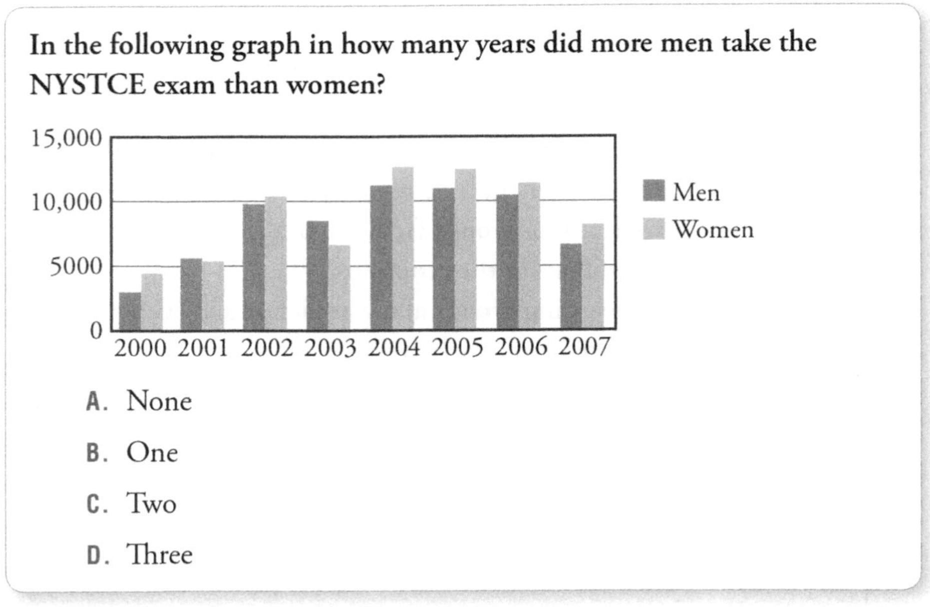

In the following graph in how many years did more men take the NYSTCE exam than women?

A. None

B. One

C. Two

D. Three

It may help you to simply circle the two years that answer the question. Make sure you've read the question thoroughly and once you've made your determination, double check your work. The correct answer is C.

SECTION 4
HELPFUL HINTS

Study Tips

1. **You are what you eat.** Certain foods aid the learning process by releasing natural memory enhancers called CCKs (cholecystokinin) composed of tryptophan, choline, and phenylalanine. All of these chemicals enhance the neurotransmitters associated with memory and certain foods release memory enhancing chemicals. A light meal or snacks of one of the following foods fall into this category:

   - Milk
   - Rice
   - Eggs
   - Fish
   - Nuts and seeds
   - Oats
   - Turkey

   The better the connections, the more you comprehend!

2. **The pen is mightier than the sword.** Learn to take great notes. A by-product of our modern culture is that we have grown accustomed to getting our information in short doses. We've subconsciously trained ourselves to assimilate information into neat little packages. Messy notes fragment the flow of information. Your notes can be much clearer with proper formatting. ***The Cornell Method*** is one such format. This method was popularized in *How to Study in College*, Ninth Edition, by Walter Pauk. You can benefit from the method without purchasing an additional book by simply looking up the method online. Below is a sample of how *The Cornell Method* can be adapted for use with this guide.

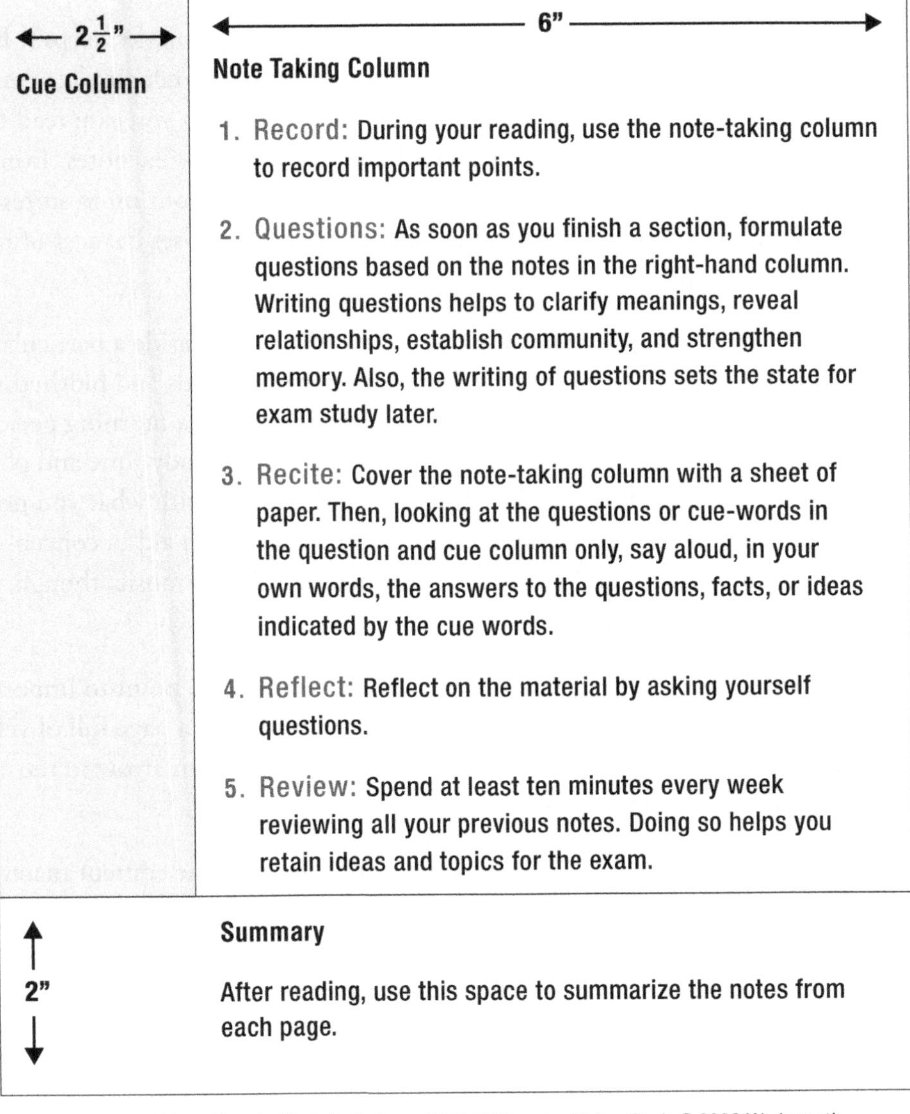

$2\frac{1}{2}$"
Cue Column
6"
Note Taking Column
1. Record: During your reading, use the note-taking column to record important points.
2. Questions: As soon as you finish a section, formulate questions based on the notes in the right-hand column. Writing questions helps to clarify meanings, reveal relationships, establish community, and strengthen memory. Also, the writing of questions sets the state for exam study later.
3. Recite: Cover the note-taking column with a sheet of paper. Then, looking at the questions or cue-words in the question and cue column only, say aloud, in your own words, the answers to the questions, facts, or ideas indicated by the cue words.
4. Reflect: Reflect on the material by asking yourself questions.
5. Review: Spend at least ten minutes every week reviewing all your previous notes. Doing so helps you retain ideas and topics for the exam.
2"
Summary
After reading, use this space to summarize the notes from each page.

**Adapted from How to Study in College, Ninth Edition, by Walter Pauk, ©2008 Wadsworth*

3. **See the forest for the trees.** In other words, get the concept before you look at the details. One way to do this is to take notes as you read, paraphrasing or summarizing in your own words. Putting the concept in terms that are comfortable and familiar may increase retention.

4. **Question authority.** Ask why, why, why? Pull apart written material paragraph by paragraph and don't forget the captions under the illustrations. For example, if a heading reads *Stream Erosion* put it in the form of a question (Why do streams erode? What is stream erosion?) then find the answer within the material. If you train your mind to think in this manner you will learn more and prepare yourself for answering test questions.

5. **Play mind games.** Using your brain for reading or puzzles keeps it flexible. Even with a limited amount of time your brain can take in data (much like a computer) and store it for later use. In ten minutes you can: read two paragraphs (at least), quiz yourself with flash cards, or review notes. Even if you don't fully understand something on the first pass, your mind stores it for recall, which is why frequent reading or review increases chances of retention and comprehension.

6. **Place yourself in exile and set the mood.** Set aside a particular place and time to study that best suits your personal needs and biorhythms. If you're a night person, burn the midnight oil. If you're a morning person set yourself up with some coffee and get to it. Make your study time and place as free from distraction as possible and surround yourself with what you need, be it silence or music. Studies have shown that music can aid in concentration, absorption, and retrieval of information. Not all music, though. Classical music is said to work best

7. **Get pointed in the right direction.** Use arrows to point to important passages or pieces of information. It's easier to read than a page full of yellow highlights. Highlighting can be used sparingly, but add an arrow to the margin to call attention to it.

The proctor will write the start time where it can be seen and then, later, provide the time remaining, typically fifteen minutes before the end of the test.

8. **Check your budget.** You should at least review all the content material before your test, but allocate the most amount of time to the areas that need the most refreshing. It sounds obvious, but it's easy to forget. You can use the study rubric above to balance your study budget.

Testing Tips

1. **Get smart, play dumb.** Sometimes a question is just a question. No one is out to trick you, so don't assume that the test writer is looking for

something other than what was asked. Stick to the question as written and don't overanalyze.

2. **Do a double take.** Read test questions and answer choices at least twice because it's easy to miss something, to transpose a word or some letters. If you have no idea what the correct answer is, skip it and come back later if there's time. If you're still clueless, it's okay to guess. Remember, you're scored on the number of questions you answer correctly and you're not penalized for wrong answers. The worst case scenario is that you miss a point from a good guess.

3. **Turn it on its ear.** The syntax of a question can often provide a clue, so make things interesting and turn the question into a statement to see if it changes the meaning or relates better (or worse) to the answer choices.

4. **Get out your magnifying glass.** Look for hidden clues in the questions because it's difficult to write a multiple-choice question without giving away part of the answer in the options presented. In most questions you can readily eliminate one or two potential answers, increasing your chances of answering correctly to 50/50, which will help out if you've skipped a question and gone back to it (see tip #2).

5. **Call it intuition.** Often your first instinct is correct. If you've been studying the content you've likely absorbed something and have subconsciously retained the knowledge. On questions you're not sure about trust your instincts because a first impression is usually correct.

6. **Graffiti.** Sometimes it's a good idea to mark your answers directly on the test booklet and go back to fill in the optical scan sheet later. You don't get extra points for perfectly blackened ovals. If you choose to manage your test this way, be sure not to mismark your answers when you transcribe to the scan sheet.

7. **Become a clock-watcher.** You have a set amount of time to answer the questions. Don't get bogged down laboring over a question you're not sure about when there are ten others you could answer more readily. If you choose to follow the advice of tip #6, be sure you leave time near the end to go back and fill in the scan sheet.

Do the Drill

No matter how prepared you feel it's sometimes a good idea to apply Murphy's Law. So the following tips might seem silly, mundane, or obvious, but we're including them anyway.

1. **Remember, you are what you eat, so bring a snack.** Choose from the list of energizing foods that appear earlier in the introduction.
2. **You're not too sexy for your test.** Wear comfortable clothes. You'll be distracted if your belt is too tight or if you're too cold or too hot.
3. **Lie to yourself.** Even if you think you're a prompt person, pretend you're not and leave plenty of time to get to the testing center. Map it out ahead of time and do a dry run if you have to. There's no need to add road rage to your list of anxieties.
4. **Bring sharp number 2 pencils.** It may seem impossible to forget this need from your school days, but you might. And make sure the erasers are intact, too.
5. **No ticket, no test.** Bring your admission ticket as well as **two** forms of identification, including one with a picture and signature. You will not be admitted to the test without these things.
6. **You can't take it with you.** Leave any study aids, dictionaries, notebooks, computers, and the like at home. Certain tests **do** allow a scientific or four-function calculator, so check ahead of time to see if your test does.
7. **Prepare for the desert.** Any time spent on a bathroom break **cannot** be made up later, so use your judgment on the amount you eat or drink.
8. **Quiet, Please!** Keeping your own time is a good idea, but not with a timepiece that has a loud ticker. If you use a watch, take it off and place it nearby but not so that it distracts you. And **silence your cell phone**.

To the best of our ability, we have compiled the content you need to know in this book and in the accompanying online resources. The rest is up to you. You can use the study and testing tips or you can follow your own methods. Either way, you can be confident that there aren't any missing pieces of information and there shouldn't be any surprises in the content on the test.

If you have questions about test fees, registration, electronic testing, or other content verification issues please visit *www.ets.org*.

Good luck!

Sharon Wynne
Founder, XAMonline

DOMAIN I
UNITED STATES HISTORY

PERSONALIZED STUDY PLAN

SKILL		KNOWN MATERIAL/ SKIP IT
1.1:	Physical geography of North America	☐
1.2:	Native American peoples	☐
1.3:	European exploration and colonization	☐
1.4:	American Revolution	☐
1.5:	Establishing a new nation	☐
1.6:	Early years of the new nation	☐
1.7:	Continued national development	☐
1.8:	Civil War era	☐
1.9:	Emergence of the modern United States	☐
1.10:	Progressive era and the First World War through the New Deal	☐
1.11:	Second World War	☐
1.12:	Post-Second World War period	☐
1.13:	Recent developments	☐

SKILL 1.1 Physical geography of North America

See Skills 1.2, 1.3, and 1.7

SKILL 1.2 Native American peoples

Tribes of North America

Native American tribes that lived throughout North America had a variety of diverse customs, different avenues of agriculture and food gathering, and variations in weapons. Their cultures were established long before European explorers arrived.

Northeastern tribes

One of the first tribes to interact with newly arrived English settlers in Plymouth, Massachusetts, was the **Wampanoag**. They were one of the Algonquian-speaking people who lived in the area from Virginia north to Hudson Bay and west to the Rocky Mountains. Their language, known as Anishinaabe or Ojibwe, became the language used for trade around the Great Lakes. The French were heavily involved in the fur trade with them.

The **Algonquians**, in what is now Canada in the Upper St. Lawrence Valley, lived in wigwams and wore clothing made from animal skins. They were proficient hunters, gatherers, and trappers. They mostly lived too far north for agriculture, although those who lived south developed corn and other crops. Conflicts with the **Iroquois** had driven them out of the Adirondack Mountains and the upper Hudson Valley.

Squanto, a Wampanoag who had been taken captive and sent to England, returned and shared his knowledge of agriculture with the English settlers; this included how to plant and cultivate corn, pumpkins, and squash.

Other famous Algonquians included **Pocahontas** and her father, **Powhatan**, both of whom are immortalized in English literature, and **Tecumseh** and **Black Hawk**, known foremost for their fierce fighting ability. The French, Dutch, and British supplied the Algonquians with firearms.

Algonquians contributed wampum (made into belts to keep records) to the Native American culture, and they celebrated the first harvest with the Pilgrims, creating the first Thanksgiving.

Powhatan

Detail from *A Map of Virginia* by Captain John Smith, 1612.

THREE SISTERS: the collective name for corn, squash, and beans, three important crops for Native Americans

Another group of tribes who lived in the Northeast were the **Iroquois**, who were fierce fighters and forward thinkers. They lived in longhouses and wore clothes made of buckskin. They, too, were expert farmers, growing the "**THREE SISTERS**" (corn, squash, and beans). Five of the Iroquois tribes formed a confederacy that was a shared form of government. **The False Face Society** was composed of a group of medicine men who shared their medical knowledge with others but kept their identities secret while doing so. Their wooden masks are an enduring symbol of the Native American era.

Southeastern tribes

Living in the Southeast were the **Seminoles** and **Creeks**, a huge collection of people who lived in chickees (open, thatch-covered houses) and wore clothes made from plant fibers. They were expert planters and hunters and were proficient at paddling dugout canoes, which they made. Their bead necklaces are considered by some to be the most beautiful on the continent. They are best known, however, for their struggle against Spanish and English settlers, especially led by the great **Osceola**.

The **Cherokee** also lived in the Southeast. One of the most advanced tribes, they lived in domed houses and wore deerskin and rabbit fur. Accomplished hunters, farmers, and fishermen, the Cherokee were known for their intricate and beautiful basketry and clay pottery. They also played a game called lacrosse, which survives to this day in countries around the world.

The Plains tribes

Between the Mississippi River to the Rocky Mountains, on the Great Plains, lived the Plains tribes, including the **Sioux**, **Cheyenne**, **Blackfeet**, **Comanche**, and **Pawnee**. When traveling, they lived in east-facing teepees made of buffalo hides, but in their villages near the streams, their homes were earth lodges. Their clothing was made from buffalo skins and deerskin. They hunted for elk, deer, and especially the buffalo. They were well known for many ceremonies, including the Sun Dance, and for war pipes and peace pipes. Some notable Plains people include **Crazy Horse** and **Sitting Bull**, authors of Gen. George Armstrong Custer's defeat at Little Bighorn, and **Sacagawea**, guide for the Lewis and Clark expedition.

Southwestern tribes

The Pueblo

Dotting the deserts of the Southwest was (and still is) a handful of tribes, including the **Acoma**, **Hopi**, **Zuni**, and **Taos**, all of whom are **Pueblo**. Their homes were made of stone or adobe. Clothing was woven from wool and cotton. Their agriculture included growing beans and domesticating turkeys; over time, they came to raise other livestock as well. One interesting cultural practice still around today are **KACHINA DOLLS**, which are given to children; the Kachina are spirits that bring rain and social good.

KACHINA DOLLS: dolls representing spirits that bring rain and social good

In 1680, a Pueblo revolt drove the Spanish out of their territories, but the Spanish reconquered them several years later. Mexican domination lasted until the close of the Mexican War, when the United States took over—and then created reservations. Pueblos are perhaps best known for the challenging vista-based villages constructed from the sheer faces of cliffs and rocks and for their adobes, mud-brick buildings that housed (and continue to house) living and meeting quarters.

Other Southwestern tribes

Another well-known southwestern tribe was the **Apache**, with their famous leader **Geronimo**. The Apache lived in homes called wickiups, which were made of bark, grass, and branches. The Apache wore cotton clothing and were excellent hunters and gatherers. Adept at basketry, the Apache believed that everything in nature had special powers and that they were honored just to be part of it all.

The **Navajo**, also residents of the Southwest, lived (and continue to live) in hogans (round homes built with forked sticks) and wore clothes of deer and rabbit skins. Their major contribution to the overall culture of the continent was in sand painting, weapon making, silversmithing, and weaving. The Navajo are known for crafting beautiful hand-woven rugs.

Northwestern Tribes

The **Northwest Coastal** tribes lived in what is now Alaska, down the coast of the Pacific Ocean to Northern California. They lived in rectangular houses constructed of cedar planks, which would be home to thirty or more people. Clothing included rain capes made from cedar. Totem poles were a mode of communication. **Chief Joseph**, the famous Nez Perce leader, tried to lead his people to Canada when they had been ordered to a reservation, and he is famous for his moving speech of surrender when the still-living among his people were trapped by the U.S. Army.

Alaska and Arctic Canada continue to be populated by the **Inuit**. Often, their homes were igloos or tents made from animal skins. Their clothes were made of animal skins, usually seal or caribou. They were excellent fishermen and hunters, crafted efficient kayaks and umiaks to take them through waterways, and made harpoons with which to hunt animals. Inuit art includes carvings from stone, whalebone, and walrus tusk, a craft extended from the creation of tools, weapons, and utensils.

SKILL 1.3 European exploration and colonization

See also Skill 2.5

AGE OF EXPLORATION: also known as the Age of Discovery, this period is marked by European world exploration and is defined as beginning in the early fifteenth century and continuing into the seventeenth century

The **AGE OF EXPLORATION** had its beginnings centuries before exploration actually took place. However, it is defined as beginning in the early fifteenth century and continuing into the seventeenth century. It is also known as the **Age of Discovery**, and it refers to European world exploration, derived from technologies for navigation, mapmaking, and advanced shipbuilding.

European Background to the Age of Exploration

The Crusades

FIRST CRUSADE: the first war waged by Christians to regain control of Jerusalem and other areas in the region; it began in 1095 CE

Prior to the period of European expansion, the rise and spread of Islam in the seventh century and its subsequent control over Jerusalem led to Pope Urban II deciding to embark on the **FIRST CRUSADE** in 1095 CE. The First Crusade resulted in Christian control of Jerusalem and other areas in the region for about two hundred years—the first western control of the region since the fall of the Roman Empire. The First Crusade marks the first organized violence against Jews. The Crusaders believed that Jews and Muslims ideally would be converted to Christianity. The Crusades, as they continued, were a political extension of Christendom.

The Rise of Italian states

As the **Byzantium Empire** declined, and Italy's city-states of **Florence**, **Genoa**, and **Venice** became wealthy from trade with Asia—spices, salt, and other luxury items. Merchant-bankers became a new rising social group who encouraged learning. A result of the decline of the Byzantium Empire was the immigration of merchants, scholars, and priests to Western Europe—along with many of the Byzantium artistic and literary treasures. One consequence was intellectual stimulation that led to the Renaissance—which began in Italy about 1300 CE.

During the ninth to twelfth centuries CE, Venice was the naval and commercial power of Europe. By the late 1200s, Venice was the most prosperous city in Europe, and it held the most valuable trade with the Muslim world. The Venetian **Marco Polo** wrote about his travels and experiences in the East. Survivors of the Crusades had made their way home from the Middle East bringing with them fascinating information about exotic lands, people, and customs, and desired foods and goods such as spices and silks.

Between sea voyages on the Indian Ocean and Mediterranean Sea and the camel caravans in central Asia and the Arabian Desert, the Italian merchants in Genoa and Venice controlled trade. Notably, the trade routes between Europe and Asia were slow, difficult, dangerous, and very expensive.

The black plague and the Renaissance

In the mid-1300s, two-thirds of the nomad Mongol population along the western trade routes came down with the **BLACK PLAGUE**. In the East, it killed two-thirds of the Chinese population. Merchants from Genoa travelled in 1346 to the Black Sea ports, caught the plague, and brought it home to Europe in 1347. Sixty percent of the population of Venice died. Approximately twenty-five million Europeans from a population of forty million died. By 1349, one-third of the people of the Islamic world were also dead from the black plague.

BLACK PLAGUE: a deadly disease that was spread through trade routes in the 14th century and killed a huge number of people worldwide

The Mongol deaths contributed to the fall of the **Mongol Empire**. The Ottoman Turks, meanwhile, were not as affected by the plague, and so the **Ottoman Empire** began to grow, while in Europe, government, trade, and commerce virtually ground to a halt.

While Jews became scapegoats for the plague, the Roman Catholic Church was also tested when people prayed in their churches and made donations, yet still lost their families to the plague. Thousands of priests and monks also died, and many people believed that God was punishing the Church.

Literate survivors in Italy began to look backward to Classical (and pagan) Rome and Greece. This inspired a renewed interest in Classical Greek culture, including:

- Art
- Architecture
- Literature
- Science
- Astronomy
- Medicine

The chaos that resulted from the plague contributed to the beginning of the **RENAISSANCE**.

RENAISSANCE: this period, named after the French word for "rebirth," is marked by a re-emergence of culture after the Dark Ages and the devastation of the black plague

Printing and navigation

Johannes Gutenberg invented the printing press in 1440 CE, and, by 1499, fifteen million books with 30,000 different titles had been published. Among those books was Ptolemy's *Geography*, which Ptolemy had first published in Egypt in 2 CE. With the advent of the printing press, numerous new maps were included in the book when it was reprinted in 1477. Maps, thus, began to reach the populace.

Just as Ptolemy had been influenced by **Hipparchus** of Greece (120–190 BCE)—who had catalogued the positions of the stars—geographers, astronomers and mapmakers of the Renaissance studied and applied the works of **Hipparchus and Ptolemy**. Notable figures in this field included the astronomer **Tycho Brahe** of Denmark and the Venetian mapmaker **Fra Mauro**.

For many centuries, maps and charts had stimulated curiosity in the West. At the same time, the Chinese were using the magnetic compass in their ships; Pacific islanders were going from island to island covering thousands of miles in open canoes navigating by sun and stars; and Arab traders were sailing all over the Indian Ocean in their **dhows**.

The Age of Exploration

These advancements in printing and navigation technologies combined with the restabilization of European culture caused the Age of Exploration to begin in earnest. By 1415, **Prince Henry of Portugal** (also called the "Navigator") encouraged, supported, and financed the Portuguese seamen who led in the search for an all-water route to Asia. A shipyard was built along with a school for teaching navigation. New types of sailing ships were built that would carry seamen safely through the ocean waters. Experiments were conducted with newer maps, newer navigational methods, and newer instruments. These included the **astrolabe** and the **compass**, enabling sailors to determine direction, as well as **latitude** and **longitude** for exact location.

Reaching the East

Although Prince Henry died in 1460, the Portuguese kept on sailing and exploring Africa's west coastline. In 1488, **Bartholomew Diaz** and his men sailed around Africa's southern tip and headed toward Asia. Diaz wanted to push on but turned back because his men were discouraged and weary from the long months at sea. Extremely fearful of the unknown, they refused to travel any further. However, the Portuguese were finally successful 10 years later in 1498 when **Vasco da Gama** and his men, continuing the route of Diaz, rounded Africa's Cape of Good Hope, sailing across the Indian Ocean, reaching India's port of Calicut (Calcutta).

Just six years after **Christopher Columbus** had sailed on his first transatlantic voyage to try to prove his theory that Asia could be reached by sailing west, reaching the New World and an entire hemisphere instead, da Gama proved Asia could be reached from Europe by sea and began the 450 years of Portuguese colonization in India, Asia, and Africa.

Long after Spain had dispatched explorers and the famed conquistadors to gather the wealth for the Spanish monarchs and their coffers, the British were searching valiantly for the **NORTHWEST PASSAGE**, a land–sea route across North America and to the open sea that would lead to the wealth of Asia. It was not until after the Lewis and Clark Expedition that Captains Meriwether Lewis and William Clark proved conclusively that there simply was no Northwest Passage. It did not exist.

NORTHWEST PASSAGE: a land–sea route across North America and to the open sea that would lead to the wealth of Asia

However, this did not deter exploration and settlement. Spain, France, and England, along with some participation by the Dutch, led the way in taking Western European civilization to the **NEW WORLD**. These three nations had strong monarchial governments and were struggling for dominance and power in Europe. Between its privateers and its defeat of Spain's mighty **Armada** in 1588, England became the undisputed mistress of the seas. Spain lost its power and influence in Europe, and it was left to France and England to carry on their rivalry.

NEW WORLD: the term used by the Europeans to refer to the Americas during the Age of Exploration

This search for passage to Asia led to eventual British control in Asia in what is now India, Pakistan, Kashmir, Sri Lanka, and Myanmar (formerly called Burma), the southern part of Yemen (formerly called Aden), the Malay Peninsula, Singapore, Hong Kong, and Kuwait.

European exploration of the New World

Columbus, a Genoan sailing for Spain, is credited with the discovery of America although he never set foot on its soil. **Magellan**, a Portuguese sailing for Spain, is credited with the first circumnavigation of the Earth. **Amerigo Vespucci**, from Florence and sailing for Spain and Portugal, recognized, unlike Columbus, that he was not in Asia when he came upon Brazil; the Americas were named after him. Other Spanish explorers made their marks in parts of what are now the United States, Mexico, and Central and South America. They included **Pizarro**, **Cortez**, **Ponce de Leon**, **Balboa**, **de Soto**, and **Coronado**.

For France, claims to various parts of North America were the result of the efforts of such men as **Champlain**, **Cartier**, **LaSalle**, **Father Marquette**, and **Joliet**. Dutch claims were based on the work of **Henry Hudson**. **John Cabot** gave England its stake in North America along with **John Hawkins**, **Sir Francis Drake**, and the half-brothers **Sir Walter Raleigh** and **Sir Humphrey Gilbert**.

Colonists from England, France, Holland, Sweden, and Spain all settled in North America, on lands populated by Native Americans. Spanish colonies were mainly in the south and west; French colonies were located in the extreme north and in the middle of the continent; and the rest of the European colonies were founded mainly in the northeast and along the Atlantic coast.

British Colonies in the New World

The English colonies were divided generally into three regions: New England, Middle Atlantic, and Southern. The culture of each was distinct and affected attitudes, ideas toward politics, religion, and economic activities. The geography of each region also contributed to its unique characteristics.

New England

NEW ENGLAND: the colonies of Massachusetts, Rhode Island, Connecticut, and New Hampshire

The **NEW ENGLAND** colonies consisted of Massachusetts, Rhode Island, Connecticut, and New Hampshire. The vast majority of the settlers shared similar origins, coming from England and Scotland. Life in these colonies centered on the towns, because town boundaries would be drawn up as soon as some residents arranged to incorporate. The predominant form of government was the town meeting, where all adult males met to make the laws, and a board of selectmen had executive authority. The legislative body, the General Court, consisted of an upper and lower house.

The meadows where pilgrims first farmed in New England were actually the farms of Native Americans who died of smallpox and measles introduced by the colonists. In addition to using these meadows, the colonists cut down forest and cleared land for farming. Short summers made for short growing seasons. Additionally, the soil was generally not superior for farming. An average farm had twenty acres; corn was the leading crop. Fish was a dietary mainstay, and ground fishing became a New England industry. In addition, New Englanders exported furs and lumber, developed granite quarries, and ultimately developed a textile industry.

The Middle Atlantic colonies

MIDDLE OR MIDDLE ATLANTIC COLONIES: the colonies of New York, New Jersey, Pennsylvania, and Delaware

The **MIDDLE** or **MIDDLE ATLANTIC COLONIES** included New York, New Jersey, Pennsylvania, and Delaware. New York and New Jersey were at one time the Dutch colony of New Netherland, and Delaware at one time was named New Sweden.

From their beginnings, these four colonies were made up of settlers from many different nations and backgrounds. The main economic activity was farming, and the settlers were scattered over the countryside cultivating their rather large farms. The Native Americans did not threaten the colonists here as much as in New England. The soil was very fertile, the land was gently rolling, and a milder climate provided a longer growing season. The farms produced a large surplus of food, which provided for the colonists themselves and was also used for export. This colonial region became known as the "breadbasket" of the New World, and the New York and Philadelphia seaports were constantly filled with ships being loaded with dried meat, wheat, flour, corn, beans, butter, and sheep and hogs bound for the West Indies in particular. At least half of all ships sailed to the

Indies to feed the population whose only crop, in many cases, was sugar. The sugar was grown to make molasses, which was made into rum in the colonists' rum distilleries in Rhode Island and Massachusetts.

Other economic activities included shipbuilding, iron mining, and the production of items such as paper, glass, textiles, kettles, pots, pans, wrought iron, stove plates, nails, and wire so that these items did not need to be imported.

In the middle colonies, there was a standard government structure, including a royal governor, a governor's council, and a colonial legislature. The legislative body in Pennsylvania was unicameral, meaning it consisted of one house. In the other four colonies, the legislative body had two houses. Unlike in the New England colonies, church and government were separate.

Southern colonies

The **SOUTHERN COLONIES** were Maryland, Virginia, North and South Carolina, and Georgia. Virginia was the first permanent successful English colony and Georgia was the last. The year 1619 was a very important year in the history of Virginia and the United States with three significant events:

SOUTHERN COLONIES: the colonies of Maryland, Virginia, North and South Carolina, and Georgia

1. Some sixty women were sent to Virginia to marry and establish families
2. About twenty Africans, the first of thousands, arrived to be slaves
3. Virginia colonists were granted the right to self-government, and they began electing their own representatives to the House of Burgesses, their own legislative body

SKILL 1.4 American Revolution

The American Revolution, or War for Independence, was largely due to economic and political changes.

European Struggle for Supremacy

After 1750 when England defeated its Armada, Spain was no longer the most powerful nation in Europe. The remaining rivalry was between Britain and France. They did not know how to coexist peacefully together; war was their solution. For nearly twenty-five years, between 1689 and 1748, these two powers had engaged in a series of armed conflicts. Those conflicts that were fought in North America are known as the **FRENCH AND INDIAN WARS.**

FRENCH AND INDIAN WARS: the name for the conflicts between the British and French colonial empires

- The War of the League of Augsburg in Europe, 1689 to 1697, also called **King William's War** and the **Nine Years War**, took place mostly in Flanders, but became the first French and Indian War

- The War of the Spanish Succession, 1702 to 1713, also called **Queen Anne's War**, became the second French and Indian War
- The War of the Austrian Succession, 1740 to 1748, also called **King George's War**, was the third French and Indian War

Britain and France fought for possession of colonies—especially in Asia, the Caribbean, and North America—and for control of the seas. But none of these conflicts was decisive.

The final conflict, which decided once and for all who was the most powerful, was the fourth French and Indian War. In Europe where it began, it is known as the **Seven Years' War** and in Canada the **War of the Conquest.** No matter what name is used, this war caused over a million deaths and, in the twentieth century, Winston Churchill called it a world war because it took place in Europe, Asia, and North America. The result was the end of France's reign as a major colonial power in North America and in Great Britain becoming the dominant power in the world.

American Colonists in the French and Indian War

In America, both sides had advantages and disadvantages. The British colonies were well established and consolidated in a smaller area than the French settlements that were scattered over roughly half of the continent. In addition, British colonists outnumbered French colonists 23 to 1. But the French settlements were united under one government and were quick to act and cooperate when necessary, while the British colonies had separate, individual governments and seldom cooperated. In Europe, France was the more powerful of the two nations. In addition, the French had many more Native American allies than did the British.

Both sides had stunning victories and humiliating defeats. If one person could be given credit for British victory, it would have to be **William Pitt.** He was a strong leader, enormously energetic, supremely self-confident, and determined on complete British victory. Despite the advantages and military victories of the French, Pitt succeeded.

Pitt got rid of the incompetents in the army and replaced them with men who could do the job. He sent more troops to America, strengthened the British Navy, and gave the officers of the colonial militia equal rank to the British officers. In short, he saw to it that Britain took the offensive and kept it until they emerged victorious.

The British victory in Canada

Of all the British victories, perhaps the most crucial was winning Canada.

The French depended on the **ST. LAWRENCE RIVER** for transporting supplies, soldiers, and messages. The river was the link between New France and France. Tied into this waterway system were the connecting links of the Great Lakes and the Mississippi River and its tributaries. Along the waterway system were scattered French forts, trading posts, and small settlements.

ST. LAWRENCE RIVER: the river that was the link between New France and France

William Pitt ordered the bombardment of **Louisburg** on Cape Breton Island in 1758, and the British captured Louisburg. This gave the British Navy a base of operations and prevented French reinforcements and supplies from getting to their troops. Under Pitt's direction, other forts fell to the British, including:

Of all the British victories, perhaps the most crucial was winning Canada.

- Frontenac
- Duquesne
- Crown Point
- Ticonderoga
- Niagara forts in the Upper Ohio Valley

Although Spain entered the war in 1762 to aid France, Quebec and finally Montreal fell to the British onslaught; the British victory was complete.

Peace and British Supremacy

In 1763, representatives from Spain, France, and Britain met in Paris to draw up the **Treaty of Paris**. Among Great Britain's prizes were most of India and all French territory in North America east of the Mississippi River, excluding New Orleans. Though Britain received control of Florida from Spain, control of Cuba and the islands of the Philippines were returned to the Spanish. France lost nearly all of its possessions in America and India but was allowed to keep islands in the Caribbean: Guadeloupe, Martinique, Haiti on Hispaniola, and St. Lucia. They also retained control of Miquelon and St. Pierre, a group of small islands off Newfoundland. France gave Spain New Orleans as well as the vast territory of Louisiana west of the Mississippi River.

British victories occurred all around the world: in India, in the Mediterranean, and in Europe.

Britain was now the most powerful nation on Earth.

The Britsh Trade System

Where did this leave the British colonies? **Colonial militias** had fought with the British and benefited, as the militias and their officers gained much fighting experience. The thirteen colonies began to realize that cooperating with each other was the best way to ensure their defense. This idea was reinforced with the eventual War for Independence and construction of a new national government.

By the end of the French and Indian War in 1763, Britain's American colonies numbered thirteen, and it had other colonies scattered around the world. Like all other countries, Britain strove to have a strong economy and a favorable balance of trade. That required wealth, self-sufficiency, and a powerful army and navy.

Imperial British legislation

The British colonies, with few exceptions, were considered commercial ventures, and their purpose was to make a profit for the Crown and for the financiers. The colonies would provide raw materials for the industries in England, and the colonies would be a market for finished products from England. The British built a strong merchant fleet to carry and protect their commodities, and this desire to dominate world trade led to the **NAVIGATION ACTS**.

NAVIGATION ACTS: laws enacted between 1607 and 1763 to help Britain get and keep a favorable trade balance

Navigation Acts

Between 1607 and 1763, the British Parliament enacted different laws to assist in getting and keeping a favorable trade balance. One series of laws required that most manufacturing be done only in England. Another law prohibited exporting any wool or woolen cloth from the colonies and the manufacture of beaver hats or iron products. There were other acts, however, that had greater impact upon the colonies.

The **Navigation Acts of 1651** put restrictions on shipping and trade within the British Empire, banning foreign ships from transporting goods to its colonies and banning foreign ships from transporting goods from elsewhere in Europe to England. These laws were directly focused upon the Dutch, who were successful in international shipping.

Those trading within the empire were also required to utilize British ships. This increased the strength of the British merchant fleet and greatly benefited the American colonists. Since they were British citizens, they could own, build, and operate their own vessels. By the end of the French and Indian War, the shipyards in the colonies were building one-third of the merchant ships under the British flag. There were quite a number of wealthy merchants among the colonists.

The **Navigation Act of 1660** and **the Staple Act of 1663** required all European goods heading for the colonies to go through an English port first. A tax was charged that raised the prices and lengthened shipping times. Britain needed to not only protect itself from the competition of European rivals but to protect its merchant ships from enemy ships and pirates as well.

The Buildup to Revolution

Triangular trade

The New England and Middle Atlantic colonies at first felt threatened by these laws since they had started producing many of the same products being produced in Britain. But they soon found new markets for their goods and began their own **triangular trade**.

Colonial vessels started the first part of the triangle by sailing for Africa, loaded with kegs of rum from colonial distilleries. On Africa's West Coast, the rum was traded for either gold or slaves. The second part of the triangle was from Africa to the West Indies, where slaves were traded for molasses, sugar, or money. The third part of the triangle was from the West Indies to home, bringing sugar or molasses to make rum and also gold and silver.

Failing British policy

The major concern of the British government was that this triangular trade violated the 1733 **MOLASSES ACT**. Planters in the British West Indies wanted the colonists to buy all of their molasses, but these islands could provide the traders with only about one-eighth of the amount of molasses needed for distilling the rum. The colonists had to buy the rest of what was needed from the French, Dutch, and Spanish islands, and they then evaded the law and did not pay the high **duty** to Britain on the molasses bought from these islands.

MOLASSES ACT: an act passed by the British government that imposed a large tax on molasses bought from non-British merchants

If Britain had enforced the Molasses Act, financial ruin would likely have occurred. So for this act and all the other mercantile laws, the British government followed the policy of **SALUTARY NEGLECT**, deliberately failing to enforce the laws.

SALUTARY NEGLECT: a policy whereby a government deliberately fails to enforce its laws

Changing British Policy

In 1763, after the French and Indian War, Britain needed money for several reasons. The important needs were:

- To pay the British war debt
- To defend the empire
- To pay for the governing of its colonies scattered across the Earth

The British government decided to adopt a new colonial policy and pass laws to raise revenue. It was reasoned that the colonists were subjects of the King, and since the King and his ministers had spent a great deal of money defending and protecting them, it was only right and fair that the colonists should help pay the costs of defense—especially the American colonists. The earlier laws passed had been for the purposes of regulating production and trade and had generally put money into colonial pockets. These new laws would take some of that rather hard-earned money out of their pockets. To the colonists, this was unjust and illegal.

As the proportion of English-born colonists decreased and the diversity of settlers increased, fewer and fewer colonists felt a cultural tie to the country that held influence over the colonies' trade and government.

As the proportion of English-born colonists decreased and the diversity of settlers increased, fewer and fewer colonists felt a cultural tie to the country that held influence over the colonies' trade and government. Divisions between the colonies became more pronounced as settlers of differing religious and national groups established themselves.

Though England's influence had been passive until this point, it remained in control of much of the colonies' political affairs as well. Each colony had a lower **legislative assembly** that was elected and a higher council and governor that were elected or appointed in different ways depending on the how the colony was organized initially. In most colonies, the **councils** and **governors** were appointed by the King of England, British property owners, or agencies. In **corporate colonies**, the council and governors were elected by colonial property owners who maintained a close connection to England.

Thus, while the colonies were allowed to determine their own taxes and regulate much of their daily lives through representation in the colonial assemblies, Britain maintained control of international affairs and international trade by controlling the upper levels of colonial government. In practice, Britain allowed the colonies to go about their business without interference, largely because the colonies were providing important raw materials to the home country.

The History of Colonial Defense

The first glimmers of dissent from the colonies came during the French and Indian War when colonial **militias** were raised to fight the French in America. Conflict arose with Britain over who should control these militias. The colonies wanted the assemblies to have authority. Britain's victory over France, and its subsequent need for funds, only increased tensions with the American colonies.

Residents of the 13 colonies had begun to speak out about how cooperation was important for their defense. Fresh in their minds was the French (and their Native American allies) defeat of **Maj. George Washington** and his militia at **Fort Necessity in 1754**. This left the entire northern frontier of the British colonies vulnerable and open to attack. In the wake of this, **Benjamin Franklin** proposed to the colonies that they unite permanently to be able to defend themselves.

Delegates from 7 of the 13 colonies met at Albany, New York, in 1754 with the representatives from the **Iroquois Confederation** at the request of British officials. But Franklin's proposal, known as the **Albany Plan of Union**, was rejected by the colonists, along with a similar proposal from the British. Delegates simply did not want each of the colonies to lose its right to act independently. However, a seed was planted.

The Buildup to Revolution

Before 1763, except for trade and supplying raw materials, the colonies had mostly been left to themselves. England looked on them merely as part of an economic or commercial empire. Little consideration was given to how they were to conduct their daily affairs, so the colonists became independent, self-reliant, and skilled at handling daily affairs. This, in turn, gave rise to leadership, initiative, achievement, and vast experience. In fact, there was a far greater degree of **independence** and **self-government** in America than could be found in Britain or the major countries on the continent or any other colonies anywhere.

Political setup in the Colonies

In America, as new towns and counties were formed, the practice of representation in government began. Representatives to the colonial **legislative assemblies** were elected from the district in which they lived, chosen by qualified property-owning male voters, and they represented the interests of the political district from which they were elected. Most of the thirteen colonies also had a royal governor appointed by the King, representing his interests in the colonies. Nevertheless, the colonial legislative assemblies controlled the purse strings by having the power to vote on all issues involving money to be spent by the colonial governments.

Political setup in England

Quite different from the colonial setup was the established government in England. Members of **Parliament** were not elected to represent their own districts. They were considered representative of classes, not individuals. If some members of a professional or commercial class or some landed interests were able to elect representatives, then those classes or special interests were represented. It had nothing at all to do with numbers or territories. Some large population centers had no **direct representation** at all, yet the people there considered themselves represented by men elected from their particular class or interest somewhere else. Consequently, it was extremely difficult for the English to understand why the American merchants and landowners claimed they were not represented; the English accepted that Parliament represented the best interests of the Empire and, therefore, the best interests of the colonies.

The colonists' protest of "**No taxation without representation**" was meaningless to the English. Parliament represented the entire nation, was completely unlimited in legislation, and had become supreme. The colonists were

There were now two different environments: the older, traditional British system and the American system with its new ideas and different ways of doing things.

QUARTERING ACT: required the colonists to provide supplies and living quarters for the British troops

PROCLAMATION OF 1763: prohibited American colonists from making any settlements west of the Appalachians until provided for by treaties with the Native Americans

SUGAR ACT OF 1764: required efficient collection of taxes on molasses brought into the colonies from other than British sources and permitted British officials to conduct searches of any suspicious premises

STAMP ACT OF 1765: levied a tax on newspapers, legal documents, and other printed material

DECLARATORY ACT: stated that Parliament had the right to make all laws for the colonies and denied their right to be taxed only by colonial legislatures

incensed at this English attitude and considered their colonial legislative assemblies equal to Parliament, a position that was totally unacceptable in England.

Contrasting traditions

In a new country, a new environment has little or no tradition, institutions, or vested interests. New ideas and traditions grew quickly in America, pushing aside what was left of the old ideas and old traditions. By 1763, Britain had changed its perception of its American colonies to their being a "territorial" empire. The stage was set and the conditions were right for a showdown.

Increasing Tensions

In 1763, Parliament decided to place a standing army in North America to reinforce British control. In 1765, the **QUARTERING ACT** was passed requiring the colonists to provide supplies and living quarters for the British troops. In addition, efforts by the British were made to keep the peace by establishing good relations with the Native Americans. The **PROCLAMATION OF 1763** prohibited any American colonists from making any settlements west of the Appalachians until provided for by treaties with the Native Americans.

The **SUGAR ACT OF 1764** required efficient collection of taxes on molasses that was brought into the colonies from other than British sources and gave British officials free license to conduct searches of the premises of anyone suspected of violating the law. Furthermore, the colonists were taxed on newspapers, legal documents, and other printed material under the **STAMP ACT OF 1765**.

Colonial response to British legislation

Nine colonies assembled in New York to call for repeal of the Stamp Act. At the same time, a group of New York City merchants organized a protest to stop the importation of British goods. Similar protests arose in Philadelphia and Boston and other merchant cities, often erupting in violence. Britain's representatives in the colonies—the governors and members of the **cabinet** and **council**—were sometimes the targets of these protests. Although a stamp tax was already in use in England, the colonists would have none of it. Hoping to curb the uproar of rioting and mob violence, Parliament repealed the tax.

Of course, great exultation resulted when news of the repeal reached America. But attached to the repeal was the small, quiet **DECLARATORY ACT**. This Act plainly and unequivocally stated that Parliament still had the right to make all laws for the colonies, and it denied their right to be taxed only by colonial legislatures.

Other acts leading up to armed conflict included the **TOWNSHEND ACTS** passed in

1767, which taxed lead, paint, paper, and tea brought into the colonies. This also increased anger and tension, resulting in the British sending troops to New York City and Boston. In Boston, mob violence provoked retaliation by the troops. The result was the deaths of five people and the wounding of eight others. The so-called **BOSTON MASSACRE** of 1770 shocked Americans and British alike.

The Tea Party and British retaliation

When Britain proposed that the **East India Company** be allowed to import tea to the colonies without customs duty, the colonists were faced with a dilemma. They could purchase the tea at a much lower price than the smuggled Dutch tea they had been drinking. However, the colonists feared that the **Tea Act** would encourage monopolies that would hurt the colonists. The **BOSTON TEA PARTY** was the result. In December 1773, a group of colonists seized a shipment of British tea in Boston Harbor and dumped it into the sea.

Britain responded punitively with a series of even more restrictive acts, driving the colonies to come together in the **First Continental Congress** to make a unified demand that Britain remove these **INTOLERABLE ACTS**, as they were called by the colonists. The punitive measures included:

- Boston's port was closed
- The royal governor of the colony of Massachusetts was given increased power
- The colonists were compelled to house and feed the British soldiers

Also in 1774, the passage of the **QUEBEC ACT** extended the limits of that Canadian colony's boundary southward to include territory located north of the Ohio River.

The colonists organize

The colonists naturally began to organize their resistance. The underground patriot organization called the **SONS OF LIBERTY** began by undermining the Stamp Act, and the **COMMITTEE OF CORRESPONDENCE** communicated opposition and resistance to Acts throughout the colonies and arranged for written communications to be distributed to foreign governments.

Delegates from 12 colonies met in Philadelphia on September 5, 1774, in the First Continental Congress. They opposed acts of lawlessness and wanted some form of peaceful settlement with Britain. They still maintained American loyalty to Britain, however, and affirmed Parliament's power over colonial and foreign affairs. They did insist on repeal of the Intolerable Acts and demanded ending all trade with Britain until this took place. The reply from **George III** was an insistence that the colonies submit to British rule or be crushed.

Britain stood firm and sought to dissolve the colonial assemblies that were coming

TOWNSHEND ACTS: laws passed in 1767 to tax lead, paint, paper, and tea brought into the colonies

BOSTON MASSACRE: an event precipitated by colonial mob violence against British troops; it resulted in the death of five people and the wounding of eight others

BOSTON TEA PARTY: a 1773 event, in which colonists dumped English tea into Boston Harbor to protest English tariffs

INTOLERABLE ACTS: a series of restrictive acts imposed by the British to punish the rebellious colonists

QUEBEC ACT: extended the limits of the Canadian colony's boundary southward to include territory located north of the Ohio River

SONS OF LIBERTY: an

COMMITTEE OF CORRESPONDENCE: a group of colonists who communicated opposition and resistance to British acts throughout the colonies and arranged for written communications to be distributed to foreign governments

forth in opposition to British policies, stockpiling weapons, and preparing militias. When the British military in America were ordered to break up the illegal meeting of the Massachusetts' assembly outside Boston, they were met with armed resistance at **LEXINGTON AND CONCORD** on April 19, 1775. The **Revolutionary War** was underway.

The Revolutionary War

The **Second Continental Congress** met in Philadelphia on May 10, 1775, to conduct the business of war and government for the next six years. Many of the delegates recommended a declaration of independence from Britain. The group established an army and commissioned George Washington as its commander.

LEXINGTON AND CONCORD: the location of first battle of the Revolutionary War, in Massachusetts on April 19, 1775

DECLARATION OF INDEPENDENCE: this document officially stated colonial independence from Britain; it was an outgrowth of ancient Greek ideas of democracy and individual rights along with the ideas of the European Enlightenment and the Renaissance

The Declaration of Independence is an important historical document because it expounds the inherent rights of all people.

The Declaration of Independence

The **DECLARATION OF INDEPENDENCE** is an outgrowth of ancient Greek ideas of democracy and individual rights along with the ideas of the European Enlightenment, the Renaissance, and, most notably, the ideology of the English political thinker **John Locke**. **Thomas Jefferson** (1743–1826), the principal author of the Declaration, borrowed much from Locke's theories and writings.

John Locke was one of the most influential political writers of the seventeenth century. He placed great emphasis on human rights and put forth the belief that when governments violate those rights, people should rebel. His book *Two Treatises of Government* (1690) had tremendous influence on political thought in the American colonies, helping to shape the Declaration of Independence and the U.S. Constitution.

Jefferson applied Locke's principles to the contemporary American situation. In the Declaration, Jefferson argued that the reigning King George Ill repeatedly violated the rights of the colonists as subjects of the British Crown.

The colonial petition for redress of grievances was guaranteed by the **Declaration of Rights of 1689**, the British Bill of Rights. According to the Declaration of Independence, King George III was establishing "an absolute Tyranny over these States." The Declaration of Independence then states: "To prove this, let Facts be submitted to a candid world," and lists the King's violations, going on to say: "That these united Colonies are, and of Right ought to be Free and Independent States, that they are Absolved from all Allegiance to the British Crown, and that all political connection between them and the State of Great Britain, is and ought to be totally dissolved."

Philosophical differences between Jefferson and Locke

Jefferson's view of **natural rights** was much broader than Locke's and less tied to the idea of **property rights**. Jefferson's famous line in the Declaration about people's right to "life, liberty and the pursuit of happiness" was based upon Locke's idea of "life, liberty, and private property." Jefferson substituted the idea that human happiness is a fundamental right that is the duty of a government to protect.

Locke and Jefferson both stressed that an individual citizen's rights are superior to and more important than any obligation to the state. Government is the servant of the people, and, likewise, the officials of government hold their positions to ensure that the rights of the people are preserved and protected by that government. The citizen comes first; the government comes second.

The military campaign begins

In June 1775, British forces had attacked patriot strongholds at **Breed's Hill** and **Bunker Hill**. Although the colonists withdrew, the British suffered heavy losses. The next month King George III declared the American colonies to be in a state of rebellion. The war began in earnest.

Although the colonial army was quite small in comparison to the British army, and although it was lacking in formal military training, the colonists had learned a new method of warfare from the Native Americans. To be sure, many battles were fought in the traditional style, with two lines of soldiers facing off and firing weapons. But the patriots had an advantage: the knowledge of **GUERILLA WARFARE**—fighting from behind trees and other defenses, and, more important, fighting on the run.

GUERILLA WARFARE: a type of warfare that includes fighting from behind trees and other defenses, and, more important, fighting on the run

By 1776, the colonists and their representatives in the Second Continental Congress realized that things were past the point of no return. On July 3, 1776, British Gen. **William Howe** arrived in New York harbor with 10,000 troops to prepare for an attack on the city. The next day, July 4, 1776, the Declaration of Independence was drafted and declared.

Turning the tide

The first American victory of the Revolutionary War was the result of a surprise attack, led by George Washington on British-Hessian troops at Trenton, New Jersey. Washington and his men crossed the icy **Delaware River** on Christmas Day 1776 and attacked the next day, completely surprising the British. It helped to restore American morale.

Washington labored against tremendous odds to wage a victorious war. Although the suffering of troops during the winter of 1777–1778 at **Valley Forge** is part of American folklore, other winter ordeals were probably worse. Valley Forge is well known because Washington stressed his army's suffering in order to gain political support. However, the army's discipline and efficiency improved during that winter, which marked a turning point in the war. Thus, the encampment became a symbol of endurance in adversity.

TREATY OF PARIS: signed in 1783, this treaty ended the Revolutionary War

The turning point in America's favor occurred in 1777 with the American victory at **Saratoga**. This victory led to the French aligning themselves with the Americans against the British. With the aid of Admiral **Francois Joseph-Paul deGrasse** and French warships blocking the entrance to Chesapeake Bay, British Gen. **Charles Cornwallis** was trapped at **Yorktown**, Virginia. He surrendered in 1781, and the war was over. The **TREATY OF PARIS** officially ending the war was signed in 1783.

SKILL 1.5 Establishing a new nation

When the war began, the colonies began to establish state governments. To a significant extent, the government that was defined for the new nation was intentionally weak. The colonies/states feared centralized government, so the first government was a very decentralized system of loosely bound states. This lack of continuity between the individual governments was confusing and economically damaging.

The Articles of Conferation

ARTICLES OF CONFEDERATION: the states' first attempt to codify self-governance after the Revolution; it was a very decentralized system, whereby states held most of the political power themselves

The **ARTICLES OF CONFEDERATION** was the first attempt of the newly independent states to reach an understanding. This was the first political system under which the newly independent colonies tried to organize themselves. It was drafted soon after the Declaration of Independence and was passed by the Continental Congress on November 15, 1777. After **ratification** by the 13 states, it took effect on March 1, 1781.

The newly independent states were unwilling to give too much power to a national government. After fighting Great Britain, they certainly did not want to replace one harsh ruler with another. After many debates, the Articles were accepted.

Government structure provided by the Articles

Each state agreed to send delegates to the **Congress**. Each state had one vote in the Congress. The Articles gave Congress the power to:

- Declare war
- Appoint military officers
- Coin money

The Congress was also responsible for foreign affairs. The Articles of Confederation limited the powers of Congress by giving the states final authority. Although Congress could pass laws, at least nine of the thirteen states had to approve a law before it went into effect. Congress could not pass any laws regarding taxes. To get money, Congress had to ask each state for it; no state could be forced to pay.

Problems with the Articles

Because the Articles created a loose alliance among the thirteen states, the **national government** was weak, in part, because it did not have a strong chief executive to carry out laws passed by the legislature. This weak national government might have worked if the states were able to get along with each other. However, many different disputes arose, and there was no way of settling them.

The government under the Articles had solved some of the postwar problems but had serious weaknesses. These included a lack of power to:

- Regulate finances
- Manage interstate trade and foreign trade
- Enforce treaties
- Coordinate military power

In addition, the delegates to Congress had no real authority, as each state carefully and jealously guarded its own interests and limited powers under the Articles. Something more efficient was needed.

CONSTITUTION: replacing the Articles of Confederation, this document provided a more centralized form of government and became the foundation of government in the United States; it serves as a model for representative government throughout the world

The Constitution

In May 1787, delegates from all states except Rhode Island began meeting in Philadelphia. At first, they met to revise the Articles of Confederation, but they soon realized that much more was needed. So they set out to write a new **CONSTITUTION**, which became the foundation of government in the United States and a model for **representative government** throughout the world.

The Constitutional Convention

The first order of business was the agreement among all the delegates that the convention would be kept secret. No discussion of the convention outside of the meeting room would be allowed. Delegates wanted to be able to discuss, argue, and agree among themselves before presenting the completed document to the American people. Also, the delegates were afraid that if the people were aware of what was taking place before it was completed, then the entire country would be plunged into argument and dissension. It would be extremely difficult, if not impossible, to settle differences and come to an agreement. The delegates were smart enough, however, to make sure that the proceedings of the event were recorded. Between the official notes kept and the complete notes of (future President) James Madison, a thorough picture of the events of the **Constitutional Convention** is available.

The delegates who went to Philadelphia represented different areas and different interests. They all agreed on the need for a **strong central government** but not one with unlimited powers. They also agreed that no one part of government could control the rest. It would be a **republican** form of government (sometimes referred to as **representative democracy**) in which the supreme power was in the hands of the voters who would elect the men that would govern for them.

VIRGINIA PLAN: a representation plan for the Constitution whereby state population would determine the number of representatives sent to Congress

NEW JERSEY PLAN: a representation plan for the Constitution whereby each state would have equal representation

GREAT COMPROMISE: also known as the Connecticut Compromise, this proposition combined both the Virginia and New Jersey Plans by creating a bicameral legislature—one body for each plan

Constitutional compromises

Representation

One of the first serious controversies was over representation in Congress and involved the small states versus the large states. Virginia's Governor **Edmund Randolph** proposed the **VIRGINIA PLAN**, stating that state population would determine the number of representatives sent to Congress. New Jersey delegate **William Paterson** countered with the **NEW JERSEY PLAN**, under which each state would have equal representation.

After much debate, **Roger Sherman** proposed the **GREAT COMPROMISE** (or Connecticut Compromise). This resulted in the **bicameral legislature**. Each state would have two **Senators**, giving states equal powers in the **Senate**. Members of the **House of Representatives** would be elected based on each state's population. Both houses could draft bills to debate and vote on, with the exception of bills pertaining to money, which must originate in the House of Representatives.

Economic differences

Another controversy arose that involved economic differences between North and South. One concern was the counting of the African **slaves** for determining representation in the House of Representatives. The southern delegates wanted the slave population to count toward representation but did not want it to determine taxes to be paid. The northern delegates argued the opposite: count the slaves for taxes but not for representation. The resulting agreement was known as the **THREE-FIFTHS COMPROMISE.** Three-fifths of the slaves would be counted for both taxes and determining representation in the House.

THREE-FIFTHS COMPROMISE: a plan whereby three-fifths of the slaves would be counted for both taxes and determining representation in the House

Another major compromise between North and South was the **COMMERCE COMPROMISE.** The economic interests of the North were ones of industry and business, whereas the South's economic interests were primarily in farming. The Northern merchants wanted the government to regulate and control commerce with foreign nations and within the states. Southern planters opposed this idea, concerned that any **tariff laws** passed would be unfavorable to them.

COMMERCE COMPROMISE: a compromise designed to soothe tensions between the differing economic interests that existed between the Northern and Southern colonies

Congress was given the power to regulate commerce with other nations and the states, including levying tariffs on **imports**. However, Congress did not have the power to levy tariffs on any **exports**. This increased Southern concern about the effect on the slave trade. The delegates finally agreed that the importation of slaves would continue for 20 more years with no interference from Congress. Any import tax could not exceed 10 dollars per person. Starting in 1808, Congress would be able to decide whether to prohibit or regulate any further importation of slaves.

Ratification of the Constitution

Once work was completed and the document presented, nine states needed to approve it for it to go into effect. **Ratification** of the U.S. Constitution was by no means a foregone conclusion. There was quite a lot of discussion, arguing, debating, and haranguing. The opposition had three major objections:

- The states felt they were being asked to surrender too much power to the national government
- The voters did not have enough control and influence over the men who would be elected by them to run the government
- There was no "bill of rights" guaranteeing hard-won individual freedoms and liberties

FEDERALISTS: citizens who wanted to see a strong central government

ANTI-FEDERALISTS: citizens who worried that a strong national government would descend into tyranny

FEDERALIST PAPERS: the collected written arguments for the Constitution as written by prominent Federalists Alexander Hamilton, John Jay, and James Madison

ANTI-FEDERALIST PAPERS: the collected written arguments against the Constitution, as written by prominent Anti-Federalists Thomas Jefferson and Patrick Henry

BILL OF RIGHTS: the first ten Amendments to the Constitution, which protect some of the most basic human rights

Federalists versus Anti-Federalists

Great debate persisted between the **FEDERALISTS** and the **ANTI-FEDERALISTS**. Those who wanted to see a strong central government were called Federalists, because they wanted to see a federal government that had enough power to hold the states together. Among the leaders of the Federalists were **Alexander Hamilton** and **John Jay**. These two, along with **James Madison**, wrote a series of letters to New York newspapers, urging that that the states ratify the Constitution. These became known as the **FEDERALIST PAPERS**.

In the Anti-Federalist camp were **Thomas Jefferson** and **Patrick Henry**. These men and many others like them were worried that a strong national government would descend into the kind of **tyranny** that they had just worked so hard to abolish. In the same way that they took their name from their opposition, they wrote a series of arguments against the Constitution called the **ANTI-FEDERALIST PAPERS**.

Compromise and ratification

In the end, both sides got most of what they wanted. The Federalists got their strong national government, which was held in place by the famous **checks and balances** system. The Anti-Federalists got the **BILL OF RIGHTS**, the first ten Amendments to the Constitution, which protect some of the most basic human rights. The promise of the Bill of Rights helped sway the opinions of the states that were not going to ratify the Constitution. Some 11 states finally ratified the document, and the new national government went into effect.

It was no small feat that the delegates were able to produce a workable document that satisfied most opinions, feelings, and viewpoints. The **separation of powers** among the three branches of government and the built-in system of checks and balances, designed to keep these powers evenly distributed, have proven to be very effective. They provided for the individuals and the states, as well as an organized central authority that helped to keep a new, inexperienced nation on track.

They created a Constitution about which **Ben Franklin** said, "Because I expect no better, and because I am not sure, that it is not the best." The Constitution has lasted over 200 years, through a civil war, foreign wars, the Depression, and various social revolutions. It is truly a living document because of its ability to remain strong and stable while allowing itself to be changed in times of utmost need.

SKILL 1.6 Early years of the new nation

Early Presidential Politics

The presidency under Washington

In 1789, the **Electoral College** unanimously elected George Washington as the first President, and the new nation was on its way. The early presidential administrations were vastly important and established forms and procedures that are still present today. For example, George Washington created the **United States Cabinet** when he appointed four people to act as his advisors and to oversee various functions of the **executive branch**.

Thomas Jefferson was Washington's **Secretary of State**, and Alexander Hamilton was his **Secretary of the Treasury**. Jefferson and Hamilton were different in many ways, not the least of which was their views on what should be the proper form of government for the United States. This difference helped to shape the parties that formed around them. By the time Washington retired from office in 1796, the new political parties would come to play an important role in choosing his successor. Each party would put up its own candidates for office.

Presidential conflict

Because he had come in second in the Electoral College when Washington was elected President, **John Adams** became the first Vice President. When it was time to elect the second President, the **Federalist Party** selected him as their first candidate for President. Thomas Jefferson (whose was a member of the Democratic-Republican party) came in second behind Adams, and so he became Adams' Vice President.

Adams' administration was marked by the new nation's first entanglement in international affairs. Britain and France were at war, and Adams' **Federalist Party** supported the British, while Vice President Thomas Jefferson's **DEMOCRATIC-REPUBLICAN PARTY** supported the French. The United States was brought nearly to the brink of war with France, which had experienced the **French Revolution** and whose military campaigns were being commanded by **Napoleon Bonaparte**. Although the United States had several naval victories, enthusiasm for war was not widespread, despite the fact that Hamilton and other Federalists were strongly in favor of it.

DEMOCRATIC-REPUBLICAN PARTY: an early American political party that supported stronger states' rights and a weaker central government

ALIEN AND SEDITION ACTS: gave the president the authority to expel noncitizens he suspected of treason and made hostile words against the government illegal

John Adams and Thomas Jefferson died on the same day—July 4, 1826.

During this time, four laws were passed known as the **ALIEN AND SEDITION ACTS.** These laws gave the president the authority to expel noncitizens he suspected of treason and made hostile words against the government illegal. The United States also began building warships and raising a **provisional army**. France decided against expanding New France and finally agreed to receive a diplomat to settle the controversies. Jefferson, who won the 1800 election, pardoned all of those that were convicted for crimes under the Alien and Sedition Acts.

Growth and Change of Political Parties

Political parties are never mentioned in the United States Constitution. In fact, Washington himself warned against the creation of "factions" in American politics that cause "jealousies and false alarms" and the damage they could cause to the body politic. Thomas Jefferson echoed this warning—yet he came to lead a party himself.

Americans had good reason to fear the emergence of political parties. They had witnessed how parties worked in Great Britain. Parties, called "factions" in Britain, were made up of a few people who schemed to win favors from the government. They were more interested in their own personal profit and advantage than in the public good. Thus, new American leaders were interested in preventing factions from forming.

Hamilton vs. Jefferson

Ironically, the disagreements between Washington's chief advisors, Thomas Jefferson and Alexander Hamilton, had spurred formation of the first political parties. Hamilton wanted the federal government to be stronger than the state governments; Jefferson believed that the state governments should be stronger than the federal government. Hamilton supported the creation of the first **Bank of the United States** to pay off debt and enable creditors to have a vital interest in the success of the new country, while Jefferson opposed the bank because he felt that it would take money from the poor and give too much power to wealthy investors.

Jefferson interpreted the Constitution strictly; he argued that nowhere did the Constitution give the federal government the power to create a **national bank**. He believed that the common people, especially the farmers, were the backbone of the nation. He thought that the rise of big cities and manufacturing would corrupt American life.

Hamilton interpreted the Constitution more loosely. He pointed out that the Constitution gave Congress the power to make all laws "necessary and proper" to carry out its duties. He reasoned that since Congress had the right to collect taxes, then Congress had the right to create the bank. Hamilton wanted the government to encourage economic growth. He also favored the growth of trade manufacturing, and cities, believing they were necessary parts of economic growth. He favored the business leaders and mistrusted the common people.

Gathering supporters and organizing the parties

At first, Hamilton and Jefferson disagreed in private. But when Congress began to pass many of Hamilton's ideas and programs, Jefferson and James Madison decided to organize support for their own views. They moved quietly and very cautiously in the beginning. In 1791, they went to New York and met with several important New York politicians including Governor **George Clinton** and **Aaron Burr**, a strong critic of Hamilton.

Before long, leaders in other states began to organize support for either Jefferson or Hamilton. Jefferson's supporters called themselves **Democratic-Republicans**. Hamilton and his supporters were known as **Federalists**, because they favored a strong federal government. The Federalists had the support of the merchants and ship owners in the Northeast and some planters in the South. Small farmers and craft workers supported Jefferson and the Democratic-Republicans.

Contentious elections

In the 1800 election, Federalist Alexander Hamilton broke the tie between Democratic-Republicans Thomas Jefferson and Aaron Burr, making Jefferson President and Burr Vice President. Election time came around again in 1804, and Hamilton thwarted Burr's attempt to be Vice President—and also thwarted Burr's attempt to become governor of New York. Burr challenged Hamilton to a duel, killing him in 1804. Burr was charged with murder but later acquitted.

Jefferson was reelected in 1804, and James Madison, another Democratic-Republican, was elected in 1808. By 1816, after losing a string of important elections, the Federalist Party ceased to be an effective political force and soon passed off the national stage.

New political parties

By the late 1820s, new political parties had grown up. The Democratic-Republican Party was the major party for several years but differences within it about the direction in which the country was headed caused a split after 1824.

Those who favored strong national growth took the name **Whigs** after a similar party in Great Britain and united around then-President **John Quincy Adams**, who had first been a Federalist and then set up a party called the **NATIONAL**

NATIONAL REPUBLICAN PARTY: an early American political party formed by John Quincy Adams following the demise of the Federalist Party

REPUBLICAN PARTY. Many business people in the Northeast, as well as some wealthy planters in the South, supported the **WHIG PARTY**.

Those who favored slower growth and were more oriented toward workers and small farmers went on to form the new **DEMOCRATIC PARTY**, with Andrew Jackson as its first leader. Jackson defeated John Quincy Adams in 1828 and became the first president from this party. It is the forerunner of today's party of the same name.

WHIG PARTY: an early American political party that supported strong national growth

DEMOCRATIC PARTY: an early American political party that supported slower national growth and was oriented toward farmers

REPUBLICAN PARTY: an early American political party that formed in the wake of the slavery debate between the North and South; it was formed by the Whig Party, Northern Democrats who opposed slavery, and other people opposed to slavery

MIDNIGHT JUDGES: federalist judges appointed by President John Adams on the night before Jefferson's inauguration

COMMISSION: a notice of appointment usually used by presidents when appointing Supreme Court justices

Slavery and the political parties

In the mid-1850s, the slavery issue was beginning to heat up. In 1854, the Whig Party, some Northern Democrats who opposed slavery, and others opposed to slavery united to form the **REPUBLICAN PARTY**. The Democratic Party was more heavily represented in the South and was, for the most part, pro-slavery.

Thus, by the time of the **Civil War**, the present form of the major political parties had taken shape. Though there would sometimes be drastic changes in their ideology and platforms over the years, no other political parties would manage to gain enough strength to seriously challenge the "Big Two" parties.

Power of the Supreme Court

Judicial review and Marbury v. Madison

Jefferson was elected in November 1800, but would not take office until March 4. President Adams, a Federalist, tried to appoint as many Federalist judges as he could before Jefferson's inauguration working long into the night of March 3. These appointees were known as the **MIDNIGHT JUDGES**. One of these judges was **William Marbury**, who was named to be Justice of the Peace for the District of Columbia.

The normal practice of making such appointments was to deliver a **COMMISSION**, or notice, of appointment. This was done by the Secretary of State. Jefferson was president when the commission was supposed to be delivered, and his Secretary of State was James Madison. Jefferson instructed Madison not to deliver the commission for Marbury.

Naturally, this led to conflict, and the issue eventually ended up in the hands of the Supreme Court. In **Marbury v. Madison, Chief Justice John Marshall** and the other Justices of the Supreme Court ruled that the power to deliver commissions to judges was not part of the Constitution. It was instead part of the **Judiciary Act of 1789**. And because the Judiciary Act conflicted with the Constitution, it was illegal, as it gave the judicial branch powers not granted to it by the Constitution. Thus, Marbury did not become Justice of the Peace in the District of Columbia. The ruling exemplifies the power of the Supreme Court to throw out unconstitutional laws. The Supreme Court always has the ultimate check on legislative and executive power.

Marbury *v.* **Madison** *was the first case to establish what has become the Supreme Court's main duty, judicial review.*

McCulloch v. Maryland

Another notable example of judicial review is **McCulloch v. Maryland**, which began as a conflict over banking. The State of Maryland voted to tax all bank business done with banks not chartered in Maryland; the law was viewed as particularly designed to target the **Second Bank of the United States**. **Andrew McCulloch**, who worked in the Baltimore branch of the Second Bank of the United States, refused to pay the tax. The State of Maryland sued, and the Supreme Court accepted the case.

McCulloch *v.* **Maryland**, *which settled a dispute involving the Second Bank of the United States, ruled that any dispute between governments at the state and federal levels would be settled in favor of the federal government.*

Supreme Court Chief Justice Marshall wrote to uphold the right of Congress to charter a national bank. Further, he wrote that a state did not have the power to tax the federal government. "The right to tax is the right to destroy," he wrote. The ruling was that states should not have the power to tax the federal government. Though the Bank of the United States did not survive after 1841, the power of **JUDICIAL REVIEW** by the Supreme Court is a practice that continues to today.

JUDICIAL REVIEW: the long-standing idea that the actions of the legislative and executive branches are subject to review and possible invalidation by the judicial branch

Effects of the Growing Nation on Native Americans

During the Revolutionary War, many Native Americans sided with the British in hopes of stopping expansion of the American colonies into lands they occupied. The **Treaty of Paris** ceded a large amount of land occupied and claimed by Native Americans to the United States; the British did not inform them of the change.

Initially, the new U.S. government tried to treat the tribes who had fought with the British as conquered people and claimed their land. This policy was later abandoned, however, because it could not be enforced.

For more information on Indian removal, check out this site:

www.pbs.org/wgbh/aia/part4/4p2959.html

In order to continue national expansion, the next phase of the government's policy toward the Native Americans was to purchase their land in treaties. This created tension, as the expansion and settlement of new territory forced the Native Americans to move farther west. The Native Americans were gradually giving up their homelands, their sacred sites, and the burial grounds of their ancestors. Some of the Native Americans chose to move west. Many, however, were relocated by force.

THE INDIAN REMOVAL ACT OF 1830: authorized the government to negotiate treaties with Native Americans to provide land west of the Mississippi River in exchange for lands east of the river

Significant legislation

THE INDIAN REMOVAL ACT OF 1830 authorized the government to negotiate treaties with Native Americans to provide land west of the Mississippi River in exchange

TREATY OF NEW ECHOTA: a treaty signed by a faction of the Cherokees in Georgia, which was designed to remove them

THE TRAIL OF TEARS: the forced removal of the Cherokees from their ancestral lands, which resulted in the deaths of more than 4,000 people

for lands east of the river. This policy resulted in the relocation of tens of thousands of Native Americans. Theoretically, the treaties were expected to result in voluntary relocation of the native people. In fact, many of the native chiefs were forced to sign the treaties.

One of the worst examples of removal was the **TREATY OF NEW ECHOTA**. This treaty was signed by a faction of the **Cherokees** in Georgia, but not by the actual leaders of the tribe. When the leaders attempted to remain on their ancestral lands, the treaty was enforced by **President Martin Van Buren**. This forced removal came to be known as **THE TRAIL OF TEARS**, which resulted in the deaths of more than 4,000 Cherokees.

SKILL 1.7 Continued National Development

For more information on the Trail of Tears, check out this site:

ngeorgia.com/history/nghisttt.html

Regional Differences

When the United States declared independence from England, the founding fathers created a unified nation while respecting the uniqueness and individual rights of each of the 13 colonies or states. Some colonists had come to America in search of **religious freedom**, others for a fresh start, and others for **economic opportunity**. As a result, each colony had a particular culture and identity.

As the young nation grew, new states were established. Religious interests, economic life, and geography defined particular regions. The **Northeast** tended toward industrial development; the **South** tended to rely on agriculture; and the **West** was an area of untamed open spaces (more accurately, space that appeared to many Americans to be "open" because they did not recognize the presence of Native Americans) where people settled and practiced agriculture. Each of these regions came to be defined, at least to some extent, on the basis of the way people made their living and the economic and social institutions that supported them.

The North

In the **industrialized** North, the factory system tended to create a division between the tycoons of business and industry and the poor industrial workers. The conditions in which the labor force worked were far from ideal—long hours, bad conditions, and low pay. Of course, life in villages, small towns, and farms was also a major part of the life in the North.

The South

In the South, the cities were centers of social and commercial life. Southern agricultural was based on the output of **plantations**, large farms owned by the wealthy and worked by indentured servants and slaves.

The Northwest Territory

The **NORTHWEST TERRITORY**, located north of the Ohio River, would become the states of Ohio (1803), Indiana (1816), Illinois (1818), Michigan (1837), Wisconsin (1848), and Minnesota (1858) where the Mississippi River begins. Land was inexpensive; fur, food, and freedom were plentiful; and the challenges poignant due to harsh weather and a lack of Eastern goods.

NORTHWEST TERRITORY: the land located north of the Ohio River that would become the states of Ohio (1803), Indiana (1816), Illinois (1818), Michigan (1837), Wisconsin (1848), and Minnesota (1858)

The Southwest Territory

The **SOUTHWEST TERRITORY**, located south of the Ohio River and east of the Mississippi River, became the states of Kentucky (1792), Tennessee (1796), Mississippi (1817), and Alabama (1819). Alabama and Mississippi were part of the **Deep South** where slavery was far more prevalent than it was in Tennessee and Kentucky.

SOUTHWEST TERRITORY: the land south of the Ohio River and east of the Mississippi River that would become the states of Kentucky (1792), Tennessee (1796), Mississippi (1817), and Alabama (1819)

The Louisiana Purchase

Because more war seemed inevitable between Britain and France, Napoleon Bonaparte decided to build barges to invade Britain and to sell **Louisiana Territory** to the United States. Jefferson had wanted to buy New Orleans, because he was concerned that either Spain or France could block American trade at that port city. To his surprise, the entire territory was offered in 1803 for only 15 million dollars. The **LOUISIANA PURCHASE** more than doubled the size of the United States. Although they lived on the land, no Native Americans were informed of the purchase.

LOUISIANA PURCHASE: the purchase of the Louisiana Territory by Thomas Jefferson, which more than doubled the size of the United States

The Louisiana Purchase was composed of land that eventually became fifteen states:

- Louisiana
- Arkansas
- Missouri
- Iowa
- Oklahoma
- Kansas
- Nebraska
- Part of Minnesota
- Most of North and South Dakota
- Part of New Mexico and Texas
- Colorado
- Wyoming
- Montana, east of the Continental Divide

The Louisiana Purchase

Territorial Acquisitions of the United States. National Atlas of the United States, http://nationalatlas.gov

Lewis and Clark Expedition

After the United States purchased the Louisiana Territory, Jefferson appointed Captains **Meriwether Lewis** and **William Clark** to explore it and to find out exactly what the nation had purchased. The expedition travelled all the way to the Pacific Ocean; the explorers returned two years later with maps, journals, and artifacts of their exploration. This led the way for future explorers to learn more about the territory, which resulted in more **westward expansion.**

The Federalists feared westward expansion, thinking it might extend slavery in the South, as well as reduce political power in the North.

Foreign Policy in the Young Nation

In the early years of the American nation, three primary ideas determined American foreign policy:

1. **Isolationism:** Although many hoped the nation would grow, this expectation did not extend to efforts to plant colonies in other parts of the world.
2. **No entangling alliances:** In his farewell address, George Washington stated that it would be in the United States' best interests to avoid

permanent alliances in any part of the world. This was echoed by Thomas Jefferson: "Equal and exact justice to all men, of whatever state or persuasion, religious or political; peace, commerce, and honest friendship with all nations—entangling alliances with none . . . We wish not to meddle with the internal affairs of any country, nor with the general affairs of Europe." For example, when James Madison led the nation into the War of 1812, he refrained from entering an alliance with France, which was also at war with England at the time.

3. **Nationalism:** Americans were united by a strong sense of nationalism—patriotic pride in one's country and a belief in one's own nation and people.

War of 1812

The United States' unintentional and accidental involvement in what was known as the **War of 1812** came about due to the political and economic struggles between France and Great Britain. Napoleon's goal was complete conquest and control of Europe, especially including Great Britain.

American involvement

Although British troops were temporarily driven off the mainland of Europe, the navy still controlled the seas, and France conducted its trade across those seas. Though America conducted trade with both nations, trade with France and its colonies was more important.

The British therefore decided to destroy American trade with France, for two primary reasons:

- Products and goods from the United States gave Napoleon what he needed to keep up his struggle with Britain, and Britain did not want the Americans to aid its enemy
- Britain felt threatened by the increasing strength and success of the U.S. merchant fleet, as Americans were becoming major competitors with the ship owners and merchants in Britain

In 1807, the British issued the **ORDERS IN COUNCIL**, a series of measures prohibiting neutral ships—including American ships—from entering any French ports, not only in Europe but also in India and the West Indies. At the same time, Napoleon began efforts for a coastal blockade of the British Isles.

ORDERS IN COUNCIL: a series of measures prohibiting neutral ships—including American ships—from entering any French ports, not only in Europe but also in India and the West Indies

Napoleon issued a series of orders prohibiting all nations (including the United States) from trading with the British. He threatened seizure of every ship entering French ports if they had stopped at a British port or colony and warned that he would enforce the seizure every ship that was inspected by British cruisers or that paid duties to the British.

At the same time, the British were stopping American ships and **impressing**—that is conscripting—American seamen to serve on British ships. Americans were outraged.

American response

EMBARGO ACT: a series of laws designed to use economic warfare instead of military warfare to protect American rights and to punish the British for forcing Americans to serve on their ships

In 1807, Congress passed the **EMBARGO ACT**, a series of laws designed to use economic warfare instead of military warfare to protect American rights and to punish the British for forcing Americans to serve on their ships. But the act led to an economic downturn in New England in particular, which led to spiraling unemployment, an antagonistic attitude toward the Democratic-Republicans, and smuggling. Many Americans did not comply with the laws and derided them by calling them, among other things, **O-grab-me** (embargo spelled backward) acts.

In 1809, the laws were withdrawn, but Congress passed two additional acts after James Madison became president. These laws attempted to regulate trade with other nations and to get Britain and France to remove the restrictions they had put on American shipping. There was a catch, however. Despite America's intention to remain neutral, the new laws said that Americans would only trade with the nation that removed its restrictions first.

Napoleon was first to remove restrictions; this prompted Madison to issue orders prohibiting trade with Britain, ignoring warnings from the British not to do so. Although Britain eventually rescinded its Orders in Council, war began in June 1812.

The war itself

Americans were divided not only about whether or not it was necessary to fight, but also over what territories should be fought for and taken. The nation was still young and not prepared for war.

For more information on the burning of Washington (August 23, 1814) from Dolly Madison's point of view, check out this site:

www.nationalcenter.org/WashingtonBurning1814.html

Two naval victories and one military victory stood out for the United States in this war. **Oliver Perry** gained control of Lake Erie, and **Thomas MacDonough** fought on Lake Champlain. Both of these naval battles prevented British invasion of the United States from Canada. However, the primary American objective to conquer Canada was unsuccessful.

In 1814, British troops traveled down the Potomac River, marched into Washington, D.C., and burned the public buildings, including the White House, home to President James Madison and First Lady Dolly Madison.

End of the war

The war ended Christmas Eve, 1814, with the signing of the **TREATY OF GHENT**. However, because news of the treaty traveled slowly, Americans continued to fight and won the **Battle of New Orleans** on January 8, 1815. Led by **Andrew Jackson**, the victory at New Orleans was a great morale booster to Americans. The treaty established peace, called for an exchange of prisoners of war, restored all occupied territory, and set up a commission to settle boundary disputes with Canada.

TREATY OF GHENT: signed in 1814, this treaty ended the War of 1812

The War of 1812 proved to be a turning point in American history. In part, this was because the United States strengthened its control of the Northwest Territory by defeating the Native Americans and the British, who had been helping them. In addition, the end of the war began a long-time alliance with Britain.

The Era of Good Feelings

The **ERA OF GOOD FEELINGS** followed the War of 1812 and the decline of the Federalist Party. This period included:

- The Missouri Compromise
- Acquisition of Florida from Spain
- The Monroe Doctrine
- Lack of partisan factions

ERA OF GOOD FEELINGS: the period of time after the War of 1812; it is marked by a general period of happiness, prosperity, and growth

The American system

After the War of 1812, **Henry Clay** and others favored economic measures that came to be known as the **AMERICAN SYSTEM**, which had three main parts.

1. A tariff would protect American farmers and manufacturers and encourage American economic growth
2. In 1816, Congress chartered the Second Bank of the United States to regulate the supply of money for the nation
3. The American System called for developing a national transportation system

AMERICAN SYSTEM: an economic system designed to capitalize on the resources within the United States and stimulate economic prosperity

Transportation

Transportation improved as Americans built roads, railroads, canals, and steamboats. New wagon trails also provided for westward migration, and travel on these trails led to the invention of the **prairie schooner**, large covered wagons.

The increased ease of travel facilitated westward movement.

Economic effects

There were economic advantages to these advances in transportation as well. The increased ease of shipping boosted the economy because shipments were faster and cheaper over larger areas. One innovation was the **ERIE CANAL**, completed in 1825, which connected the interior and Great Lakes with the Hudson River and the coastal port of New York. Canals connected many other natural waterways, and travel became far easier.

ERIE CANAL: a canal that connects the interior and Great Lakes with the Hudson River and the coastal port of New York City

The steam engine

The invention of the steam engine resulted in many changes. John Fitch developed the steamboat, and Robert Fulton's *Clermont*, was the first commercially successful steamboat. **Steam-powered railroads** eventually became the most important transportation method and helped to open the West. Expansion into the interior of the country resulted in America's becoming the leading agricultural nation in the world.

The innovations in transportation and the advent of the steam engine allowed American farmers produced a vast surplus for export in commodities such as:

- Cotton
- Grain
- Flour
- Livestock

Tools like the **cotton gin** and the **reaper** made farm production more efficient.

Jacksonian Democracy

As the United States expanded, its political system continued to evolve. The election of Andrew Jackson as president in 1828 signaled a swing of the political pendulum from government influence of the wealthy, aristocratic Easterners to the interests of the Western farmers and pioneers. It came to be called the era of the "common man," with equal political power for all. For example, every white man, not just property owners, was extended the right to vote, as had been the case before.

On the other hand, Jackson favored some controversial policies as well: he supported increased **executive power**, the **patronage system**, strict **constitutional interpretation**, and the removal of Native Americans from the Southeast.

Laissez faire economics

Upon becoming President, Jackson fought to get rid of the Second Bank of the United States because he believed it favored the wealthy. Congress voted in 1832 to renew the Bank's charter, but Jackson **vetoed** the bill, withdrew the government's money, and the bank finally collapsed.

The nullification crisis

Jackson also faced a **nullification crisis** during his presidency. The **DOCTRINE OF NULLIFICATION** says that the states have the right to "nullify"—declare invalid—any act of Congress they believe to be unjust or unconstitutional. The doctrine of nullification was based on the assumption that the United States was a union of independent commonwealths and that the general government was merely their agent.

DOCTRINE OF NULLIFICATION: says that the states have the right to "nullify"—declare invalid—any act of Congress they believe to be unjust or unconstitutional

In 1828, Congress had passed a law that the South called the **TARIFF OF ABOMINATIONS**. Signed by President John Quincy Adams, this law placed high tariffs on goods imported into the United States.

TARIFF OF ABOMINATIONS: placed high tariffs on goods imported into the United States

Southerners, led by **John C. Calhoun** (from South Carolina and Vice President under Adams and then Jackson), felt that the tariff favored the manufacturing interests of New England and the Northeast. The tariff was lowered in 1832 but not low enough to satisfy South Carolina, which promptly threatened to secede from the Union. Although Jackson agreed with the rights of states, he also believed in preservation of the Union, so he signed the **FORCE BILL**, which enabled him to send troops to South Carolina to force it to obey all federal laws.

FORCE BILL: signed by Andrew Jackson, this bill enabled him to send troops to South Carolina to force it to obey all federal laws

Compromise and aftermath

The **COMPROMISE TARIFF OF 1833**, designed by Henry Clay, lowered the tariffs and averted secession for the time being. Tariff laws continued to pass, however, exemplifying another difference between the Southern Democrats and the Northern Whigs.

COMPROMISE TARIFF OF 1833: designed by Henry Clay, this act lowered the tariffs that were causing the nullification crisis and averted secession

The nullification crisis led then-President Jackson, a Southern Democrat, to say in his "Proclamation to the People of South Carolina" that the Constitution derives its authority from the people, not from the states. He said that "each State, having expressly parted with so many powers as to constitute, jointly with the other States, a single nation, cannot, from that period, possess any right to secede, because such secession does not break a league, but destroys the unity of a nation."

MONROE DOCTRINE: informed the powers of the Old World that the American continents were no longer open to European colonization and that any effort to extend European political influence into the New World would be considered by the United States "as dangerous to our peace and safety"

Monroe Doctrine

During the early years of the Republic, European events had profoundly shaped U.S. policies, especially foreign policies. These experiences had created a profound wariness among Americans. On December 2, 1823, President James Monroe delivered what is known as the **MONROE DOCTRINE**.

The Monroe Doctrine informed the powers of the Old World that the American continents were no longer open to European colonization and that any effort to extend European political influence into the New World would be considered by the United States "as dangerous to our peace and safety." Nor would the United States interfere in European wars or internal affairs—and they expected Europe to stay out of American affairs.

MANIFEST DESTINY: the belief in the divinely given right of the nation to expand westward to the Pacific Ocean

Manifest Destiny

American Progress. John Gast, 1872.

Mass migration westward put the U.S. government on a collision course with the Native Americans, Great Britain, Spain, and Mexico.

Manifest Destiny

At the same time that the United States stated its intention to bar European nations from expanding into the Americas, it pursued its own policy of expansion westward. The nineteenth century is sometimes called the age of **MANIFEST DESTINY**, the belief in the divinely given right of the nation to expand westward to the Pacific Ocean. The **Northwest Ordinance** (1787) and the **Louisiana Purchase** (1803), for example, were parts of westward expansion and expressions of Manifest Destiny.

The last unresolved tension between Great Britain and the United States was over the shared **Oregon** country in the Northwest. By the 1840s, with the conflict of free and slave states and the demand of the western settlers for government by the United States, the conflict had to be resolved. In an 1846 treaty, just before the outbreak of the war with Mexico, President **James Polk** accepted a compromise with the U.S. boundary at the **49th parallel**.

Mexican-American War

The struggle for territory continued in the Southwest, however, and Americans used Manifest Destiny to justify the **Mexican-American War** (1846–1848), which resulted in the United States annexing Texas, California, and much of the Southwest.

The Spanish and Mexican southwest

Spain first claimed land in the region in the 1540s. The claim had spread northward from **Mexico City**, and in the 1700s, Spain had established:

- Missions
- Forts

- Villages
- Towns
- Large ranches

After the United States purchased the Louisiana Territory in 1803, which included some of Texas, Americans began moving into Spanish territory. A few hundred American families were allowed to live there, but they had to agree to become Spanish subjects.

In 1821, Mexico successfully revolted against Spanish rule and won independence. The new **Republic of Mexico** was tolerant toward the American settlers and traders, encouraging extensive trade and settlement, especially in Texas. Many of the new settlers were southerners who brought their slaves with them. Although slavery was outlawed in Mexico (and therefore in Texas), the Mexican government looked the other way.

Buildup to war

With Americans swarming into western lands, friction between the two nations increased. The clash was not only political but also cultural and economic. Spanish influence permeated all parts of Southwestern life, including law, language, architecture, and customs.

Some were concerned that an American state might develop within Mexico. Settlement restrictions, cancellation of land grants, the forbidding of slavery, and increased military activity brought everything to a head. The Mexican government also owed debts to U.S. citizens whose property had been damaged or destroyed during the struggle for independence from Spain. Mexico became bitter over the American expansion into Texas and then by the **Texas Revolution** in 1836—after which Texas considered itself an independent republic.

In the 1844 Presidential election, the Democrats pushed for annexation of Texas (and Oregon also), which President Jackson had opposed. Now, under President Tyler, the procedure to admit Texas to the Union began. When statehood occurred in 1845 under President Polk, diplomatic relations between the United States and Mexico ended.

Polk's attempts at peace

President Polk supported Manifest Destiny and desired U.S. control of the entire southwest from Texas to the Pacific Ocean. The Whigs were largely opposed to the notion of Manifest Destiny and war with Mexico, while the Southern Democrats favored it, especially with the idea of an expansion of slave states.

President Polk sent a diplomatic mission to Mexico with an offer to purchase New Mexico and Upper California and to forgive the $4.5 million that Mexico owed U.S. citizens, but the Mexican government, which was chaotic and in conflict, refused to receive the diplomats.

The war begins

Two members of Congress, John Quincy Adams and Abraham Lincoln, remained firm in their opposition to the war, but President Polk's declaration of war passed; in 1846, the United States and Mexico were formally at war. The **WILMOT PROVISO**, an amendment to the war funding bill which stipulated that none of the territory acquired in the Mexican War should be open to slavery, revealed the continuing conflict over slavery in the nation.

WILMOT PROVISO: an amendment to the war funding bill which stipulated that none of the territory acquired in the Mexican War should be open to slavery

The treaty that ended the Mexican-American War, signed in 1848, and a subsequent treaty in 1853 completed the southwestern boundary of the United States. It extended to the Pacific Ocean, as President Polk had wished. Completed in 1854 for lands south of the Gila River and west of the Rio Grande, the **GADSDEN PURCHASE** added property for the purpose of building a transcontinental railroad. All together, the United States added land that became the states of California, Nevada, and Utah, as well as parts of Arizona, Colorado, New Mexico, and Wyoming.

GADSDEN PURCHASE: the 1854 purchase of land south of the Gila River and west of the Rio Grande

Gadsen Purchase

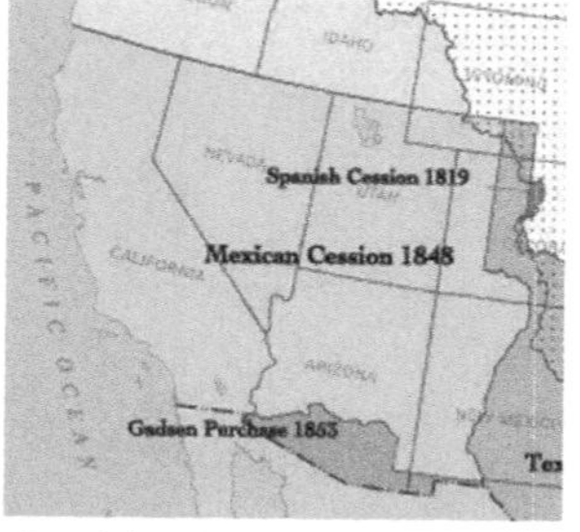

Detail from Territorial Acquisitions of the United States.
National Atlas of the United States, http://nationalatlas.gov

American Slavery

Equality for everyone, as stated in the Declaration of Independence, did not yet apply to African Americans or Native Americans. Voting rights and the right to hold public office were also restricted in varying degrees in each state.

Differences between North and South came to a head over the issue of slavery. The rise of the abolitionist movement in the North, the publication of *Uncle Tom's Cabin* by **Harriet Beecher Stowe**, and issues of trade all coalesced around the issue of slavery. As the South defended its lifestyle, its economy, and the right of the states to be self-determining, the North became stronger in its criticism of slavery.

Brief history of slavery in America

Slavery in the English colonies had begun in 1619 when 20 Africans arrived in the colony of Virginia at Jamestown. From then on, slavery had a foothold, especially in the agricultural South, where the operation of large plantations relied on slave labor. In part, the reliance on slave labor was based on the fact that free men refused to work for wages on plantations when they could move west and settle their own land on the frontier. Plantation owners believed that using

indentured servants and slave labor was the only profitable course they could take. In addition, the South had become increasingly dependent on one crop: **cotton**.

Cotton production increased from 150,000 pounds a year in the early 1800s to nearly four million pounds a year in 1855; the slave population rose accordingly, from about 1.2 million in 1810 to over four million in 1860.

One of the slavery compromises at the **Constitutional Convention** had been the **three-fifths compromise**, which determined that three-fifths of the slaves would be counted for both taxes and representation. Another compromise over slavery in those early days regarded disputes over how much regulation the central government would have over the slave trade. Southerners were worried about the taxing of slaves coming into the country and the possibility of Congress prohibiting the slave trade altogether. The compromise allowed the states to continue importation of slaves for the next 20 years until 1808, at which time Congress would make the decision about the future of the slave trade. During the 20-year period, a tax of no more than $10 per person could be levied on slaves coming into the country.

By 1808, cotton had become increasingly important in the primarily agricultural South, and the institution of slavery had become firmly entrenched in Southern culture. It was also evident that as early as the Constitutional Convention, active anti-slavery feelings and opinions were very strong, leading to extremely active groups and societies.

By 1808, cotton had become increasingly important in the primarily agricultural South, and the institution of slavery had become firmly entrenched in Southern culture.

The abolition movement

The **abolitionists**' efforts to end slavery were intense and controversial. The abolitionist movement had political fallout, affecting admittance of states into the Union and the government's continued efforts to keep a balance between total numbers of free and slave states. Congressional legislation after 1820 reflected this. Eventually, the efforts to end slavery split the country, hardened Southern defense of slavery, and led to a four year bloody civil war.

AMERICAN COLONIZATION SOCIETY: a society founded in 1816 with the goal of sending free black people to Africa

Anti-slavery organizations

Anti-slavery sentiment increased in the first half of the 1800s, and numerous organizations took up the cause. The **AMERICAN COLONIZATION SOCIETY** was founded in 1816 with the goal of sending free black people to Africa. Reformers' motives varied; some wanted to abolish slavery, while others believed that there was no place in American society for free blacks. The society created the colony of Liberia.

AMERICAN ANTI-SLAVERY SOCIETY: an important abolitionist society founded by Quaker William Lloyd Garrison, who started a newspaper named *The Liberator*

The **AMERICAN ANTI-SLAVERY SOCIETY** was founded by Quaker **William Lloyd Garrison**, who also started a newspaper named *The Liberator*. The newspaper was an important voice for the abolitionist movement, and Garrison was a controversial figure with both supporters and enemies around the country.

Women also formed their own abolitionist organizations when they were denied full access to existing groups. **Margaretta Forten**, for example, cofounded the **PHILADELPHIA FEMALE ANTI-SLAVERY SOCIETY**, a group of black and white women, because the American Anti-Slavery Society would not grant women full membership.

PHILADELPHIA FEMALE ANTI-SLAVERY SOCIETY: a group of abolitionist black and white women, cofounded by Margaretta Forten

The **ANTI-SLAVERY CONVENTION OF AMERICAN WOMEN** held its first meeting in Philadelphia in 1838. Pennsylvania Hall, the building chosen to be the site of their meetings, was burned down by a proslavery mob, but the fire did not stop the women. They continued meeting at **Sarah Pugh**'s schoolhouse. Many women joined the **FEMALE VIGILANT SOCIETY**, a group that raised money for food, transportation, and other assistance for refugee slaves.

ANTI-SLAVERY CONVENTION OF AMERICAN WOMEN: a women's abolitionist group whose meeting building, Pennsylvania Hall, was burned down by a proslavery mob

FEMALE VIGILANT SOCIETY: a group that raised money for food, transportation, and other assistance for refugee slaves

Other Reform Movements

Abolition was just one of many reform movements that took root and flourished during the nineteenth century. This spirit of reform found expression in the effort to expand and protect rights and opportunities for all.

Education

A new understanding of education led to major efforts for **public education** for all children. In Massachusetts, **Horace Mann** published the *Common School Journal*, so the public could become more familiar with the importance of education. He and other members of the common school movement argued that free public schools were essential for educating citizens who would be capable of sustaining American democracy. Further, they believed that common schools would help create a more unified American society and increase the wealth of individuals, communities, and the nation.

For more information on the history of public education, check out this site:

www.pbs.org/kcet/publicschool/index.html

As public schools were established, more people became **literate**. This meant that there was more participation in literature and the arts. The more literate society broadly appreciated newspapers and works of literature, art, and live entertainment. Education also helped people become more informed about previously unknown areas, including the West.

By the end of the nineteenth century, free public elementary school was available for all children in America.

By the end of the nineteenth century, free public elementary school was available for all children in America.

Early labor movement

Before 1800, most **manufacturing** activities were accomplished in small shops or in homes. However, starting in the early 1800s, the ability to build machines resulted in factories that made it easier to produce goods faster. More industries required more labor. Women, children, and, at times, entire families worked long hours and days in mills and factories, and employers began hiring **immigrants** who were coming to America in huge numbers.

As the nature of work changed in the nineteenth century, workers began their efforts for reform. By the 1830s, many labor organizations began a struggle for a 10-hour workday. In 1844, in Lowell, Massachusetts, female textile employees organized the **LOWELL FEMALE LABOR REFORM ASSOCIATION** to demand shorter hours, higher wages, and better working conditions.

LOWELL FEMALE LABOR REFORM ASSOCIATION: a group organized by female textile employees whose purpose was to shorten working hours, obtain higher wages, and improve working conditions

The Second Great Awakening

Religious belief also fueled the spirit reform. The **FIRST GREAT AWAKENING** had taken place in the 1730s and 1740s, and the **SECOND GREAT AWAKENING** took place about 60 years later, between 1790 and 1830. The Second Great Awakening was an **evangelical Protestant** revival preaching that **salvation** was available to everyone, not just a chosen few. Inspired by the idea that it was possible to gain salvation, adherents subscribed to a strong work ethic, avoided being wasteful, and abstained from drinking. Further, the idea of creating a more Godly society inspired reform efforts aimed at improving conditions in the United States.

FIRST GREAT AWAKENING: a period of religious activity in the American colonies that took place in the 1730s and 1740s

SECOND GREAT AWAKENING: an evangelical Protestant revival that took place between 1790 and 1830; it preached that salvation was available to everyone, not just a chosen few

Interdenominational missionary groups began, such as the **American Home Missionary Society** in 1826. Some publishers of Christian literature included the **American Bible Society** and the **American Tract Society**.

Preachers traveled the country spreading the gospel of social responsibility. This point of view then extended to mainline Protestant adherents, who began to believe that the Christian faith should be expressed for the good of society. Preachers argued that people should see God as one who looks after and cares for the individual and for society. They preached that sin is selfishness, behavior should be benevolent, and people needed to purify for the arrival of the coming Kingdom when Jesus would return to Earth. **Methodists** and **Baptists** also gained large numbers of new followers. Some of the new denominations of the period were the **Disciples of Christ**, **Latter Day Saints**, and **Seventh-Day Adventists**.

Temperance

Closely allied to the Second Great Awakening was the **TEMPERANCE MOVEMENT**, which began as early as the 1820s. Perhaps the largest and most influential temperance organization was the **Women's Christian Temperance Union** (WCTU) founded in 1874. Under the banner of "home protection," WCTU members advocated not just temperance, but all kinds of reform that would protect women and children from the effects of men who drank alcohol.

TEMPERANCE MOVEMENT: a social movement that was against the use of alcohol

Other Notable People and Events

Horace Mann

Horace Mann grew up a poor child with little opportunity for education except for his small community library. He took full advantage of it, however, and was admitted to Brown University, from which he graduated in 1819. Mann practiced law for several years and served in the Massachusetts House of Representatives. He served on the committee of the first school funded by public tax dollars in Dedham, Massachusetts, and was appointed secretary to the newly formed State Board of Education in 1837. Mann became an outspoken proponent of educational reform and fought for better resources for schools and teachers. Mann planned the Massachusetts Normal School system for training new teachers. The compulsory public education that is taken for granted today was a new idea in **antebellum** America, and Mann faced opposition to his ideas. Shortly after Massachusetts adopted this system, New York followed suit, laying the foundation for the present state-based educational system.

Dorothea Dix

Dorothea Dix was an advocate for public treatment and care for the mentally ill. In the early 1840s, Dix called attention to the deplorable treatment and conditions to which the mentally ill in Massachusetts were subjected in a pamphlet titled *Memorial to the Legislature of Massachusetts.* Her efforts resulted in a bill that expanded the state hospital. Dix traveled to several other states, encouraging and overseeing the founding of state mental hospitals. Dix proposed federal legislation that would have sold public land with the proceeds being distributed to the states to fund care for the mentally ill. Congress approved the legislation. Using public money for social welfare, however, was a contentious issue, and President **Franklin Pierce** vetoed it on these grounds.

Other notable issues

Other social issues were also addressed. It was during this period that efforts were made to transform the **prison system** and its emphasis on punishment into a **penitentiary system** that attempted **rehabilitation**.

Other notable people

The following is a partial list of well-known Americans who contributed their leadership and talents in various fields and reforms:

- Emma Willard, Catharine Beecher, and Mary Lyon: education for women
- Dr. Elizabeth Blackwell: the first woman doctor

- Antoinette Louisa Blackwell: the first female minister
- Elihu Burritt and William Ladd: peace activists
- Henry Barmard, Calvin E. Stowe, Caleb Mills, and John Swett: public education
- Benjamin Lundy, David Walker, William Lloyd Garrison, Isaac Hooper, Arthur and Lewis Tappan, Theodore Weld, Frederick Douglass, Harriet Tubman, James G. Birney, Henry Highland Garnet, James Forten, Robert Purvis, Harriet Beecher Stowe, Wendell Phillips, and John Brown: abolition of slavery and the Underground Railroad
- Louisa Mae Alcott, James Fenimore Cooper, Washington Irving, Walt Whitman, Henry David Thoreau, Ralph Waldo Emerson, Herman Melville, Richard Henry Dana, Nathaniel Hawthorne, Henry Wadsworth Longfellow, John Greenleaf Whittier, Edgar Allan Poe, Oliver Wendell Holmes: famous writers

Women's Rights

The first American women's rights movement began in the 1840s. Among the early leaders of the movement were **Elizabeth Cady Stanton**, **Lucretia Mott**, and **Ernestine Rose**. At the time, very few states recognized women's rights to vote, own property, sue for divorce, or execute contracts.

The **SENECA FALLS CONVENTION**, held in the New York mill town of Seneca Falls in 1848, was the first women's rights convention in the United States. Lucretia Mott had attended the **World Anti-Slavery Society** in Britain in 1840, but she was not allowed to speak from the floor nor be seated as a delegate. This led to the discussion of how women could neither vote nor hold important positions in American government. **Abigail Adams** had even addressed this subject with her husband John Adams many years before when the Constitution was being written.

Some 300 people attended the convention, which culminated in the publication of a **DECLARATION OF SENTIMENTS**, largely written by Stanton and signed by 68 women and 32 men. **Frederick Douglass** described it as the "grand basis for attaining the civil, social, political, and religious rights of women." Others thoroughly objected. The structure of the document was based on the Declaration of Independence: "We hold these truths to be self-evident: that all men and women are created equal."

In 1869, **Susan B. Anthony**, Ernestine Rose, and Elizabeth Cady Stanton founded the **National Woman Suffrage Association**.

SENECA FALLS CONVENTION: the first women's rights convention in the United States

For a timeline of women's rights, check out this site:

www.infoplease.com/spot/womenstimeline1.html

DECLARATION OF SENTIMENTS: an important document in the women's rights movement, largely written by Elizabeth Cady Stanton and signed by 68 women and 32 men at the Seneca Falls Convention

SKILL 1.8 **Civil War era**

National Tension and the Buildup to the Civil War

The buildup to the Civil War took decades. The first serious clash between the North and South occurred in 1819–1820 during the presidency of **James Monroe** and concerned admitting **Missouri** as a state.

In 1819, the United States consisted of twenty-one states: eleven free states and ten slave states. **Alabama** had been admitted as a slave state and that had balanced the Senate, with the North and South each having twenty-two senators. The Missouri Territory allowed slavery and, if admitted, would cause an imbalance in the number of U.S. Senators in states with and without slavery.

FIRST MISSOURI COMPROMISE: a compromise that attempted to resolve the slavery conflict by approving admission of the northern part of Massachusetts as the free state of Maine and Missouri as a slave state

SECOND MISSOURI COMPROMISE: this proposal stated that the Constitution of the United States guaranteed protections and privileges to citizens of states, and Missouri's proposed constitution could not deny these to any of its citizens

POPULAR SOVEREIGNTY: doctrine stating that people living in territories and states should be allowed to decide for themselves whether or not slavery should be permitted

The Missouri Compromises

The **FIRST MISSOURI COMPROMISE** resolved the conflict by approving admission of the northern part of Massachusetts as the free state of Maine and Missouri as a slave state—thus maintaining the balance of power in the Senate with the same number of free and slave states. An additional provision of this compromise was that with the admission of Missouri, slavery would not be allowed in the rest of the Louisiana Purchase territory north of latitude 36 degrees 30'. This was acceptable to the slave-state congressmen since it was not profitable to grow cotton on land north of this latitude anyway.

It looked as though the crisis had been resolved, but Missouri's proposed state constitution barred the immigration of free blacks into the state.

Anti-slavery Congressmen were determined to exclude Missouri from the Union. **Henry Clay**, known as the **Great Compromiser**, then proposed a **SECOND MISSOURI COMPROMISE**, which was acceptable to everyone. His proposal stated that the Constitution of the United States guaranteed protections and privileges to citizens of states, and Missouri's proposed constitution could not deny these to any of its citizens. The acceptance in 1820 of this second compromise opened the way for Missouri's statehood. This reprieve was only temporary.

More compromises and more tension

The slavery issue continued to flare. In addition to the two factions of those who opposed slavery and those who supported it, a third faction supported the doctrine of **POPULAR SOVEREIGNTY**, which stated that people living in territories and states should be allowed to decide for themselves whether or not slavery should be permitted. When California applied for admittance to the Union in 1849, the furor began anew.

The result of this conflict was the **COMPROMISE OF 1850**, a series of laws designed as a final solution to the issue. To satisfy those who opposed slavery, the compromise admitted California as a free state and abolished slave trading in Washington, D.C. To satisfy those who supported slavery, it called for stricter measures to capture runaway slaves. And as for popular sovereignty, New Mexico and Utah territories would decide for themselves whether or not to permit slavery.

COMPROMISE OF 1850: a series of laws designed as a final solution to the issue of admitting new states as either free or slave states

A few years later, Congress took up consideration of new territories between Missouri and present-day Idaho. Again, heated debate over permitting slavery in these areas flared up.

Those opposed to slavery used the Missouri Compromise to prove their point, showing that the land being considered for territories was part of the area the compromise had designated as prohibiting slavery. But on May 25, 1854, Congress passed the infamous **KANSAS-NEBRASKA ACT**, which nullified this provision, created the territories of **Kansas** and **Nebraska**, and allowed the two territories to decide for themselves whether or not to permit slavery.

KANSAS-NEBRASKA ACT: nullified the provision that prohibited slavery in the area, created the territories of Kansas and Nebraska, and allowed the two territories to decide for themselves whether or not to permit slavery

Kansas-Nebraska Act 1854

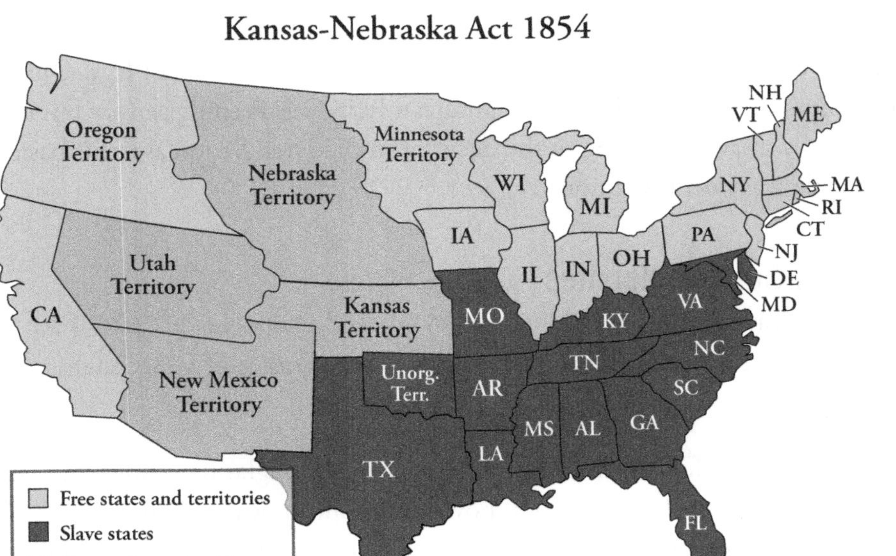

Adapted from Slavery in the Field. *New York Tribune*, January 6, 1854.

Feelings of both sides of the issue were so deep and divided that any further attempts to compromise would meet with little, if any, success. Political and social turmoil swirled everywhere. Kansas came to be called **Bleeding Kansas** due to the violence and bloodshed throughout the territory, as two governments existed there—one proslavery and the other anti-slavery. Then, in 1857, the Supreme Court handed down a decision guaranteed to cause explosions throughout the country.

For more information on Bleeding Kansas, check out this site:

www.pbs.org/wgbh/aia/part4/4p2952.html

The Dred Scott decision

Dred Scott was a slave whose owner had taken him from the slave state of Missouri to the free state of Illinois, to the Minnesota Territory (which was free under the provisions of the Missouri Compromise), and then finally back to Missouri. Abolitionists presented a court case on Scott's behalf; they believed that since Scott, whose owner had by then died, had previously lived in free territory, he was a free man.

For more information on the history of the Whig Party, check out this site:

www.us-civilwar.com/whig.htm

One lower court ruled in favor of freedom, and one lower court ruled against. In 1857, the Supreme Court decided that residing in a free state and free territory did not make Scott a free man because Scott and all other slaves were not U.S. citizens or state citizens of Missouri. Therefore, he did not have the right to sue in state or federal courts.

The Supreme Court went a step further and ruled that the old Missouri Compromise was now unconstitutional because Congress did not have the power to prohibit slavery in the territories.

The only way to ban slavery in new areas was by a Constitutional amendment, requiring ratification by three-fourths of all states; this was impossible because of Southern opposition.

The Compromise of 1850, along with the deaths of Daniel Webster and a division of pro- and anti-slavery members, put the Whig Party on its last legs. One of the platforms of the newly formed Republican Party was keeping slavery out of the territories. Now, according to the decision in the Dred Scott case, this basic party principle was unconstitutional.

Lincoln-Douglas debates

In 1858, former Whig **Abraham Lincoln** and Democrat **Stephen A. Douglas** were running against each other for the office of U.S. Senator from Illinois.

Lincoln viewed the Kansas-Nebraska Act, which Douglas had sponsored, as being immoral and disturbing. Lincoln, now a Republican, was not an abolitionist, but he believed that slavery was morally wrong. Lincoln supported the Republican Party's principle that slavery must not be permitted to extend any further.

Douglas, on the other hand, had originated the doctrine of popular sovereignty and was responsible for supporting and pushing the inflammatory Kansas-Nebraska Act through Congress. Douglas, up for reelection, knew that if he won this race, he had a good chance of becoming President in 1860.

In the course of the debates, Lincoln challenged Douglas to show that popular sovereignty reconciled with the Dred Scott decision. Whichever way he answered Lincoln, Douglas would lose crucial support from one group or the other. If he supported the Dred Scott decision, Southerners would support him, but he would lose Northern support. If he stayed with popular sovereignty, Northern support would be his, but Southern support would be lost.

His reply to Lincoln, stating that territorial legislatures could exclude slavery by refusing to pass laws supporting it, gave him enough support and approval to be reelected to the Senate; however, it cost him the Democratic nomination for president in 1860. Southern Democrats realized that Douglas was devoted to popular sovereignty but not necessarily to the expansion of slavery.

Lincoln received the nomination of the Republican Party for President.

Abolitionist John Brown

In 1859, in what is now West Virginia, abolitionist **John Brown** and his followers seized the federal arsenal at **Harper's Ferry**. Brown's purpose was to take the guns stored in the arsenal, give them to slaves nearby, and lead them in a widespread rebellion. He and his men were captured by **Col. Robert E. Lee** of the U.S. Army; tried and found guilty, he was hanged.

It was not the first illegal effort Brown had been part of. He and his sons murdered five men who were pro-slavery, in response to the sacking of Lawrence, Kansas, which was largely anti-slavery. Brown and his sons escaped, and he went on to solicit wealthy abolitionists to create a colony for runaway slaves.

Most Southerners felt that the majority of Northerners approved of Brown's actions, and Southern newspapers frequently quoted the small, but well-known, minority of abolitionists who applauded Brown's actions. Northern abolitionists viewed Brown's execution as an example of the government's support for slavery.

When economic issues and the issue of slavery came to a head, the North declared slavery illegal.

Presidential election of 1860

Candidates from four political parties vied for the Presidency in 1860.

- **Southern Democrats**, who endorsed slavery, nominated John Breckenridge
- **Republicans**, who denounced slavery, nominated Abraham Lincoln
- **Northern Democrats**, who said democracy required the people themselves to decide on slavery locally, nominated Stephen Douglas
- **The Constitutional Union Party**, which prioritized the survival of the Union, nominated John Bell

Although Lincoln received less than 40 percent of the popular vote, he won the electoral vote by a large margin and became the new president. But the fact that Lincoln did not win a popular majority or a single Southern state fueled Southerners' dissatisfaction. They increasingly felt that the federal government did not represent them.

The Southern states secede

The doctrine of nullification that had come up during Jackson's presidency resurfaced in the debate over slavery. The South asserted that states could **secede** from the union and form their own government just as Texas had seceded from Mexico. The North saw the doctrine of nullification as the assumption that the United States was a league of states rather than a union, as the founders had intended when they acknowledged that the Articles of Confederation did not work well. The North saw secession as a violation of the nation that could not be torn apart because of differences in component parts of it; they claimed that both Federalists and Anti-Federalists, North and South alike, had come to agreement on this in the constitutional period.

The doctrine of nullification that had come up during Jackson's presidency resurfaced in the debate over slavery.

After Lincoln's election, the Southern states returned to their earlier proposition that they had the right to secede from the union, and one by one they voted to do so. South Carolina was the first state to secede from the Union; the first shots of the war were fired on **Fort Sumter** in Charleston Harbor in April 1861. The North and South sides quickly prepared for war.

The Civil War

Northern Advantages

The North boasted superiority in the following areas:

- Population
- Finances
- Transportation facilities
- Manufacturing
- Agriculture
- Natural resources

The North also possessed most of the nation's gold, had about 92 percent of all industries, and claimed almost all known supplies of copper, coal, iron, and various other minerals. Since most of the nation's railroads were in the North and Midwest, men and supplies could move more easily wherever needed. Trade with nations overseas could continue due to Northern control of the U.S. Navy and the merchant fleet.

There were 24 Northern states, including the western states of California and Oregon; the border states of Maryland, Delaware, Kentucky, Missouri, which did not secede; and West Virginia, an area that seceded from Virginia after it seceded from the Union. (Nevada became a Union state during the Civil War.)

Southern Advantages

Some eleven Southern states made up the Confederacy: South Carolina, Georgia, Florida, Alabama, Mississippi, Louisiana, Texas, Virginia, North Carolina, Tennessee, and Arkansas.

Although outnumbered in population, the South was completely confident of victory. The rationale was that fighting a defensive war and protecting their own territory would lead the North—which had to invade and defeat an area almost the size of Western Europe—to tire of the struggle and give up.

A number of the South's best military officers had graduated from the U.S. Military Academy at **West Point** and had long years of army experience. Some of them had held commissions in the Indian wars and the war with Mexico. Further, many Southern men were conditioned to living outdoors in a warm climate and, because of lifestyle, were more familiar with horses and firearms than men from northeastern cities. Finally, because cotton was such an important crop, Southerners believed that British and French textile mills, dependent on raw cotton, would certainly side with the Confederacy in the war.

The major aims of the Confederacy never wavered. Their goals were:

- To win independence
- To win the right to govern themselves as states as they wished
- To preserve slavery

Strategies for the Civil War

The war strategies for both sides were relatively clear and simple.

Southern strategy

The **South** planned a defensive war, wearing down the North until it agreed to peace on Southern terms. It aimed to gain control of Washington, D.C., and to go north through the Shenandoah Valley into Maryland and Pennsylvania in order to drive a wedge between the Northeast and Midwest. This would interrupt the lines of communication, which they hoped would end the war quickly.

Northern strategy

For its part, the **North** planned to blockade the Confederate coastline in order to cripple the South and seize control of the Mississippi River, the interior railroad lines, and the Confederate capital of Richmond, Virginia. Then the Union planned to head south to join with Union forces coming east from the Mississippi Valley.

EMANCIPATION PROCLAMATION: Lincoln's1863 presidential proclamation that freed slaves

The 1863 **EMANCIPATION PROCLAMATION** that freed slaves became part of the Union's strategy. It resulted in aggressive recruitment of blacks; more than 180,000 of them fought in the Union army and more than 10,000 in the navy.

Military engagements

Initial battles

BATTLE OF BULL RUN: the first major battle of the Civil War, occurring in July 1861

It was at Bull Run that **Gen. Thomas Jackson** *got the nickname Stonewall Jackson, for taking such a strong stand against the Union.*

In July 1861, the first **BATTLE OF BULL RUN** was the first major battle of the war. Less than 40 miles from Washington, D.C., this battle was observed by picnickers, who came out to watch and cheer on the troops. The carnage they witnessed, however, changed the general opinion of war as a sporting event. In this first major battle, 2,900 Northern troops were killed, wounded, captured, or missing, as were 2,000 Southern troops. Both sides realized that the war was not going to be fought and won quickly; they prepared for a protracted struggle.

The war raged in the South. **Gen. Ulysses Grant** captured Fort Henry, Tennessee, located on the Tennessee River, in February 1862. This was the first major Union victory of the war.

Gettysburg

BATTLE OF GETTYSBURG: from July 1 to July 3, 1863, in Gettysburg, Pennsylvania, this battle proved to be a turning point in the war

The 1863 **BATTLE OF GETTYSBURG** proved to be a turning point in the war. After success at **Chancellorsville**, Gen. Robert E. Lee's **Amy of Northern Virginia** headed through the Shenandoah Valley, aiming toward Philadelphia. They met with the Union troops in Gettysburg, Pennsylvania; the fighting lasted from July 1 to July 3, 1863.

Lee's troops suffered a strategic disadvantage at Gettysburg, because Union troops gained the best positions and the best ground first, which allowed the Union troops to more easily make a stand there. Lee's overconfidence may also have undermined his efforts.

On the third and last day of the battle, Lee launched a final attempt to break Union lines. **Gen. George Pickett** sent his division of three brigades under Generals **Garnet**, **Kemper**, and **Armistead** against Union troops on Cemetery Ridge under command of **Gen. Winfield Scott Hancock**. The Union lines held, and Lee and the defeated Army of Northern Virginia made their way back to Virginia. Casualties numbered nearly 50,000.

The Union successfully turned back the Confederate charge. However, Lincoln's commander, **George Meade**, and his troops did not pursue Lee and the Confederate soldiers.

The battle of Gettysburg was the turning point in the war for the North. After this, Lee never again had the troop strength to launch a major offensive.

The day after the Battle of Gettysburg ended, on July 4, 1863, Vicksburg, Mississippi, surrendered to Grant, severing the western Confederacy from its eastern counterpart.

Final stages of the war

The Confederacy won its last important victory at **Chickamauga** in September 1863. That November, the Union victories in **Chattanooga, Tennessee**, at **Lookout Mountain** and **Missionary Ridge** made it possible for Union troops to go into Alabama and Georgia, completely splitting the eastern Confederacy in two.

Lincoln gave U. S. Grant command of all Northern armies in March 1864. The **OVERLAND CAMPAIGN** began at the inconclusive battle at **Wilderness of Spotsylvania**, where Lee eliminated the Union's artillery advantage. Casualties were high throughout the campaign, but by keeping Confederate forces engaged in battle, Grant forced Lee into the position that led to the end of the war.

OVERLAND CAMPAIGN: an offensive launched by General Grant in Virginia in mid-1864

Joining Grant, **Gen. Philip Sheridan** smashed through the Confederate lines at **Five Forks** in Virginia on April 1, 1865, necessitating the evacuation of both Petersburg and **Richmond**, the Confederate capital. Confederate General Pickett's losses led to the retreat to **Appomattox**.

Meanwhile, the other armies under Grant's direction tore the Confederacy apart. The Union won a battle at **Mobile Bay**, and in May 1864, **William Tecumseh Sherman** began his march to demolish Atlanta and burn his way on to Savannah. Sherman and his troops then turned northward through the Carolinas to meet with Grant in Virginia.

On April 9, 1865, Lee formally surrendered to Grant at the **Appomattox Courthouse** *in Virginia.*

On April 9, 1865, Lee formally surrendered to Grant at the **Appomattox Courthouse** in Virginia.

Aftermath of the Civil War

Assassination of President Lincoln

Five days after the surrender, on April 14, 1865, Lincoln and his wife, Mary, went to **Ford's Theater** in Washington, D.C. to see the play *Our American Cousin*. During the third act of the play, **John Wilkes Booth** shot Lincoln in the head. Doctors moved Lincoln from the theater to a house across the street, but he never regained consciousness. He died at 7:22 the next morning.

Results of the war

The Civil War took more American lives than any other war in America's history.

The Civil War took more American lives than any other war in America's history—more than 618,000 men died, with the South losing one-third of its soldiers in battle and the North losing about one-sixth. More than half of those deaths were caused by disease and the horrendous conditions of field hospitals. Both sides paid a tremendous economic price, but the South also suffered severely from direct damages because most battles were fought in the South.

The Civil War changed methods of waging war. It introduced weapons and tactics that, when improved later, were used extensively in the wars that followed. Civil War soldiers were the first to:

- Fight in trenches
- Fight under a unified command
- Wage a defense called "major cordon defense," a strategy of advance on all fronts
- Use repeating and breech-loading weapons
- Utilize observation balloons during the war along with submarines, ironclad ships, and mines
- Communicate by telegraph
- Travel by railroad

The Civil War is considered a "modern war" because of the vast destruction it caused and it was considered "total war" because it involved the use of all resources of the opposing sides.

FREEDMEN'S BUREAU: created during Reconstruction to help four million freed slaves become self-sufficient and protect them from being taken advantage of by others

RECONSTRUCTION: the period between 1865 and 1877 when the federal and state governments debated and implemented plans to provide civil rights to freed slaves and to set the terms under which the former Confederate states might once again join the Union

Reconstruction

The Freedmen's Bureau

The economic and social chaos in the South after the war was incredible. Disease especially was rampant. Although the U.S. Army provided some relief in the form of food and clothing, the responsibility primarily fell to the **FREEDMEN'S BUREAU**. Though Bureau agents helped southern whites, their main responsibility was to help four million freed slaves (freedmen) become self-sufficient and protect them from being taken advantage of by others. Many Northerners looked on it as a real, honest effort to help the South out of the chaos it was in. Most white Southerners, however, accused the Bureau of deliberately encouraging freedmen to consider former slave owners as enemies.

Defining Reconstruction

RECONSTRUCTION refers to the period between 1865 and 1877 when the federal and state governments debated and implemented plans to provide civil rights to freed slaves and to set the terms under which the former Confederate states might once again join the Union. Reconstruction had three phases:

1. Presidential Reconstruction
2. Congressional Reconstruction
3. The Redemption

Lincoln's moderate plan for Reconstruction had been part of his effort to win the war. Lincoln and the moderates had thought that if it remained easy for states to return to the Union and if moderate proposals on black suffrage were made, the Confederate states involved in the hostilities might be swayed to rejoin the Union rather than continue fighting the war.

After Lincoln's death, **moderate Republicans** wanted to allow all but former Confederate leaders to vote, while the **Radical Republicans** wanted to require an oath from all eligible voters stating they had never borne arms against the United States (thus excluding all former rebels).

Radical Republican control

Radical Republicans in Congress, such as **Charles Sumner** in the Senate, viewed the Southern states as being in the same position as any unorganized territory. House leader **Thaddeus Stevens** said: "It would be best for the South to remain 10 years longer under military rule, and that during this time we would have Territorial Governors, with Territorial Legislatures, and the government at Washington would pay our general expenses as territories, and educate our children, white and colored." But President **Andrew Johnson** was conciliatory toward the South. He supported Black Codes, vetoed renewal of the Freedman Bureau, and vetoed the Civil Rights bill.

In response, when the Radical Republicans—who had been abolitionists before the war—gained control of both houses of Congress in 1868, they attempted to impeach Johnson, falling one vote short of conviction. The Republicans in Congress favored the extension of **voting rights** to black men but were divided as to how far to extend the right. Moderate Republicans wanted only literate African Americans and those who had fought for the Union to be allowed to vote. Radical Republicans wanted to extend the vote to all African-American men. **Conservative Democrats** did not want to give African Americans the vote at all.

Radical Republican legislation

Not surprisingly, Southerners took measures to make sure that freedmen stayed under white control. **BLACK CODES** in the South made it illegal to let freedmen

BLACK CODES: laws that prohibited freedmen from testifying against whites, bearing arms, or having large gatherings; they mandated segregated schools; created provisions for arresting unemployed black vagrants, and prohibited freedmen from serving on juries

CIVIL RIGHTS ACT OF 1866: legal measures submitted to congress to counter the Black Codes

RECONSTRUCTION ACTS: legal measures that placed the governments of the southern states under the control of the federal military in order to ensure black's rights

THIRTEENTH AMENDMENT: ensures that neither slavery nor involuntary servitude would ever exist again in the United States

FOURTEENTH AMENDMENT: defines American citizenship, requires equal protection under the law by all states to all persons within their jurisdiction, and guarantees the right to sue or serve on a jury

FIFTEENTH AMENDMENT: guarantees that the right of citizens of the United States to vote shall not be denied or abridged by the United States or by any state on account of race, color, or previous condition of servitude

testify against whites, bear arms, or have large gatherings; mandated segregated schools; set rules that unemployed blacks would be arrested for vagrancy and then hired out as cheap labor; and prohibited freedmen from serving on juries.

The **CIVIL RIGHTS ACT OF 1866** was submitted to counter the Black Codes. Although Johnson vetoed it, Congress overrode the veto, and the bill became a law. In 1866, the Radical Republicans passed the **RECONSTRUCTION ACTS**, which placed the governments of the Southern states under the control of the federal military. Also, the Radical Republicans began to implement policies such as granting all black men the vote and denying the vote to former Confederate soldiers.

General Ulysses Grant was elected president in 1868 and served two scandal-ridden terms until 1877. Military control of the South continued throughout Grant's administration, despite growing conflict both inside and outside the Republican Party.

Constitutional amendments during Reconstruction

Three Amendments to the Constitution were part of Reconstruction. The **THIRTEENTH AMENDMENT** ratified on December 18, 1865 ensured that "neither slavery nor involuntary servitude" would ever exist again in the United States.

The **FOURTEENTH AMENDMENT**, which overturned the Dred Scott decision, was ratified on July 9, 1868. It defines American citizenship and requires equal protection under the law by all states to all persons within their jurisdiction and guarantees the right to sue or serve on a jury.

The **FIFTEENTH AMENDMENT**, ratified on February 3, 1870, guarantees that "the right of citizens of the United States to vote shall not be denied or abridged by the United States or by any State on account of race, color, or previous condition of servitude."

Ratification of the Thirteenth, Fourteenth, and Fifteenth Amendments was a condition for Southern states to be readmitted to the Union. Republicans found support in the South among **SCALAWAGS**, southern whites who joined the Republican Party during Reconstruction and joined into a coalition with freedmen and newcomers from the North for control of the local and state governments. The newcomers from the North were called **CARPETBAGGERS** and arrived in the South for humanitarian reasons and/or to personally gain economically.

End of Reconstruction

Reconstruction officially ended when the last federal troops left the South in 1877 after the election of **Rutherford B. Hayes**.

Without the military support, the Republican governments were replaced by so-called **REDEEMER GOVERNMENTS**. The rise of the Redeemer governments marked the beginning of the **Jim Crow laws** and official segregation. Blacks still had the legal right to vote, but white Southern leaders found ways—such as literacy tests, poll taxes, and physical violence—to make it difficult for them to do so.

Reconstruction did set up public school systems and expanded the legal rights of black Americans through amendments to the Constitution. However, in terms of its goals of reunification of the South with the North and guaranteeing civil rights to freed slaves, Reconstruction was only a limited success.

SCALAWAGS: southern whites who joined the Republican Party during Reconstruction and joined into a coalition with freedmen and newcomers from the North for control of the local and state governments

CARPETBAGGERS: newcomers from the North who arrived in the South for humanitarian reasons and/or to personally gain economically

SKILL 1.9 Emergence of the modern United States

The conclusion of the Civil War opened the floodgates for westward migration and settlement of new land. The availability of cheap land and the expectation of great opportunity, spurred on by the discovery of gold in California in 1849, had already prompted many to travel to the **Great Plains** and the **West Coast**. After the Civil War, the numbers increased. In 1867, Russia ceded more than 500,000 square miles of land to the United States for $7,200,000. **Alaska** was more than twice the size of Texas.

REDEEMER GOVERNMENTS: governments that replaced Reconstruction efforts after federal troops left the South; they marked the beginning of the Jim Crow laws and official segregation

Railroads

While Americans had begun building railroads before the Civil War, it was only after the war ended that the railroads expanded across North America. The **Union Pacific** and **Central Pacific Railroads** completed the first section of the **TRANSCONTINENTAL RAILROAD** from Omaha, Nebraska, to Sacramento, California, in 1869. A majority of the railroad workers in the West were Chinese, and much of the work they did was extremely dangerous.

TRANSCONTINENTAL RAILROAD: a railroad that spanned the North American continent

Railroad development resulted in efficient transportation of products across the nation. However, as the railroads developed, so did the effort to reward larger shippers with rebates and other incentives, often charging more for shipping products short distances. Consequently, smaller, family farms suffered.

For more information on the Central Pacific Railroad, check out this site:

cprr.org/Museum/Chinese.html

Immigration

Between 1870 and 1916, more than 25 million immigrants came into the United States. The three main reasons for immigration to the United States at this time were:

- Economic opportunity
- Freedom from religious discrimination
- Refuge from political unrest and war

Nationalities of immigrants

NATURALIZATION ACT OF 1870: limited U.S. citizenship to "white persons and persons of African descent"

CHINESE EXCLUSION ACT OF 1882: restricted immigration of Chinese immigrants into the United States

The **NATURALIZATION ACT OF 1870** limited U.S. citizenship to "white persons and persons of African descent," and the **CHINESE EXCLUSION ACT OF 1882** restricted immigration of Chinese immigrants into the United States. The act resulted in widening the ratio of Chinese men to Chinese women to 27:1.

Along with the arrival of the Chinese, between 1800 and 1880, more than 10 million immigrants came from Northern Europe, especially from England, Ireland, and Germany. The Irish generally stayed on the East Coast, while the Germans tended to move west. During the 1850s, the primary focus of the **Know-Nothing Party** had been demanding laws to reduce this immigration.

During the 1870s, the United States suffered a recession, but immigration continued. Between 1891 and 1910, approximately 12 million immigrants arrived from all over the world—particularly from eastern and southern Europe. Prejudice increased against Roman Catholics, Jews, and the Japanese.

Legislating immigration

IMMIGRATION ACT OF 1882: created a 50-cent tax on immigrants when they arrived

EMERGENCY QUOTA ACT: limited the number of immigrants to the United States to three percent of the foreign-born people of that nationality who already lived in the United States in 1910

The **IMMIGRATION ACT OF 1882** created a 50-cent tax on immigrants when they arrived. The funds generated were used for regulating immigration, paying immigration agents, and caring for immigrants after they arrived. It also denied accepting immigrants who were convicts and "persons likely to become public charges." The numbers of immigrants coming to cities at this time were especially high. In 1892, **Ellis Island** opened as the processing center for immigrants arriving in New York, and it served more than 12 million immigrants over the next 50 years.

In 1921, the first immigration quota act was passed, the **EMERGENCY QUOTA ACT** also known as the Johnson Quota Act. It limited the number of immigrants allowed to three percent of the foreign-born people of that nationality who lived in the United States in 1910.

Agriculture

Legislating agriculture

In 1862, the **Department of Agriculture** was created. The same year, the **MORRILL LAND-GRANT ACTS**, which allowed for the creation of land-grant colleges, were passed. The **HATCH ACT OF 1887** set up agricultural experiment stations in connection to the land grant colleges. The **SMITH-LEVER ACT OF 1914** set up a nonformal educational program or cooperative to help citizens become knowledgeable about agriculture, food, home economics, environment, and community development. Agricultural extension programs were funded to increase farm yields.

MORRILL LAND-GRANT ACTS: allowed for the creation of land-grant colleges

HATCH ACT OF 1887: set up agricultural experiment stations in connection to the land grant colleges

Agricultural technology

There were many advances in agricultural technology in the nineteenth century. The benefits of **irrigation** were discovered, and during the mid-1800s, advances were introduced for cultivation, breeding, use of fertilizers, and crop rotation. In 1892, the first successful **gasoline-powered tractor** was introduced in Iowa. (By the 1900s, one tractor could substitute for 17 men and 50 horses.) In 1893, 42 patented insecticides were sold to farmers. The steel plow made it possible for widespread cultivation on the dense soil of the Great Plains, an area that used to be called the **Great American Desert**. Ranches developed in the Southwest, primarily for raising cattle, including the longhorn, which can survive where no other breed can.

SMITH-LEVER ACT OF 1914: set up a nonformal educational program or cooperative to help citizens become knowledgeable about agriculture, food, home economics, environment, and community development

Other developments in farming and ranching were the **reaper**, the **silo**, **deep-well drilling**, **barbed wire**, the **combine**, and **cream-separators**.

Agricultural decline

During the late 1800s, however, prices for farm goods, especially for wheat and cotton, fell drastically. Family farms were facing detrimental railroad strategies, which included rebates to larger agricultural producers. This preferential treatment for larger businesses was one factor that led to the formation of the **Populist Party** in 1892.

While 90 percent of the people in the United States had been farmers in 1790, by 1890, those who worked on farms were 43 percent of the labor force. By 1930, it was 21 percent; by 1990, it was 2.5 percent.

Business and Industry

At the end of the Civil War, industry in America was small. After the war, however, dramatic changes took place with the production of machines. The following is a limited list of American inventers who helped bring America into the future:

- Walter Hunt, Elias Howe, and Isaac Singer: the sewing machine
- Alexander Graham Bell: the telephone

- George Eastman: the camera
- Thomas Edison: the phonograph, the incandescent light bulb, and the motion picture
- Samuel Morse: the telegraph
- Cyrus McCormick: the reaper
- Charles Goodyear: vulcanized rubber
- Nikola Tesla: alternating current and the radio
- George Westinghouse: the transformer and air brake
- Richard Gatling: the machine gun
- Orville and Wilbur Wright: the airplane

Between 1860 and 1900, inventors registered almost 700,000 new patents.

The Gilded Age

GILDED AGE: the popular name for the period from the end of the Civil War to the beginning of World War I

The popular name for the period from the end of the Civil War to the beginning of World War I is the **GILDED AGE** or the Second Industrial Revolution. The new nation had the potential of enormous economic expansion as it moved from agriculture and mercantilism to industrialism, a system built on large industries instead of farming and craftsmanship.

The following is a list of major industrialists and financiers, their locations, and their industries:

- Philip Armour, Chicago: meatpacking
- John Jacob Astor IV, New York: inherited fortune, writer, businessman, hotelier
- Andrew Carnegie, Pittsburgh: railroads, steel; also contributed libraries
- Jay Cooke, Philadelphia: finance
- Charles Crocker, Monterey: dry goods, railroads
- Daniel Drew, New York: cattle, finance, brokerage
- James Buchanan Duke, Durham, NC: tobacco
- James Fisk, New York: smuggler, stockbroker, railroads
- Henry Flagler, New York/Palm Beach: real estate, railroads, Standard Oil
- Henry Ford, Dearborn/Detroit: inventor, automobile, mass production
- Henry Clay Frick, Pittsburgh/New York: steel

- John Warne Gates, Texas: wire, railroads, oil
- Jay Gould, New York: railroads, gold; involved in Tammany Hall and Boss Tweed
- E. H. Harriman, New York: railroads
- James J. Hill, St. Paul, MN: railroads, exports
- Mark Hopkins, San Francisco: railroads
- Collis P. Huntington, Sacramento/Richmond: railroads
- Andrew Mellon, Pittsburgh: oil, steel, ships, aluminum, banking
- J. Pierpont Morgan, New York: banking
- John D. Rockefeller and William Rockefeller, Cleveland: Standard Oil
- Jacob Schiff, New York: banking
- Leland Stanford, Sacramento/San Francisco: railroads
- Cornelius Vanderbilt, New York: railroads, shipping

While respected for business acumen and success, these men were also condemned for exploitation of workers and questionable business practices. They were also feared because of their power.

During the Gilded Age, banks were established, department stores began, the chain store was born, and trusts developed.

Trusts

After the Civil War, government encouraged the growth of business. **TRUSTS** were developed when the stockholders of many competing companies would give the control of the stock to a group of trustees who would operate all the companies as if they were one company and pay the profits to the stockholders.

TRUSTS: developed when the stockholders of many competing companies would give the control of the stock to a group of trustees who would operate all the companies as if they were one company and pay the profits to the stockholders

For example, more than 70 oil companies' stockholders gave control of the stock to—or had that control seized by—the nine trustees of Standard Oil. Thus, nine men were in charge of 90 percent of all oil production in the U.S.

At the same time was a rise of **monopolies**. An owner of one successful company would buy all the other companies engaged in the same product(s). Similarly, it was not uncommon that the owners would drive other owners out of business. One method for doing this was to lower prices so the competition could not make a profit. Once all competition was quashed, prices could skyrocket. Additionally, those companies with little or no competition would require their suppliers to supply goods at a low cost; but they would sell the finished products at high prices. Monopolists also reduced the quality of the product to save money—and the consumer would have no choice but to buy because there would be no alternative.

Growth of Cities

The growth of industry, the pace of capital investments, and the movement of large numbers of workers led to the growth of cities. Populations were shifting from rural agricultural areas to urban industrial areas. This had both advantages and disadvantages.

Chicago

Chicago was a perfect example of a city that offered advantages and disadvantages. In 1871, wooden buildings, ships on the Chicago River, wood-plank sidewalks, and lumberyards were all destroyed and hundreds were killed when strong winds carried a huge fire through the city. In 1903, another fire at the Iroquois Theater killed 600. The high population and urban clutter of the city no doubt contributed to the impact of these fires.

In 1893, however, the World Exposition in Chicago celebrated the 400th anniversary of Columbus' landing. This event brought world exposure and prosperity to the city.

Urban migration

By the early 1900s, a third of the nation's population lived in cities.

By the early 1900s, a third of the nation's population lived in cities. Industrialization also brought immigrants, many of whom lived in cities. High rates of immigration led to the creation of communities in various cities such as "Chinatown," "little Russia," or "little Italy." Increased urban populations, frequently packed into dense tenements, often without adequate sanitation facilities, led to public health challenges that required cities to establish sanitation, water, and public health departments to cope with and prevent epidemics.

Political organizations also saw the advantage of mobilizing the new industrial working class and created vast patronage programs that sometimes became notorious for corruption in big-city machine politics. One example is **Tammany Hall** in New York led by **William "Boss" Tweed**, who stole hundreds of thousands of dollars from the taxpayers.

Panic of 1873

COINAGE ACT OF 1873: changed to the gold standard and demonetized silver

The boom in the railroad industry had attracted speculators. When the banks of **Jay Cooke** and others went bankrupt because they had invested too much in the railroads, factories closed and credit evaporated. Workers endured great cuts in pay. The cause can be attributed, in part, to the change in money—the **COINAGE ACT OF 1873** changed to the gold standard and demonetized silver.

The next economic recession hit the West and South before it hit the cities in the 1890s. Drought struck and farm prices dropped, especially for cotton. Farmers then found themselves deeply in debt; tenant farmers especially suffered. All in all, the **Farmers' Alliance** had the benefit of uniting poor rural people into a political force.

For more information on Farmers' Alliance in Nebraska, check out these sites:

www.nebraskastudies.org/0600/frameset_reset.html?

www.nebraskastudies.org/0600/stories/0601_0302.html

The Populist Party

The **Populist Party** was officially formed by joining the Farmers' Alliance and the **Knights of Labor**. The platform of the Populist Party included:

- A national currency and unlimited coinage of silver and gold
- Graduated income tax
- Government ownership and operation of the railroads
- Government ownership of telegraph and telephone
- Secret ballot system
- Liberal pensions to ex-Union soldiers and sailors
- Restriction of immigration
- Abolition of Pinkerton system
- Limits to one term for president and vice president
- Direct vote for election of senators
- Abolition of subsidies to private corporations
- Reclamation of railroad lands by government

The Panic of 1893 and the Labor Movement

The **Panic of 1893** was a worldwide economic crisis that affected the United States. Railroads went bankrupt and unemployment in factories was as high as 25 percent. Industrial areas in cities, rural areas, and mill towns were hit hard. President **Grover Cleveland** repealed the **Sherman Silver Purchase Act** because he thought it caused the Panic.

The Panic led to a few significant social and political changes. First, it brought the Republican Party to power. Also, Americans began to view poverty as a broad economic failure rather than as God's punishment of the individual. Last, the labor movement expanded. Numerous boycotts and strikes became violent when the police or militia were called in to stop them.

HOMESTEAD STRIKE: took place between the Amalgamated Association of Iron and Steel Works (AA) and Carnegie Steel Company

PULLMAN STRIKE: took place between the American Railway Union and the Pullman Place Car Company, in response to a 28 percent pay cut

For more information on the Homestead and Pullman strikes, check out these sites:

www.pbs.org/wgbh/amex/carnegie/peopleevents/pande04.html

www.pbs.org/newshour/bb/business/september96/labor_day_9-2.html

MOTHER JONES: an activist and labor leader in the early 1900s

Labor advances and strikes

The 1890s economic recession struck the industrial areas of the cities; factory workers shared farmers' views against the industrialists. The goal of the Knights of Labor, formed in 1869 under **Uriah Stephens** and then **Terence Powderly**, was to organize all workers—whether skilled or unskilled, black or white, male or female—into one union united for the rights of all workers. Their goals included:

- The eight-hour workday
- Equal pay for women
- The elimination of child labor
- Cooperative ownership of factories and mines

Strikes

The 1892 **HOMESTEAD STRIKE** took place between the Amalgamated Association of Iron and Steel Works (AA) and Carnegie Steel Company. There was gunfire between the strikers and the Pinkerton strikebreakers, and the Carnegie Steel Company eliminated a union at the plant.

The 1894 **PULLMAN STRIKE** was called in response to a 28 percent pay cut. **George Pullman** had built a company town, and while workers surely appreciated it for a time, some compared it to a feudal society where everything was controlled and inspected by the feudal lord. The Pullman Strike was led by **Eugene Debs**, leader of the **American Railway Union**. Army troops were called in by President **Grover Cleveland** to break the strike, saying it interfered with the mail. Debs ran for President of the United States five times.

Mother Jones

MOTHER JONES—or Mary Harris Jones—was involved with the **United Mine Workers of America** (UMWA). She organized a Children's Crusade in 1903, marching children to President **Theodore Roosevelt**'s home in Oyster Bay, New York, to protest child labor. She was also one of the founders of the **Industrial Workers of the World** (IWW).

The Native Americans after the Civil War

Tribes of the West

Nomadic Native American tribes of the Great Plains followed vast herds of buffalo, their main food source. These tribes included the following:

- Cheyenne
- Lakota

- Arapaho
- Comanche
- Kiowa and Plains Apache
- Crow
- Blackfoot
- Assiniboine
- Liban
- Plains Cree
- Sarsi
- Tonkaw
- Shosone

Others for whom the **buffalo** were important were the following seminomadic Plains tribes:

- Arikara
- Hidatsa
- Iowa
- Kansa
- Mandan
- Omaha
- Osage
- Otoe
- Pawnee
- Ponca
- Wichita

Buffalo, or the American bison, were vital to these tribes. The white settlers usually killed this animal for the hides, but sometimes people would just shoot as many as possible from passing trains. Either way, the carcasses were left on the prairie to decay.

INDIAN WARS: numerous conflicts that broke out between the U.S. army and many different native tribes

BATTLE OF LITTLE BIGHORN: the battle in 1876 in which native people defeated General Custer and his forces

The Indian Wars

Numerous conflicts, often called the **INDIAN WARS**, broke out between the U.S. Army and many different native tribes. Though many treaties were signed with the various tribes, most were broken by the U.S. government. One of the most known conflicts was the 1876 **BATTLE OF LITTLE BIGHORN** (sometimes also known as Battle of the Greasy Grass and Custer's Last Stand), in which native people defeated Gen. George Custer and his forces.

Lead up to Little Bighorn

In 1871, **Chief Sitting Bull**'s Hunkpapas learned that the **Northern Pacific Railway** intended to make a railway route directly through their lands. The Panic of 1873, however, which caused Jay Cooke's bank to go under, eliminated this plan. But then General Custer came to the Black Hills to seek gold and select a site for a fort. When gold was found, the government insisted that all Sioux move to the Sioux reservation. When they refused, the government termed them "hostile." More than 3,000 Native Americans left their reservations to follow Sitting Bull. The result was the Battle of Little Bighorn and the death of General

For information on "Our Indian Wards," check out this site:

etext.virginia.edu/railton/roughingit/map/bufmaypenny.html

DAWES ACT OF 1887: intended to break up the Native American communities and bring about assimilation into white culture by deeding portions of reservation lands to individual Native Americans who were expected to farm the land

INDIAN BOARDING SCHOOLS: schools intended to "civilize" Native American children by assimilating them into mainstream American culture

For more information on Indian boarding schools, check out these sites:

www.kporterfield.com/aicttw/articles/boardingschool.html#section2

www.english.uiuc.edu/maps/poets/a_f/erdrich/boarding/index.htm

Custer. The government came down even harder on the tribes. Chief Sitting Bull escaped to Saskatchewan, came back to surrender, spent some time in jail, and then joined Buffalo Bill Cody's Wild West Show.

Reservations and Assimilation

In 1876, the U.S. government ordered all surviving Native Americans to move to **reservations**. Continued conflict led to passage of the **DAWES ACT OF 1887**. This was in response to the recognition that confinement to reservations was not working. The law was intended to break up the Native American communities and bring about assimilation into white culture by deeding portions of the reservation lands to individual Native Americans who were expected to farm their land. The policy continued until 1934.

In addition, during the late nineteenth century, the avid reformers of the day instituted a practice of trying to "civilize" Native American children by educating them in **INDIAN BOARDING SCHOOLS**. The children were forbidden to speak their native languages, required to convert to Christianity, and generally forced to give up all aspects of their native culture and identity. There are numerous reports of child abuse at these schools.

From resistance to preservation

Armed resistance essentially came to an end in 1890 as a result of the well-known massacre of Native Americans at **Wounded Knee**. The surrender of **Geronimo** and the massacre at Wounded Knee led to a change of strategy by the Native Americans. Thereafter, the resistance strategy was to preserve their culture and traditions.

SKILL 1.10 Progressive era and the First World War through the New Deal

The Progressive Era

The **Progressive Era** began in the 1890s and lasted until the end of World War I. **Progressives** opposed waste and corruption and advocated for workers' rights and safety. Progressives also believed that science could resolve many issues, government could help to endorse fairness and repair social problems, and more people could be directly involved in the political process.

Genesis of the Progressive Movement

One factor that led to the Progressive movement was the disparity between rich and poor, which resulted in a public call for reform. At the same time, there was an outcry for governmental reform to address political corruption and elitism. Several political parties were formed out of this philosophy, including:

- The Greenback Party
- The Populist Party
- The Farmer-Labor Party
- The Progressive Party
- The Union Party

In addition, a **SINGLE TAX MOVEMENT** sought to "abolish all taxation save that upon land values."

SINGLE TAX MOVEMENT: sought to "abolish all taxation save that upon land values"

MUCKRAKERS, who published scathing exposés of political and business wrongdoing and corruption, fueled attitudes toward reform and change. Some notable muckrakers included investigative journalists **Ida Tarbell**, **Jacob Riis**, and **Lincoln Steffens**, as well as novelist **Upton Sinclair**. Muckrakers used their writings to address such issues as child labor laws, workers' compensation, and trust-busting.

MUCKRAKERS: publishers of scathing exposés of political and business wrongdoing and corruption

Progressive reforms

Although Progressive leaders came from many different backgrounds and were driven by different ideologies, they shared a common fundamental belief that government should work toward eradicating social ills and promoting the common good. Among their reforms were:

- **Seventeenth Amendment:** Provided for the popular election of U.S. Senators
- **Eighteenth Amendment:** Provided for the prohibition of alcohol
- **Nineteenth Amendment:** Provided women the right to vote
- **Sherman Antitrust Act:** Opened the door for breaking up trusts and monopolies
- **Elkins Act and Hepburn Act:** Regulated railroads
- Initiative and referendum laws at a state level: Enabled citizens to put propositions before the public to vote on
- Recall laws: Enabled the recall of elected officials
- **Food and Drugs Act:** Required accurate labeling and prohibited poisonous additives

- **Meat Inspection Act:** Regulated the meat industry to protect the public against tainted meat
- **Department of Commerce and Labor:** Created to oversee industry

Environmental reforms

Responding to concern over the environmental effects of the timber, ranching, and mining industries, Theodore Roosevelt set aside 238 million acres of federal lands to protect them from development. Wildlife preserves were established, the national park system was expanded, and the **National Conservation Commission** was created. The **NEWLANDS RECLAMATION ACT** also provided federal funding for the construction of irrigation projects and dams in semiarid areas of the country.

NEWLANDS RECLAMATION ACT: established wildlife preserves, expanded the national park system, created the National Conservation Commission, and provided federal funding for the construction of irrigation projects and dams in semi-arid areas of the country

Economic reforms

The **Woodrow Wilson** administration carried out additional reforms. The **FEDERAL RESERVE ACT OF 1913** created a national banking authority, providing a stable money supply. The **SHERMAN ANTITRUST ACT** and **THE CLAYTON ANTITRUST ACT** defined unfair competition, made corporate officers liable for the illegal actions of employees, and exempted labor unions from antitrust lawsuits. The **Federal Trade Commission** was established to enforce these measures. Finally, the Sixteenth Amendment was ratified, establishing a graduated income tax. This measure was designed to relieve the poor of a disproportionate burden in funding the federal government and make the wealthy pay a greater share of the nation's tax burden.

FEDERAL RESERVE ACT OF 1913: created a national banking authority, providing a stable money supply

SHERMAN ANTITRUST ACT AND THE CLAYTON ANTITRUST ACT: defined unfair competition, made corporate officers liable for the illegal actions of employees, and exempted labor unions from antitrust lawsuits

Notable progressives

Some notable Progressives were:

- Jane Addams: Chicago social reformer and first woman to win the Nobel Peace Prize
- Robert La Follette: Wisconsin politician opposed corruption and entry into World War I
- W.E.B. Du Bois: Civil rights activist and leader
- John R. Mott: YMCA leader and Nobel Prize winner
- Booker T. Washington: Educator who began life as a slave
- Margaret Sanger: Birth control activist
- William Jennings Bryan: Supporter of prohibition and opponent of Darwinism

- Thorstein Veblen: Sociologist and economist
- Walter Lippman: Investigative journalist
- Ida B. Wells: Antilynching and women's rights advocate

Expanding Overseas

During the late nineteenth and early twentieth centuries, the United States began to expand abroad. **Captain Brooks** of the Hawaiian barque, Gambia, discovered **Midway Island** and named the islands "Middlebrook." Then Capt. **William Reynolds** of the **USS Lackawanna** took possession of the islands in 1867, marking the first acquisition of an island by the United States. Elsewhere in the Pacific, the United States lent its support to American sugar planters and assisted in overthrowing the **Kingdom of Hawaii.**

By the 1880s, Secretary of State **James G. Blaine** favored a **PAN-AMERICAN CONGRESS**, which refers to economic, commercial, social, military, and political cooperation throughout the Americas. In the 1890s, President Grover Cleveland interpreted the Monroe Doctrine to mean there were American interests everywhere in the Western Hemisphere. The United States became involved in a border dispute between Great Britain and Venezuela, taking Venezuela's side to improve relations between the United States and Venezuela.

PAN-AMERICAN CONGRESS: refers to economic, commercial, social, military, and political cooperation throughout the Americas

The Spanish-American War

Background of the war

During the 1890s, Spain still controlled land overseas, including Puerto Rico, the Philippines, and Cuba. Spain had taken over the island of Cuba after Columbus discovered it, and then decimated the island's population by forcing them to work in gold mines. When the native people became too feeble, the Spanish imported slaves from Africa. The slaves revolted several times, but the Spanish had put down the revolts and continued to use and demand cheap products from them. When slavery ended in 1886, the Cubans were prepared to revolt.

The Spanish-American War marked the start of the United States becoming a world power.

In 1853, during Franklin Pierce's presidency, the United States had offered Spain $130 million for Cuba. The offer was not accepted; at the time of the Cuban revolt America's interest had not waned.

The media played a major part in this continued interest in Cuba. **William Randolph Hearst** and **Joseph Pulitzer** were news tycoons. Because of their practice of **YELLOW JOURNALISM**, a method for pleasing the customer with melodrama, newspapers reported what was happening in Cuba. This influenced Progressives to favor helping the Cubans. At the same time, industrialists had an

YELLOW JOURNALISM: a method for pleasing the customer with melodrama

economic interest in the island. It was obvious that Cuba was strategically important because the British had used the Caribbean waters during the Revolution and the War of 1812.

The Maine and fighting the war

President **William McKinley**, who had won the presidential campaign against **William Jennings Bryan**, initially refused to recognize the Cubans' rebellion but affirmed the possibility of American intervention, believing that there could be a good base in Cuba for U.S. Navy ships. However, his preference was for Cuba to be free and he wanted to negotiate rather than become involved in a war. Then the U.S. battleship **The Maine** was blown up in Havana Harbor; 260 lives were lost.

Though people today dispute the cause of the explosion, evidence at the time indicated that Spain had caused it. Two months later, Congress declared war on Spain, and less than four months later, in August 1898, the war was over. In the Philippines, Commodore **George Dewey** had sunk every Spanish ship in Manila Bay. Theodore Roosevelt and the **Rough Riders** took possession of San Juan Hill near Santiago de Cuba, and the Spanish surrendered. In defeating Spain the United States instantly became a world power.

The aftermath

TELLER AMENDMENT: stated that the United States could not annex Cuba but must leave "control of the island to its people"

PLATT AMENDMENT: ceded Cuba's Guantanamo Bay to the United States

CUBAN-AMERICAN TREATY: provided that Guantanamo Bay be perpetually leased to the U.S. for coaling and naval stations

Victory over Spain proved fruitful for American territorial ambitions. Although in response to McKinley's war message, Congress had passed the **TELLER AMENDMENT**, which stated that the United States could not annex Cuba but must leave "control of the island to its people." The United States did gain control of the Philippines and various other Pacific islands formerly possessed by Spain.

The decision to occupy the Philippines rather than grant it independence led immediately to a guerrilla war. The Filipinos, who wanted independence from the Americans, struggled for three years, until **Emilio Aguinaldo**, their leader, was finally captured. He gained his freedom by taking an oath of allegiance to the United States and continued to benignly rule the Philippines until 1942.

The peace treaty that ended the Spanish-American War in 1898 also gave the United States possession of Puerto Rico, Guam, and Hawaii. The **PLATT AMENDMENT** to the Army Appropriations Act in 1901 ceded Cuba's Guantanamo Bay to the United States. Under President Theodore Roosevelt, the **CUBAN-AMERICAN TREATY** ensured that Guantanamo Bay would be perpetually leased to the United States for coaling and naval stations.

Panama Canal

Although the idea of building a canal in Panama goes back to the early sixteenth century, actual work did not begin until 1880 by the French, who had built the Suez Canal to join the Mediterranean and Red Seas. The effort collapsed, and the United States completed the task. The **Panama Canal** opened in 1914.

The construction was an enormous, complex engineering task. Because the area is mountainous, the canal was built as a lock-and-lake canal, meaning that ships are lifted on the locks to travel across a manmade lake. The 40-mile-long canal was built by cutting through the isthmus that joins North and South America to connect the Atlantic and Pacific Oceans. Ships no longer neede to make the trip around Cape Horn, saving 8,000 nautical miles. The United States helped Panama win independence from Colombia in exchange for control of the Panama Canal Zone.

For more information on the building of the Panama Canal, check out this site:

www.sil.si.edu/Exhibitions/Make-the-Dirt-Fly/index.html

Changing Foreign Relations

The Open Door Policy

The **OPEN DOOR POLICY** was developed after the United States won control of the Philippines because this acquisition created an American foothold in East Asia Japan and the European powers had created **spheres of influence** throughout China as they had defeated Chinese armies, and the United States sent 2,500 sailors and marines to China to assert power there. This policy was developed by Secretary of State **John Hay**, serving under President Theodore Roosevelt, who wanted to guarantee equal trading rights for all engaged in China. He also recommended protecting the integrity of the Chinese empire.

OPEN DOOR POLICY: a policy that guaranteed equal trading rights for all engaged in China

Roosevelt's Big Stick

BIG STICK DIPLOMACY was a term Theodore Roosevelt used to describe his foreign policy; he attributed its name to an African proverb: "Speak softly and carry a big stick." The **ROOSEVELT COROLLARY** rose from this statement of the United States' police power. The intention was to safeguard American economic interests in Latin America and to prevent European domination.

These new approaches to foreign policy led to the expansion of the U.S. Navy and to greater involvement in world affairs. The United States felt that it had both the right and the obligation to intervene if any nation in the Western Hemisphere became vulnerable to European control because of political or economic instability. Thus, the United States intervened in Cuba, Nicaragua, Haiti, and the Dominican Republic in the years before World War II.

BIG STICK DIPLOMACY: the term used to describe Theodore Roosevelt's opinion of the United States' police power; he attributed it to an African proverb: "Speak softly and carry a big stick"

ROOSEVELT COROLLARY: a foreign policy plan intended to safeguard American economic interests in Latin America and to prevent European domination

Taft and Dollar Diplomacy

DOLLAR DIPLOMACY: describes the U.S. efforts under President William Howard Taft to extend its foreign policy goals in Latin America and East Asia through economic power

DOLLAR DIPLOMACY describes the U.S. efforts under President **William Howard Taft** to extend its foreign policy goals in Latin America and East Asia through economic power. The name for this diplomatic approach came from Taft's claim that U.S. interests in Latin America had changed from "warlike and political" to "peaceful and economic" (hence, "dollar"). Taft justified this policy in terms of protecting the Panama Canal. The practice of dollar diplomacy, however, was anything but peaceful at times, particularly in Nicaragua. When revolts or revolutions occurred, the United States sent troops to resolve it. Immediately upon resolution, bankers were sent in to loan money to the new regimes. The policy persisted until the election of President **Woodrow Wilson** in 1913.

Wilson and moral diplomacy

MORAL DIPLOMACY: an American foreign policy approach dedicated to the interests of all humanity rather than merely American national interests

Wilson repudiated the dollar diplomacy approach to foreign policy within weeks of his inauguration. Wilson's **MORAL DIPLOMACY** became the model for American foreign policy and exists to this day.

Wilson envisioned a federation of democratic nations, believing that democracy and representative government were the foundation of world stability. Specifically, he saw Great Britain and the United States as the champions of self-government and the promoters of world peace. Wilson's beliefs and actions set in motion an American foreign policy that was dedicated to the interests of all humanity rather than merely American national interests. Wilson promoted the power of free trade and international commerce as the key to acquiring a voice in world events.

Wilson believed that democratic states would be less inclined to threaten U.S. interests, and he advocated:

- Maintaining a combat-ready military to meet the needs of the nation
- Promoting democracy abroad
- Improving the U.S. economy through international trade

The First World War

Staying neutral

WORLD WAR I: a global military conflict fought mostly in Europe between 1914 and 1918

WORLD WAR I (also known as the First World War or WWI) was a global military conflict fought mostly in Europe between 1914 and 1918. When the war began in 1914, triggered by the assassination of Austrian Archduke **Francis Ferdinand** and his wife in Sarajevo, President Wilson declared that the United States was neutral. Most Americans were opposed to involvement and wanted to stay out of the war.

Then, in 1915, a German **U-boat** sank the British luxury passenger liner **RMS Lusitania**, killing more than 1,000 civilians, more than 100 of them Americans. This attack outraged the American public and turned public opinion against Germany. The attack on the Lusitania became a rallying point for those advocating U.S. involvement in the European conflict.

U.S. entrance into the war

Wilson's 1916 presidential campaign was based on the slogan "He kept us out of war." He continued efforts to end the war, but German submarines began unlimited warfare against American merchant shipping. The development of the German unterseeboat, or U-boat, allowed Germans to efficiently attack merchant ships from Canada and the United States that were supplying Germany's European enemies. Then the British intercepted a telegram, known as the **ZIMMERMAN NOTE**, sent by Germany to the ambassador of Germany in the United States, instructing him to solicit the Mexican government for an alliance an invasion of the United States if America were to enter the war. This, along with the continued destruction of American ships by German forces, resulted in the United States entering into the war.

ZIMMERMAN NOTE: a telegram sent by Germany to the German ambassador in the United States, which instructed him to solicit the Mexican government to invade the United States

The economy was directed to the war effort, and more than four million Americans served in the military with over two million of them serving overseas. Nearly 50,000 Americans lost their lives and an additional 221,000 were wounded in the conflict.

The War effort at home

Railroads and communication

In December 1917, the government assumed control of all of the railroads in the nation and consolidated them into a single system with regional directors. The goal was to increase efficiency and enable the rail system to meet the needs of both commerce and military transportation. The understanding was that private ownership would be restored after the war. (This restoration occurred in 1920. In 1918, telegraph, telephone, and cable services were also taken over by the federal government; they were returned to private ownership in 1919.)

Medical volunteers

The **American Red Cross** and the volunteers who supported their effort knitted garments for both the U.S. Army and the U.S. Navy. In addition, they prepared surgical dressings, hospital garments, and refugee clothing. More than eight million people participated in this effort.

Liberty Bonds

To secure the huge sums of money needed to finance the war, the government sold **Liberty Bonds**. Nearly $25 billion worth of bonds were sold in four bond issues.

The first Liberty bond was issued at 3.5 percent; the second at 4 percent; and the remaining two at 4.25 percent. More than one-fifth of U.S. residents bought bonds. For the first time in their lives, millions of people had begun saving money. After the war, **Victory Bonds** were sold.

War production

The war effort required massive production of weapons, ammunition, radios, and other equipment of war. For example, at the beginning of the war, the United States had little overseas shipping, as attacks by German submarines destroyed ships faster than their replacements could be built. Scores of shipyards were quickly constructed to build both wooden and steel ships. At the end of the war, the United States had more than 2,000 ships. By April 30, 1919, the cost of the war was over 22.5 billion dollars.

Ending the war

FOURTEEN POINTS: authored by Woodrow Wilson, these points were aimed at bringing World War I to an end with an equitable peace settlement

President Wilson proposed his **FOURTEEN POINTS** to Congress in January 1918. His hope was to bring the war to an end with an equitable peace settlement. Five points set out general ideals; the next eight points pertained to immediately resolving territorial and political problems; and the fourteenth point counseled establishing an organization of nations to promote world peace.

In November 1918, Germany agreed to an armistice, assuming that the peace settlement would be drawn up on the basis of the Fourteen Points. There were many debates about how to punish Germany and its allies for their aggressive acts, however, at the peace conference in Paris in 1919. Wilson did insist that the **League of Nations** be included in the Treaty of Versailles.

Italy, France, and Great Britain demanded retribution, and so peace treaties punished the Central Powers (the name for Germany and its allies), taking away arms and territories and requiring payment of reparations. Germany was punished more than the others and was forced to assume responsibility for causing the war.

In 1918, Senator **Henry Cabot Lodge** of Massachusetts, Senate Majority Leader and Foreign Relations Committee Chairman, demanded Germany's unconditional surrender. Wilson ignored Lodge and took no senators along to the peace proceedings in Paris. In November, Lodge sent the treaty to the Senate floor with 14 reservations, but Wilson was unwilling to negotiate. On November 19, 1919, the Senate rejected the peace treaty, and the United States did not become a member of the League of Nations.

The 1920s

The decade from 1920 to 1930 saw tremendous changes. There was a significant shift from farm life to city life for many Americans. Income and wealth also increased, though there were still millions living below the poverty line of $2,000 per year, many Americans experienced prosperity.

Cultural changes

The boom in the automobile and entertainment industries resulted in the fast-paced **ROARING TWENTIES**, also known as the Jazz Age. Movie stars, sports figures, and national heroes, such as aviator **Charles Lindbergh**, influenced Americans to admire, emulate, and support individual accomplishments. Sports such as professional boxing provided new entertainment for the public.

ROARING TWENTIES: the name for the decade from 1920-1930, marked by post-war prosperity

Laissez-faire economics, mass production, electrification, the building of roads, and the invention of the radio all had an influence on the cultural changes of the decade. Telephone lines and indoor plumbing for many homes became commonplace. Skyscrapers were built, and mass transit systems were developed and expanded.

HARLEM RENAISSANCE: a literary and artistic movement that began when large numbers of African Americans left the rural South and migrated to the North in search of opportunity; many settled in Harlem in New York City

Harlem Renaissance

The **HARLEM RENAISSANCE** literary and artistic movement also began at this time. Large numbers of African Americans left the rural South and migrated to the North in search of opportunity, and many settled in Harlem in New York City. By the 1920s, Harlem had become a center of African American life. The artistic expressions that emerged from this community in the 1920s and 1930s celebrated black experience, black traditions, and the voices of black America. Major writers and works of this movement included Langston Hughes (*The Weary Blues*), Nella Larsen (*Passing*), Zora Neale Hurston (*Their Eyes Were Watching God*), Claude McKay, Countee Cullen, and Jean Toomer.

For more information on speakeasies, check out this site:

www.pbs.org/jazz/exchange/exchange_speakeasies.htm

Prohibition

The **EIGHTEENTH AMENDMENT**, known as the Prohibition Amendment, had been ratified in 1917 and prohibited selling alcoholic beverages throughout the United States. This led to a rise in bootlegging, organized crime, and the creation of **speakeasies**. As an offshoot of this underground culture, the Charleston dance and the "flapper look" became popular.

EIGHTEENTH AMENDMENT: an amendment to the Constitution that prohibited selling alcoholic beverages throughout the United States

Music

The decade was a time of optimism and exploration of new boundaries and a clear movement away from conventionalism in many ways. The musical style of

JAZZ: a musical style that uses free-flowing improvisation on a simple theme with a four-beat rhythm

jazz perfectly typified the mood of society. **JAZZ** is essentially free-flowing improvisation on a simple theme with a four-beat rhythm. Jazz originated in the poor districts of New Orleans as an outgrowth of the Blues. The leading jazz musicians of the time included:

- Buddy Bolden
- Joseph "King" Oliver
- Duke Ellington
- Louis Armstrong
- Jelly Roll Morton

The era of the **Big Band** began by the mid-1920s and developed into **Swing Jazz** by the early 1930s. Some notable musicians were:

- Bing Crosby
- Frank Sinatra
- Don Redman
- Fletcher Henderson
- Count Basie
- Benny Goodman
- Billie Holiday
- Ella Fitzgerald
- The Dorsey Brothers

THE ASHCAN SCHOOL: developed around the work and style of Robert Henri, the artists of this style focused on facets of everyday urban life, presented without adornment or glamour

THE AMERICAN SCENE PAINTERS: produced a tight, detailed style of painting that focused on images of American life that were understandable to all

Art

In painting and sculpture, the new direction of the decade was **realism**. In the early years of the twentieth century, American artists had developed several realist styles.

THE ASHCAN SCHOOL developed around the work and style of **Robert Henri**. These artists' subjects were the various facets of everyday urban life, presented without adornment or glamour. **THE AMERICAN SCENE PAINTERS** produced a tight, detailed style of painting that focused on images of American life that were understandable to all. In the Midwest, a school within this group was called **regionalism**. One of the leading artists of **regionalism** was **Grant Wood**, best known for American Gothic. Other important realists of the day were **Edward Hopper** and **Georgia O'Keeffe**.

NINETEENTH AMENDMENT: an amendment to the Constitution that guaranteed women the right to vote

Women in society

In 1920, the **NINETEENTH AMENDMENT**, which guaranteed women the right to vote, was ratified. Roles and opportunities for women grew, and more of them sought careers outside the home. **Amelia Earhart** flew solo across the Atlantic; **Greta Garbo** was a favorite movie star; **Jeanette Rankin** was a pacifist, politician, and social activist who helped make sure the Nineteenth Amendment passed.

Religion and science

In Tennessee, **William Jennings Bryan**, three-time presidential candidate for the Southern Democrats, led the Fundamentalist position for banishing Darwin's theory of evolution from schools. **H. L. Mencken**, editor of the *American Mercury* and reporter for *The Baltimore Sun*, covered the story of the **Monkey Trial** in which young biology teacher **John Scopes** was defended by attorney **Clarence Darrow**. In the end, Scopes was found guilty and fined $100 for teaching evolution in a Tennessee science class.

For more information on the Scopes Monkey Trial, check out this site:

www.npr.org/templates/story/story.php?storyId=4723956

Overall, the decade witnessed an increase in a religious tradition known as **revivalism** or emotional preaching.

Immigration

The **NATIONAL ORIGINS ACT OF 1924**, also known as Johnson-Reed Act, limited immigration to two percent of the number of foreign-born persons of any nationality that had been in the United States in 1890. Asians were prohibited from immigrating, and there were far fewer Italians admitted than Germans. Following the war and the Bolshevik Revolution in Russia, there was fear of **anarchists**, **communists**, and immigrants.

NATIONAL ORIGINS ACT OF 1924: also known as Johnson-Reed Act, limited immigration to two percent of the number of foreign-born persons of any nationality that had been in the United States in 1890

Political atmosphere

The administration of President **Warren G. Harding** was marked by widespread corruption and scandal, although many Americans were demanding law and order. President Harding promised a return to "normalcy" following World War I. But under his administration the **TEAPOT DOME** scandal broke, when his Secretary of the Interior, Albert Fall, made a secret deal with two oilmen to pump oil out of the fields and sell it for themselves and reward him. Others in Harding's "Ohio Gang," as it was termed by his detractors, accepted bribes. Harding's contentious period in office was cut short, however, as a heart attack took his life; Vice President **Calvin Coolidge** assumed the Presidency.

TEAPOT DOME: a Harding administration scandal in which the Secretary of the Interior, Albert Fall, made a secret deal with two oilmen to pump oil out of the fields, sell it for themselves, and reward him

Working class unrest

During World War I, about nine million people worked in war-related industries. An additional four million served in the military. When the war ended, most of these people were jobless, which contributed to a small depression in 1920–1921. Two groups were highly visible during this time: the **International Workers of the World** (IWW) and the **Socialist Party** led by Eugene Debs.

During World War I, work hours were shortened, wages increased, and working conditions improved. In the 1920s, a huge wave of labor strikes sought a return to these wartime trends of preferable workday length, wages, and conditions. A number of these labor strikes turned violent. Many viewed the early strikes as the work of radicals, who were labeled "reds" (communists). As the news spread and other strikes occurred, the **RED SCARE** swept the country. Some Americans feared a Bolshevik-type revolution in America. As a result, people were jailed for expressing views that were considered anarchist, **communist**, or **socialist**. In an attempt to control the potential for revolution, **civil liberties** were ignored and thousands of people were deported. The Socialist party came to be viewed as a group of anarchist radicals.

RED SCARE: widespread fear of a communist revolution and takeover in America

Several state and local governments passed a variety of laws designed to reduce radical speech and activity. Congress considered more than 70 antisedition bills, though none were passed. Within a year, the Red Scare had essentially run its course.

The Ku Klux Klan

In 1866, veterans of the Confederate Army formed the **KU KLUX KLAN** (KKK or the Klan) to resist Reconstruction. The beliefs of this group included white supremacy, anti-Semitism, racism, anti-Catholicism, and nativism. Typical methods of intimidation used by the Klan included terrorism, violence, and cross burning. The Klan enjoyed a renaissance beginning in 1915. The new medium of film spread the Klan's message in **D.W. Griffith**'s *Birth of a Nation*. Klan members also published a number of anti-Semitic newspaper articles.

KU KLUX KLAN: a group formed in 1866 by veterans of the Confederate Army to resist Reconstruction; they believed in white supremacy, anti-Semitism, racism, anti-Catholicism, and nativism

These attempts to spread their message were successful—although the KKK began in the South, at its peak, membership extended into the Midwest, the Northern states, and even into Canada. Membership during the 1920s reached approximately four million—20 percent of the adult white male population in many regions and as high as 40 percent in some areas. The group's political influence was significant because members essentially controlled the governments of Tennessee, Indiana, Oklahoma, and Oregon as well as some southern legislatures. Klan membership did not begin to decline until the 1930s.

Race issues

Marcus Garvey, an English-educated Jamaican, established an organization to build African-American nationalism and independence called the **Universal Negro Improvement Association (UNIA)**. By 1920, its followers numbered about four million, and by the early 1920s there were 700 branches established in 38 states.

For more information on Marcus Garvey, check out this site:

www.pbs.org/wgbh/amex/garvey/

The National Association for the Advancement of Colored People (NAACP) was founded in 1909. One struggle was to eliminate **Jim Crow laws**, and members protested *Birth of a Nation*. The NAACP helped enable black men to become officers in the military during WWI. The group organized voters to oppose Woodrow Wilson's efforts to weave racial segregation into federal government policy. During the 1920s, the NAACP, led by **James Weldon Johnson**, helped combat lynchings, and in the 1930s, it lent support for the **Scottsboro Boys**, who were accused of rapes they did not commit.

Social activist groups

The **American Civil Liberties Union** was founded in 1920. It was an outgrowth of the **American Union Against Militarism**, which had opposed American involvement in WWI and provided legal advice and assistance for conscientious objectors and those being prosecuted under the Espionage Act of 1917 and the Sedition Act of 1918. The agency attempted to:

- Protect immigrants threatened with deportation and citizens threatened with prosecution for communist activities
- Oppose efforts to repress the Industrial Workers of the World and other labor unions

The Anti-Defamation League was created in 1913 to stop discrimination against Jewish people. Its charter states, "Its ultimate purpose is to secure justice and fair treatment to all." The organization has historically opposed all groups considered anti-Semitic or racist, including the Ku Klux Klan.

The Great Depression

The **1929 STOCK MARKET CRASH** was the powerful event that generally marks the beginning of the **GREAT DEPRESSION** in America. The stock market crash had identifiable causes. The 1920s had been a decade of social and economic growth, but the attitudes and actions of the 1920s regarding wealth, production, and investment created several trends that quietly set the stage for the 1929 disaster.

1929 STOCK MARKET CRASH: the rapid decline of stock market's overall value, generally marking the beginning of the Great Depression in America

GREAT DEPRESSION: beginning with the stock market crash of 1929, this period of American history was a time of severe economic hardship

Causes

The decline of agriculture

During WWI, the government subsidized farms and paid high prices for grains. Farmers had been encouraged to buy and cultivate more land and to use new technology to increase production to feed much of Europe during and in the aftermath of the war. When the war ended, these farm policies were discontinued. Prices plummeted, farmers fell into debt, and farm prices declined. The agriculture industry already was on the brink of ruin before the stock market crash.

Uneven distribution of wealth

In the 1920s, the distribution of wealth between the upper and middle classes was grossly unequal. In 1929, the combined income of the top 0.1 percent of the population was equal to the combined income of the bottom 42 percent. The top 0.1 percent of the population controlled 34 percent of all savings, while 80 percent of American had no savings.

Between 1920 and 1929, the top 0.1 percent of the population enjoyed an increase in disposable income of 75 percent; for the rest of the population, the increase was 9 percent. Average worker productivity in manufacturing increased 32 percent during this period, yet wages in manufacturing increased only 8 percent. As production costs fell and prices remained constant, profits soared. Many believed that **capitalism** was enriching the wealthy at the expense of the workers.

REVENUE ACT OF 1926: significantly reduced income taxes for the wealthy

To make matters worse, the legislative and executive branches during Coolidge's presidency tended to favor business and the wealthy. The **REVENUE ACT OF 1926** significantly reduced income taxes for the wealthy. For example, a person with a million-dollar income would have seen taxes reduced from $600,000 to $200,000. Also, despite an increase in labor union membership, even the Supreme Court ruled in ways that further widened the gap between the rich and the middle class. For example, in the case of **Adkins v. Children's Hospital** (1923), the Supreme Court ruled that minimum wage legislation was unconstitutional.

The distribution of wealth between the rich and the middle class mirrored the uneven distribution of wealth between industries. In 1929, just 200 companies controlled half of all corporate wealth. The automotive industry was growing exceptionally quickly, but agriculture was steadily declining. In fact, in 1921 food prices dropped about 70 percent due to surplus. The average income in agriculture was only about one-third of the national average across all industries.

Increased availability of credit and excessive spending

Disparity in distribution of wealth weakened the economy. Along with this, the concept of buying on **credit** caught on quickly. Buying on credit, however, created artificial demand for products people could not have ordinarily afforded. This had three effects in time:

1. Less need to purchase products because they have already been bought
2. Paying for previous purchases on credit makes it impossible to purchase new products
3. Surplus goods

The economy also relied heavily on **investment** and **luxury spending** by the rich in the 1920s. Luxury spending, however, only occurs when people are confident about the economy and the future. Should people lose confidence, luxury spending would come to an abrupt halt. This is precisely what happened when the **stock market** crashed in 1929.

Investment in business produces returns for the investor and during the 1920s, investing was very healthy. Investors, however, began to expect even greater returns on their investments, which prompted many to make speculative investments in risky opportunities.

Two industries—automotive and radio—drove the economy in the 1920s. The government tended to support these new industries rather than support agriculture. The concentration of production and economic stability in the automotive industry and the production and sale of radios was expected to last forever. But there came a point when the growth of an industry slowed due to market saturation. When these two industries declined, due to decreased demand, they caused the collapse of other industries upon which they were dependent (e.g., rubber tires, glass, fuel).

The stock market

Risky speculative investments in the stock market contributed to the crash of 1929. Stock market speculation was spectacular throughout the 1920s. In 1929, shares traded on the New York Stock Exchange reached 1,124,800,410. In 1928 and 1929, stock prices doubled and then tripled. For example, RCA stock prices rose from \$85 to \$420 within one year. The opportunity to achieve such profits was irresistible.

In the same way that buying goods on credit became popular in the 1920s, buying stock on **margin** allowed people to invest a very small amount of money in the hope of receiving exceptional profit. This created an investing craze that drove the market higher and higher. But brokers also charged higher interest rates on margin loans (nearly 20 percent). If the price of the stock dropped, the investor owed the broker the amount borrowed plus interest. Another factor contributing to the Great Depression was that the Federal Reserve increased interest rate in 1929.

In September 1929, stock prices began to slip somewhat, yet people remained optimistic. On Monday, October 21, prices began to fall quickly. The volume traded was so high that the tickers were unable to keep up. Investors started selling quickly, which caused further collapse. Then, for the next two days, prices stabilized somewhat.

On **Black Thursday**, October 24, prices plummeted again, and on Monday, October 28, they declined by 13 percent in one day. The next day, **Black**

Tuesday, October 29, saw 16.4 million shares traded. Stock prices fell so far that many were unwilling to buy at any price.

The stock market crash of 1929 led to financial ruin for many investors, a weakening of the nation's economy, and fuel for the Great Depression of the 1930s. The Depression included bank failures, job losses, production cutbacks, and a sharp decline in consumer spending. This affected businesses, factories, and stores. Farm products were no longer affordable, so farmers suffered. Foreign trade sharply decreased, and in the early 1930s, the United States and European economies were effectively paralyzed.

Without demand for products, other businesses and industries collapsed. This set in motion a domino effect, bringing down the businesses and industries that provided raw materials or components to these industries. Unemployment quickly reached 25 percent nationwide. Hundreds of thousands became jobless, and the jobless often became homeless.

People thrown out of their homes created makeshift domiciles of cardboard, scraps of wood, and tents. With unmasked reference to President **Herbert Hoover**, who was quite obviously overwhelmed by the situation and unable to effectively deal with it, these communities were called **HOOVERVILLES**.

HOOVERVILLES: communities created by people thrown out of their homes following the stock market crash; they consisted of makeshift domiciles of cardboard, scraps of wood, and tents, and were so named to belittle President Hoover

Families stood in bread lines, rural workers left the plains to search for work in California, and banks failed. More than 100,000 businesses failed between 1929 and 1932.

Natural disasters

The economic disaster was then worsened by **natural disaster**. The Florida Keys were hit by the **Labor Day Hurricane** in 1935. This was one of only three hurricanes in history to make landfall as a Category 5 storm. More than 400 died in the storm, including 200 WWI veterans who were building bridges for a public works project. In the Northeast, the **Great Hurricane of 1938** struck Long Island, causing more than 600 fatalities, demolishing much of Long Island, and resulting in millions of dollars in damage to the coast from New York City to Boston.

DUST BOWL: caused by a severe and prolonged drought in the Great Plains and reliance on inappropriate farming techniques, this disaster was marked by a series of dust storms that ruined crops and destroyed farms in the 1930s

By far though, the worst natural disaster of the decade was the **DUST BOWL**. A severe and prolonged drought in the Great Plains and inappropriate farming techniques led to a series of **dust storms** in the 1930s. Plowing the plains removed the grass and exposed the soil. When the drought occurred, the soil dried out and became dust. Crops were ruined, the land was destroyed, and people either lost or abandoned homes and farms. Between 1934 and 1939 winds blew the soil into dust storms, called "black blizzards." These huge clouds of dust were visible all the way to Chicago and as far east as the Atlantic Ocean. The story of this natural disaster and its toll in human suffering is poignantly preserved in the photographs of **Dorothea Lange**.

In Texas, Arkansas, Oklahoma, New Mexico, Kansas, and Colorado over half a million people were homeless. Some 15 percent of Oklahoma's population left the state. The estimates of the number of people displaced by this disaster range from 300,000 to 2.5 million. The migrants came to be called "**Okies**" no matter where they came from. Many of these people journeyed west in the hope of making a new life in California.

President Hoover was urged to provide government relief for Dust Bowl victims, but he responded by urging the nation to be patient.

President Hoover was urged to provide government relief, but he responded by urging the nation to be patient. By the time he signed relief bills in 1932, it was too late.

The New Deal Era

Franklin D. Roosevelt's election

During President Hoover's first campaign, prohibition and religion had been the primary concerns. Hoover had run against **Al Smith**, a Catholic, on the slogan "A chicken in every pot and a car in every garage," and he had favored continuing prohibition.

Hoover's bid for reelection in 1932 failed. **Franklin D. Roosevelt** won the White House on his promise to the American people of a **NEW DEAL**.

NEW DEAL: a series of innovative reforms designed to end the Great Depression

Relief efforts begin

Upon assuming the office, Roosevelt and his advisers immediately launched a massive program of innovation to bring the Depression to an end. Congress gave the president unprecedented power to act. During the next eight years, the most extensive and broad-based legislation in the nation's history was enacted. The legislation was intended to accomplish three goals:

1. Relief
2. Recovery
3. Reform

The first step in the New Deal was to relieve suffering. This was accomplished through a number of job-creation projects, such as the **Civilian Conservation Corps**. This contrasted with Hoover's approach based on the belief that the government should neither provide direct aid to citizens nor be directly involved in the economy. The second step, the recovery aspect, was to stimulate the economy.

The third step was to create social and economic change through innovative legislation.

New Deal organizations and legislation

The **National Recovery Administration** attempted to accomplish several goals:

- Restore employment
- Increase general purchasing power
- Provide character-building activity for unemployed youth
- Encourage decentralization of industry and thus divert population from crowded cities to rural or semirural communities
- Develop river resources in the interest of navigation and cheap power
- Complete flood control on a permanent basis
- Enlarge the national program of forest protection and develop forest resources
- Control farm production and improve farm prices
- Assist home builders and home owners
- Restore public faith in banking and trust operations
- Recapture the value of physical assets, whether in real property, securities, or other investments

Among the "alphabet organizations" set up to work out the details of the recovery plan:

- **Agricultural Adjustment Administration (AAA):** Designed to readjust agricultural production and prices, thereby boosting farm income
- **Civilian Conservation Corps (CCC):** Designed to provide wholesome, useful activity in the forestry service to unemployed young men
- **Works Progress Administration (WPA):** Designed to move individuals from relief rolls to work projects or private employment
- **Tennessee Valley Authority (TVA):** Designed to improve the navigability of the Tennessee River and increase productivity of the timber and farm lands in its valley; also built 16 dams that provided water control and hydroelectricity
- **Public Works Administration (PWA)** and **Civil Works Administration (CWA):** Employed Americans on over 34,000 public works projects at a cost of more than $4 billion; among these projects was

the construction of a highway that linked the Florida Keys and Miami, the Boulder Dam (now the Hoover Dam), and numerous highway projects

To provide economic stability and prevent another crash, Congress passed the **GLASS-STEAGALL ACT**, which separated banking and investing. The **Securities and Exchange Commission (SEC)** was created to regulate dangerous speculative practices on Wall Street. The Wagner Act guaranteed a number of rights to workers and unions in an effort to improve worker-employer relations. The **SOCIAL SECURITY ACT OF 1935** established pensions as well as a system of unemployment insurance.

GLASS-STEAGALL ACT: separated banking and investing

SOCIAL SECURITY ACT OF 1935: established pensions as well as a system of unemployment insurance

Regulating business operations, from activities of corporations to labor problems, included:

- Protecting bank depositors and the credit system of the country
- Employing gold resources and currency adjustments to aid permanent restoration of normal living
- Establishing a line of subsistence below which no citizen would be permitted to sink

In addition to responding to economic crisis, the Roosevelt administration also responded to the ecological disaster of the Dust Bowl during the first 100 days in office. One action was the formation of the **Soil Conservation Service** (now the Natural Resources Conservation Service).

Controversy

The New Deal was controversial. A number of concerns surfaced during its early years, including:

- The deaths of the WWI veterans in the Labor Day Hurricane, who were employed by a public works project, resulted in a Congressional investigation into possible negligence
- The Central Valley Project upset farmers who lost tillable land and some water supply because of the construction of the Hoover Dam
- Tennesseans were concerned with the changes in river flow and navigation when the Tennessee Valley Authority began constructing dams and directing water to form reservoirs and to power hydroelectric plants
- Some businesses and business leaders did not appreciate minimum wage laws, restrictions and controls on working conditions, and limitation of work hours
- The numerous import/export tariffs of the period caused unease

Many would argue, however, that much of what was accomplished under the New Deal had positive long-term effects on economic, ecological, social, and political issues for the next several decades. The Tennessee Valley Authority and the Central Valley Project in California provided a reliable source and supply of water to major cities, as well as electrical power to meet the needs of an increasingly electricity-dependent society. For the middle class and the poor, the labor regulations, the establishment of the **Social Security Administration**, and the separation of investment and banking have served the nation for more than six decades.

Organized labor during the New Deal

WAGNER ACT: a New Deal act that provided the legal basis for unions and set the rules and protections for collective bargaining

Because the National Recovery Administration lacked clarity regarding unions, Congress passed the **WAGNER ACT** (the National Labor Relations Act) that:

- Established a legal basis for unions
- Set collective bargaining as a matter of national policy required by the law
- Provided for secret ballot elections for choosing unions
- Protected union members from employer intimidation and coercion

The Supreme Court upheld the Wagner Act in 1937.

Strikes

One of the most common tactics of the union was the **strike**. Half a million Southern mill workers walked off the job in the Great Uprising of 1934, based on the premise that without workers, industry could not move forward. Then, in 1936, the United Rubber Workers staged the first **sit-down strike** where instead of walking off the job, they stayed at their posts but refused to work. The **United Auto Workers** used the sit-down strike against General Motors in 1936–1937.

ANTI-STRIKEBREAKER ACT: made it illegal to transport or aid strike-breakers in interstate or foreign trade

Strikes were met with varying degrees of resistance by the companies. Sometimes, **scabs** were brought in to replace the striking workers. In 1936, the **ANTI-STRIKEBREAKER ACT** (the Byrnes Act) made it illegal to transport or aid strikebreakers in interstate or foreign trade. In part, this was an attempt to stem the violence often associated with management's attempts to bully the workers back to work.

As the leaders of industry were often powerful community figures, they sometimes employed law enforcement to disrupt the strikes. In 1937, during a strike of the Steel Workers Organizing Committee against Republic Steel, police attacked a crowd gathered in support of the strike, killing 10 and injuring 80. This came to be called the **Memorial Day Massacre**.

Legislating labor

A number of acts were designed to provide fair compensation and other benefits to workers. Some of these were:

- The **DAVIS-BACON ACT**, passed in 1931, provided that employers of contractors and subcontractors on public construction should be paid the prevailing wages. Individual states also provided measures; Wisconsin created the first unemployment insurance act in the country in 1932.
- The Public Contracts Act or **WALSH-HEALEY ACT** of 1936 established labor standards, including minimum wages, overtime pay, child and convict labor provisions, and safety standards on federal contracts.
- The **FAIR LABOR STANDARDS ACT** created a minimum wage and stipulated time-and-a-half pay for work over 40 hours per week.
- The Social Security Act was approved in 1935.
- The Supreme Court upheld the **RAILWAY LABOR ACT** in 1930, including its prohibition of employer interference or coercion in the choice of bargaining representatives.
- The **GUFFEY ACT** stabilized the coal industry and improved labor conditions in 1935, but a year later, it was declared unconstitutional because it enabled the federal government to control prices.

Further federal labor efforts included:

- The **ANTI-INJUNCTION ACT OF 1932** prohibited federal injunctions in most labor disputes.
- The **WAGNER-PEYSER ACT** created the United States Employment Service within the Department of Labor in 1933.
- The Secretary of Labor in 1934 called for the first National Labor Legislation Conference to get better cooperation between the federal government and the states in defining a national labor legislation program.
- The United States joined the International Labor Organization (also in 1934).
- The **NATIONAL APPRENTICESHIP ACT** established the Bureau of Apprenticeship within the Department of Labor in 1937.

Specific labor unions

General Motors recognized the **United Auto Workers** and US Steel recognized the **Steel Workers Organizing Committee**, both in 1937. Then, in 1938, the Merchant Marine Act created a **Federal Maritime Labor Board**.

DAVIS-BACON ACT: (1931) provided that public construction contractors should be paid prevailing wages

WALSH-HEALEY ACT: established labor and safety standards on federal contracts

FAIR LABOR STANDARDS ACT: created a minimum wage and stipulated time-and-a-half pay for work over 40 hours per week

RAILWAY LABOR ACT: prohibited employer interference or coercion in the choice of bargaining representatives

GUFFEY ACT: enabled the federal government to control prices in order to stabilize the coal industry and improve labor conditions (was ultimately ruled unconstitutional)

ANTI-INJUNCTION ACT OF 1932: prohibited federal injunctions in most labor disputes

WAGNER-PEYSER ACT: created the United States Employment Service within the Department of Labor in 1933

NATIONAL APPRENTICESHIP ACT: established the Bureau of Apprenticeship within the Department of Labor in 1937

For more information on the AFL-CIO, check out this site:

www.aflcio.org/

One of labor's biggest unions was formed in 1935. The **Committee for Industrial Organization (CIO)** was formed within the **American Federated Labor Union (AFL)** to carry unionism to the industrial sector. By 1937, however, the CIO had been expelled from the AFL over charges of dual unionism or competition. It then became known as the **Congress of Industrial Organizations**.

Ending the Depression

Many scholars believe that the steps taken by the Roosevelt administration alleviated the economic disaster of the Great Depression by enacting controls to mitigate the risk of another stock market crash and providing greater security for workers. The nation's economy, however, did not fully recover until America entered World War II.

SKILL 1.11 Second World War

World War II: 1939 to 1945

Interventionalists

After the war began in Europe, President Roosevelt announced that the United States would remain neutral. Many Americans, although hoping for an Allied victory, wanted the United States to stay out of the war.

President Roosevelt and his supporters were called **interventionists** because they favored all aid—except outright war—to the Allied nations fighting Axis aggression. Interventionists were concerned that an Axis victory would seriously endanger all democracies. Roosevelt's plan was to defeat the Axis nations by sending the Allied nations the equipment needed to fight—ships, aircraft, tanks, and other war materials. The **American Neutrality Act** was amended in November of 1939 to permit the Allies to have "cash and carry" purchases.

Between 1941 and 1945, under the **Land Lease project**, more than $50 billion worth of supplies were shipped to the allies.

Isolationists

The **isolationists** were against any U.S. aid being given to the warring nations and accused President Roosevelt of leading an unprepared United States into a war. America First Committee spokesman Charles A. Lindbergh said that it was best to stay out of the war in Europe and argued that:

- The United States must build an invulnerable national defense
- No foreign power, nor group of powers, can successfully attack an America that is prepared
- American democracy can be preserved only by keeping out of the war in Europe
- "Aid short of war" weakens national defense at home and threatens to involve America in war abroad

U.S. entry to the war

When Japan invaded China in 1937, the United States stopped exports to Japan. Japan's industry depended on importing petroleum, scrap metal, and other raw materials. Then Roosevelt refused the Japanese request to withdraw its funds from American banks.

Pearl Harbor and the Pacific war

General Tojo became Japanese Premier in October 1941. On December 7, 1941, the Japanese bombed **Pearl Harbor** in Hawaii, destroying many aircraft and much of the U.S. Pacific Fleet. On December 8, 1941, congress approved U.S. entry into the war against Japan.

In the six months after it attacked Pearl Harbor, Japanese forces had moved across Southeast Asia and the western Pacific Ocean. By August 1942, the Japanese Empire stretched northeast to Alaska's Aleutian Islands, west to Burma, and south to what is now Indonesia. Invaded and controlled areas included Hong Kong, Guam, Wake Island, Thailand, and part of Malaysia, Singapore, and the Philippines.

The raid of **General Doolittle**'s bombers on Japanese cities, the American naval victory at **Midway**, and the fighting in the **Battle of the Coral Sea** helped turn the tide against Japan. The Island-hopping strategy employed by the U.S. Seabees and Marines succeeded in pushing the Japanese back.

The war in Europe

In 1939, Hitler and Stalin signed a **nonaggression pact** that indicated Germany and the U.S.S.R. would split up Poland and Eastern Europe between them. Hitler violated the agreement in 1941 by invading the Soviet Union.

The scope of the war again expanded at the end of 1941. Germany, Italy, and Japan had created the **TRIPARTITE PACT**, which formalized the Axis Powers. The pact said that, except for the U.S.S.R., any country that attacked an Axis Power would be at war with all three. When the United States declared war on Japan,

TRIPARTITE PACT: an agreement between Germany, Italy, and Japan that formalized the Axis powers in 1941

Germany and Italy declared war on the United States; Hungary and Bulgaria declared war two days later.

The United States quickly involved itself in Europe, when Roosevelt joined **Winston Churchill**, and **Josef Stalin** in planning the military strategy in the European theater. They decided to concentrate on defeating Germany first, and then turn their attention to Japan.

True to this strategy, in the summer of 1942, an Allied push began in North Africa to drive the Axis forces off the continent. This ended successfully in May 1943. As the Allies drove the Axis powers out of Africa, the German army suffered a major defeat at Stalingrad. Trapped in winter conditions, German troops died by starvation and freezing. It marked a turning point in the war.

For more information on the Yalta Conference, check out this site:

library.thinkquest.org/10826/yalta.htm

The liberation of Italy began in July 1943 and ended on May 2, 1945. The next part of the European strategy was **D-Day**, June 6, 1944, when the Allies invaded France at the beaches of Normandy. At the same time, starting in January 1943, the Soviets began pushing the German troops back into Europe. By April 1945, Allies occupied positions beyond the Rhine, and the Soviets moved on to Berlin, surrounding it by April 25th. Germany surrendered on May 7, and the war in Europe was finally over.

The end of the European war

YALTA CONFERENCE: a gathering in February 1945 between the Allied leaders Winston Churchill, Franklin Roosevelt, and Joseph Stalin to decide how to manage post-war Europe

The **YALTA CONFERENCE** took place in Yalta in February 1945, between the Allied leaders Winston Churchill, Franklin Roosevelt, and Joseph Stalin. With the defeat of Nazi Germany in sight, the three allies met to determine the shape of post-war Europe. Germany was to be divided into **four zones of occupation**, as was the capital city of Berlin. Germany was also to undergo demilitarization and to make reparations for the war. Poland was to remain under control of Soviet Russia. Roosevelt also received a promise from Stalin that the Soviet Union would join the new **United Nations**.

POTSDAM CONFERENCE: a gathering in July 1945 between Clement Attlee, Harry Truman, and Josef Stalin to finalize the administration of post-war Germany

Following the surrender of Germany in May 1945, the Allies called the **POTSDAM CONFERENCE** in July, between Clement Attlee, Harry Truman, and Stalin. The goals were to finalize the administration of post-war Germany. The **Security Council** of the United Nations was determined to be the United States, United Kingdom, U.S.S.R., China, and France. Germany was demilitarized, and Japan was asked to surrender. If the country did not surrender, the Potsdam declaration stated, "The alternative for Japan is prompt and utter destruction."

The end of the Pacific war

The United States had dropped two atomic bombs on the cities of **Hiroshima** and **Nagasaki** to finally end the war in the Pacific. Japan formally surrendered on September 2, 1945, aboard the U.S. battleship Missouri, anchored in Tokyo Bay.

For more information on the Potsdam Conference, check out this site:

www.trumanlibrary.org/teacher/potsdam.htm

The Aftermath of World War II

German consequences

In the aftermath of the war, the Allies agreed on the following:

- Germany's armed forces would be abolished
- The **Nazi Party** would be outlawed
- The territory east of the Oder and Neisse Rivers would be taken away
- Nazi leaders would be accused of war crimes and brought to trial

Many Germans were also relocated from areas of Germany and from territories that Germany had claimed in the war. Others in various Central and Eastern European countries were also relocated. The United States and United Kingdom viewed this as necessary to create ethnic homogeneity and prevent violence.

Japanese consequences

After Japan's defeat, the Allies began a military occupation directed by American General **Douglas MacArthur**, who introduced a number of reforms that rid Japan of its military and transformed it into a democracy.

A constitution was drawn up in 1947 that transferred all political rights from the **emperor** to the people. The constitution also granted women the right to vote and denied Japan the right to declare war. War crimes trials for 25 war leaders and government officials were also conducted. The United States did not sign a peace treaty with Japan until 1951. The treaty permitted Japan to rearm in self-defense but took away its overseas empire.

The United Nations

The United Nations, with the goal of working to promote peace around the earth, was set up. The charter was constructed and signed by the four Allied powers in October 1945.

American Minorities During the WWII Era

ALIEN REGISTRATION ACT OF 1940: required the fingerprinting and registration of all aliens over the age of 14

The **ALIEN REGISTRATION ACT OF 1940**, also known as the Smith Act, required the fingerprinting and registration of all aliens over the age of 14. Aliens were also required to report any change of address within five days. Almost five million aliens registered under the provisions of this Act.

Japanese tensions

From the dawn of the twentieth century, there had been tension between Caucasians and Japanese in California. A series of laws had discouraged Japanese immigration and prohibited land ownership by Japanese.

This tension was worsened by the Japanese attack on Pearl Harbor (on December 7, 1941), as it raised suspicion that Japan was planning a full-scale attack on the West Coast. Many believed that American citizenship did not necessarily imply loyalty. Some authorities feared sabotage of both civilian and military facilities within the country.

WAR RELOCATION CAMPS: camps in federally created zones where aliens suspected of subversive activities could be isolated and held

By February 1942, presidential executive orders had authorized the arrest of all aliens suspected of subversive activities and the creation of exclusion zones where people could be isolated and held. Here, they could not damage national infrastructure. These **WAR RELOCATION CAMPS** were used to isolate about 120,000 Japanese and Japanese Americans (62 percent of them were citizens) during World War II.

442ND REGIMENTAL COMBAT TEAM: WWII combat unit composed of Japanese Americans who fought in Europe

Despite the suspicions and relocations, Japanese Americans also served in the American military during the war. The **442ND REGIMENTAL COMBAT TEAM** was one such unit composed of Japanese Americans; they fought in Europe. This unit was the most highly decorated unit of its size in the history of the U.S. Army. This self-sufficient force served with great distinction in North Africa, Italy, southern France, and Germany. The medals earned by the group include 21 Congressional Medals of Honor (the highest award given). The unit was awarded 9,486 purple hearts for being wounded in battle. The casualty rate, combining those killed in action, missing in action, and wounded and removed from action, was 93 percent.

African American contributions

THE TUSKEGEE AIRMEN: a group of African-American aviators who made a major contribution to the war effort

THE TUSKEGEE AIRMEN were a group of African-American aviators who made a major contribution to the war effort. Although they were not considered eligible for the gold wings of a navy pilot until 1948, these men completed standard army flight classroom instruction and the required flying time. These fliers were the first blacks permitted to fly for the military. They flew more than 15,000 missions, destroyed over 100 German aircraft, and earned more than 150 Distinguished Flying Crosses and hundreds of Air Medals.

Native American contributions

The **NAVAJO CODE TALKERS** have been credited with saving countless lives and accelerating the end of the war. More than 400 Navajos served in all six Marine divisions from 1942 to 1945. The job of these men was to talk and transmit information on tactics, troop movements, orders, and other vital military information. At the time, fewer than 30 non-Navajos were able to speak the Navajo language. Because it was a very complex language and not a code, it was unbreakable by the Germans and the Japanese. It is generally accepted that without the Navajo Code Talkers, Iwo Jima could not have been taken.

NAVAJO CODE TALKERS: a group of Navajo soldiers who transmitted information on tactics, troop movements, orders, and other vital military information in their native language, which enemy forces could not decipher

Minority statistics

MINORITY REPRESENTATION IN WWII	
African Americans	1,056,841
Chinese	13,311
Japanese	20,080
Hawaiians	1,320
Native Americans	19,567
Filipinos	11,506
Puerto Ricans	51,438

*Statistics were not kept on how many Hispanics served in the war.

Advancements During WWII

Gender Advancements

Women served in the military as drivers, nurses, communications operators, clerks, soldiers, and pilots. The **Army Nurses Corps** was also created at the beginning of the war.

At home, war required people to build planes, tanks, ships, bombs, torpedoes, and other items. A vast campaign combining patriotism and emotions was launched to recruit women to these tasks. One of the most famous recruiting campaigns featured **Rosie the Riveter**.

For more information on women and war jobs, check out this site:

www.adcouncil.org/default.aspx?id=128

By the middle of 1944, an estimated 18 million women had entered the work force. Women did many jobs, including:

- Building planes and tanks
- Operating large cranes to move heavy equipment
- Loading and firing machine guns and other weapons to ensure that they were in working order
- Operating hydraulic presses
- Serving as volunteer fire fighters, welders, riveters, drill press operators, and cab drivers

Women worked all manufacturing shifts making everything from clothing to fighter jets. Most women and their families tended **VICTORY GARDENS** to produce food items that were in short supply.

VICTORY GARDENS: personal gardens designed to produce food items that were in short supply

Aircraft advancements

The years between WWI and WWII produced significant advancement in aircraft technology, but the pace of aircraft development and production was dramatically increased during WWII. Some major developments included:

- Flight-based weapon delivery systems such as the long-range bomber
- First jet fighter
- First cruise missile
- First ballistic missile (although the cruise and ballistic missiles were not widely used during the war)
- Glider planes (heavily used in WWII because they were silent upon approach)
- Broad use of paratrooper units
- Hospital planes to extract the seriously wounded from the front to hospitals for treatment

Other technological advancements

Weapons and technology in other areas also improved rapidly during the war. These advances were critical in determining the outcome of the war. Used for the first time were:

- Radar
- Electronic computers

- New tank designs
- Nuclear weapons

More new inventions were registered for patents than ever before. Ironically, most of these new ideas were aimed to either kill or prevent people from being killed.

Weaponry

The war began with essentially the same weaponry that had been used in WWI. But soon the aircraft carrier joined the battleship; the primary landing craft was invented; light tanks were developed to meet the needs of a changing battlefield; and other armored vehicles were developed. Submarines were also perfected during this period.

Numerous other weapons were also developed or invented to meet the needs of battle during WWII:

- Bazooka
- Rocket-propelled grenade
- Antitank weapons
- Assault rifles
- The tank destroyer
- Mine-clearing flail tanks
- Flame tanks
- Submersible tanks
- Cruise missiles
- Rocket artillery
- Air-launched rockets
- Guided weapons
- Torpedoes
- Self-guiding weapons
- Napalm

The atomic bomb

The **atomic bomb** was surely the most profound military development of the war years. This invention made it possible for a single plane to carry a single bomb that was sufficiently powerful to destroy an entire city.

The United States believed that the bomb would serve as a deterrent to agression by any nation because to do otherwise would be a decision to commit mass suicide. Developing and using nuclear weapons marked the beginning of a new age in warfare that made the act of killing remote but also made impossible to minimize the effects of war on noncombatants.

Developing and using nuclear weapons marked the beginning of a new age in warfare that created greater distance from the act of killing and eliminated the ability to minimize the effects of war on noncombatants.

The two nuclear bombs dropped in 1945 on Nagasaki and Hiroshima caused the immediate deaths of 100,000 to 200,000 people and far more deaths over time. This has been a controversial decision. Those who opposed the use of the atom bomb argued that was an unnecessary act of mass killing. Proponents argued that by ending the war sooner, it resulted in fewer casualties on both sides. Regardless of the arguments, the use of U.S. nuclear weapons quickly led to the development of similar weapons by other nations leading to fears of such effects as **radiation poisoning** and **nuclear winter**.

SKILL 1.12 Post-Second World War period

The nation had faced two major crises: the Great Depression and World War II. During both crises, the government had assumed greater responsibility for ensuring the basic needs of its citizens, promoting economic opportunity for all, and managing economic growth. The government had also taken on the role of ensuring security of the nation against foreign enemies. Both the size and the reach of the federal government had expanded.

Increased Federal Power

A shared identity

This marked the culmination of a major change in the role of the federal government that many have called "the rise of the **welfare state**." Since the **Progressive Era**, regulatory agencies had been created to control the actions of big business, to protect labor, and to protect the rights and privileges of minorities. In addition, a truly national culture had emerged from:

- The shared hardships
- The growth of the railroad and the radio
- The introduction of the automobile
- The war effort itself

These factors had smoothed out many of the regional—if not racial and ethnic—differences that previously divided the social and cultural interests of the American people.

Bringing the nation through the Depression and the war had required experimentation. Franklin Roosevelt and his administration drew upon past experience and trial and error to sustain the nation through crisis. Roosevelt's use of the radio to speak to the American people in his **fireside chats** permitted him to rally the public and persuade them to consider new ideas and new approaches to the problems of the day. Essentially, Roosevelt convinced the nation that a more active role for the federal government both internationally and at home would prevent another depression or world war.

This transition was important in American history and in the national ethos. Americans had traditionally distrusted a centralization of authority in the federal government. They had also traditionally repudiated international alliances and commitments. Yet both of these changes came about in the years following WWII.

In many ways, the period from 1945 to 1972 was a time of unprecedented prosperity in the nation. Wages, car and home ownership, and average educational levels all increased when the veterans of the war took full advantage of the opportunity to receive a college education paid for by their **G.I. BENEFITS**. People were willing to give the government this major role in perpetuating this prosperous society.

G.I. BENEFITS: federal benefits available to veterans when they returned home from war

Domestic Policy: Presidents of the 1950s and 1960s

Harry S. Truman

Harry Truman became president near the end of WWII. He is credited with some of the most important decisions in history. When Japan refused to surrender, Truman authorized the dropping of atomic bombs on Japanese cities dedicated to war support: Hiroshima and Nagasaki.

Truman also presented a 21-point plan to Congress that came to be known as the **FAIR DEAL**. It included:

FAIR DEAL: Harry Truman's 21-point plan to improve America

- Expansion of Social Security
- A full-employment program
- Public housing
- Slum clearance
- Permanent Fair Employment Practices Act

Dwight David Eisenhower

Dwight Eisenhower succeeded Truman. His domestic policy was middle of the road. He continued most of the programs introduced under both the New Deal and the Fair Deal. When school integration began, he sent troops to Little Rock, Arkansas, to enforce court-ordered desegregation. During his administration, the Department of Health, Education, and Welfare was established and the **National Aeronautics and Space Administration (NASA)** was formed.

John F. Kennedy

John F. Kennedy is widely remembered for his inaugural address in which he stated, "Ask not what your country can do for you—ask what you can do for your country." His campaign pledge was to get America moving again. He wanted the United States to again take up the mission as the first country committed to the evolution of human rights. Through the **Alliance for Progress** and the **Peace Corps**, the hopes and idealism of the nation reached out to assist developing nations. He was deeply involved in the cause of equal rights for all Americans, and he drafted new civil rights legislation. He also drafted plans for a broad attack on the systemic problems of poverty. He believed that the arts were critical to a society and instituted programs to support them.

Lyndon B. Johnson

A GREAT SOCIETY: Lyndon Johnson's plan for America; he defined it as "a place where the meaning of man's life matches the marvels of man's labor"

Lyndon Johnson assumed the presidency after the assassination of Kennedy in 1963. His vision for America was called **A GREAT SOCIETY**. He won support in Congress for the largest group of legislative programs in the history of the nation. These included programs Kennedy had been working on at the time of his death, including a new civil rights bill and a tax cut. He defined the "great society" as "a place where the meaning of man's life matches the marvels of man's labor." The legislation enacted during his administration included:

- Urban renewal
- Medicare
- Aid to education
- Conservation and beautification
- Development of economically depressed areas
- The War on Poverty
- Voting rights for all
- Control of crime and delinquency

Johnson also encouraged space exploration. During his administration, the Department of Transportation was formed, and **Thurgood Marshall** became the first African American to be appointed to the Supreme Court.

Domestic Policy: The Civil Rights Movement

The economic boom following the war led to prosperity for many Americans in the 1950s. However, this prosperity did not extend equally to African Americans. Eventually, efforts began to end discrimination in education, housing, and jobs, and to eliminate widespread poverty. Taking inspiration from similar struggles in India in the 1940s, led by **Mahatma Ghandi**, the Civil Rights movement began to gain momentum.

Important Civil Rights figures

Some key people in the Civil Rights movement are:

- **Emmett Till:** Till was a teenage boy who was murdered in Mississippi in August 1955 while visiting from Chicago. The crime of which he was accused was "whistling at a white woman in a store." He was beaten and murdered, and his body was dumped in a river. His two white abductors were apprehended and tried. They were acquitted by an all-white jury. After the acquittal, they admitted their guilt, but remained free because of double jeopardy laws. Emmett Till's death became one of the key events in the movement.
- **Rosa Parks:** In December 1955—just months after Emmett Till's murder—Parks, an NAACP member from Montgomery, Alabama, refused to give up her seat on the bus to a white man. This event is generally understood as a spark that lit the fire of the Civil Rights Movement.
- **Martin Luther King Jr.:** King was the most prominent member and leader of the Civil Rights movement and promoted nonviolent methods of opposition to segregation. His "Letter from Birmingham Jail" explains nonviolent action and injustice to the clergy of Birmingham, Alabama. King led the march on Washington in 1963, at which he delivered his "I Have a Dream" speech. He received the 1968 Nobel Prize for Peace. He was assassinated in 1968 in Memphis, Tennessee.
- **James Meredith:** In 1962, Meredith was the first African American to enroll at the University of Mississippi.
- **Ralph Abernathy**: Abernathy was major figure in the Civil Rights Movement who succeeded Martin Luther King, Jr. as head of the Southern Christian Leadership Conference
- **Malcolm X:** Malcolm X was a African American nationalist and prominent Muslim.
- **Stokely Carmichael:** Carmichael was a leader who called for independent development of political and social institutions for blacks and for black pride and maintenance of black culture. He was a member of the Student Nonviolent Coordinating Committee, participated in the Freedom Rides, and coined the term **Black Power**.
- **Adam Clayton Powell Jr.:** Powell was a leader in the Harlem civil rights movement who led efforts for jobs and housing and was chairman of the **Coordinating Committee for Employment.** He became the first African American to represent New York in the House of Representatives.

- **Jesse Jackson:** Just a young man when King selected him as head of the Chicago Operation Breadbasket in 1966, Jackson went on to organize boycotts to pressure businesses to hire blacks for jobs and to work with black contractors.

Important events in Civil Rights

Following the example of Gandhi, Civil Rights activists took the approach of using nonviolent resistance and civil disobedience, most notably in the years from 1955 to 1965. These **direct actions** consisted of such events as bus boycotts, sit-ins, and freedom rides.

Rosa Parks and the Montgomery bus boycott, 1955–1956

After refusing to give up her seat on a bus in Montgomery, Alabama, **Rosa Parks** was arrested, tried, and convicted of disorderly conduct and violating a local ordinance. When word reached the black community, a bus boycott was organized to protest the segregation of blacks and whites on public buses. The boycott lasted 381 days, until the ordinance was lifted.

Formation of the Southern Christian Leadership Conference, 1957

This group was formed by Martin Luther King Jr., John Duffy, Rev. C. D. Steele, Rev. T. J. Jemison, Rev. Fred Shuttlesworth, Ella Baker, A. Philip Randolph, Bayard Rustin, and Stanley Levison. The group provided training and assistance to local efforts to fight segregation. Nonviolence was its central doctrine and its major method of fighting segregation and racism.

The Desegregation of Little Rock schools, 1957

Following the decision of the Supreme Court in *Brown vs. Board of Education*, the Arkansas school board voted to integrate the school system. The NAACP chose Arkansas as the place to push integration because it was considered a relatively progressive Southern state. Governor **Orval Faubus** called up the National Guard to prevent nine black students from attending Little Rock's Central High School. In response, President Eisenhower sent the 101st Airborne to patrol the school, accompany the black students to classes, and ensure that court-ordered integration took place.

Sit-ins

In 1960, students began to stage sit-ins at local lunch counters and stores as a means of protesting the refusal of those businesses to desegregate. The first was in Greensboro, North Carolina. This led to similar campaigns throughout the South. Demonstrators began to protest segregation of parks, beaches, theaters, museums, and libraries. When arrested, the protesters made "jail-no-bail" pledges; this put the financial burden of providing jail space and food on the cities.

Freedom rides

Activists traveled by bus throughout the South to desegregate bus terminals. Many buses were firebombed, and protestors were attacked and beaten by the KKK. They were crammed into small, airless jail cells and mistreated in many ways. Key figures in this effort included:

- John Lewis
- James Lawson
- Diane Nash
- Bob Moses
- James Bevel
- Charles McDew
- Bernard Lafayette
- Charles Jones
- Lonnie King
- Julian Bond
- Hosea Williams
- Stokely Carmichael

The Birmingham Campaign, 1963–1964

A campaign was planned to use sit-ins, kneel-ins in churches, and a march to the county building to launch a voter registration campaign. The city obtained an injunction forbidding all such protests. The protesters, including Martin Luther King Jr., believed the injunction was unconstitutional and defied it. They were arrested. While in jail, King wrote his famous "Letter from Birmingham Jail."

More than 600 students skipped school to protest Reverend King's being jailed and were also jailed. This was called the **Children's Crusade**. The next day, when a thousand more students joined the protest, police dogs were brought out, and fire hoses were used to knock protesters down.

The media broadcast vivid pictures of the protest and response, to a shocked nation. This resulted in the Kennedy administration's intervention, still the motel where the members of the Southern Christian Leadership Coalition (SCLC) were staying was burned, and four months later, the Ku Klux Klan bombed the **Sixteenth Street Baptist Church**, killing four African American girls who were attending Sunday school that morning. Two years later, **J. Edgar Hoover**, director of the FBI, closed the case, saying that conviction would be "remote."

The March on Washington, 1963

This march on the capital was a call for reforms and improved civil rights in many facets of society. It was a combined effort of all major civil rights organizations. The goals of the march were:

- Meaningful civil rights laws
- A massive federal works program
- Full and fair employment
- Decent housing
- The right to vote
- Adequate integrated education

It was at this march that Martin Luther King Jr. made his famous "I Have a Dream" speech.

Mississippi Freedom Summer, 1964

Students came from other states to Mississippi to assist local activists in registering voters, teach in "Freedom Schools," and form the Mississippi Freedom Democratic Party. In an attempt to curb this influx of activists, three workers were abducted and murdered by the KKK. It took six weeks to find their bodies. The national uproar forced President Johnson to send in the FBI. Court prosecution of the accused was difficult in the 1960s, however, and none of the men found guilty served more than six years for the murders. Some 41 years later, on June 21, 2005, Edgar Ray "Preacher" Killen was finally convicted of three cases of manslaughter.

It was during this time that Congress passed the **Civil Rights Act of 1964.**

Selma to Montgomery marches, 1965

Attempts to obtain voter registration in Selma, Alabama, had been largely unsuccessful due to opposition from the city's sheriff. Because of this, Reverend King came to the city to lead a series of marches. He and over 200 demonstrators were arrested and jailed. Police met each successive march of King and his followers with violent resistance.

In March, a group of over 600 intended to walk 54 miles from Selma to Montgomery. Six blocks into the march, state and local law enforcement officials attacked the marchers with billy clubs, tear gas, rubber tubes wrapped in barbed wire, and bull whips. The marchers were driven back to Selma. National broadcast of the footage provoked an outraged national response. Civil right activists were victorious, though, as the **Voting Rights Act of 1965** was signed into law on August 6, 1965.

The Assassinations of Martin Luther King Jr. and Robert Kennedy

The assassination of Martin Luther King in Memphis, Tennessee, on April 4, 1968, sparked racial riots in many American cities.

Senator **Robert F. Kennedy** is remembered for the speech he gave after the assassination to try to bring calm to the African American community. Kennedy himself was assassinated in Los Angeles on June 6, 1968, after winning the California Democratic Primary. It was likely that he would have won the Democratic Party's nomination for president, running on an antiwar platform.

Important Civil Rights legislation

Some key civil rights policies, legislation, and court cases included:

- **Brown v. Board of Education, 1954:** In this case, the Supreme Court declared that *Plessy v. Ferguson*, the ruling that had established "Separate but Equal" and was the basis for segregation, was unconstitutional. With this decision, the Supreme Court ordered immediate desegregation.
- **Civil Rights Act of 1964:** This act bars discrimination in public accommodations, employment, and education.
- **Voting Rights Act of 1965:** This law suspended poll taxes, literacy tests, and other voter tests for voter registration. This law irrevocably changed the political landscape of the South.

Foreign Policy: The Cold War

Defining the Cold War

Declaring itself the **arsenal of democracy**, the United States entered the World War II and emerged not only victorious but also as the strongest power on the Earth. It then had a permanent and leading place in world affairs.

U.S. foreign policy from the end of World War II to 1990 was the post-war struggle between non-Communist nations led by the United States and the Communist nations led by the Soviet Union. It was referred to as a **COLD WAR** because its conflicts did not lead to a major war of fighting, or a hot war between the two superpowers.

COLD WAR: the post–World War II struggle between non-Communist nations, led by the United States, and the Communist nations, led by the Soviet Union

Domestic implications of the Cold War

Just as WWII had united Americans in a common commitment to the purpose of supporting the troops and winning the war, they again rallied together to support the government in the Cold War.

Both the Soviet Union and the United States embarked on an arsenal buildup of atomic and **hydrogen bombs**. Both nations had the capability of destroying each other, but because of the continuous threat of nuclear war and accidents, both sides exercised extreme caution.

The Cold War on the world stage

Following the end of the war in 1945, social and economic chaos continued in Western Europe. The **MARSHALL PLAN** sent economic aid to Europe in the aftermath of the Second World War aimed at preventing the spread of communism.

MARSHALL PLAN: sent economic aid to Europe in the aftermath of the Second World War aimed at preventing the spread of communism

CONTAINMENT: a policy designed to contain the expansion of Soviet communist policies and activities

TRUMAN DOCTRINE: a policy that provided support for Greece and Turkey when they were threatened by the Soviet Union

For more information about the National Security Act, check out this site:

www.texascollaborative.org/SilverblattModule/act2-1.php

BERLIN AIRLIFT: the flying in of food and supplies to West Berlin by Allied air forces in response to Russian roadblocks attempting to prevent German reunification

In 1946, Josef Stalin stated that capitalism and its development of the world's economy made international peace impossible. In response, **George F. Kennan**, an American diplomat in Moscow, proposed a statement of U.S. foreign policy that would come to be known as **CONTAINMENT**. The goal of this policy was for the United States to contain the expansion of Soviet communist policies and activities.

In foreign policy, the **TRUMAN DOCTRINE** provided support for Greece and Turkey when they were threatened by the Soviet Union. The Marshall Plan, named for Secretary of State **George Marshall**, stimulated economic recovery for Western Europe. Truman participated in the negotiations that resulted in the formation of the **North Atlantic Treaty Organization (NATO).** He and his administration believed it necessary to support South Korea when the communist government of North Korea threatened it. But he contained American involvement in Korea so as not to risk conflict with China or Russia.

The **National Security Act of 1947** established the **Department of Defense**, the **National Security Council**, and the **Central Intelligence Agency (CIA)**.

The Struggle for Germany

Germany, which was still in pieces from the aftermath of World War II, would also become an area of Cold War struggle. Britain and the United States combined their two zones in February 1948; France joined them in June. This provided a united front for America's Cold War allies.

The Soviets, on the other hand, were opposed to German unification. In April 1948, the Soviets blocked all road traffic access to West Berlin from West Germany.

To avoid armed conflict, from June 1948 to mid-May 1949, Allied air forces flew in food and supplies for the West Berliners, in an event known as the **BERLIN AIRLIFT**. As a result of the airlift, the Soviets lifted their blockade and permitted vehicles access to the city.

Treaties and alliances

The **North Atlantic Treaty Organization (NATO)** was formed in 1949. The United States and several Western European nations, for the purpose of opposing communist aggression, stated: "The Parties of NATO agreed that an armed attack against one or more of them in Europe or North America shall be considered an attack against them all."

In response, the **WARSAW PACT** was signed in 1955 by Albania, Bulgaria, Czechoslovakia, East Germany, Hungary, Poland, Romania, and the Soviet Union stating that they would aid each other if attacked.

These pacts played out geographically as well. The **Berlin Wall**, dividing Germany into east and west parts, was built in 1961. The **IRON CURTAIN** referred to the ideological, symbolic, and physical separation of Europe between East and West.

WARSAW PACT: signed in 1955 by Albania, Bulgaria, Czechoslovakia, East Germany, Hungary, Poland, Romania, and the Soviet Union stating that they would aid each other if attacked

IRON CURTAIN: ideological, symbolic, and physical separation of Europe between East and West

Non-European alliances

In Asia, the Soviet Union's allies were China, North Korea, and North Vietnam. The allies of the United States were Japan, South Korea, Taiwan, and South Vietnam.

The arms race

The main symbol of the Cold War was the **ARMS RACE**, a continual buildup of missiles, tanks, and other weapons that became ever more technologically advanced and increasingly more deadly. Spending on weapons and defensive systems eventually occupied great percentages of the budgets of the United States and the U.S.S.R. Some historians argue that this high level of spending played a large part in bringing about the end of the Soviet Union.

ARMS RACE: a continual buildup of missiles, tanks, and other weapons that became ever more technologically advanced and increasingly more deadly

The Korean War

The first "hot war" in the post-World War II era was the Korean War; it began on June 25, 1950, and ended July 27, 1953. It was the first war in which a world organization played a major military role, and it presented quite a challenge to the United Nations, which had only been in existence five years.

Background

Korea had been under control of Japan from 1895 to the end of World War II in 1945. At war's end, the Soviet and U.S. military troops moved into Korea. The U.S. troops mobilized to the southern half, and the Soviet troops went to the northern half; the **38 DEGREE NORTH LATITUDE** line was the boundary between the two sides.

38 DEGREE NORTH LATITUDE: the boundary between North and South Korea

Invasion and war

The **General Assembly** of the U.N. in 1947 ordered elections throughout all of Korea to select one government for the entire country. The Soviet Union would not allow the North Koreans to vote, so they set up a communist government. The South Koreans set up a democratic government. Both, however, claimed the entire country. At times, there were clashes between Korean troops from

1948 to 1950. After the United States removed its remaining troops in 1949 and announced in early 1950 that Korea was not part of its defense line in Asia, troops from communist North Korea invaded democratic South Korea in an effort to unite both sections under communist control.

The United Nations asked member nations to furnish troops to help restore peace. Many nations responded and President Truman sent American troops to help the South Koreans. The war dragged on for three years and ended with a **truce**, not a **peace treaty**. Korea remains divided to this day.

Participants

The participants in Korean War were:

- North and South Korea
- United States of America
- Australia
- New Zealand
- China
- Canada
- France
- Great Britain
- Turkey
- Belgium
- Ethiopia
- Colombia
- Greece
- South Africa
- Luxembourg
- Thailand
- The Netherlands
- The Philippines

Ending the war

For more information on the Korean War, check out this site:

www.koreanwar-educator.org/home.htm

Eisenhower obtained a truce in Korea in 1953, and an **armistice agreement** was signed, ending the fighting. A permanent treaty of peace has never been signed, and the country remains divided between the communist North and the democratic South. The war destroyed villages and homes, displacing and/or killing millions of people. Hoping to avoid future conflicts of this type, Eisenhower worked to mitigate the tension of the Cold War during his two terms. He had some success; when Stalin died, he was able to negotiate a peace treaty with Russia that neutralized Austria.

CUBAN MISSILE CRISIS: a Cold War event that resulted from Soviet installation of nuclear missiles in Cuba, which endangered the United States

Cuban Missile Crisis

In October 1962, American U-2 spy planes photographed suspicious activities on the island of Cuba. The photographs showed the construction of missile bases, touching off the **CUBAN MISSILE CRISIS**. Because both the United States and the

U.S.S.R. had nuclear weapons capabilities, for a week tension and anxiety gripped the world.

Soviet fears

Russian Premier **Nikita Khrushchev** and the Soviets were concerned about American missiles installed in Turkey that were aimed at the U.S.S.R. They were also concerned about an invasion of Cuba, which had just experienced a change in its power structure. Khrushchev wanted to demonstrate to the Russian and Chinese critics that despite his policy of peaceful coexistence, he was tough and not to be intimidated.

American fears

At the same time, the Americans feared that if Russia launched nuclear missiles located just 90 miles off our coast there would not be enough time for adequate warning. Furthermore, they would originate from a direction that radar systems could not detect. This Soviet presence endangered American security.

President Kennedy had not attempted to prevent the erection of the Berlin Wall and was reluctant to commit American troops to invade Cuba. The Soviets peceived this as a weakness and decided they could install the missiles without any interference.

U.S. action and resolution

For the United States the only recourse was the removal of the missile sites and the prevention of further construction. Kennedy announced that the United States had set up a **quarantine** of Soviet ships heading to Cuba. It was, in reality, a blockade, a word that could not be used publicly because a blockade was actually considered an act of war. Soviet ships carrying missiles to the Cuban bases turned back, and the crisis eased.

In turn, American missiles in Turkey were removed. A telephone **hot line** was set up between Moscow and Washington to make it possible for the two heads of government to have instant contact with each other. As a final act of resolution, the United States also agreed to sell its surplus wheat to the Soviets.

The Vietnam War Era

Brief history of Vietnam

Vietnam had been part of the French colony of Indochina since 1861, along with Laos and Kampuchea (Cambodia). When France fell to Hitler in 1940, the Japanese seized Vietnamese rice and millions starved to death. Vietnamese continued to fight French troops for control of the country after the war.

GENEVA CONFERENCE OF 1954: granted Vietnam independence from France and divided the country into northern and southern zones

The **GENEVA CONFERENCE OF 1954** (which the United States did not participate in) granted Vietnam independence from France and divided the country into northern and southern zones. The Vietnamese believed that unification would follow. They considered their war one of national liberation, a struggle to avoid dominance and influence of a foreign power.

The United States' aid and influence in the region continued as part of the Cold War foreign policy to help any nation threatened by communism. The United States was particularly concerned about communism in China and thus had been aiding the French there. About a half-million Catholic Vietnamese moved south when the CIA spread messages such as "The Virgin Mary is moving south," indicating a threat of communist encroachment in the north.

A country divided

When the Vietnam War started, it divided the American public. Many saw as it the first war fought on foreign soil in which U.S. combat forces were unable to achieve objectives.

1968 DEMOCRATIC NATIONAL CONVENTION: during this convention, the deep divisions in the country over the Vietnam War were exemplified; while debate raged on the floor inside the hall, thousands protested the war outside

The debate over the war soon became heated, and many began to actively demonstrate against it. This conflict is exemplified in the **1968 DEMOCRATIC NATIONAL CONVENTION** in Chicago, both on the floor of the convention hall and outside, where thousands had gathered to protest the Vietnam War. Vice President **Hubert H. Humphrey** became the party's nominee, but he led a divided party.

The Tet Offensive

TET OFFENSIVE: a major offensive launched by the North Vietnamese communists between January and September 1968, attacking more than 100 cities and resulting in thousands of deaths and the destruction of homes

The turning point of the war itself was the **TET OFFENSIVE**, which occurred between January and September 1968. The communist North attacked over 100 cities, which resulted in thousands of deaths and destruction of homes. In the United States, advisors to President Johnson concluded that the war would go on as an endless violent stalemate.

Unrest at home

President **Richard Nixon**, who took office in 1969, began the secret bombing of Cambodia. This escalation of the war led to more antiwar demonstrations, and following the invasion of Cambodia, students demonstrating at **Kent State** in Ohio were killed by the National Guard. Student protests grew even larger. Protest of the military draft led to the end of the draft in 1973.

Meanwhile, returning veterans faced not only readjustment to normal civilian life but also bitterness, anger, and rejection at home. The escalation of drug abuse, the weakening of the family unit, homelessness, poverty, and mental trauma experienced by the Vietnam veterans all contributed to the divisions in the country.

End of the war

A cease-fire was called in January 1973, and a few months later, U.S. troops left Vietnam. The South Vietnamese continued to fight, but this ended on April 30, 1975. With the surrender of South Vietnam, the entire country was united under communist rule.

The Cold War Ends

The Cold War drew to a close in the late 1980s with the introduction of **Mikhail Gorbachev**'s reform programs and the fall of the Berlin Wall. The Soviet Union ceded its power over Eastern Europe and was dissolved in 1991.

The 15 republics of the former U.S.S.R. became independent nations with varying degrees of freedom and democracy in government, and together they formed the **COMMONWEALTH OF INDEPENDENT STATES (CIS)**. The former communist nations of Eastern Europe also emphasized their independence with democratic forms of government.

COMMONWEALTH OF INDEPENDENT STATES (CIS): the collection of 15 republics of the former U.S.S.R. that became independent nations with varying degrees of freedom and democracy

Technology in the Post-War Years

Discoveries and innovations in science and technology are directed to enhancing life and building up military. In the United States following World War II, there were significant advances in preventing and curing disease.

Life expectancy increased, along with the desire to develop new enhancements for living. In 1900, life expectancy for U.S. males was age 47; in 1950, it was age 64 for men and 67 for women; in 2001, age 75 for men and 80 for women.

The Soviet Union was first to begin a program of space flight and exploration, launching **SPUTNIK** in 1957 and putting the first man in space, **Yuri Gagarin**, in 1961. In 1969, the United States landed space crews on the moon.

SPUTNIK: the first manned vessel to be sent into space, it was launched by the Russians in 1961

Major post-war technological developments

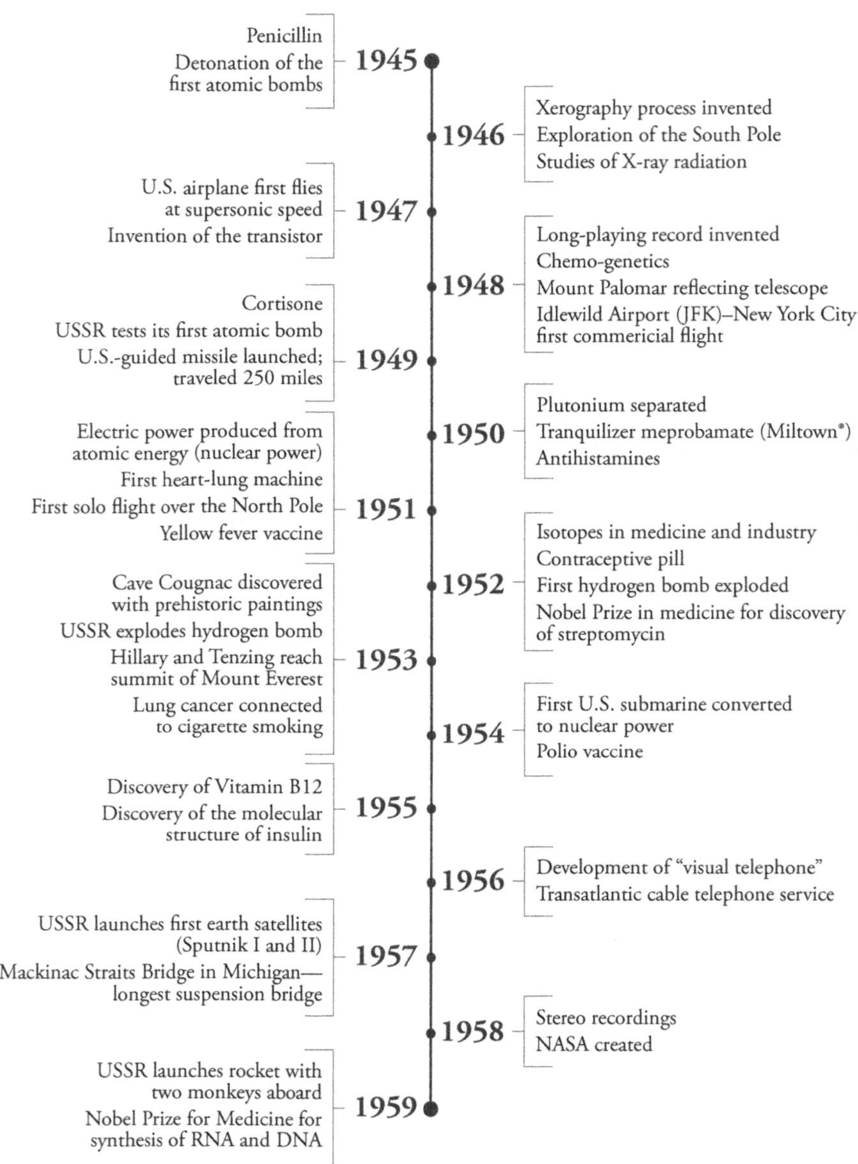
Major Technological Developments Between 1945 and 1960
1945
Penicillin
Detonation of the first atomic bombs
1946
Xerography process invented
Exploration of the South Pole
Studies of X-ray radiation
1947
U.S. airplane first flies at supersonic speed
Invention of the transistor
1948
Long-playing record invented
Chemo-genetics
Mount Palomar reflecting telescope
Idlewild Airport (JFK)–New York City first commericial flight
1949
Cortisone
USSR tests its first atomic bomb
U.S.-guided missile launched; traveled 250 miles
1950
Plutonium separated
Tranquilizer meprobamate (Miltown®)
Antihistamines
1951
Electric power produced from atomic energy (nuclear power)
First heart-lung machine
First solo flight over the North Pole
Yellow fever vaccine
1952
Isotopes in medicine and industry
Contraceptive pill
First hydrogen bomb exploded
Nobel Prize in medicine for discovery of streptomycin
1953
Cave Cougnac discovered with prehistoric paintings
USSR explodes hydrogen bomb
Hillary and Tenzing reach summit of Mount Everest
Lung cancer connected to cigarette smoking
1954
First U.S. submarine converted to nuclear power
Polio vaccine
1955
Discovery of Vitamin B12
Discovery of the molecular structure of insulin
1956
Development of "visual telephone"
Transatlantic cable telephone service
1957
USSR launches first earth satellites (Sputnik I and II)
Mackinac Straits Bridge in Michigan—longest suspension bridge
1958
Stereo recordings
NASA created
1959
USSR launches rocket with two monkeys aboard
Nobel Prize for Medicine for synthesis of RNA and DNA

For more information on immigration, check out this site:

www.digitalhistory.uh.edu/historyonline/immigration_chron.cfm

INTERNATIONAL REFUGEE ORGANIZATION: created in 1946, this organization relocated over a million European refugees who had been made homeless by World War II

Immigration after World War II

After WWII, the United States and Canada began to distinguish between economically motivated immigrants and **political refugees**. The United Nations created the **INTERNATIONAL REFUGEE ORGANIZATION** in 1946. Over the next three years, this organization relocated over a million European refugees who had been made homeless by the war. Fear of persecution caused massive migrations, and immigration policy in the United States was carefully aligned with foreign policy.

History of immigration legislation

President Truman proposed the **Displaced Persons Act**, Congress passed it in 1948. The act facilitated the admission of more than 400,000 displaced persons from Europe who were survivors of concentration camps and refugees of the Soviet-occupied regions of Europe.

The **Internal Security Act of 1950**, also known as the **McCarran-Wood Act**, set up required registration with the Attorney General's office for anyone who was a member of the American Communist Party, made it illegal if a member of that Party concealed it if seeking a job with the government, and prohibited such individuals from using a U.S. passport. Communists could be deported. Truman vetoed that act and also the **McCarran-Walter Act Immigration Nationality Act of 1952**, but Congress overrode his vetoes. The 1952 act maintained the quota system at the rate of one-sixth of one percent of each nationality's population in the United States in 1920. It also set up a racial quota for Asians.

Refugees from Communist Europe were admitted to the United States under the **President's Escapee Program** of 1952 and the **Refugee Relief Act** of 1953. Under these measures, 200,000 nonquota visas were granted to Europeans, many of who were Hungarians.

The Migration and Refugee Assistance Act of 1962 provided for refugee assistance, and the **Immigration Act of 1965** abolished the national-origin quotas. This latter has resulted in a decline of the relative proportion of the white population.

A more recent act was the **Immigration Reform and Control Act (IRCA) of 1986**. Signed by President Reagan, the act granted amnesty to about three million illegal immigrants and made it illegal to knowingly hire illegal immigrants.

Contributions of immigrants

Many immigrants were highly trained and skilled scientists, teachers, inventors, and executives. Their migration added to the American **melting pot** experience, and provided new sources of labor for a booming economy and the introduction of new cultural ideas.

SKILL 1.13 Recent developments

Presidents of the 1970s

The Nixon years

When Richard Nixon became president in 1969, he inherited racial unrest and the Vietnam War. His administration is probably best known for:

- Ending the Vietnam War
- Improving relations with China
- Appointing conservative justices to the Supreme Court
- Introducing new anticrime legislation
- Enacting the **National Environmental Policy Act** and legislation on clean air, national parks, endangered species, pesticides, coastal protection, and ocean dumping restrictions
- Revenue sharing legislation, which blocked grants that permitted state and local government to receive financial assistance
- Ending the draft
- The Watergate scandal

Chinese relations

After withdrawal of troops from Vietnam, Nixon first sent his Secretary of State **Henry Kissinger** on a secret trip to Peking (Beijing), China. The United States had not recognized Communist China and maintained that **Chiang Kai-shek**, exiled on the island of Taiwan, was China's legitimate leader. In 1972, President Nixon and the First Lady traveled to China and met with the Communist leaders. In 1979, the United States formally recognized Communist China.

Roe v. Wade

ROE V. WADE: a 1973 Supreme Court decision that legalized abortion

A landmark Supreme Court case during the Nixon years, 1973's **ROE V. WADE** legalized abortion.

Oil and energy

In 1973, the decision of the **Organization of Petroleum Exporting Countries (OPEC)** ministers to cut back on oil production raised the price of a barrel of oil and created a fuel shortage. Energy and fuel conservation became necessary as Americans experienced shortages of fuel oil for heating and gasoline for cars and other vehicles.

Watergate

In 1972, Nixon was involved in the **WATERGATE SCANDAL** when members of his administration broke into the Democratic National Committee headquarters in the Watergate Hotel to plant listening devices. This resulted in the first resignation of an American president. Not only did Nixon resign in 1974, but his Vice President, **Spiro Agnew**, later resigned as well, for tax evasion.

WATERGATE SCANDAL: a scandal that occurred when members of the Nixon Administration broke into the Democratic National Committee headquarters in the Watergate Hotel to plant listening devices; this led to Nixon's resignation in 1974

Gerald Ford

Gerald Ford was the first vice president selected under the Twenty-fifth Amendment. Ford was appointed by Nixon and approved by Congress. When Nixon resigned, Ford became the 38th president. He pardoned Nixon and appointed **Nelson Rockefeller** as his vice president.

The challenges that faced his administration included:

- Depressed economy
- Inflation
- Energy shortages
- *Détente*, or lessening aggression

Ford tried to reduce the role of the federal government. He did so by decreasing business taxes and lessening the government controls on business. His international focus was on preventing a major war in the Middle East. He negotiated with Russia regarding limitations on nuclear weapons.

Jimmy Carter

Jimmy Carter is the third U.S. president to win the Nobel Peace Prize (which he won in 2002, decades after his presidency). When Carter took office in 1977, he faced unemployment, a budget deficit, inflation, and high interest rates. Carter's presidency is known for:

- National energy policy
- Removing price controls from domestic petroleum production
- Pursuing Camp David Accords
- Pursuing Panama Canal Treaties
- **Strategic Arms Limitation Talks (SALT)**
- Iran hostage crisis (and botched helicopter rescue effort)
- Deregulation of trucking and airline industries
- Appointment of women and minorities to government jobs

Israel-Egypt peace

Egyptian President **Anwar el-Sadat** and Israeli Prime Minister **Menachem Begin** met at presidential retreat **Camp David** in 1978 and agreed to sign a formal treaty of peace between the two countries, as they had been in a state of war since 1948. The Camp David Accords led directly to the 1979 Israel-Egypt peace treaty.

Iran hostage crisis

In 1979, 53 American hostages were captured in Iran. The Shah had been deposed, and control of the government and the country was in the hands of Islamic cleric **Ayatollah Ruhollah Khomeini.**

OPERATION AJAX: a CIA-sponsored operation in which Iran's Mossadegh government was overthrown in a coup d'état

The United States' relationship with Iran had been friendly for decades. In 1953, Iran's **Mossadegh** government was overthrown in a coup d'état, sponsored by the CIA undertaking known as **OPERATION AJAX**. The CIA trained Shah **Mohammad Reza Pahlavi**'s secret police force; when the exiled Shah was allowed into the United States for medical treatment, 52 U.S. diplomats were held hostage for 444 days by Iranian college students who supported the revolution.

For more information on the attempt to rescue American hostages being held in Iran, check out this site:

www.defenselink.mil/news/newsarticle.aspx?id=31346

President Carter froze all Iranian assets in the United States, set up trade restrictions, and approved a risky rescue attempt. The attempt failed, resulting in the deaths of eight U.S. servicemen.

Khomeini ignored U.N. requests for releasing the Americans, and Europeans refused to support the embargo so as not to risk losing access to Iran's oil. The hostages were released on the day of President Ronald Reagan's inauguration in January 1981.

Presidents of the 1980s

Ronald Reagan

Ronald Reagan was the first president whose career included being a professional actor. He was also the first divorced president and the oldest president, elected at the age of 69. A two-term president, Reagan is known for:

- **Reagonomics**, also known as supply-side or "trickle-down" economics
- Curbing inflation
- Increasing employment, following the peak unemployment rate of 10.8 percent in December 1982
- Signing **Economic Recovery Tax Act of 1981** (also known as ERTA or the Kemp-Roth Tax Cut), resulting in one percent decrease in government revenues or three percent of GDP

- Nominating **Sandra Day O'Connor**, first female justice on the Supreme Court.
- Contributing to **Iran-Contra scandal**
- Declaring war on **Grenada**
- Negotiation with Soviet Premier Mikahail Gorbachev to reduce nuclear weapons
- Surviving an assassination attempt by **John Hinkley Jr.**
- Breaking the air traffic controllers union
- Increasing national debt from $600 billion to $3 trillion, or 48.1 percent of GDP
- Presiding over the end of Cold War
- The stock market crash of 1987
- The War on Drugs, with the slogan "Just Say No"

Employment and inflation

When Reagan took office, inflation was at 11.83 percent and unemployment at 7.1 percent. Increases in federal budget deficits and the national debt were used to reduce these numbers.

Defense spending

Defense spending increased by 40 percent between 1981 and 1985. Much of the budget was to fund the B-1 bomber program, the MX "Peacekeeper" Missile, and the **Strategic Defense Initiative** (SDI, also known as "Star Wars").

Savings and loan crisis

The savings and loan industry (S&L) was deregulated and began to make risky loans along with other unsafe financial activities. More than 1,000 savings and loan institutions failed during this time.

For more information on the savings and loan crisis, check out this site:

www.nysscpa.org/cpajournal/old/08033828.htm

Iran-Contra affair

U.S. involvement in the domestic revolutions of El Salvador and Nicaragua continued into Reagan's second term. Congress held televised hearings on the **IRAN-CONTRA AFFAIR**: not only were members of his administration selling arms to Iran, but there were allegations of drug dealing as well. The cover-up was exposed, showing that profits from secretly selling military hardware to Iran had been used to support rebels, called **Contras**, who were fighting in Nicaragua.

IRAN-CONTRA AFFAIR: this scandal involved members of the Reagan Administration illegally selling arms to Iran and using the profits to fund Contra rebels in Nicaragua

Air traffic controllers strike

On August 3, 1981, federally employed air traffic controllers went on strike, demanding better pay, shorter hours, and improved conditions. Reagan said that the striking air traffic controllers had to report to work within 48 hours or they would "have forfeited their jobs and will be terminated." On August 5, 1981, Reagan fired the 11,345 striking air traffic controllers and broke the union.

Attack on peacekeeping forces

In 1983, 241 American Marines who were serving as part of a peacekeeping force in Lebanon were killed when an Islamic suicide bomber drove an explosive-laden truck into U.S. Marine headquarters located at the airport in Beirut. This tragic event came as part of the unrest and violence between the Israelis and the **Palestinian Liberation Organization (PLO)** forces in southern Lebanon.

Granada

In the same month, 1,900 U.S. Marines landed on the island of **Grenada** to rescue a small group of American medical students and depose the leftist government.

George H. W. Bush

George H. W. Bush served as vice president under President Reagan. His prior career had been in the oil industry and government. His involvement in the national political stage began when Nixon asked Bush to chair the Republican National Committee. After this, he served as chief of the U.S. Liaison Office in China and then as director of the CIA. He then became chairman of the First International Bank in Houston and an adjunct professor at Rice University. During the Reagan Administration, Bush held responsibility for anti-drug programs and federal deregulation.

When Bush ran for president against Massachusetts governor Michael Dukakis, his **thousand points of light** speech moved him forward in the polls.

Significant events during the Bush years

Some events that occurred during the Bush Administration included:

- Invasion of Panama Canal and capture of dictator **Manuel Noriega**
- Iraq's invasion of Kuwait
- Gulf War, known as **Desert Storm**
- Fall of the Berlin Wall
- Unification of Germany
- Break-up of Soviet Union
- Establishment of independent nations
- Tiananmen Square massacre in Beijing

For more information on corruption in Washington, D.C., check out this site:

www.pbs.org/newshour/indepth_coverage/law/corruption/history.html

- Exxon Valdez oil spill of 11 million gallons of crude oil
- First World Wide Web page created
- Ruby Ridge confrontation with the Weaver family and federal agents
- Seizure of Lincoln Savings and Loan, a company that cost taxpayers about $200 billion

The Panama invasion

President Bush sent U.S. troops to invade Panama in December 1989 and arrest the Panamanian dictator, Manuel Noriega. Although he had periodically assisted CIA operations with intelligence information, Noriega also laundered money from drug smuggling and gunrunning through Panama's banks. When a political associate tried unsuccessfully to depose him and an off-duty U.S. Marine was shot and killed at a roadblock, Bush acted. Noriega was brought to the United States, where he stood trial in Miami and was convicted on 8 out of 10 drug and racketeering charges.

Involvement in the Iraq-Iran War

During the Iraq-Iran war, the United States and most of Iraq's neighbors supported Iraq. In a five-year period, **Saddam Hussein** received $500 million worth of American technology, including lasers, advanced computers, and special machine tools used in missile development from the United States. Iraq also received $14 billion from its supportive neighbor Kuwait.

The Iraq-Iran war resulted in a stalemate with a U.N. truce, and it officially ended.

The First Gulf War

Iraq intended to pay off its war debt with oil earnings by raising the prices of oil. However, Kuwait, a member of the OPEC, prevented a global increase in petroleum prices by increasing its own petroleum production, thus lowering the price and preventing recovery of the war-crippled Iraqi economy.

The drop in oil prices upset Saddam Hussein, who was deeply in debt from the war and totally dependent on oil revenues. Iraq invaded Kuwait on August 2, 1990. Consequently, the United States made extensive plans to carry out **OPERATION DESERT STORM**, the liberation of Kuwait. It was a joint effort of many nations with the backing of the United Nations.

Operation Desert Storm began with airstrikes on January 16, 1991. The next day Iraq shot scud missiles into Israel. The United States persuaded Israel not to retaliate. When the Iraqi soldiers retreated from Kuwait on February 28, they set fire to Kuwaiti oil fields.

For more information on Desert Storm, check out this site:

www.gwu.edu/~nsarchiv/NSAEBB/NSAEBB39/

OPERATION DESERT STORM: the military operation designed to the liberate Kuwait during the first Gulf War

Modern Presidents

William Clinton

William Clinton won the 1992 presidential election against Bush and **Ross Perot**. He was the first **baby boomer** president. Despite his being only the second president to be impeached after President Andrew Johnson, he left office with a high approval rating.

Significant events during Clinton's terms

Some actions during his two terms include:

- **Family and Medical Leave Act**
- The "Don't Ask, Don't Tell" military policy
- First female Secretary of State
- **North American Free Trade Agreement (NAFTA)**
- Brady Bill
- Earned Income Tax Credit
- The Elián González affair
- Policy of "regime change" against Iraq
- Operation Allied Force with NATO in Bosnia
- Oslo Accords
- Defense of Marriage Act
- Extraordinary rendition and irregular rendition approval
- Waco siege

Clinton's domestic accomplishments include the lowest inflation rate in 30 years, the lowest unemployment rate, the highest rate of home ownership, lower crime rates in many places, smaller welfare rolls, a balanced budget, and a budget surplus.

Foreign affairs

Clinton sent U.S. troops to Haiti to support **Jean-Bertrand Aristide**, a former Roman Catholic priest who had been elected President of Haiti and was overthrown by a military coup.

Clinton also sent troops to Bosnia to assist U.N. peacekeeping forces from 1992 to 1995. He also sent U.S. troops to Somalia in December 1992 to support U.N.

efforts to end the starvation of the Somalis and restore peace. The efforts were successful at first but eventually failed due to the severity of the intricate political problems within the country. After U.S. soldiers were killed in an ambush along with 300 Somalis, American troops were withdrawn and returned home.

Domestic disturbances

In Waco, Texas, in 1993, the FBI held a 51-day siege on the **Branch Davidian Seventh Day Adventist Church** headed by **David Koresh** after the Bureau of Alcohol, Tobacco, and Firearms had attempted to serve a warrant on the group. On April 19, 76 residents, along with 21 children, died in a fire.

This would not be the last significant loss of life in the Clinton Era; there was also an attack on the **Murrah Federal Building** in Oklahoma City on April 19, 1995. This act of domestic terrorism killed 168 people.

Clinton also had to deal with economic trouble. Numerous savings and loans institutions failed and others went into bankruptcy due to customer default on loans and mismanagement. Congressional legislation helped rebuild the industry, costing taxpayers billions of dollars.

For more information on the cost of the savings and loan crisis, check out this site:

www.fdic.gov/bank/analytical/banking/2000dec/brv13n2_2.pdf

The Environment

As the population of the United States has increased, so have the nation's industries. Harmful pollution of the environment is an unfortunate result of this expansion. Factory smoke, automobile exhaust, and industrial waste all combine to create hazardous air, water, and ground pollution. Many scientists argue that if this pollution is not brought under control and significantly diminished, it could endanger all life on Earth.

Some prominent environmental threats of the modern era include the **Exxon Valdez** oil spill off the Alaskan coast, the nuclear accident and meltdown at the Ukrainian nuclear power plant at **Chernobyl**, and the near nuclear disaster at **Three Mile Island Nuclear Plant** in Pennsylvania.

Changing Policies and Legislation

The United States has a long history of expanding the rights guaranteed by the Constitution. Various civil rights movements have sought to guarantee that individual rights are not denied on the basis of being part of a minority group. The effects of these movements may be seen in guarantees of minority representation and affirmative action programs.

Significant Civil Rights legislation

Since 1941, Congress has passed a number of anti-discrimination. These acts have protected the civil rights of several groups of Americans. These laws include:

- Fair Employment Act of 1941
- Civil Rights Act of 1964
- Immigration and Nationality Services Act of 1965
- Voting Rights Act of 1965
- Civil Rights Act of 1968
- Age Discrimination in Employment Act of 1967
- Age Discrimination Act of 1975
- Pregnancy Discrimination Act of 1978
- Americans with Disabilities Act of 1990
- Civil Rights Act of 1991
- Employment Non-Discrimination Act

Different Civil Rights movements

Numerous groups have used various forms of protest, attempts to sway public opinion, legal action, and congressional lobbying to obtain full protection of their civil rights under the Constitution.

DISABILITY RIGHTS MOVEMENT: guaranteed equal access and equal protection under the law to disabled American citizens

Disabled rights

Many minority rights movements began after the Civil Rights movement of the 1950s, 1960s, and 1970s. The **DISABILITY RIGHTS MOVEMENT**, for example, resulted in a guaranteed access to public buildings and transportation; equal access to education and employment; and equal protection under the law in terms of access to insurance, and other basic rights of American citizens. Public buildings and public transportation must be accessible to persons with disabilities. Discrimination in hiring or housing on the basis of disability is also illegal.

PRISONERS' RIGHTS MOVEMENT: ensured the basic human rights of people incarcerated for crimes

Prisoners' rights

A **PRISONERS' RIGHTS MOVEMENT** has helped to ensure the basic human rights of persons incarcerated for crimes.

IMMIGRANT RIGHTS MOVEMENTS: fought for employment and housing rights and preventing hate crimes

Immigrant rights

IMMIGRANT RIGHTS MOVEMENTS have provided for employment and housing rights, as well as preventing abuse of immigrants through hate crimes. In some states, immigrant rights movements have led to bilingual education and public information access.

Gay rights

Another group movement seeking to obtain equal rights is the **LESBIAN, GAY, BISEXUAL AND TRANSGENDER (LGBT) MOVEMENT**. This movement seeks equal housing, freedom from social and employment discrimination, and equal recognition of gay relationships under the law.

LESBIAN, GAY, BISEXUAL AND TRANSGENDER (LGBT) MOVEMENT: seeks equal housing, freedom from social and employment discrimination, and equal recognition of gay relationships under the law

Women's rights

The **WOMEN'S RIGHTS MOVEMENT** is concerned with the rights and freedoms of women that at times have been suppressed or prohibited in American culture.

WOMEN'S RIGHTS MOVEMENT: the movement concerned with securing and protecting the rights and freedoms of women

By the 1960s, the word **feminism** came to describe the movement. The **National Organization for Woman (NOW)** began in 1966 with the purpose of getting the **Equal Rights Amendment** passed. This amendment said that "equality of rights under the law shall not be denied or abridged by the United States or any state on account of sex." In 1982, the amendment died, however, because not enough states had ratified it.

Some of the most famous leaders in the women's movement since the 1960s are:

- Shirley Chisolm
- Coretta Scott King
- Katha Pollett
- Betty Friedan
- Gloria Steinem
- Adrienne Rich
- Naomi Wolf
- Ana Castillo

For more information on the National Organization for Women (NOW), check out this site:

www.now.org/

DOMAIN II
WORLD HISTORY

PERSONALIZED STUDY PLAN

SKILL		KNOWN MATERIAL/ SKIP IT
2.1:	Human society to approximately 3000 BCE	☐
2.2:	Development of early civilizations: circa 3000–1500 BCE	☐
2.3:	Ancient empires and civilizations: circa 1700 B.C.E.–500 CE	☐
2.4:	Disruption and reversal: circa 500–1400 CE	☐
2.5:	Emerging global interactions: circa 1400–1800 CE	☐
2.6:	Political and Industrial Revolutions, Nationalism: 1750–1914	☐
2.7:	Conflicts, ideologies, and evolutions in the 20th century: 1900–1991	☐
2.8:	Contemporary trends: 1991–present	☐

SKILL 2.1 Human society to approximately 3000 BCE

Prehistory

PREHISTORY is defined as the period of human achievement prior to the development of writing. The three different periods of prehistory are:

- **Lower Paleolithic Period:** use of crude tools, mostly made of stone
- **Upper Paleolithic Period:** a greater variety of better-made tools, implements, and weapons made out of a variety of materials; starting fires through friction; emergence of clothing, organized group life, and art
- **Neolithic Period:** agriculture with domesticated animals and raising crops; the arts of knitting, spinning, and weaving cloth; building houses rather than living in caves; the development of institutions including the family, religion, and government; and the origin of the state

PREHISTORY: the period of human achievement prior to the development of writing

Anthropology

ANTHROPOLOGY is the scientific study of human culture and humanity and the relationship between humans and their culture. Anthropologist **Eric Wolf** defined it as "the most scientific of the humanities, and the most humanistic of the sciences."

ANTHROPOLOGY: the scientific study of human culture and humanity and the relationship between humans and their culture

Anthropologists study:

- Different groups
- How groups relate to other cultures
- Patterns of behavior
- Similarities and differences among cultures

Anthropological research is two-fold: **cross-cultural** and **comparative**. The major method of study is referred to as **PARTICIPANT OBSERVATION**. An anthropologist studies and learns about the people by living among them and participating with them in their daily lives. Anthropology is divided into: biological and cultural anthropology, archaeology, and linguistics.

PARTICIPANT OBSERVATION: method of study in which an anthropologist studies and learns about people by living among them and participating with them in their daily lives

Archaeology

ARCHAEOLOGY is the scientific study of past human cultures by studying the remains they left behind including pottery, bones, buildings, tools, and artwork.

ARCHAEOLOGY: the scientific study of past human cultures by studying the remains they left behind

Archaeologists locate and examine any evidence to help explain the way that people lived in past times. They use special equipment and techniques to gather the evidence and keep detailed records of their findings. Unfortunately, the rigors of their research may sometimes result in destruction of the remains being studied.

Archaeological process

The first step of the process is to locate an archaeological site. Next, the site is surveyed, starting with a detailed description of the area with notes, maps, photographs, and the collection artifacts from the surface. **Excavating** follows, either by digging for buried objects or by diving and working in submersible decompression chambers when underwater. The archaeologists record and preserve the evidence for eventual classification, determination of date, and evaluation of their find.

Archaeology and early humanity

Sources of knowledge about early humans include:

- Fossils derived from burial pits
- Occasional bones found in rock deposits
- Archaeological excavations of tools, pottery, paintings
- The study of living primitives

Although written records go back only about 4,500 years, scientists have pieced together evidence that documents the existence of humans (or "man-apes") as many as 600,000 years ago. The first man-like primates arose about one million years ago. These primates developed and discovered fire and tools. They had human-sized brains and produced the **Cro-Magnon** (25,000 years ago), from which **Homo sapiens** descended.

Primitive humans demonstrated wide behavior patterns and great adaptability.

Primitive humans demonstrated wide behavior patterns and great adaptability. There is little is known about many details of early humanity, including when language began to develop. They are believed to have lived in small communities that developed on the basis of the need to hunt. Cave paintings may suggest that early humans believed that magic pictures of animals could conjure up real ones. Unearthed figurines indicate belief in fertility gods and goddesses, and their concept of an afterlife is evidenced by burial formalities.

For more information about Paleolithic art, check out this site:

www.culture.gouv.fr /culture/arcnat/lascaux/en/

Archaeological evidence points to the use of hatchets, awls, needles, and cutting tools in the Lower Paleolithic or Old Stone Age (one million years ago). Artifacts of the Upper Paleolithic or New Stone Age (6000-8000 BCE) that have been discovered indicate the use of polished tools, domesticated animals, the wheel, and some agriculture. Pottery and textiles have been found dating to the end of the New Stone Age (Neolithic period). The discovery of metals in the **Bronze Age** (3000 BCE) is concurrent with the establishment of what are believed to be the first civilizations. The **Iron Age** rapidly developed next.

Early Civilizations

By 4000 BCE, humans lived in villages, engaged in animal husbandry, grew grains, sailed in boats, and practiced religions. Civilizations arose earliest in the fertile river valleys of the Nile, Mesopotamia, the Indus, and the Hwang Ho.

The prerequisites of civilization include:

- Use of metals rather than stone for tools and weapons
- A system of writing
- A calendar
- A territorial state

The Fertile Crescent

The earliest known civilizations developed in the **Tigris-Euphrates valley** of Mesopotamia (modern Iraq) and the **Nile valley** of Egypt between 4000 BCE and 3000 BCE. The **FERTILE CRESCENT**, named by **James Breasted**, a University of Chicago archaeologist, described the part of the Near East that extended from the Persian Gulf to the Sinai Peninsula. It included Mesopotamia, Syria, and Palestine. Geography, especially the physical environment played a critical role in the rise and the survival of civilizations. They are also known as **FLUVIAL CIVILIZATIONS**, as rivers provided a source of water that would sustain life. The hunters had ample access to a variety of animals, to provide food, hides, bones, and antlers from which clothing, tools, and art could be made. Proximity to water enabled domesticating animals, which could be herded and bred to provide a stable supply of food and animal products. Rivers also usually flooded, leaving behind a deposit of very rich soil. This soil was fertile, and water was readily available to produce sizeable harvests. In time, the people developed systems of irrigation that channeled water to the crops.

FERTILE CRESCENT: site of the first known civilizations; this part of the Near East extended from the Persian Gulf to the Sinai Peninsula and included Mesopotamia, Syria, and Palestine

FLUVIAL CIVILIZATIONS: civilizations centered on rivers, as they provided a source of water that would sustain life

This region was marked by **invasions** and **migrations**. The invaders and migrants may have destroyed existent cultures or absorbed and supplemented the civilization that existed before their arrival. In the Fertile Crescent, civilization developed quickly into an advanced culture.

The Fertile Crescent

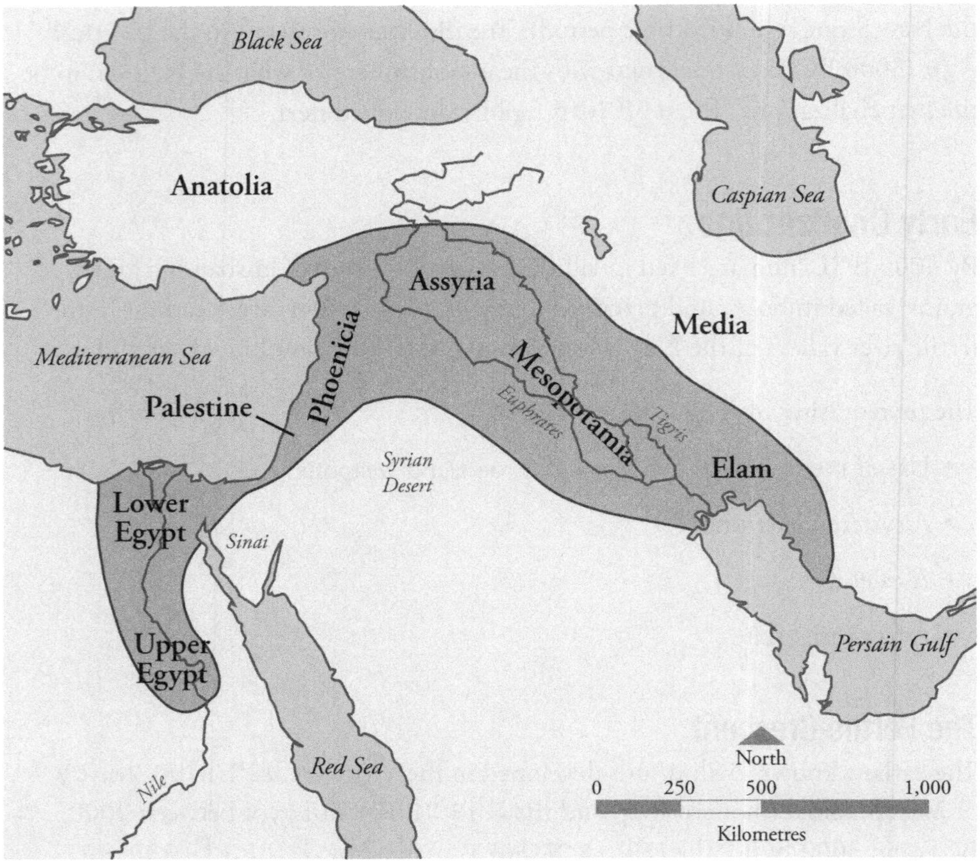

For more information on the Saraswati River, check out this site:

www.gisdevelopment.net/application/archaeology/site/archs0001.htm

India

In India, the **Indus Valley culture** was primarily urban and traded with Sumer. Along the now-dry Saraswati River, archaeologists are discovering many ancient towns and cities.

For more information on ancient Chinese technology, check out this site:

www.library.thinkquest.org/23062/

China

The Neolithic Era of China took place about 12,000 years ago, and civilization centered on the Yangtze River and Yellow River. The atmosphere there was far wetter than it is today. Silk production was active, and the **Yangshao** had the pottery wheel. The **Lungshan** created black pottery. **Millet** was grown south of the Yellow River.

SKILL 2.2 Development of Early Civilizations: Circa 3000–1500 BCE

In the 1500 years between 3000 BCE and 1500 BCE, cultures developed all over the world, including:

- Mesopotamia in the Middle East
- Egypt and Kush in Africa
- Greece in Southern Europe
- India in Asia
- China in Asia
- Japan in Asia
- Americas in the Western Hemisphere

Notable Civilizations

The civilizations of the Sumerians, Amorites, Hittites, Assyrians, Chaldeans, and Persians controlled various areas of the land known as Mesopotamia. The cultures of Mesopotamia were autocratic, with a single ruler at the head of the government who, in many cases, was also the head of the religion. With few exceptions, tyrants and military leaders controlled trade, religions, and law. Many cultures had a handful of gods, and it was common to have a national worship structure, with high priests centered in the capital city as advisors to the tyrant. Trade was vastly important to these civilizations since they had access to some, but not all, of the things that they needed to survive. Some trading agreements led to the occupation of cities, as was the case with Egypt and the Phoenician cities, who were powerful and regular trading partners of the various Mesopotamian cultures.

SUMER was the southern half of Mesopotamia; **AKKAD** was the northern half.

SUMER AND AKKAD: the southern and the northern halves of Mesopotamia, respectively

Civilizations of Mesopotamia

Sumer

Sumer was composed of 12 **city-states**, which had their own gods, with the city-state's leader doubling as the high priest. Sumerians made advances in astronomy, mathematics, and irrigation; improved the wheel (both for making pottery and for transportation) and the sailboat; invented glass and bronze; devised the first system of writing (cuneiform); and learned to divide time. Their society is credited for the first-known epic poem, *The Epic of Gilgamesh*. The Sumerians did not build walls around their cities to protect their advancements.

For more information on Sumer, check out this site:

www.history-world.org/sumeria.htm

Sargon and the Akkadian Empire

For more information on Sargon the Great, check out this site:

www.history-world.org/sargon_the_great.htm

The first empire was probably in Mesopotamia: the Akkadians led by **Sargon**, conqueror of Sumer. Sargon of Akkad is known for conquering these areas in the south, such as **Syria**, **Anatolia**, and **Elam**, and for establishing the first **Semitic** dynasty. Semites include Akkadians, Phoenicians, Hebrews, and Arabs.

Ur

Ur, an ancient city in Sumer was at one time led by Ur-Nammu who developed the Code of Ur-Nammu, which preceded the Codes of Hammarubi by about 300 years. The third dynasty of Ur was taken over by the Elamites in about 1950 BCE.

The Assyrians

ASSYRIANS: an ancient Mesopotamian people, thought to be warlike and aggressive and who had a highly organized military that used horse-drawn chariots

Evidence indicates that the ancient **ASSYRIANS** were probably warlike and aggressive, with a highly organized military that used horse-drawn chariots. Using their advanced military, the Assyrians conquered and ruled northern Mesopotamia around 1300 BCE. Their expanded empire ultimately included Egypt and the Fertile Crescent, and their presence in that region preceded the Persian Empire. There was more to their culture than war though; the Assyrian leader **Ashurbanipal** instituted the first library dedicated to preserving knowledge. Agriculture and breeding horses were also important to their societies, but their record of impaling and beheading enemies is perhaps more known.

The Hebrews

HEBREWS: an ancient Mesopotamian people who instituted monotheism, which is the worship of one god

The **HEBREWS**, also known as the ancient Israelites, practiced **monotheism**, which is the worship of one god, Yahweh, who provided the ten commandments.

The Babylonians

BABYLONIANS: an ancient Mesopotamian people known for their Amorite leader Hammurabi—who devised the famous Code of Hammurabi—and for conquering and exiling the Jews

BABYLONIANS are remembered for the Amorite leader **Hammurabi** who devised the famous Code of Hammurabi, a code of law. He was emperor around 1810 BCE. Also, **Nebuchadnezzar**, leader of the Chaldeans, is remembered for building the **Hanging Gardens of Babylon** and the Babylonian Captivity around 597 BCE, when he conquered Judah and Jerusalem, destroyed the Temple, and banished Jews to Babylon.

Egypt

Most know that Egypt built the great pyramids. Some of their other significant contributions include:

- Development of hieroglyphic writing
- Preservation of bodies after death
- Making of paper from papyrus

- Contributing to developments in arithmetic and geometry
- Completion of a solar calendar
- Laying of a foundation for science and astronomy

The Egyptian civilization encompassed many cities up and down the Nile River in northeastern and east-central Africa. Egyptian goods flowed from ports and trade centers to locations all over the Mediterranean area and into central Asia. The **PHARAOHS**, who were the autocrats of Egypt and therefore in command of all aspects of the lives of the Egyptian people, were also heads of the various religions. Even though each Egyptian god had its own temple and each temple had its own priests, the pharaoh was the liaison between the people and their gods

PHARAOHS: the monarchs of ancient Egypt, they commanded all aspects of the lives of the Egyptian people and the heads of the various religions

The Hittites

The **HITTITE EMPIRE**, centered in what is now Turkey, extended from Mesopotamia to Palestine and Syria. They conquered the Babylonians and over time adopted Babylonian laws and religion. The height of the Hittite empire was 1600 to 1200 BCE. The Hittite rulers were less despotic than other rulers in the region, and they practiced an early form of religious tolerance, seeing all gods as legitimate and incorporating them into their religion. Militarily they were strong, but they were met with a formidable foe in Ramesses II of Egypt. The war between these two empire would considerable weaken both sides. Hittite independence continued until 700 BCE when they were taken over by the Assyrians.

HITTITE EMPIRE: centered in what is now Turkey, this empire extended from Mesopotamia to Palestine and Syria; it also conquered the Babylonians, but, over time, adopted Babylonian laws and religion

For more information on the Hittite empire, check out this site:

www.specialtyinterests.net/hittites.html

The Persians

The ancient **PERSIANS** developed an alphabet; contributed the religions/philosophies of **Zoroastrianism**, **Mithraism**, and **Gnosticism**, and allowed conquered peoples to retain their own customs, laws, and religions.

PERSIANS: a significant ancient empire that developed an alphabet, contributed to various religions and philosophies, and allowed conquered people to retain their own customs, laws, and religions

Kush

The earliest historical record of **KUSH** is in Egyptian sources. Kush (also known as Cush) was located in the southern part of modern Egypt and the northern part of Sudan. During the time when the Kush empire ranged from near **Khartoum** to the Mediterranean Sea, it was the largest empire on the Nile River. Its people were called Ethiopians, but that does not refer to modern-day Ethiopia.

KUSH: a civilization located in the southern part of modern Egypt and the northern part of Sudan; at its peak, it was the largest empire on the Nile River

Neolithic Kush

The Neolithic civilization of Kush was characterized by a settled way of life in fortified mud-brick villages with hunting and fishing, herding cattle, and raising grain.

Language and culture

Skeletal remains suggest that the people were a blend of Negroid and Mediterranean peoples. The Kush spoke **Nilo-Saharan** languages, and the capital city was **Kerma**, a major trading center.

The descent of the king was determined through the mother's line (as in Egypt), and the Kushites were ruled by a series of female heads of state called **KANDAKE** or Kentake.

KANDAKE: also called Kentake, the female heads of the Kush state

Religion

The Kushite religion was **polytheistic**, including all of the primary Egyptian gods. There were, however, regional gods who were the principal gods in their regions. Along with other African cultures, there was a lion warrior god.

For more information on Ancient Egypt and Nubia, check out these sites:

www.wysinger.homestead.com/chronology.html

www.nubianet.org/

The fall of Kush

The Assyrians and Persians invaded Kush and forced them south. Kush was conquered by the Nubian Kingdom around 800 BCE.

The Phoenicians

The **PHOENICIANS** were sea traders well known for manufacturing skills in glass, and metals, and for the development of their famous purple dye. They were proficient with navigation, so they were able to sail by the stars at night. Further, they devised an alphabet using symbols to represent single sounds, which was an extension of the cuneiform writing system from Mesopotamia.

PHOENICIANS: sea traders well known for manufacturing skills in glass and metals and for the development of their famous purple dye

The Minoans

The Bronze Age Minoan civilization developed on the island Crete about 2700 BCE and lasted until approximately 1450 BCE. They developed a writing system known as **Linear A** and later **Linear B**, but A is not yet translatable. **MINOANS** were traders and used their writing system of symbols to represent syllables in words. They built palaces that contained multiple levels with many rooms, water and sewage systems with flush toilets, bathtubs, hot and cold running water, and bright paintings on the walls. In about 2000 BCE and again in 1450 BCE, there was widespread destruction of Minoan settlements. There is evidence that this destruction might have been caused by earthquakes as well as volcanoes, such as the Thera volcano.

MINOANS: this ancient civilization, which existed on the island Crete from around 2700 to 1450 BCE, was famous for trade and used their writing system of symbols to represent syllables in words

India

In ancient times, India had the shining light of **Mohenjo-Daro**, which was a planned community with wide, straight streets, advanced plumbing, and other features that many would consider "modern" innovations. Indian goods also found their way to western ports through trade with the ancient Mediterranean civilizations. The major religions of **Hinduism** and **Buddhism** had their genesis in India. The Hindu doctrine of reincarnation made it nearly impossible for anyone to change his or her fortune.

Indo-European languages

The northern Indian languages evolved from Old Indo-Aryan such as Sanskrit. Indo-Uralic languages are being examined. The Finno-Ugric languages are separate from the Indo-sources.

China

China is considered by some historians to be the oldest uninterrupted civilization in the world. Chinese writing goes back to 1500 BCE. Their Neolithic age is traced back 10,000 years, and evidence of agriculture dates back 7,000 years. The Yellow River Valley is where the earliest settlements are found. Cliff carvings dating back 6,000 years have also been discovered at Ningxia.

Ancient Americans

An agricultural society existed in Peru more than 5,000 years ago. It is referred to as the Norte Chico civilization, and it included 20 communities.

For more information on Ancient America, check out this site:

www.precolumbia.com/bearc/CAAS/ancient_america.html

SKILL 2.3 Ancient empires and civilizations: circa 1700 BCE–500 CE *(India, China, Ancient Western Asia, Mediterranean, Africa)*

The Mycenaeans

The **MYCENAEANS** were Europe's first major civilization. It included the city-states of **Sparta**, **Metropolis**, and **Corinth**, and its success made it a target for the Persian Empire. Their writing was the Minoan Linear B, and it continues to be transcribed to reveal more about this ancient culture. Tablets show that the Mycenaeans were involved in trade, agriculture, industry, and war and that they worshipped the gods that became Zeus and the other gods and goddesses of Mount Olympus. Archaeology has continued to provide information about them. For example, it has been discovered that in **Peloponnesus**, a town of the Bronze Age, was deserted in about 1150 BCE and then reborn 125 years later.

MYCENAEANS: Europe's first major civilization, it encompassed Sparta, Metropolis, and Corinth

The destruction of Mycenae

There is evidence of the palaces and cities of the Mycenaean being destroyed around 1200 BCE, about the same time that the Hittite culture (located in what is now Turkey) was destroyed. The ancient Greek writer **Homer** puts the date for the destruction of Troy at 1220 BCE. The site **Hisarlik** is thought to be in the area of ancient Troy.

It is assumed that the destruction was because of a **Dorian invasion**, but the answer is not known. Hittite records indicate that the destruction occurred by "the people of the Aegean." The Dorian invasion is spoken about as "return of the sons of Heracles" when Greek invaders came in from the north. The destruction is also blamed upon the "Sea People," and there are numerous conjectures as to who they might be.

This destruction led to the **Greek Dark Ages**, which lasted from 1100 BCE to 750 BCE.

Contributions of the Greek City States

For more information on Ancient Greece, check out this site:

www.ling.ohio-state.edu/~bjoseph/articles/gancient.htm

Strong, independent, city-states, such as Athens and Sparta, developed in Greece. For example, **Cleisthenes** of **Athens** is responsible for the birth of democracy in 510 BCE. He created a system that gave every man a vote. Other important intellectual areas that the Greeks are credited with influencing include:

- Drama
- Epic and lyric poetry
- Fables
- Astronomy
- Science
- Myths, centered on the many gods and goddesses
- Medicine
- Mathematics
- Philosophy
- Art
- Architecture
- The recording historical events.

The tradition of theater was born in Greece, with the plays of **Aristophanes** and others. In the field of mathematics, **Pythagoras** and **Euclid** laid the foundation of geometry and **Archimedes** calculated the value of pi. **Herodotus** and **Thucydides** were the first to apply research and interpretation to written history.

In sculpture, the Greeks achieved an idealistic aesthetic that had not been perfected before that time. The Greek alphabet was derived from the Phoenician letters, which formed the basis for the Roman alphabet and our present-day alphabet. Extensive trading and colonization resulted in the spread of the Greek civilization.

PELOPONNESIAN WAR: a war fought among the Greeks, in which Athens fought against Sparta and its allies

Though the Greek societies were able to achieve much together, they also came into conflict with one another. The most prominent example of this was the **PELOPONNESIAN WAR** in which Athens fought against Sparta and the other Peloponnesian cities.

Greek and Persian Tensions

The Greek city-states located on the coast of Asia Minor were under the control of the Lydian king **Croesus** in the middle of the sixth century BCE. When the Persians under Cyrus conquered Lydia, they took control of all their subject states also. **Miletus**, a Greek city-state under the leader Aristagoras, appealed to the Spartans and Athenians to help him, but the Athenians went to the Sardis, the capital of Lydia, and conquered it. Other city-states on the coast of Asia Minor then joined in—until Persia put an end to it. This would not be the last time that Persia and Greek city-states would clash.

The Persian Wars

The **Median Empire** (600 BCE) reached from the Black Sea to Afghanistan and Central Asia. It was the first Iranian empire and became the Persian Empire of **Cyrus the Great**. He also took Egypt in 539 BCE and was followed by **Darius** who became king in 522 BCE. Darius remade the ancient trade route into the Persian **Royal Road**. When Darius died; the Persian Empire was at its zenith.

The Persians and Greeks engaged in the **PERSIAN WARS** (499-448 BCE). This struggle includes the battles of **Marathon**, which the Greeks won despite being vastly outnumbered; **Thermopylae**, in which Spartans held off thousands of Persian warriors for several days; **Salamis**, a naval battle that the Greeks won despite being outnumbered; and **Plataea**, in which the Greeks outnumbered the Persians. These victories convinced the Persians not to attempt another invasion of Greece, but it did not mean the end of the Persian Empire.

PERSIAN WARS: wars between the Persian Empire and the Greek city-states, occurring between 499–448 BCE

Alexander the Great

That end came at the hands of **ALEXANDER THE GREAT**, whose father was **Philip II of Macedon**. **Aristotle** was Alexander's tutor. Alexander was a Macedonian general who conquered Greece, Persia, and eventually Egypt, Phoenician cities, and part of India. He created an empire that was staggering in its geography, impact, and cultural exchange. It brought the Greek or **Hellenic** way of life to people in the East while also bringing exotic goods and customs of the East to Greece. Until this time, the East and West exchanged goods and customs in small ways, but Alexander changed all that, bringing both sides together under one banner and beginning an exchange of ideas, beliefs, and goods that would capture the imagination of rulers for years after his death.

ALEXANDER THE GREAT: a Macedonian general who conquered Greece, Persia, and eventually Egypt, Phoenician cities, and part of India

He was 32 years old when he died. **PTOLEMY**, a general under Alexander who had been appointed satrap of Egypt and the founder of the Great Library of Alexandria, declared himself king after Alexander's death. His family ruled Egypt until the Romans came.

PTOLEMY: a general under Alexander who had been appointed satrap of Egypt

The Maurya Empire

MAURYA EMPIRE: an empire in India that lasted from 322 to 185 BCE

CHANDRAGUPTA: brought the subcontinent of India together after Alexander the Great's armies withdrew

ASOKA: a ruler of the Mauryans who was a great believer in the practices and power of Buddhism, sending missionaries throughout Asia to preach the ways of the Buddha

In India, the **MAURYA EMPIRE** lasted from 322 to 185 BCE. **CHANDRAGUPTA** brought the subcontinent of India together after the Alexander the Great's armies withdrew. The empire established a common economic system. Waterworks were built, and the Mauryans traded with the selling silk goods, spices, and exotic foods to the Greeks and others. Their trade extended into Southeast Asia, and private corporations were common. Religion developed with Buddhism and Jainism. Not only was there protection of civil and social rights, but there was protection of animals, too. **ASOKA**, was more of a peaceful ruler but powerful nonetheless. He was also a great believer in the practices and power of Buddhism, sending missionaries throughout Asia to preach the ways of the Buddha.

The Dynasties of China

In 221 BCE, China became unified into an empire under Qin Shi Huang. The dynasties that followed for the next 700 years were:

- **The Qin Dynasty:** 221–206 BCE
- **The Han Dynasty:** 206–220 CE
- **The Jin Period:** 265–420 CE
- **The Southern and Northern Dynasties:** 420–589CE

China expanded, rivaling even Rome in breadth and accomplishments by the time of the famous Han Dynasty. The foundation of their government was a strong emphasis on the rule of law. The Chinese became proficient at producing and exporting beautiful artworks and silks. China was also responsible for many inventions, including paper, printing, paper money, and gunpowder.

The Roman Empire

ROME: site of a civilization famous for uniting most of the known European and Middle Eastern world

For more information on the Roman empire, check out this site:

www.crystalinks.com/romanempire.html

ROME built itself from one town that borrowed from its Etruscan neighbors into a worldwide empire, reaching from the wilds of Scotland to the shores of the Middle East. The ancient civilization of Rome lasted approximately 1,000 years, including the periods of the Roman Republic and the Roman Empire. It mythically began with two kings—Remus and Romulus, and Romulus slew Remus. The Roman Empire, which began in 27 BCE, ended in about 476 CE when Emperor **Romulus Augustus** was deposed.

Cultural aspects of the Romans

There was a sharp contrast between the curious, imaginative, inquisitive Greeks and the practical, simple, down-to-earth, no-nonsense Romans. The population of the city of Rome may have reached a million or more, but 80 percent of Roman citizens lived in smaller communities and in rural areas, and there were also many slaves. The early religion of the Roman Empire had been one of many gods and goddesses, representing the various parts of the natural world. As Rome conquered various people with various religions, however, their religion changed as they assimilated the religions of those people.

Building on the Hellenic principles, Rome imported and exported goods and customs, melding the production capabilities and the belief systems of all it conquered into a heterogeneous yet distinctly Roman civilization. Trade, religion, science, political structure—all were incorporated into the Roman Empire with all of the benefits that assimilation brought being passed on to the Empire's citizens.

Trade, religion, science, political structure—all were incorporated into the Roman Empire with all of the benefits that assimilation brought being passed on to the Empire's citizens.

Political organization of Rome

In government, Rome used an **autocratic** form of government with a limited administrative system. That meant that officials were local people in the provinces, and this was key to the length of survival for the empire.

For more information on the culture and economy of Rome, check out this site:

www.pbs.org/empires/romans/educators/lesson8.html

The wars of the Romans

Rome fought three wars against Carthage, known as the **PUNIC WARS**. Rome destroyed Carthage in 146 BCE, and then refounded it because it had an excellent position on the Mediterranean.

PUNIC WARS: the collective name for Rome's three wars against Carthage, which Rome ultimately won

Some other Roman conflicts included:

- Wars with Germanic tribes
- The Roman conquest of Britain
- The Parthian Wars
- The Jewish wars
- Numerous civil wars
- The battle against the Gothic invasions

The End of Unified Rome

The Roman emperor **Diocletian** split the empire into two portions in the early fourth century because it had grown too large to administer easily. This weakened the western empire but strengthened the eastern part of the empire, closer to Asia and farther away from Germany.

SKILL 2.4 **Disruption and reversal: circa 500–1400 CE** *(nomadic migrations [Huns to Mongols], Byzantine Empire, Eastern Europe, rise and expansion of Islam, feudalism in North and Central Europe, Mayans and Chavin culture)*

The Byzantine Empire

BYZANTINE EMPIRE: the successor to the Roman Empire in the East and protected Western Europe from invaders such as the Persians and Ottomans

Constantine moved the capital of Rome to Constantinople in 330 CE, and the eastern portion of the Roman Empire became The **BYZANTINE EMPIRE**. It was close to the Middle East, and therefore more readily incorporated traditions of Mesopotamia and Persia, in addition to the Greek influences that shaped Rome initially. These Near Eastern influences were not part of the culture of the Western Empire. The Byzantine Empire (353–1453 CE) was the successor to the Roman Empire in the East and protected Western Europe from invaders such as the Persians and Ottomans.

Contributions of the Byzantine Empire

CODE OF JUSTINIAN: Roman law collected into a clear and well-stated system

The Byzantines made important contributions in art and preserved Greek and Roman achievements including architecture (especially in Eastern Europe and Russia) and the **CODE OF JUSTINIAN**, which was Roman law collected into a clear and well-stated system. Byzantium was known for exquisite artwork including the famous church **Hagia Sophia**. Uniquely situated at the gateway to both West and East, Byzantium could control trade going in both directions. The Eastern Empire was much more centralized and rigid in its enforcement of its policies than the feudal West.

Byzantine culture and religion

The Byzantine Empire was a Christian nation that incorporated Greek philosophy, language, and literature along with Roman government and law. They also had a strong infantry, cavalry, and engineering corps and excellent morale among its soldiers.

CONFERENCE OF NICEA: held in 325 CE, this conference was aimed at making a uniform Christian doctrine

The **CONFERENCE OF NICEA** was held in 325 CE, and one matter discussed was the Trinity. A uniform Christian doctrine was created with the **Nicene Creed**. After the Council of Chaledon in 451, there was no more debate—to speak out against the Trinity was considered blasphemy or heresy.

Later religious conflict

A problem developed regarding the issue of iconoclasm: Byzantine Emperor **Leo III** (685-741 CE) ordered that the image of Jesus on the Chalke Gate at the entrance to the Constantinople Palace be replaced with a cross and order that all icons across the empire be destroyed. **Pope Gregory III** (731–741 CE) called a **synod**, and it was agreed to take strong measures against anyone who would destroy images of Jesus, Mary, or the saints. Leo then attempted to kidnap the Pope, but a storm destroyed Leo's ships.

The Germanic Tribes

The power of the German Tribes was considerable; they had played a major role in the fall of the Western Roman Empire, along with the increasing sprawl of the empire and the spread of dissatisfaction of the empire's residents with the administration of the vast social, economic, and political network.

Germanic tribes ranged over most of Europe. The five major tribes were the:

1. Visigoths
2. Ostrogoths
3. Vandals
4. Saxons
5. Franks

The Ostrogoths, Visigoths, and Vandals converted to **Arianism**, which does not adhere to the Nicene Creed, so the Roman Catholic Church viewed them as heretics. The Germanic tribes battled among themselves, made alliances, and separated again. **Theodoric** led the Ostrogoths and Visigoths, but they separated soon after his death.

Byzantine Emperor **Justinian I** declared war on the Vandals, and afterward they fled or became slaves. The Saxons invaded Britannia in the fifth century along with fellow tribe the Angles. They immigrated onto the island that became known as England. Later they joined to fight against invading Vikings.

The Franks

One of those most important Germanic tribes was the Franks. In 711, the Muslims conquered Spain, and they planned to continue their expansion. The Franks, under the leadership of **Charles Martel**, successfully stopped this Muslim advance into southern Europe by defeating them at the Battle of Tours in 732 CE. The Muslim advance continued; in 805 CE, Muslims captured Rhodes and Cyprus; in 816 CE, the island of Corsica; and in 969 CE, Egypt. Despite their successes elsewhere, the Frankish victory at Tours kept them out of Europe.

In 768 CE, the grandson of Charles Martel, **Charlemagne**, became king of the Franks. A man of war, Charlemagne also respected and encouraged learning. He is remembered for efforts to rule fairly and ensure just treatment for the people.

Islam

Before Mohammed

BEDOUINS: native people of the Arabian peninsula who lived in scattered tribes

Except for the coastal areas on the Red Sea, the Arabian Peninsula was a vast desert of rock and sand, populated by nomadic wanderers called **BEDOUINS** who lived in scattered tribes. Tribal leaders engaged in frequent war with one another over pastures, camels, horses and especially the critical resource, water. The tribe was made up of related families and was the social and political unit under the authority of the head of the family.

As these Arabs settled near oases or in fertile valleys, many became traders. Through regular contact with Christians and Jews, they were introduced to new religions but remained polytheistic. Arabs came from all parts of the country in annual pilgrimages to **the Kaaba** (Cube) in Mecca during the sacred months when warfare was prohibited. For this reason, Mecca was considered the center of Arab religion.

The coming of Mohammed

MOHAMMED: the father of Islam, who claims to have had a revelation of God's will

A few years after the death of the Emperor Justinian, **MOHAMMED** was born (570 CE) in a small Arab town near the Red Sea. According to Islamic tradition, Mohammed had a revelation in 610 and soon began preaching about it. His new religion was called **Islam** (submission to the will of God), and his followers were called **Muslims**. His first converts were members of his family and his friends. They soon met with opposition and persecution from the Arabs who feared the new religion and the possible loss of the profitable trade with the pilgrims who came to the Kaaba every year.

The Hijrah and Islamic growth

HIJRAH: the name for the flight of Mohammed from Mecca to Medina

Islam slowly found followers, although persecutions of Muslims became severe around Mecca. In 622, Mohammed and his close followers fled the city and found refuge in **Medina** to the North. His flight is called the **HIJRAH**. This event marks the beginning of the Muslim calendar. The town accepted Islam and became its center, with Mohammed as its religious and political leader.

In the years that followed, Islam grew significantly. It attracted many converts from the Bedouin tribes. By 630, Mohammed conquered Mecca and made it the religious center of Islam, toward which all Muslims turned to pray, and the

Kaaba, the most sacred **MOSQUE** or temple. Medina remained the political capital. By the time of Mohammed's death in 632 CE, most of the people of the Arabian Peninsula had become at least nominal adherents of Islam.

MOSQUES: the worship places of Islam

Mohammed left behind a collection of divine revelations (**surahs**) that he claimed were delivered by the angel Gabriel. These were collected and published in a book called the **KORAN** (Qur'an), which is the holy scripture of Islam. The revelations were not kept in chronological order, however. Rather, after the prophet's death, they were organized by length (in diminishing order). The Koran was written in classical Arabic and concerns all aspects of life.

KORAN: the holy book of Islam

Principles of Islam

Islam has five basic principles, known as the **PILLARS OF ISLAM**:

PILLARS OF ISLAM: the five basic principles of Islam

- **Faith:** The oneness and omnipotence of God; **Allah** with Mohammed as the prophet of Allah to whom all truth has been revealed by God; to each of the previous prophets (Adam, Noah, Abraham, Moses, and Jesus) a part of the truth was revealed
- **Prayer:** One should pray five times a day at prescribed intervals, facing Mecca
- **Charity:** A religious tax for the welfare of the community
- **Fasting:** From sunrise to sunset every day during the holy month of **Ramadan** to cleanse the spirit
- **The Hajj** or Pilgrimage to Mecca: This should be made once in a lifetime if possible and if no one suffers thereby

Some principles of Islam are: to practice charity, humility, and patience toward fellow Muslims; to forgive enemies; to condemn murder, stealing, adultery, and lying; and never to drink alcohol, eat pork, or gamble.

On the Day of Judgment all souls will be judged. The infidel will be condemned to a **gehennem** with perpetual fire, and the good/faithful will go to **Paradise**, a beautiful place of cool waters, sensual delights, and ease. In some ways, the Koran elevated the level of women. A man could marry as many as four wives if he loved them equally. Divorce was easy, but the wife had to be given a dowry.

The death of Mohammed and expansion

Mohammed died with neither a political nor a religious succession plan. His cousin, **Ali**, who had married Mohammed's daughter, **Fatima**, believed his kinship and his heroism as a warrior gave him a natural claim to leadership. But **Abu Bakr** was chosen, and he took the title of **Caliph**. The title was retained throughout the duration of the Muslim Empire.

These Muslim Arabs immediately launched a series of conquests that, in time, extended the empire from the Indus to Spain. It has often been said that these conquests were motivated by religious fanaticism and the determination to force Islam upon the infidel. However, the motives were also economic and political.

UMAYYAD: an aristocratic family of Mecca that took over the caliphate after Ali's death

During the period of expansion, a brief civil war occurred when Ali was proclaimed Caliph at Medina. He was opposed by an aristocratic family of Mecca called the **UMAYYAD**. Ali was assassinated in 661, and the Umayyads emerged supreme, handing the caliphate down in their family for nearly a century. Because their strongest support was in Syria, they moved the capital from Medina to Damascus. The **Byzantine-Arab Wars** began in 629 CE and lasted until the twelfth century. Finally, in the middle of the thirteenth century, the Muslim Empire was overcome by a fresh invasion from Asia: the Mongols.

Cultural aspects of Islam

Despite these political divisions, the Muslim world maintained strong economic, religious, and cultural unity throughout this period. Mohammed had taught that all Muslims are brothers, equal in the sight of God. Conversion to Islam erased the differences between peoples of different ethnic origin.

There was a blending of cultures, facilitated by a common language, a shared religion, and a strong economy. This allowed learning, literature, science, technology, and art to flourish, so that it surpassed anything found in the Western Christian world during the Early Middle Ages. Interestingly, the most brilliant period of Muslim culture was from the eighth century through the eleventh, coinciding with the West's darkest cultural period.

Literacy

Reading and writing in Arabic, the study of the Koran, arithmetic, and other elementary subjects were taught to children in schools attached to mosques.

Reading and writing in Arabic, the study of the Koran, arithmetic, and other elementary subjects were taught to children in schools attached to the mosques. In larger and wealthier cities, the mosques offered more advanced education in literature, logic, philosophy, law, algebra, astronomy, medicine, science, theology, and the tradition of Islam. Books were produced for the large reading public. The wealthy collected private libraries and public libraries arose in large cities.

The most popular subjects were theology and the law, but the more important field of study was philosophy. The works of the Greek and Hellenistic philosophers were translated into Arabic and interpreted with commentaries. These were later passed on to the Western Christian societies and schools in the twelfth and thirteenth centuries. The basis of Muslim philosophy was Aristotelian and Neoplatonic ideas, which were transmitted without creative modification.

Science

The Muslims were also interested in natural science. They translated the works of Galen and Hippocrates into Arabic and added the results of their own experience in medicine. **AVICENNA** was regarded in Western Europe as one of the great masters of medicine. They also adopted the work of the Greeks in the other sciences and modified and supplemented them with their own discoveries. Much of their work in chemistry was focused on alchemy, the attempt to transmute base metals into gold.

AVICENNA: regarded in Western Europe as one of the great masters of medicine

Mathematics

Adopting the heritage of Greek mathematics, the Muslims also borrowed a system of numerals from India. This laid the foundation for modern arithmetic, geometry, trigonometry, and algebra.

Art and architecture

Muslim art and architecture tended to be mostly uniform in style, allowing for some regional modification. They borrowed from the Byzantine Empire, Persia, and other sources. The floor plans of the mosques were generally based on Mohammed's house at Medina. The notable unique elements were the tall minarets from which the faithful were called to prayer. This interior decoration became the style now called **arabesque**. Because Mohammed had banned paintings or other images of living creatures, they continued to be absent from mosques, although they occasionally appeared in book illustration and secular contexts. Their skilled craftsmen also produced the finest art in jewelry, ceramics, carpets, and carved ivory.

Prose and poetry

The Muslims also produced sophisticated literature in both prose and poetry. The flexibility of the Arabic language was very well adapted to poetry. Little, however, of their poetry or prose has been translated into Western languages. The best-known works of this period are the short stories known as the **Arabian Nights** and the poems of **Omar Khayyam**.

Other Cultures

Vikings

Anther major civilization in this era was the **VIKINGS**. They had spread their ideas and knowledge of trade routes and sailing, accomplished first through their conquests and later through trade. They were Scandinavian seafaring warriors who raided and colonized wide areas of Europe from the eighth to the eleventh century. Overpopulation at home, ease of conquest abroad, and their extraordinary capacity as shipbuilders and sailors inspired their adventures. Some Vikings settled in Northern France, becoming the **NORMANS**.

VIKINGS: Scandinavian seafaring warriors who raided and colonized wide areas of Europe from the eighth to the eleventh century

NORMANS: Vikings who settled in Northern France

In 865 CE, Vikings conquered major centers in England. Under **Alfred the Great**, the English made a truce in 878 that led to Danish control of much of England. Alfred and his successors retook many of the lands, although renewed Viking raids in 980 brought England into the empire where it remained until 1042, when the Vikings were finally pushed out. The Vikings permanently affected English social structure, dialect, and names, and subsequently European cultures at large. In the western seas, Vikings had settled in Iceland by 900, after which they traveled to Greenland and North America. As traders they made commercial treaties with the Byzantines and served as mercenaries in Constantinople. Viking activity came to an end in the eleventh century.

Feudalism

FEUDALISM: an economic and social system in Europe during the Middle Ages

During the early Middle Ages (from about 500–1100 CE), the system of **FEUDALISM** was an economic and social system in Europe. Feudalism began as a way to ensure that a king or nobleman could raise an army when needed. In exchange for the promise of loyalty and military service, **lords** would be granted a section of land, called a **fief**, to a **vassal**, as those who took this oath of loyalty were called. The vassal was then entitled to work the land and benefit from its proceeds or to grant it, in turn, as a fief to another. At the bottom of this ladder were the **peasants** or **serfs**, who actually worked the land. At the top was the king, to whom all lands legally belonged, and he ensured loyalty among his advisors by giving them use of large sections of land that they in turn could grant as fiefs.

Serfs and Lords

The strong—the lord or noble—protected the weak—the serf—who returned the service with farm labor, military service, and loyalty.

It was a system of loyalty and protection. The strong—the lord or noble—protected the weak—the serf—who returned the service with farm labor, military service, and loyalty. In practical effect, the serf was considered property owned by his lord with few or no rights at all. The lord's sole obligation to the serfs was to protect them so they could continue to work for him (in most cases, though not all, lords were men). Improved tools and farming methods made life more bearable for serfs, although most never left the manor nor traveled away from their village during their lifetime. This system would last for many centuries in Europe. In Russia, it would even last until the 1860s.

Manorialism

MANORIALISM: similar to feudalism in structure, but consisted of self-contained manors that were often owned outright by a nobleman

MANORIALISM, which also arose during the Middle Ages, is similar to feudalism in structure, but consisted of self-contained manors that were often owned outright by a nobleman. Some manors were granted conditionally to their lords, and some were linked to the military service and oaths of loyalty found in feudalism, meaning that the two systems overlapped somewhat.

Manors usually consisted of a large house for the lord and his family, surrounded by fields and a small village that supported the activities of the manor. The lord of the manor was expected to provide certain services for the villagers and laborers associated with the manor, including the support of a church.

The culture of feudal Europe

Knighthood and its code of chivalry (good manners and loyalty to the king) grew in importance. Knighthood was not inherited but rather bestowed.

There was also the tremendous influence of the Roman Catholic Church. Until the Renaissance, the Church was the main source for an education. The Bible and other books were hand-copied by monks in monasteries. Cathedrals were built and were decorated with art that depicted religious subjects.

As trade and travel increased, cities sprang up and grew. When craft workers in cities developed their skills, they eventually organized **GUILDS** to protect the quality of their work and to regulate the buying and selling of their products. City government developed with strong town councils and the support of the wealthy businessmen who made up the rising middle class

GUILDS: organizations created by skilled laborers to protect the quality of their work and to regulate the buying and selling of their products

Changes resulting from the Black Death

The outbreak and spread of the infamous Black Death, which killed over one-third of the total population of Europe, ended the feudal/manorial system in Western Europe. Wars and trade decreased, as did the amount of land under cultivation. Those who survived the Black Death and were skilled in any job or occupation were in demand, and many serfs or peasants found freedom and wages, which gave them a decidedly improved standard of living.

The Crusades

The eleventh century is regarded as the beginning of the **High Middle Ages**. The **CRUSADES** were a series of military campaigns by European Christians, beginning in the eleventh century, against the encroaching Muslim Empire, particularly in the holy land of Palestine and the city of Jerusalem. They continued into the thirteenth century as Jerusalem and other holy cities changed hands between Christian and Muslim forces. Several crusades took place within Europe, as well, such as the efforts to reconquer portions of the Muslim-occupied Iberian Peninsula. Not only were the Crusades against Muslims but also against Greek Orthodox Christians and pagan Slavs.

CRUSADES: a series of military campaigns by European Christians, beginning in the eleventh century, against the encroaching Muslim Empire, particularly in the holy land of Palestine and the city of Jerusalem

For more information on the Crusades, check out this site:

www.fordham.edu/halsall/sbook1k.html

The beginning of the Crusades

The Christian Byzantine Empire was centered in Constantinople. The empire was under attack from Seljuk Turk forces that had taken Palestine and threatened Constantinople. The eastern emperor, **Alexius I**, called on his western counterpart, **Pope Urban II**, for assistance. Urban saw the situation as an opportunity to reunite Christendom, which was still in the throes of schism between the Eastern Orthodox and the Western Catholic sects, and to invest the papacy with religious authority.

The first and second Crusades

In 1095, Urban called on all Christians to rally behind the campaign to drive the Turks out of the Holy Land. Participation in the crusade, Urban said, would count as full penance for sin in the eyes of the Church.

Many responded, and in 1099, a force of crusaders marched to Jerusalem and captured it, massacring the inhabitants. Along the way, several small Crusader states were established. A second crusade was led against Damascus in 1145 and included forces from Western Europe and the Holy Roman Empire. It was unsuccessful.

The third and fourth Crusades

In 1187, **Saladin**, the Sultan of Egypt, recaptured Jerusalem, and Pope Gregory VIII called for a third Crusade. This Crusade fell short of its goal to recapture Jerusalem. The fourth Crusade took place in 1202, under Pope Innocent III. Originally, the intention of the fourth Crusade was to recapture Jerusalem, but the plan was changed and forces were diverted to Constantinople.

The legacy of the Crusades

The marches of the crusaders opened new routes between Europe and the East along which culture, learning, and trade could travel. Also, the Crusades established and reinforced the political and military authority of the Catholic Church and the Roman Pope. The religious fervor spurred on by the Crusades would eventually culminate in such movements as the Inquisition in Spain and the expulsion of the Moors from Europe.

The Eastern World

Between the fourth and ninth centuries, Asia was a story of religions and empires, of kings and wars, and of increasing and decreasing contact with the West. The imposing mountains to the northwest of India served as a deterrent to Chinese expansion. Most of India's invaders came from the East. The Indian people were also vulnerable to the powerful monsoons, which came driving up from the south a few times every year, bringing howling winds and devastation in their wake.

The Guptas

In India, the **GUPTAS** began their long rule of India and brought prosperity and international recognition to their people. The Guptas were great believers in science and mathematics, especially applying their uses to the production of goods. They invented the decimal system and used the concept of zero, and were ahead of the rest of the world in the field of mathematics. Their medical practices were likewise more advanced than those in Europe and elsewhere in Asia at the time. Extensive trade brought these inventions and innovations, as well as many trade goods, throughout Asia and Europe.

GUPTAS: long-time rulers of India, they were great believers in science and mathematics, especially their uses in the production of goods

The idea of a united India continued after the Gupta Dynasty ended. It was especially favorable to the invading Muslims, who took over in the eleventh century, ruling the country for hundreds of years through a series of sultanates.

Islam in India

The Muslim leader **Tamerlane** or **Timur Lenk** founded India's Mogul Dynasty and created a huge empire across Central Asia. One of Tamerlane's ancestors, **Akbar**, is considered the greatest Mogul emperor. He believed in freedom of religion and is perhaps most well-known for the series of buildings that he had built, including mosques, palaces, forts, and tombs, some of which are still standing today. During the years that Muslims ruled India, Hinduism was still practiced, although it was a minority religion. After the twelfth century, Buddhism died out almost entirely from the country that begot its founder, **SIDDHARTHA GAUTAMA**.

SIDDHARTHA GAUTAMA: the founder of Buddhism

China's dynasties

During this time, Chinese dynasties controlled various parts of what is now China and Tibet. The **Tang Dynasty** (618-907) was one of the most proficient, promoting the idea of civil service and the practice of block printing.

During the **Song Dynasty**, some of the world's greatest paintings and porcelain pottery was produced. In the tenth century, gunpowder was used in a battle for the first time. China was eventually taken over by the Mongols, led by **Genghis Khan** and his most famous grandson, **Kublai**.

The Mongols

For more information about Ghengis Khan, check out this site:

www.accd.edu/sac/history/keller/Mongols/empsub1.html

At its height, the Mongol Empire was the largest the world has ever seen, encompassing all of China, Russia, Persia, and central Asia.

Mongol Ghengis Khan, born in about 1167, grew up to be a warrior and was known as a conqueror. He overran China then moved on to battle in Caucasia, with Russians and Turks. His legacy went on after his death. His grandsons founded dynasties in Russia, Persia, and China, and his descendants continued to rule for centuries.

At its height, the Mongol Empire was the largest the world has ever seen, encompassing all of China, Russia, Persia, and central Asia.

One grandson, Kublai Khan, was the first Mongol emperor of China, founding the Yuan dynasty. It improved travel within China, but resentful Chinese eventually rebelled against their foreign Mongol rulers.

Japan

The other major power in Asia was **Japan**. Early Japanese society focused on a divine emperor who could do no wrong and served for life. The **Shinto** faith was strong, and most people lived on farms. Although fairly closed to outsiders, Japan was influenced by China, from which it borrowed many ideas, including religion (Buddhism), the characters for writing, their calendar, and even fashion.

The Sea of Japan protected Japan from Chinese invasion, including Kublai Khan's attempted invasions, both of which were ended by typhoons. The Shinto priests called these typhoons **kamikaze** or "divine wind." Japan's isolation lasted until the sixteenth century.

Feudalism in Japan

DAIMYO: land-controlling lord of Japanese feudalism

SAMURAI: the loyal soldiers of a Daimyo, known for their strict code of honor

Feudalism lasted longer in Japan than in Europe. As the power of the emperor declined, and it was usurped by the **Shoguns**. These military leaders had the real power over the **DAIMYO**, or land-controlling lords. This, in turn, gave them power over the loyal soldiers of each Daimyo, the **SAMURAI**, who are famous for their strict code of honor.

As with European feudalism, the land was worked by the peasants. The main economic change between imperial and feudal Japan was that the money that the profit from the tightly controlled trade no longer went into the emperor's coffers but rather into the pockets of the Daimyos.

Religion of Japan

Japan flourished economically and culturally during many of these years, although the policy of isolation kept the rest of the world from knowing about Japan's success. Buddhism and local religions were joined by Christianity in the sixteenth century, when Europeans came into Japan. But it was not until the mid-nineteenth century that Japan joined the international community.

Africa

Most of northern coastal Africa was under Muslim control. Because parts of Africa's geography are uninhabitable, African settlements were restricted to specific areas.

Some societies managed to flourish, however. Zimbabwe was a trading empire between the eleventh and fifteenth centuries and brought gold and other goods to the Indian Ocean. **GHANA**, a Muslim-influenced trading empire, arose in the seventh century and sent gold and salt to northern Africa over the Sahara in caravans.

GHANA: a Muslim-influenced trading empire that arose in the seventh century

Mali took eventually over Ghana's route, and **Timbuktu** developed into a major trading center on the Saharan caravan route. Gold, slaves, and ivory were sent to Northern Africa and later to the western African coast. The **Songhai** continued this trading tradition. The Muslim religion grew in importance in these civilizations.

SKILL 2.5 Emerging global interactions: circa 1400–1800 CE

See also Skill 1.3

The Ottoman Empire

By 1400, the **Ottoman Turks** in Anatolia were conquering Byzantine territory in Macedonia and Bulgaria. They struggled to take Constantinople again and again, and finally in 1453, they were successful and renamed the city **Istanbul**. This was the end of the Byzantine Empire.

Success of the Ottomans

The Ottoman Empire is noted for its ability to unite highly varied populations as it grew through conquest and treaty arrangement. This ability can be attributed to military strength, a policy of strict control of recently invaded territories, and an Islamic-inspired philosophy that stated that all Muslims, Christians, and Jews were related because they were all "People of the Book." This religious and ethnic tolerance was the basis upon which a **heterogeneous culture** was built. It quickly transformed a Turkish empire into the Ottoman Empire.

Diversity of the Ottomans

The major religious groups were permitted to construct their own semi-autonomous communities. Conquering armies immediately repaired buildings, roads, bridges, and aqueducts and even built them where needed. They also constructed modern sanitary facilities and linked the city to a supply structure that was able to provide for the needs of the people.

The attitude of tolerant blending and respect for diverse ethnic and cultural groups in time produced a rich mix of people that was reflected in multicultural and multireligious policies that were based on recognition and respect for different perspectives.

The attitude of tolerant blending and respect for diverse ethnic and cultural groups in time produced a rich mix of people that was reflected in multicultural and multireligious policies that were based on recognition and respect for different perspectives. Ottoman architecture, although influenced by **Seljuk**, Byzantine, and Arab styles, developed a unique style of its own.

Additionally, music was important to the elites of the empire. The two primary styles of music that developed were Ottoman classical music and folk music. Again, both styles reflect a basis in the diversity of influences that came together in the unified empire.

Government structure

Government had an absolute authority in the monarch or **sultan**. The Ottomans viewed justice as distributive, fair, and vital to building a successful society. It maintained a strong nave to protect its profitable trade routes.

China

Confucianism, Taoism, and ancestor worship—the staples of Chinese society for hundreds of years—continued to flourish during all this time.

In China, following the **Mongol Yuan Dynasty**, the **Ming** and **Manchu Dynasties** developed. At first, the Ming looked outward but soon focused on a more closed society, as did the Manchu. This did not preclude some trade, but there was limited cultural diffusion. As a result, the Chinese knew very little of the outside world at the end of the eighteenth century, and vice versa. Ming artists created beautiful porcelain pottery, but not much of it saw its way into the outside world until after this period of isolation. The Manchus were known for their focus on farming and road building, two practices they developed to deal with their expanding and increasingly dense population. Confucianism, Taoism, and ancestor worship—the staples of Chinese society for hundreds of years—continued to flourish during all this time.

The European Renaissance

The word Renaissance literally means "rebirth," and this period in European history signaled the rekindling of interest in the glory of ancient classical Greek and Roman civilizations. This era marked the start of many ideas and innovations that would lead to what is considered the modern age. In the areas of art, literature, music, and science, the Western world grew. Much of its ideas came from looking at the world as it was and not in religious, ideal, or economic terms.

The beginning of the Renaissance

A combination of a renewed fascination with the classical world and new infusion of money into the hands of those who were fascinated brought on the Renaissance. Specifically, it began in Florence, Italy, as the infamous **Medici** family fostered scholars and artists.

Notable artists

Important Renaissance artist **Giotto** was the first to portray people as they really looked, not as an artist imagined them to be. **Leonardo da Vinci** was not only an artist but also a scientist and inventor. **Michelangelo** was a sculptor, painter, and architect. Other Italian artists included:

- Raphael
- Donatello
- Titian
- Tintoretto

The spread of the Renaissance

From Italy, the Renaissance moved across Europe. Many people in the Low Countries, Germany, Spain, and England contributed to the growth of knowledge and skills. From all over Europe, artists contributed new works, skills, and ideas. These included:

- Durer
- Holbein
- van Eyck
- Breughel the Elder
- El Greco
- de Morales

Humanism

HUMANISTS, including Petrarch, Boccaccio, Erasmus, and Sir Thomas More, advanced the idea of being interested in life here on Earth and the opportunities it can bring, rather than constantly focusing on heaven and its rewards. Sir Francis Bacon wrote and taught philosophy and was inspired by Vesalius. The political writings of Machiavelli influenced European leaders.

HUMANISTS: advanced the idea of being interested in life here on Earth and the opportunities it can bring, rather than constantly focusing on heaven and its rewards

The printing press and the Renaissance

In Germany, Gutenberg's invention of the printing press with movable type facilitated the rapid spread of Renaissance ideas, writings, and innovations, thus ensuring the enlightenment of most of Western Europe. The availability of books changed education. Education was expanded to the merchant class and now reading, writing, math, the study of law, and the writings of classical Greek and Roman writers were all included.

Literature grew during the Renaissance and was available to more people. The monumental works of Shakespeare, Dante, and Cervantes found their origins in Renaissance ideas. Other writers include:

- Rabelais
- de Montaigne
- De Vega
- Chaucer
- Spenser
- Marlowe
- Jonson

Music during the Renaissance

The Renaissance changed music as well. No longer just a religious experience, music could be fun and composed for its own sake, to be enjoyed in fuller and more humanistic ways than in the Middle Ages. Musicians could work for themselves, rather than just for the churches, and so could command good money for their work, increasing their prestige.

Legacies of the Renaissance

The Renaissance ushered in a time of curiosity, learning, and incredible energy, as people began to see the world in a new, more realistic way.

The Renaissance ushered in a time of curiosity, learning, and incredible energy, as people began to see the world in a new, more realistic way. It sparked a desire for trade for exotic products and better, faster, cheaper trade routes.

As geographers, astronomers, and mapmakers made important contributions and studied and applied the work of such men as Hipparchus of Greece, Ptolemy of Egypt, Tycho Brahe of Denmark, and Fra Mauro of Italy, they were able to go out into the world and expand travel and trade.

The Reformation

The Reformation period consisted of two phases: the Protestant Reformation and the Catholic Counter-Reformation.

The first phase

The **PROTESTANT REFORMATION** came about because of religious, political, and economic reasons.

> **PROTESTANT REFORMATION:** a response to the abuses in the Catholic Church, this religious movement resulted in the establishment of Protestant churches

Religious reasons

The religious reasons stemmed from the questioning of the Catholic Church's authority (which was encouraged by the Humanists). These exposed abuses in the Catholic Church included the clergy and their exorbitant lifestyles; the sale of religious offices, **indulgences**, and **dispensations**; different theologies within the Church; and frauds involving sacred relics.

Political reasons

The political reasons for the Reformation included the increase in the power of rulers who were considered "absolute monarchs." They desired to increase their power and control, especially over the Church. The growth of "**nationalism**" or patriotic pride in one's own country was another contributing factor.

Economic reasons

Economic reasons included the greed of ruling monarchs wishing to possess and control the Church's lands and wealth, the deep animosity against the burdensome papal taxation, the rise of an affluent middle class and its clash with medieval Church ideals, and the increase of an active system of mercantilism.

People in the Protestant Reformation

The Protestant Reformation began in Germany with the revolt of **Martin Luther** against Church abuses. It soon spread to Switzerland, where **John Calvin** (Jean Cauvin) led its efforts. In England, it began with the efforts of **King Henry VIII** to have his marriage to **Catherine of Aragon** annulled so he could wed another for a male heir. The Protestant Reformation had the increasing support of many Europeans, even nobles and some rulers.

> **CATHOLIC COUNTER-REFORMATION:** undertaken by the Church in response to the Protestant Reformation

The second phase

The **CATHOLIC COUNTER-REFORMATION** was undertaken by the Church in response to the Protestant Reformation. Its goal was to strengthen the Catholic Church and keep Catholics from converting to Protestant religions. To achieve this goal, the **Council of Trent** and the **Jesuits** introduced some major reforms.

> *The Reformation and Counter-Reformation led to the establishment of a number of Protestant churches, a religiously and politically divided Europe, an increase in religious wars, and an increase in religious persecution.*

The Scientific Revolution and the Enlightenment

The Scientific Revolution and the Enlightenment resulted in a new sense of self-examination and a wider view of the world than ever before. People began to look for new ways to think about things, rather than fitting ideas and observations into the old ways. The Catholic Church wielded tremendous power at this time, including the power to banish people or sentence them to prison or even death for heresy. Scientists and philosophers had to work in private and follow church dictates, or the church punished them.

The scientific revolution

SCIENTIFIC REVOLUTION: a shift in focus from belief to evidence

The **SCIENTIFIC REVOLUTION** was a shift in focus from belief to evidence. Scientists used a new approach, the scientific method.

Copernicus

A Polish astronomer, **Nicolaus Copernicus**, began the scientific revolution. He crystallized a lifetime of observations into a book that was published around the time of his death. In this book *Revolutions of the Celestial Spheres*, Copernicus argued that the Sun, not the Earth, was the center of a solar system and that other planets revolved around the Sun, not the Earth. Since this flew in the face of established, Church-mandated doctrine, Copernicus worked in private and only published his work near his death.

Brahe and Kepler

The Danish astronomer **Tycho Brahe** was the first to catalog his thousands of observations of the night sky. Building on Brahe's data, German scientist **Johannes Kepler** used mathematical formulas to verify that data and create his **Laws of Planetary Motions**. His work confirmed Copernicus's observations and argument that the Earth revolved around the Sun.

Galileo

The most famous defender of this idea was **Galileo Galilei**, an Italian scientist who conducted many famous experiments in the pursuit of science. He is most well known for his defense of the **heliocentric** (sun-centered) idea. He wrote a book comparing the two theories, but most readers could tell easily that he favored the new one. He was convinced of this mainly because of what he had seen with his own eyes, as he had used the relatively new invention of the telescope to see four moons of Jupiter. Those moons did not revolve around the Earth, so why should everything else?

The Church did not favor Galileo's ideas. The Church put Galileo on trial and placed him under house arrest. There, he continued his experiments, especially in physics.

Newton

Galileo died under house arrest, but his ideas did not die with him. He influenced the English scientist **Isaac Newton** who developed the law of gravity. He also was a pioneer in the study of optics (light), calculus, and physics. Newton believed in a **mechanistic** view of the world where people can see and prove how the world works through observation.

Other important figures

Medicine also changed during these years. The Brussels-born **Andrea Vesalius**, who earned himself the title of "father of anatomy," investigated science and medicine. He had a profound influence on the Spaniard **Michael Servetus**, and the Englishman **William Harvey Paracelsus**.

The Enlightenment

The **ENLIGHTENMENT** was a period of intense self-study that focused on applying reason to all manner of problems, such as God and nature. More so than at any time before, scientists and philosophers questioned widely held beliefs in an attempt to discover the world within. "I think, therefore I am" ("Cogito ergo sum" in Latin) was said by **Rene Descartes**, a French scientist-philosopher whose dedication to logic and the rigid rules of observation were a blueprint for the thinkers who came after him.

ENLIGHTENMENT: a period of intense self-study that focused on applying reason to all manner of problems, such as God and nature

Locke and Hume

John Locke contended that people were formed by the experiences that happened in their lives. Scotland's **David Hume** built on Locke's doctrine of **EMPIRICISM**, a theory of experience as truth. Hume believed in the value of **SKEPTICISM**. He was suspicious of things that other people told him to be true and constantly set out to discover the truth for himself. These two related ideas influenced many later thinkers, and the works of both writers continue to inspire philosophers to this day.

EMPIRICISM: a theory of experience as truth

SKEPTICISM: a belief that rejects absolute truth unless one experiences something first hand

Kant

Immanuel Kant of Germany was a philosopher and a scientist who developed new perspectives on human knowledge and thinking. He wrote the famous essay "Answering the Question: What Is Enlightenment?" In his work he tried to reconcile the ideas of the rationalists and those of the empiricists. Kant believed that humans were rational and still capable of creative thought and intense self-evaluation. He encouraged self-examination and observation of the world. Kant believed that the source of morality lay not in the nature of the grace of God but in the human soul itself. He believed that man believed in God for practical, not religious or mystical, reasons.

The social contract

The idea of **SOCIAL CONTRACT** was the belief that government existed because people wanted it to, and that the people had an agreement with the government that they would submit to it as long as it protected them and did not encroach

SOCIAL CONTRACT: the belief that government existed because people wanted it to, and that the people had an agreement with the government that they would submit to it as long as it protected them and did not encroach on their basic human rights

on their basic human rights. The Frenchman **Jean-Jacques Rousseau**, England's John Locke, and America's **Thomas Jefferson** all believed in it, and it would influence the political revolutions to come.

SKILL 2.6 Political and Industrial Revolutions, Nationalism: 1750–1914

Political Revolutions

The period of the 1700 and 1800s was characterized in Western countries by the political ideas of democracy and nationalism.

The period of the 1700 and 1800s was characterized in Western countries by the political ideas of democracy and nationalism. This resulted in strong nationalistic feelings and people of common cultures asserting their belief in the right to have a part in their government.

The American Revolution

The **American Revolution** resulted in the successful efforts of the English colonists in America to win their freedom from Great Britain. After more than 100 years of mostly self-government, the colonists began to resent the increasing British control. They declared their freedom, won their war for independence with aid from France, and formed a new independent nation.

The French Revolution

FRENCH REVOLUTION: a revolt of the middle and lower classes against the political and economic excesses of the rulers and the supporting nobility

The **FRENCH REVOLUTION** was a revolt of the middle and lower classes against the political and economic excesses of the rulers and the supporting nobility. Conditions leading to this revolt included:

- Extreme taxation
- Inflation
- Lack of food
- The total disregard by the nobility, government, and church for the deplorable living conditions of the common people

Its goal was to overthrow the ruling society and its outdated traditions. Coming at the end of the eighteenth century, it ended the thousand-year rule of kings in France and established the nation as a republic, the first in a series of French Republics.

The beginning of the Revolution

The revolution began in 1789, after **King Louis XVI** had convened the French parliament to deal with an enormous national debt. The common people's division of the parliament declared itself the true legislature of France, and when the king seemed to resist, a crowd destroyed the royal prison, the **BASTILLE**. A constitutional monarchy then was set up. After King Louis and his queen, **Marie Antoinette**, tried to flee the country, they were arrested, tried for treason, and executed on the guillotine.

BASTILLE: the royal prison of France

The Reign of Terror and Bonaparte's rise

Control of the government passed to **Robespierre** and other radicals, the extreme Jacobins, and the **REIGN OF TERROR** followed from 1793 to 1794, when thousands of French nobles and others considered enemies of the revolution were executed. After the Terror, Robespierre himself was executed, and a new ruling body, the **Directory**, came into power. Its incompetence and corruption allowed **Napoleon Bonaparte** to emerge as dictator in 1799 and, eventually, to become emperor. Napoleon's ascent to power is considered the official end of the revolution.

REIGN OF TERROR: the period of the French Revolution, from 1793 to 1794, when thousands of French nobles and others considered enemies of the revolution were executed

Comparing the revolutions

The American Revolution and the French Revolution were similar yet different. Both liberated people from unwanted government interference and installed a different type of government. They were both based on writings and ideas of the Enlightenment. Both Revolutions proved that people could expect more from their government and that such rights as self-determination were worth fighting and dying for.

The American Revolution and the French Revolution were similar yet different.

Despite these similarities, there are several differences between these two revolutions. Their causes were different, as British colonists were striking back against unwanted taxation and other sorts of "government interference," while the French were striking back against an autocratic regime that ignored the country's deep social and economic inequities. How they were fought differed too. The American Revolution involved whole armies in several years of bloody battles, skirmishes, and stalemates over a huge geographic area. On the other hand, the French Revolution was bloody in a more personal way and was mostly contained in one area. The results were also different. The American Revolution resulted in a **representative government**, which marketed itself as a beacon of democracy for the rest of the world, while the French Revolution resulted in a **consulship**, a generalship, and then an emperor.

The Industrial Revolution

The **INDUSTRIAL REVOLUTION**—which began in Great Britain and spread elsewhere—was the era during which complex machinery powered by coal and steam was developed. This led to the accelerated growth of manufacturing, with large factories replacing homes and small workshops as work centers. The lives of people changed drastically, and a largely agricultural society changed to an industrial one.

INDUSTRIAL REVOLUTION: the era during which complex machinery powered by coal and steam was developed

First phase

The first phase of the Industrial Revolution (1750–1830) saw the mechanization of the **textile** industry, vast improvements in mining, the invention of the **steam engine** (and its application in various industries), and numerous improvements in transportation, including turnpikes, canals, and the railroad.

Second phase

During the second phase (1830–1910), vast improvements were made in a number of already mechanized industries, such as the Bessemer steel process and the invention of steam ships. Technologies such as photography, electricity, and chemical processing created new industries. New sources of power were harnessed and applied, including **petroleum** and **hydroelectric** power. Precision instruments were developed and engineering grew. It was during this second phase that the Industrial Revolution spread to other European countries, Japan, and the United States.

Later, during the late 1800s and early 1900s, power based on electricity and internal combustion replaced coal and steam. This resulted in even greater production and changes in transportation, daily life, trade, and the exchange of ideas and knowledge.

Legacy of the Industrial Revolution

The Industrial Revolution completely changed life for people all over the world.

The Industrial Revolution completely changed life for people all over the world. In industrial countries, this included political changes such as the expansion of the franchise and, eventually, government agencies aimed at regulating businesses' excesses. Huge social changes also occurred, including:

- Mass education
- The increase and reorganization of populations
- The rise of big cities
- The development of trade unions
- The growth of the middle class

New technology was applied to agriculture, sanitation, medicine, and leisure pursuits. These changes led to a faster tempo of life and increased stress from monotonous work routines. The emancipation of women, the decline of religion, the rise of scientific materialism, and even Darwin's theory of evolution were influenced by the industrial revolution. Due to increased mobility and opportunities in industrial countries, widescale immigration occurred.

New forms of business created a rich and powerful class of businessmen with interests all over the world. It also created the **factory system**, **mass production**, **monopolies**, and more opportunities for more people.

Nationalism

During the eighteenth and especially the nineteenth centuries, **NATIONALISM**, or the belief in one's own nation and people, emerged as a powerful force in Europe and elsewhere in the world. More so than in previous centuries, the people in contiguous areas in Europe began to think in terms of a nation of people who had similar beliefs, concerns, and needs; this was partly a reaction to a growing discontent with their governments. Unifying smaller political entities into larger countries created Italy and Germany. Although many of these smaller entities shared a common language, history, and culture, some did not like being assimilated into the larger country. They wanted to remain a separate cultural and political entity.

NATIONALISM: the belief in one's own nation and people

Nationalism spreads

The time from 1830 to 1914 especially is characterized by the extraordinary growth and spread of patriotic pride expressed as nationalism. There were revolutions in Austria and Hungary, and the Franco-Prussian War was waged. In industrial countries, nationalism combined with industrialism increased imperialism. Europeans looked to Africa and Asia as rich sources of goods, trade, and cheap labor. Sometimes they took control of a country as a colony, and other times they interfered in their internal politics and economics. France, Great Britain, Italy, Portugal, the Netherlands, Spain, Germany, and Belgium together controlled the entire African continent except for Liberia and Ethiopia. In Asia and the Pacific Islands, only China, Japan, and present-day Thailand (Siam) kept their independence. The others were controlled by the strong European nations.

The time from 1830 to 1914 is characterized by the extraordinary growth and spread of patriotic pride expressed as nationalism.

In the Western Hemisphere, the United States supported Spanish and Portuguese colonies in their successful wars for independence. However, it also expanded westward under the banner of "Manifest Destiny," fought the Mexican War, the Spanish-American War, and became an imperialistic power, as well.

The Russian Revolution

Reasons for revolution

Centuries of dismal conditions in Russia led up to the turmoil of the twentieth century. Russia's harsh climate, tremendous size, and physical isolation from the rest of Europe, along with the brutal, despotic rule and control of the Czars over enslaved peasants, all contributed to the explosive conditions that ignited the revolution. Despite the tremendous efforts of **Peter the Great** to bring his country up to the social, cultural, and economic standards of the rest of Europe, Russia always remained a hundred years or more behind. All of the following contributed to conditions that made Russia susceptible to revolution:

- Autocratic rule
- The system of serfdom or slavery of peasants
- Lack of money
- Defeats in wars
- Lack of adequate food and food production
- Harsh working conditions in the small amount of industrialization

Czars

CZARS: the autocratic rulers of prerevolutionary Russia

Until the early years of the twentieth century, Russia was ruled by a succession of **CZARS**. The Czars ruled as autocrats or, sometimes, despots. Society was essentially feudalistic and was structured in three levels:

1. The Czar
2. The rich nobles who held government positions and owned vast tracts of land
3. The remaining people who lived in poverty as peasants or serfs

There were several unsuccessful attempts to revolt during the nineteenth century, caused largely by discontent, especially on the part of the peasants, but they were quickly suppressed. The two revolutions of the early twentieth century in 1905 and 1917, however, were quite different.

The 1905 Revolution

The causes of the **1905 Revolution** include discontent with the social structure, the horrendous living conditions of the peasants, and the deplorable working and living conditions of factory workers. The **Russo-Japanese War** (1904–1905) aggravated this general discontent. Peasants who had been able to eke out a living prior to the war were now starving. Men and battles were lost due to poor leadership, lack of training, and inferior weaponry, but Czar **Nicholas II** refused to end the war.

In 1905, a trade union leader, Father **Gapon**, organized a protest to demand an end to the war, industrial reform, more civil liberties, and a constituent assembly. On **Bloody Sunday**, over 150,000 peasants demonstrated outside the Czar's

Winter Palace. Before the demonstrators even spoke, the palace guard opened fire on the crowd and many were killed. This destroyed the people's trust in the Czar.

Illegal trade unions and political parties formed and organized strikes to gain power. The strikes eventually brought the Russian economy to a halt. This led Czar Nicholas II to sign the **OCTOBER MANIFESTO**, which created a constitutional monarchy, extended some civil rights, and gave the parliament limited legislative power. But in a very short period of time, the Czar disbanded the parliament and violated the promised civil liberties. This violation of the October Manifesto would help foment the **1917 Revolution**.

OCTOBER MANIFESTO: created a constitutional monarchy, extended some civil rights, and gave the parliament limited legislative power

The 1917 Revolution

The Czar's behavior triggered more unrest. He continued to appoint unqualified people to government posts, which intensified his political incompetence. He also listened to his wife **Alexandra**'s advice, and she was strongly influenced by **Rasputin**, a mystic healer.

There were other factors as well. Defeats on the battlefields of World War I caused discontent, loss of life, and a popular desire to withdraw from the war. The war had caused another surge in prices and the scarcity of many items. Most peasants could not afford to buy bread. In addition, workers in Petrograd went on strike in March 1917 over the lack of food. The Czar again ordered troops to suppress the strike. This time, however, the troops sided with the workers.

The Czar was forced to abdicate, and parliament created a provisional government. The military and the workers also created local councils and governments called **SOVIETS**.

SOVIETS: local councils and governments created to rule Russia after the Czar abdicated

Revolutionary control

The revolutionary leaders, previously driven underground or into exile, returned. **Vladimir Lenin's Bolshevik Party** won the support of the peasants and the exhausted military with the promise of "Peace, Land, and Bread." The government reorganized four times from March to October. In October, Lenin and the Bolshevik party, with the support of the **Red Guard**, overthrew the provisional government, took control of Russia, and established a new communist government. A civil war continued until 1921, as Lenin solidified his power and that of his **Communist Party**. The people of Russia had simply exchanged one autocratic dictatorial system for another.

SKILL 2.7 Conflicts, ideologies, and evolutions in the 20th century: 1900–1991

World War I: 1914 to 1918

Nationalism and rivalries ran high in early twentieth century Europe, and minor disputes were magnified into major ones. The **Balkan Peninsula** was an especially volatile and fertile ground for trouble. There were a few attempts to keep a war from starting, but these efforts were futile.

Causes for World War I

One of the major causes of the war was the tremendous surge of nationalism. People of the same nationality or ethnic group sharing a common history, language, or culture began uniting or demanding the right of unification, especially in Eastern Europe, in places like Russia, the Ottoman Empire, and the Austria-Hungary Empire.

Other causes were the increasing military capabilities, massive colonization for the procurement of raw materials, and military and diplomatic alliances.

Assassination

The political climate was tense; one tiny spark was all it would take to set off an explosion. On June 28, 1914, a Bosnian Serb student named **Gavrilo Princip** assassinated **Archduke Frantz Ferdinand**, heir to the Austria-Hungarian throne, and his wife, **Sophie Chotek**, while on a state visit to Sarajevo. Princip was a member of the Black Hand, a Serbian Nationalist Secret Society. Ferdinand's death set in motion a series of events that culminated in the world's first global war, World War I.

Three weeks later, Austria-Hungary issued an ultimatum to Serbia, certain that Serbia would reject the terms. Austria-Hungary was prepared to launch a limited war against Serbia. What it intended as a brief war against Serbia, rapidly escalated into a conflict between all of the major world powers.

Making and honoring alliances

Eventually, nearly 30 nations were involved in the war, which continued until 1918. Austria-Hungary, unhappy with Serbia's response to their ultimatum, immediately declared war on Serbia. After this, the war declarations fell like dominoes. Russia, bound by its treaty to Serbia, brought its immense army to her defense. Germany, allied to Austria-Hungary by treaty, viewed the Russian mobilization as an act of war against Austria-Hungary and declared war on Russia. France was bound by treaty to Russia and so found itself at war against Germany.

Britain, allied to France by a loosely worded treaty that stated a "moral obligation" to defend France, soon declared war against Germany. Japan honored a military agreement with Britain and declared war on Germany, though largely for its own interests. Austria-Hungary responded by declaring war on Japan. Italy was committed to both Germany and Austria-Hungary, which allowed it to remain neutral for a short period of time but eventually Italy joined the Allies against her two former allies. The Ottoman Empire joined the **Central Powers**, hoping to obtain land from Russia. Britain's colonies and dominions (Australia, Canada, India, New Zealand, and the Union of South Africa) offered financial and military assistance. President Woodrow Wilson declared the United States absolutely neutral but finally entered the war in 1917 on the side of the **Allies**.

Staying true to the military alliances, the **ALLIES** (chiefly, Britain, France, and Russia) opposed the **CENTRAL POWERS** (primarily Austria-Hungary, Germany, and the Ottoman Empire). Eventually, the war spread outside of Europe as the war went to colonies and allies for assistance.

ALLIES: one of the warring factions in World War I, consisting mainly of Britain, France, and Russia

CENTRAL POWERS: one of the warring factions in World War I, consisting mainly of Austria-Hungary, Germany, and the Ottoman Empire

The two fronts

Much of the fighting in World War I took place along the **Western Front**, which ran from the North Sea to the border Switzerland. On the **Eastern Front** were the vast eastern plains. The two opposing fronts were composed of a complex system of manned trenches and fortifications, separated by unoccupied land called "no man's land." By the war's end, each side had dug at least 12,000 miles of trenches.

Deadly weapons

World War I saw the introduction of such warfare as use of tanks, airplanes, barbed wire, machine guns, submarines, poison gas, and flamethrowers. The atrocities of war took everyone by surprise and led to much of the animosity that marked the terms of the end of the war. It would lead to ban on certain weapons, particularly poison gas, and leave the nations of Europe unwilling to go to war again.

War's end

Before the official **ARMISTICE** was declared on November 11, 1918, nine million people had died on the battlefields. The Allies defeated the Central Powers, but the conflicts underlying the war had not been solved.

ARMISTICE: an agreement declared on November 11, 1918, that brought about the end of WWI

Consequences of the war

World War I seriously damaged the economies of the European countries, both the victors and the defeated, leaving them deeply in debt. Both sides had difficulty paying off war debts and loans. People found it difficult to find jobs, and some countries, like Japan and Italy, found themselves without enough raw materials to produce anything of worth. They solved these problems by expanding colonial territory to get more materials, which merely set the conditions for war later.

Germany suffered from runaway inflation, which ruined the value of its money and wiped out the savings of millions. Despite U.S. loans to Germany that helped the government restore some order and provided some economic stability in Europe, the soon-to-begin Great Depression would undo any good done with these loans. Mass unemployment, poverty, and despair greatly weakened the democratic governments that had been formed and significantly strengthened the increasing power and influence of extreme political movements such as communism, fascism, and socialism.

Socialist Movements

SOCIALISM: the belief that society, as a whole, should control the means of production

SOCIALISM is the belief that society, as a whole, should control the means of production. It advocates public rather than private ownership over means of production. **Communism** is a form of socialism. Another form is **democratic socialism**, which developed in Western European industrial countries. It advocates public control of some industries and for the government to protect the welfare of the individual. These economic and political philosophies have grown and changed since the mid-1800s.

Utopian Socialists

Mid-nineteenth century **utopian socialists** repudiated the private-property system with its economic inefficiency and social injustice. They established settlements based on their beliefs, but their criticisms eclipsed their achievements. They envisioned industrial capitalism as becoming increasing inhumane and oppressive. They could not imagine the mass of workers prospering in such a system.

The influence of Karl Marx

In the same period, German philosopher **Karl Marx** developed his theory that included the need for industrial workers to overthrow capitalism and work toward a society without a government or class divisions. Other socialists, by contrast, advocated reforming present societies.

Marx became an active member in the first **Socialist International** in 1864. This radical leftist organization died, but in 1889 the **Second Socialist International** met. However, by this time, serious factions were developing in the socialist movement:

- **Anarchists** wanted to tear down everything

- Communists wanted to tear down the established order and build another in its place
- The **Democratic socialist** majority favored reforms through peaceful political action

Struggling for internal peace and cohesion right up to the World War I, socialism would remain largely ineffectual at this critical international time.

Post-war surges

After the war, a huge rift was evident between Lenin's communists and reform-minded socialists. They no longer had common ground, so, in 1919, Lenin created The **Communist International**. His goal was to encourage revolutions among the world's industrial workers. It was abolished by Stalin in 1943 but returned in 1947 as **Cominform** and lasted until 1956. These organizations affected countries all over the world, especially former colonies.

The decade following World War II saw tremendous growth in socialism. In 1951 the **Congress of Socialists International** was held in Frankfurt, Germany. It adopted a document entitled "Aims and Tasks of Democratic Socialism." A summary of its objectives expresses the ideals of modern democratic socialism. Economic planning and the nationalization of industry was undertaken in many countries, though a subsequent return to confidence in private business has frequently weakened the socialist majority or reduced it to the status of an opposition party. This political balance leaves most industrialized countries with a mixed socialist-capitalist economy.

Fascism

Conditions leading to Fascism

Nationalism, which had been a major cause of World War I, grew even stronger after the war ended. The political, social, and economic unrest fueled nationalism and allowed dictators to gain and maintain power from the 1930s to the end of World War II in 1945. Totalitarian regimes tightly control all aspects of life. After World War I, Italy, Germany, and Russia developed totalitarian governments. Russia, which became the Union of Soviet Socialist Republics, had a communist government that was totalitarian. Joseph Stalin succeeded in gaining political control and establishing a strong, harsh dictatorship. In Japan, although Emperor **Hirohito** was considered the ruler, actual control and administration of government came under military officers.

FASCISM: an aggressive form of nationalism that glorifies the state and a single party system with an absolute ruler

Due to these conditions, Italy and Germany developed fascist governments. **FASCISM** has an aggressive form of nationalism that glorifies the state and a single party system with an absolute ruler. However, unlike communism, it encourages businesses with regulation.

Italian Fascism

In Italy, where fascism first arose, **Benito Mussolini** and the **Fascist Party** promised prosperity and order, gained national support, and set up a strong government. He sought to create a "corporate" state that would, in theory, run the economy like a corporation for the benefit of the whole country. It would be centrally controlled and managed by an elite group who would ensure that its benefits would be shared. The propertied interests and the upper classes, fearful of revolution, gave their support based on promises by fascist leaders to maintain the status quo and safeguard property. However, under fascism, capital is regulated as much as labor. Also, fascism often ignores legal or constitutional guarantees.

Fascists declared themselves to be an uncompromising enemy of communism, but many of their actions, methods of organization, and propaganda techniques were taken from the early Russian communists, along with the belief in a single strong political party. Secret police were another shared feature.

Once established, a fascist regime ruthlessly crushes all opposition parties, whether communist, socialist, or democratic.

Once established, a fascist regime ruthlessly crushes all opposition parties, whether communist, socialist, or democratic. It regiments the propertied interests to its national goals and wins the potentially revolutionary masses to fascist programs by substituting a rabid nationalism for class conflict. Thus, fascism is sometimes an extreme defensive expedient adopted by a nation that is faced with the sometimes-illusionary threat of communism or revolution.

German Fascism

Germany was purposefully hard hit by the **Treaty of Versailles**, which ended World War I. It left Germans dissatisfied with the government and their standing in the world and with economic, social, and military problems. The German economy suffered horribly as runaway inflation ruined the value of its money and wiped out the savings of millions. Its government and economy were unstable. U.S. reconstruction loans eventually dried up. All of these situations enabled **Adolf Hitler** and his National Socialist, or **Nazi**, party to gain complete power and control.

Then, problems were made worse when the Depression hit Europe. In Germany, large numbers of unemployed, dissatisfied urban workers joined communist and fascist paramilitary organizations. They promised dramatic action, economic restructuring, and the improvement of Germany's standing in the world. It was out of this climate that the Nazi Party emerged.

An early attempt at a coup put many Nazi leaders, including Adolf Hitler, in jail. Upon his release, Hitler took leadership again and built the fascist Nazi party into a political party that won seats in the German Parliament. Then, in 1933, Hitler was named Chancellor of Germany. He used his position to implemented policies of military expansion and aggression that culminated in the Second World War.

Fascist aggression

Germany, Italy, and Japan initiated a policy of aggressive territorial expansion. In 1931, Japanese forces seized control of **Manchuria**, a part of China with rich natural resources, and in 1937 began an attack on the rest of China, occupying most of eastern China by 1938. Italy invaded **Ethiopia** in Africa in 1935, gaining complete control by 1936. The Soviet Union did not invade or take over any territory but actively participated in the **Spanish Civil War** along with Italy and Germany, using it as a proving ground to test tactics and weapons, setting the stage for World War II.

RIBBENTROP–MOLOTOV PACT OF 1939: an agreement between Germany and Russia stating that if either country went to war, both countries would remain neutral and refrain from acts of aggression against the other

The Soviet-German **RIBBENTROP–MOLOTOV PACT OF 1939** stated that if either country went to war, both countries would remain neutral and refrain from acts of aggression against the other. There was also a secret clause about partitioning Poland, with Stalin taking the east and Hitler the west. Of course, when Hitler invaded Poland, the agreement was nullified. During the period of alliance created by the treaty, Italy, Germany, and their satellite countries ceased their anti-communist propaganda and attacked the western democracies.

Europe: World War II: 1939 to 1945

See also Skill 1.11

Buildup to war

Almost immediately after taking power and in direct violation of the World War I peace treaty, Hitler began a buildup of the armed forces. He sent troops into the Rhineland in 1936, invaded Austria in 1938, and united it with Germany. In 1938, he seized control of the Sudetenland, part of western Czechoslovakia populated largely by Germans, followed by the rest of Czechoslovakia in March 1939. Despite his territorial designs, the other nations of Europe made no move to stop Hitler.

Preferring not to embark on another costly war, the European powers opted for a policy of **appeasement**, believing that once Hitler had fulfilled his desire for land he would be satisfied, and war could be averted. Then, on September 1, 1939, Hitler invaded Poland, which touched off World War II.

Early German success

In 1940, Germany invaded and controlled Norway, Denmark, Belgium, Luxembourg, the Netherlands, and France. German military forces struck in what came to be known as the **BLITZKRIEG** or "lightning war." These shock attacks relied on surprise, speed, and superiority in firepower. The German blitzkrieg coordinated land and air attacks to paralyze the enemy by disabling its communications and coordination capacities.

BLITZKRIEG: a military tactic employing shock attacks that rely on surprise, speed, and superiority in firepower

When France fell in June 1940, the Franco-German armistice divided France into two zones: one under German military occupation and one under nominal French control (the southeastern two-fifths of the country). The National Assembly, summoned at Vichy, France, ratified the armistice and granted **Philippe Pétain** control of the French State. The **VICHY GOVERNMENT** then collaborated with the Germans, eventually becoming little more than a rubber stamp for German policies. Germany would occupy the whole of France in 1942, and by early 1944, a **resistance** movement created a period of civil war in France. The Vichy regime was abolished after the liberation of Paris.

VICHY GOVERNMENT: the French governmental body that collaborated with the German invaders, eventually becoming little more than a rubber stamp for German policies

With the continent safely conquered, Hitler turned his sights to England. The **BATTLE OF BRITAIN** (June 1940–April 1941) was a series of intense raids directed against Britain by the **Luftwaffe**, Germany's air force. Intended to prepare the way for invasion, the air raids were directed against British ports and **Royal Air Force (RAF)** bases. In September 1940, London and other cities were attacked in the **blitz**, a series of bombings that lasted for 57 consecutive nights. Sporadic raids continued until April 1941. The RAF was outnumbered but succeeded in blocking the German air force, and eventually Hitler abandoned his plans for invasion; this was Germany's first major setback in the war.

BATTLE OF BRITAIN: a series of intense raids directed against Britain by the Luftwaffe

The war expands

A second front was opened when Japan attacked Pearl Harbor in 1941 and drew the United States into the war. Hard-fought battles continued in the Pacific and Asia until 1945.

After success in North Africa (1942) and Italy (1943), and following the D-Day Invasion (1944), the Allied forces faced a protracted campaign across Europe. Each gain was hard won, and both the weather and local terrain at times worked against them. The **BATTLE OF THE BULGE**, also known as Battle of the Ardennes (December 16, 1944 to January 28, 1945), was the largest World War II land battle on the Western Front, and the last major German counteroffensive of the war. Launched by Adolf Hitler himself, the German army's goal was to cut Allied forces in half and to retake the crucial port of Antwerp. Secretly massed Panzer tank-led units launched their assault into the thinnest part of the Allied forces.

BATTLE OF THE BULGE: the largest World War II land battle on the Western Front and the last major German counteroffensive of the war

Though surprised and suffering tremendous losses, Allied forces still managed to slow the Germans. American tanks moved swiftly to counterattack and cut German supply lines. The attack resulted in a bulge 70 miles deep into Allied lines, but all forward momentum for the Germans was essentially stopped by Christmas. It took another month before the Allies could push back to the original line. Both sides suffered great casualties, but the Germans' losses were a crushing blow, as the troops and equipment lost were irreplaceable.

War's end

During WWII, Allied forces flew extensive bombing raids deep into German territory. Launching from bases in England, both American and RAF bomber squadrons attacked German factories and cities. Although the raids were dangerous, with many planes and lives lost both to the Luftwaffe and anti-aircraft artillery, they continued throughout the war. German cities were reduced to rubble by war's end. The impact on Germany's production capacity and transportation lines helped swing the tide of war.

Even before war in Europe had ended, the Allies had agreed on a military occupation of Germany. It was divided into four zones, with Great Britain, France, the Soviet Union, and the United States each occupying one zone; all four powers jointly administered Berlin. After the war, the Allies agreed to abolish Germany's armed forces, outlaw the Nazi Party, and take away German territory east of the Oder and Neisse Rivers. Nazi leaders were also accused of war crimes and brought to trial at **Nuremburg**.

During the war, the Soviet Union took control of Lithuania, Estonia, Latvia, and, by mid-1945, parts of Poland, Czechoslovakia, Finland, and Romania. It helped communist governments gain power in Bulgaria, Romania, Hungary, Czechoslovakia, Poland, and North Korea. Also, China fell to **Mao Zedong**'s communist forces in 1949.

Consequences of the war

The major consequences of the war include:

- Horrendous death and destruction
- The displacement of millions of people
- The strengthening and spreading of Communism
- The beginning of Cold War tensions

World War II ended more lives and caused more devastation than any other war.

World War II caused more death and devastation than any other war that had been fought. In addition to staggering military casualties, cities, houses, and factories were reduced to ruin and rubble, and communication and transportation systems were destroyed. Millions of civilian died of famine, especially in China and the Soviet Union.

The world after World War II was a complicated place. Germany and Japan were completely defeated; Great Britain and France were seriously weakened; and the Soviet Union and the United States became the world's leading powers. Although allies during the war, the alliance fell apart as the Soviets pushed Communism in Europe and Asia. In spite of the tremendous destruction it suffered, the Soviet Union seemed stronger than ever.

Communism takes over

The American **Marshall Plan** helped the nations of Western Europe get back on their feet. The Soviet Union helped the Eastern European nations return to greatness by putting Communist governments at the helm. The nations of Asia were rebuilt as well, with Communism taking over China, while Japan and Taiwan were more influenced by American culture and policy. East and West struggled for control in this arena, especially in Korea and Southeast Asia. When Communism eventually fell in the U.S.S.R. and Eastern Europe, it remained in China, North Korea, and Vietnam.

Beginning of the Cold War

Until the fall of the Berlin Wall in 1989 and the dissolution of communist governments in Eastern Europe and Russia, the United States and the Soviet Union faced off in what was known as the Cold War. The possibility of the terrifying destruction by nuclear weapons loomed over both nations.

Genocide and the Holocaust

GENOCIDE: the intended extinction of one people by another

GENOCIDE, or the intended extinction of one people by another, is not a new concept. However, in the twentieth century, it has reached great heights—and depths.

Armenian genocide

ARMENIAN GENOCIDE: an attempted extermination of a huge number of Armenians at the hands of the *Young Turks*

In the early 1900s was the **ARMENIAN GENOCIDE**, an attempted extermination of a huge number of Armenians at the hands of the **Young Turks**, who inherited Turkey from the Ottoman Empire. More than one million Armenian people (nearly half of their population) died between 1915 and 1917 because they were blamed for defeats at the hands of Russia and its allies. Armenians were forcibly moved and kept in harsh conditions elsewhere. Some 25 concentration camps are believed to have existed. Turkish authorities claimed that the Armenian people had agitated for separation from the Ottoman Empire and that the relocation fulfilled the goals of both parties; others disagree. Some sources blame other causes for these deaths, but most scholars agree that it was a determined attempt to exterminate an entire group of people.

The Holocaust

The most well-known genocide of the twentieth century, however, is the **HOLOCAUST**, which took place before and during World War II. Much of the atrocity occurred in Germany, although the practice spread throughout German-occupied countries during the war. German authorities capitalized on hundreds of years of distrust of the Jewish people and invented what they saw as "the **Final Solution** of the Jewish Question:" the extermination of the Jewish people.

HOLOCAUST: the Nazi German–instituted genocide of Jews during the World War II era

Germans in charge of this Final Solution constructed a vast, complicated system of transport to concentration camps where Jews were imprisoned, forced to work, and killed in increasingly large numbers. Due to the Germans' efficiency and extensive record keeping, thousands of pages of documents describe in excruciating detail how thorough and determined Nazi authorities were in pursuing their goals.

German doctors also carried out experiments on their Jewish prisoners, pursuing radical cures for diseases and, more often than not, new methods of torture and mistreatment of prisoners of war. Worse still, torture and killing were not restricted to the able-bodied. Children, the elderly, the disabled, the mentally ill, and the near dead were all subject to the harshest treatment imaginable. One common practice was the forced march from one location to another, miles away, without food. These "**death marches**" left many of the prisoners dead or near death.

The number of Jews killed during the Holocaust is generally said to be six million. This figure includes people from all over Europe. The Holocaust did not kill just Jews, however. Gypsies, communists, homosexuals, Jehovah's Witnesses, Catholics, psychiatric patients, and even common criminals were systematically incarcerated and, in many cases, executed for being "enemies of the state." The number of concentration camps in Nazi-controlled lands during World War II was more than 40. Although the most famous ones, including **Auschwitz**, were death camps, some were not.

The number of Jews killed during the Holocaust is generally said to be six million.

The Holocaust ended with Germany's defeat in World War II. The troops of the West and East who liberated the concentration camps found the lists of those killed by the Nazis. Much of the meticulous German record system remained intact, preserving for the entire world the horrors that the Nazis had wrought.

Criticism of the Allies

The Allied powers were sharply criticized during WWII for their failure to act to save the European Jews. Many organizations and individuals did not believe reports of the abuse and mass genocide that was occurring in Europe. Many nations did not want to accept Jewish refugees. Even some relief organizations, such as the International Red Cross, discounted reports of atrocities.

One particular point of criticism was the failure of the Allied Powers to bomb the death camp at **Auschwitz-Birkenau** or the railroad tracks leading there. Military leaders argued that their planes did not have the range to reach the camp; they also argued that they could not provide sufficiently precise targeting to safeguard the inmates. Critics have claimed that even if Allied bombs killed all inmates at Auschwitz at the time, the destruction of the camp would have saved thousands of other Jews. Regardless of post-facto arguments, it is very likely that even if the Allies had destroyed the camp, the Nazis would have turned to other methods of extermination.

It was not until after the war that the **Nuremberg Trials** redefined genocide as a crime against humanity. This redefined morality attained popular currency, and individuals, rather than governments, were held accountable for war crimes.

World Restructuring

The **United Nations (U.N.)**, a more successful heir to the League of Nations—which couldn't prevent World War II—began in the waning days of the war. It brought the nations of the world together to discuss their problems rather than fight about them. Its agencies worked to help countries with a variety of economic, social, and political problems. In 1948, the U.N. recognized that its charter was insufficiently precise as to the rights it protected, so its General Assembly unanimously passed the **Universal Declaration of Human Rights**.

Nation building

DECOLONIZATION: the period after World War II when many African and Asian colonies and protectorates gained independence from the powers that had colonized them

DECOLONIZATION refers to the period after World War II when many African and Asian colonies and protectorates gained independence from the powers that had colonized them. The independence of India and Pakistan from Britain in 1945 marked the beginning of an especially important period of decolonization that lasted through 1960. Several British colonies in eastern Africa and French colonies in western Africa and Asia also formed as independent countries during this period.

NATION BUILDING: the process of organizing new nations out of the remains of former colonies

Colonial powers had found it efficient to draw political boundaries across traditional ethnic and national lines, thereby dividing local populations and making them easier to control. With the yoke of colonialism removed, many new nations found themselves trying to reorganize into politically stable and economically viable units. The role of nationalism was important in this reorganization, as formerly divided people had an opportunity to reunite. This process of organizing new nations out of the remains of former colonies is called **NATION BUILDING**.

Failures of nation building

Nation building in this fashion did not always result in the desired stability. Pakistan, for example, eventually split into Bangladesh and Pakistan along geographic and religious lines. Ethnic conflicts in newly formed African nations arose and are still flaring in some areas. As the United States and the Soviet Union emerged as the dominant world powers, these countries encouraged dissent in post-colonial nations such as Cuba, Vietnam, and Korea, which eventually became arenas for Cold War conflict.

The Middle East has been an especially violent part of the world since the war and the recreation of the State of Israel. The struggle for supremacy in the Persian Gulf area has brought about a handful of wars as well. Oil, needed to power the world's large transportation and power industries, is king of all resources.

International organizations

With the emergence of so many new independent nations, the role of **international organizations** such as the newly formed United Nations grew in importance. Although the United Nations was formed to establish peaceful ties between countries, the organizers of the United Nations provided for the ability to deploy peacekeeping troops and to impose sanctions and restrictions on member states. Other international organizations arose to take the place of former colonial connections. The British Commonwealth and the French Union, for example, maintained connections between Britain and France and their former colonies.

With the emergence of so many new independent nations, the role of international organizations such as the newly formed United Nations grew in importance.

Global migrations

Global migration increased in the years during and following World War II. Before and during the war, many Jews left the hostile climate under Nazi Germany for the United States and Palestine. After the war, displaced European Jews flocked to Palestine, soon to be called Israel. Following the war, the Allied countries agreed to force German people living in Eastern Europe to return to Germany, affecting over 16 million people. In other parts of the world, instability in post-colonial areas often led to migration. Also, colonial settlers, who had enjoyed the protection of a colonial power, sometimes found themselves in hostile situations as native people gained independence and ascended to power. This spurred migration to more friendly nations. Economic instability in these newly forming countries also created incentives for people to seek opportunity in other countries.

Korean War 1950 to 1953

Korea was under control of Japan from 1895 to the end of World War II in 1945. At this war's end, the Soviet and U.S. military troops moved into Korea, with the

U.S. troops in the southern half and the Soviet troops in the northern half. The 38-degree North Latitude line was the boundary.

Reasons for war

In 1947, the **General Assembly** of the U.N. ordered elections throughout all of Korea to select one government for the entire country. The Soviet Union would not allow the North Koreans to vote and set up a communist government there. In contrast, the South Koreans set up a democratic government, and both countries claimed the entire peninsula as their country. The Soviet troops withdrew from North Korea in 1948. Clashes continued between North and South Korea from 1948 to 1950. The U.S. removed its remaining troops in 1949. The communists received Stalin's permission to act and invaded the south. This was the first actual war of the Cold War period.

The U.N. Security Council voted to organize an army to oppose the invasion. Participant countries in this war were:

- North and South Korea
- United States of America
- Australia
- New Zealand
- China
- Canada
- France
- Great Britain
- Turkey
- Belgium
- Ethiopia
- ColombiaGreece
- Greece
- South Africa
- Luxembourg
- Thailand
- The Netherlands
- The Philippines

It was the first time that a world organization played a major military role during a war, and it presented quite a challenge to the U.N. (which had only been in existence five years).

Course of the war

The war began June 25, 1950. Later that year, after **General MacArthur** had led U.N. troops to the Chinese border, China entered into the war, and the U.N. troops retreated south. By the winter of 1951, troops were fighting along the 38th parallel. When MacArthur publically threatened to attack China, President Harry Truman relieved MacArthur from duty for insubordination.

Truce but no peace

A truce was drawn up and on July 27, 1953, an armistice agreement was signed ending the fighting. A permanent treaty of peace has never been signed, and the country remains divided between the communist north and the democratic south. It was a very costly and bloody war, destroying villages and homes and displacing and killing millions of people.

The Vietnam War

Background

Conflict in this region began with what is often called the **French Indochina War**, which waged from 1946 to 1954. This conflict involved France, which had ruled Vietnam as its colony (French Indochina), and the newly independent Democratic Republic of Vietnam under **Ho Chi Minh**. On May 7, 1954, at a French military base known as **Dien Bien Phu**, Vietminh troops emerged victorious after a 56-day siege and ended France's involvement in Indochina. After the Vietnamese victory, the country was divided into the communist-dominated north and the U.S.-supported south. Almost inevitably, war soon broke out between the two as Americans poured massive aid into South Vietnam.

A controversial war

In the fighting that ensued, soldiers trained in the north (the **VIET CONG**) waged a guerrilla war against U.S.-supported South Vietnamese forces. North Vietnamese forces would later join the fighting, supported by Soviet advisors and equipment. At the height of U.S. involvement, there were more than half a million U.S. military personnel in Vietnam. The **Tet Offensive of 1968**, in which the Viet Cong and North Vietnamese attacked over 100 South Vietnamese cities and towns, marked a turning point in the war.

VIET CONG: soldiers trained and fighting for North Vietnam during the Vietnam War

Many in the U.S. opposed the war on moral and practical grounds. In response to the large-scale civil unrest the war was creating, President Lyndon B. Johnson, and later President Richard Nixon, decided to shift to a policy of **deescalation** or "**Vietnamization**." American troops were withdrawn, and the South Vietnamese military took more responsibility for the war.

In 1968, peace talks began in Paris. Between 1969 and 1973, U.S. troops were withdrawn from Vietnam, although the war expanded into Cambodia and Laos in 1970 and 1971. Peace talks, which had reached a stalemate in 1971, started again in 1973, producing a cease-fire agreement. Even without U.S. troops, however, fighting continued, and there were numerous truce violations. In 1975, the North Vietnamese launched a full-scale invasion of the South. The

More than 2,000,000 people (including 58,000 Americans) died over the course of the Vietnam War, about half of them civilians.

South surrendered later that year, and in 1976, the country was reunited as the **Socialist Republic of Vietnam**. More than 2,000,000 people (including 58,000 Americans) died over the course of the Vietnam War, about half of them civilians.

Conflicts related to the war

In a related conflict, Cambodia experienced its own civil war between communists and non-communists during that period, which was won by the communist **Khmer Rouge** in 1975. After several years of horrifying atrocities under **Pol Pot**, the Vietnamese invaded Cambodia in 1978 to end border incidents and installed a puppet government. Fighting between the Khmer Rouge and the Vietnamese continued throughout the 1980s; Vietnam withdrew its troops by 1989. In 1993, U.N.-mediated elections established a coalition government that reestablished Cambodia's monarchy. In Laos, North Vietnam's victory over South Vietnam brought the communist **Pathet Lao** into complete control in Laos.

SKILL 2.8 Contemporary trends: 1991–present *(changing geopolitical map of the world, regional and global economic and environmental interdependence, the welfare state, liberation movements, and globalization)*

Regional Tensions

Yugoslavia

In the modern era, ethnic issues have created a vicious cycle of changing borders, migration, and fostered genocide in several regions. Yugoslavia was a melting pot of ethnic peoples, all of whom were struggling for meager resources and living space. After World War II, this country was held together by its strong leader, **Josip Broz Tito**. After his death, political and ethnic issues melded and led to Yugoslavia's break-up into several smaller states. In the 1990s, it also led to **ethnic cleansing** in several of them: Kosovo, Croatia, and Bosnia.

Slobodan Milosevic was a Serb in Serbia, one of Yugoslavia's republics. His rabidly nationalistic leadership led to violence, huge numbers of displaced people, and the deaths of both Serbs and Muslim Albanians between 1989 and the intervention of NATO and the U.N. in the late 1990s. A final accord outlined Serbian troop withdrawals and the return of nearly 1,000,000 ethnic Albanian refugees to Serbia, as well as 500,000 displaced within the province. Milosevic was put on trial for crimes against humanity. In other Yugoslavian republics, Bosnia and Croatia, outside forces also had to come in to stop the violence and ethnic cleansing.

Rwanda

The African **RWANDAN GENOCIDE** in 1994 was the mass extermination of hundreds of thousands of ethnic **Tutsis** and moderate **Hutu** sympathizers and was the largest atrocity of the Rwandan Civil War. Two extremist Hutu militia groups carried out this genocide from April 6 through mid-July 1994. Hundreds of thousands of people were slaughtered.

RWANDAN GENOCIDE: the 1994 mass extermination of hundreds of thousands of ethnic Tutsis and moderate Hutu sympathizers

After the Rwandan Genocide, the United Nations and the international community drew severe criticism for its inaction. Despite international news media coverage of the violence as it unfolded, most countries, including France, Belgium, and the United States, declined to intervene or speak out against the massacres. Canada continued to lead the UN peacekeeping force in Rwanda. However, the U.N. Security Council did not authorize direct intervention or the use force to prevent or halt the killing.

Despite international news media coverage of the violence as it unfolded, most countries, including France, Belgium, and the United States, declined to intervene or speak out against the massacres in Rwanda.

The genocide ended when a Tutsi-dominated expatriate rebel overthrew the Hutu government and seized power. Fearing reprisals, millions of Hutu and other refugees fled into neighboring countries. Although many have returned, some remain in eastern Zaire (now the Democratic Republic of the Congo) and are working toward retaking Rwanda. These issues fueled the First (1996–1997) and Second (1998–2003) **Congo Wars**. Rivalry between Hutu and Tutsi tribal factions is also a major factor in the **Burundi Civil War**.

Globalization

GLOBALISM is defined as the principle of the interdependence of all the world's nations and their peoples. This socio-economic system says people, goods, and ideas should cross national lines without a problem, allowing free trade and free access to ideas. It also realizes that events within a country affect other countries worldwide, so this should be a consideration before action is taken.

GLOBALISM: the principle of the interdependence of all the world's nations; it dictates that people, goods, and ideas should cross national lines and allow free trade and free access to ideas

Economic globalism

Economically, no one nation has all of the resources needed for production, so trade with other nations is required to obtain what is needed for production, to sell what is produced, to buy finished products, and/or to earn money to maintain and strengthen the nation's economic system. The global economy has changed with the advent of faster, safer transportation by sea, air, trains, and roads. Goods (especially perishable foods) can travel farther and wider than ever before. Being able to ship goods quickly and efficiently means that overseas business can be done much more easily than ever before.

Many nations have joined regional or **international trade organizations** to increase their power in the global community. International systems of banking

A large number of businesses have investments in countries around the world, and financial transactions are now easily and quickly completed across international borders.

and finance have been devised to assist governments and businesses in setting policies and for exchanging currencies. A large number of businesses have investments in countries around the world, and financial transactions are now easily and quickly completed across international borders.

Economic growth and development is vital to a country. Businesses, labor, and governments share common interests and goals in its nation's economic status. Nations also grapple with the issues of placing tariffs and quotas on imports.

Resources and globalization

NONRENEWABLE RESOURCES: finite resources

An increase in demand for something is not always a good thing, however, especially if what is being demanded has a limited supply; such is the case with **NONRENEWABLE RESOURCES**. Some of these resources, like coal and oil, are in growing worldwide demand, but the supplies will not last forever. By making it easier to ship these resources, demand continues to grow—this raises concerns about the danger of these resources becoming extinct.

Technology and medicine

Globalization has also brought positive developments, such as those in the field of epidemiology. Vaccines and other cures for diseases can be shipped quickly all around the world. This has made it possible for HIV vaccines to reach the remotest areas on the Earth. Conversely, the preponderance of global transportation has also meant a very real threat of spreading a disease internationally.

Not only goods are being exchanged, but also belief systems, customs, and practices.

Another example of technology contributing to globalization is the development of the **Internet**. Instant communication between people thousands of miles apart is possible just by plugging in a computer and connecting to the Internet. Information, business interactions, and financial transactions are done instantaneously. Cell phones, with their ever-increasing capacity, have helped bring political events to the immediate attention of people worldwide, as they did after Iran's elections in 2009.

Globalization and migration

The movement of people across international borders has also increased in recent years. As people in less-developed nations see what is available in other places, they want to move there in order to take advantage of all that more-developed nations have to offer. Other people become refugees because of economic, ethnic, or political problems within their country. Also, with increasing economic opportunities in developing countries, many people are moving from a harsh, rural subsistence life to jobs within an urban area.

The Middle East

The **MIDDLE EAST** (once called the Near East) is defined by its name and its geographic position in the world. This position enables it to exert tremendous influence in global affairs, as much international trade passes through its realm of influence. From the beginnings of civilization, the Middle East has been an active cultural, economic, and religious region. Its countries continue to play an important role in the cultural, religious, political, and economic life of the world.

MIDDLE EAST: a region of the world with tremendous influence on trade and whose countries play an important worldwide role in cultural, religious, political, and economic life

Oil

A critical element in the power of the Middle East is its oil reserves. Saudi Arabia, most notably, but also Iran, Iraq, Kuwait, Qatar, Dubai, and the United Arab Emirates are huge exporters of oil. In some cases the amount of oil that one of these countries exports exceeds 90 percent of its total economic outflow. In order to optimize their economic power, oil producing countries created an international organization, the **Organization of the Petroleum Exporting Countries** or **OPEC**. Its members (not all of them in the Middle East) are:

A critical element in the power of the Middle East is its oil reserves.

- Algeria
- Angola
- Indonesia
- Iran
- Iraq
- Kuwait
- Libya/Nigeria
- Qatar
- Saudi Arabia
- United Arab Emirates
- Venezuela
- Ecuador

Most of the world requires oil in large quantities to run machines, especially vehicles such as cars, trucks, airplanes, and buses. Oil is also the raw material needed for the production of many commonplace goods, such as plastic. The vast majority of the world's developing and developed nations would be helpless without oil, and so nations will pay nearly any price to keep that oil flowing from the Middle East into their countries. The oil-rich exporters of the Middle East can hold the rest of the world hostage by increasing the price of oil even slightly, since the consumption for even a small, developed nation numbers in the billions of gallons every month.

Israel

A second area of international importance in the Middle East is the issue of **Israel**. Muslims claim **Jerusalem**, capital of the ancient civilization of Israel, as a holy city in the same way that Jews and Christians do. Muslims held **Palestine** and Jerusalem for many years, prompting the Christian Crusades that sent armies from Europe to regain the Holy Land. For hundreds of years after Christendom's failure, Muslim leaders and armies ruled these lands. After World War I, the British controlled the area and divided it in to Palestine and Jordan. In 1948, after World War II, the modern state of Israel was created.

Israel adds a religious conflict to the Middle East, not only with the Palestinians, but also with the Arab people of neighboring Egypt and Syria, and other Muslim nations. In the last 40 years, Israel has won four major wars with its neighbors, and there is some sort of armed conflict in that region on nearly a daily basis.

DOMAIN III
GOVERNMENT/CIVICS/ POLITICAL SCIENCE

PERSONALIZED STUDY PLAN

SKILL		KNOWN MATERIAL/ SKIP IT
3.1:	Political theory	☐
3.2:	United States government and politics	☐
3.3:	Comparative government and politics	☐
3.4:	International relations	☐

SKILL 3.1 Political theory: major political concepts, major political theorists, political orientations *(e.g., liberal, conservative)*

Political Science

POLITICAL SCIENCE is the study of government, including international relations, political thought and activity, and comparison of governments.

POLITICAL SCIENCE: the study of government, including international relations, political thought and activity, and comparison of governments

In addition, political science studies include values such as justice, freedom, power, and equality. There are six main fields of political study in the United States:

- Political theory and philosophy
- Comparative governments
- International relations
- Political behavior
- Public administration
- American government and politics

Political science is also important in the fields of:

- History
- Anthropology (how government affects a group's culture and relationship with other groups)
- Economics (governmental influence and regulation of producing and distributing goods and products)
- Sociology (insight into how social developments affect political life)

Important figures in political science

Aristotle and Plato

Aristotle and **Plato** were Greek philosophers who believed that politics, which was a practical science, would result in political order and that this political order would ensure maximum justice and stability.

Saint Thomas Aquinas

Saint Thomas Aquinas elaborated on Aristotle's theories and adapted them to the Christianity, emphasizing certain duties and rights of individuals in governmental processes. He also stressed government rule according to those rights and duties. Aquinas helped lay the foundation of the idea of **MODERN CONSTITUTIONALISM** by stating that government was limited by law.

MODERN CONSTITUTIONALISM: a theory that states that government is limited by law

Machiavelli

Niccolò Machiavelli was a famous politician and writer (*The Prince*) from Florence, Italy, who disregarded the ideals of Christianity in favor of realistic power politics.

For more information on Machiavelli, check out this site:

www.plato.stanford.edu/entries/machiavelli/

Thomas Hobbes

Thomas Hobbes believed that a person's life was a constant, search for power and he believed in the state's supremacy to combat this. His most famous work was *Leviathan* (1651), which was actually written as a reaction to the disorders caused by the English civil wars that had culminated with the execution of King Charles I. Hobbes perceived people as rational beings, but unlike John Locke (see below) and Thomas Jefferson (see Domain I), he had no faith in their abilities to live in harmony with one another without a government. The trouble, as Hobbes saw it, was that people are selfish, and the strong would take from the weak. However, the weak (being rational) would in turn band together against the strong. For Hobbes, the natural state of humanity is a chaotic one in which every person becomes the enemy of every other. It would become a war of all against all, with terrible consequences.

John Locke

John Locke was an important thinker on the nature of democracy. He regarded the mind of man at birth as a **tabula rasa**, a blank slate upon which experience imprints knowledge and behavior. He did not believe in the idea of intuition or theories of innate knowledge. Locke also believed that all men are born good, independent, and equal, that it is their actions that will determine their fate. Locke's views, espoused in his most important work, **Two Treatises of Civil Government** (1690), attacked the theory of the divine right of kings and the nature of the state as conceived by Thomas Hobbes. Locke argued that sovereignty did not reside in the state but with the people. The state is supreme, but only if it is bound by civil, and what he called, **natural law**.

Many of Locke's political ideas, such as those relating to natural rights, property rights, the duty of the government to protect these rights and the rule of the majority, were embodied in the Constitution of the United States.

Many of Locke's political ideas, such as those relating to natural rights, property rights, the duty of the government to protect these rights and the rule of the majority, were embodied in the Constitution of the United States. He further held that revolution was not only a right but also often an obligation. Locke also advocated a system of checks and balances in government. He envisioned a government comprised of three branches of which the legislative would be more powerful than either the executive or the judicial. He also believed in the separation of the church and state. All of these ideas were to be incorporated in the Constitution of the United States. Thus, Locke is considered in many ways the true founding father of the United States Constitution and government system.

Montesquieu and Rousseau

Montesquieu and **Rousseau** were proponents of **LIBERALISM**, the willingness to change ideas, policies, and proposals to solve current problems. They also believed that individual freedom was just as important as any community's welfare. Rousseau especially was one of the most famous and influential political theorists before the French Revolution. His most important and most studied work is *The Social Contract* (1762). He was concerned with what should be the proper form of society and government. However, unlike Hobbes, Rousseau did not view the state of nature as one of absolute chaos.

LIBERALISM: the willingness to change ideas, policies, and proposals to solve current problems, and the belief on the emphasis of individual rights

The problem as Rousseau saw it was that the natural harmony of the state of nature was due to people's intuitive goodness and not to their actual reason. Reason only developed once a civilized society was established. The intuitive goodness was easily overwhelmed, however, by arguments for institutions of social control, which likened rulers to father figures and extolled the virtues of obedience to such figures. To a remarkable extent, strong leaders, in Rousseau's judgment, have already succeeded not only in extracting obedience from the citizens that they ruled, but also in justifying such obedience as necessary.

Rousseau's most direct influence was upon the French Revolution (1789–1815). In the *Declaration of the Rights of Man and The Citizen* (1789), it explicitly recognized the sovereignty of the general will as expressed in the law. In contrast, to the American Declaration of Independence, it contains explicit mention of the obligations and duties of the citizen, such as consenting to taxes to support the military or police forces for the common good. In modern times, ideas such as Rousseau's have often been used to justify the ideas of authoritarian and totalitarian systems.

Hume and Bentham

David Hume and **Jeremy Bentham** believed that "the greatest happiness of the greatest number was the goal of politics." Hume was a pioneer of the doctrine of **empiricism**, the theory that things should be believed only when one has seen the proof forwith their own eyes. Hume was also a prime believer in the value of **skepticism**; in other words, he was naturally suspicious of things that other people told him to be true and constantly set out to discover the truth for himself.

John Stuart Mill

John Stuart Mill wrote extensively about the liberal ideas of his time. He was a progressive British philosopher and economist whose ideas came closer to socialism than to the classical capitalist ideas of **Adam Smith**. Mill constantly advocated for political and social reforms, including emancipation for women, labor organizations, and farming cooperatives.

Fitche and Hegel

Johann Gottlieb Fichte and **Friedrich Hegel** were German philosophers who contributed significantly to eighteenth century thought. Fitche and Hegel supported a liberalism that included ideas about nationalism and socialism.

SKILL 3.2 United States government and politics: constitutional underpinnings; federalism; powers, structure, and processes of national political institutions; civil liberties and civil rights, political beliefs and behaviors; political parties, interest groups, and mass media

Branches of the U.S. Government

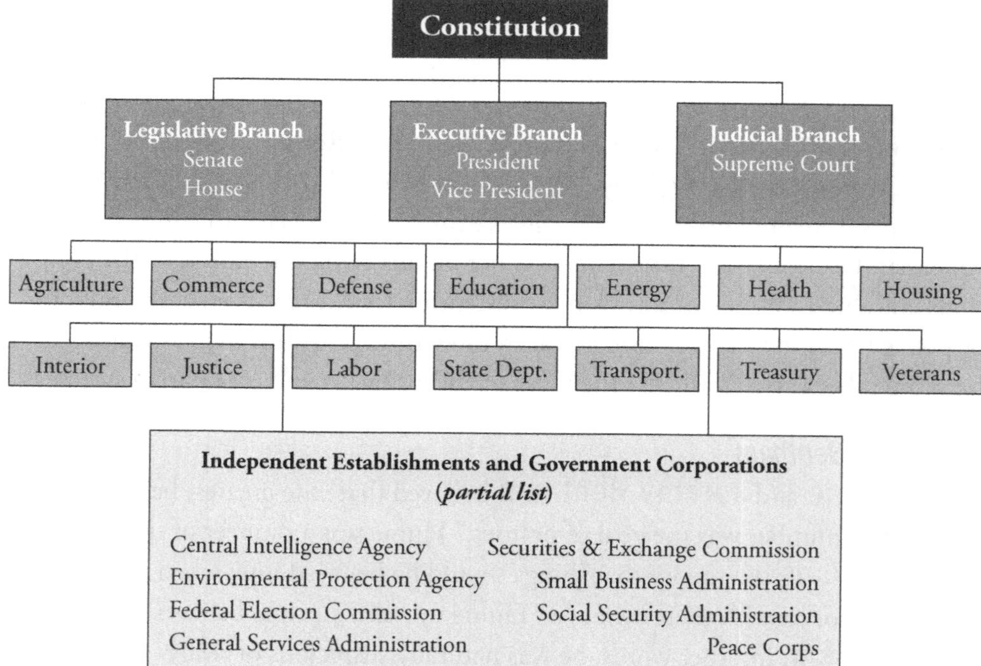

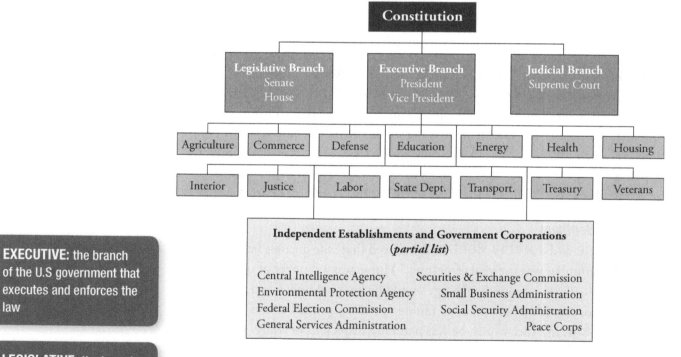

EXECUTIVE: the branch of the U.S government that executes and enforces the law

LEGISLATIVE: the branch of the U.S government that creates and establishes the law

JUDICIAL: the branch of the U.S government that interprets the law

In the United States, there are three branches of the federal government, the **EXECUTIVE**, the **LEGISLATIVE**, and the **JUDICIAL**.

Legislative

Article I of the Constitution establishes the legislative or law-making branch of the government called **Congress**. It is made up of two houses, the **House of Representatives** and the **Senate**. Voters in all states elect the members who serve in each respective House of Congress. The legislative branch is responsible for:

- Making laws
- Raising and printing money
- Regulating trade
- Establishing the postal service
- Establishing federal courts
- Approving president's appointments
- Declaring war
- Supporting the armed forces

Congress also has the power to amend the Constitution (with state ratification) and to **IMPEACH** (bring charges against) the President. Charges for impeachment are brought by the House of Representatives and are tried in the Senate.

IMPEACH: to bring charges against the sitting President

Executive

Article II of the Constitution creates the executive branch of the government. The **president** is the head of this branch, and he recommends new laws and can veto bills passed by the legislative branch. As chief of state, the president is responsible for:

- Carrying out the laws of the country
- Making treaties with advice and consent of the senate
- Appointing federal judges
- Serving as commander-in-chief of the military when it is called into service
- Appointing cabinet members
- Appointing ambassadors

Article II also explains how the president is elected. The **Electoral College** system requires citizens to vote for electors; these electors then cast their votes for a presidential candidate. In rare situations, a candidate may win the popular vote but lose the election because of the Electoral College vote.

Other members of the executive branch include the vice president (who is elected along with the president), various presidential advisors, members of the armed forces, and other civil servants of government agencies, departments and bureaus. Although the president appoints many of these positions, the legislative branch must approve them.

Judicial

Article III of the Constitution establishes the judicial branch of government headed by the **Supreme Court**. The Supreme Court has the power to rule that a law passed by the legislature or an act of the executive branch is illegal and unconstitutional. Citizens, businesses, and government officials can ask the Supreme Court to review a decision made in a lower court if someone believes that the ruling by a judge is unconstitutional.

The judicial branch also includes the federal district courts established by Congress. These courts try lawbreakers and review cases that are referred from other courts.

Federal Power versus State Power

One notable aspect of the United States government is the balance between federal and state power. The following table outlines some of the major powers possessed by each.

DELEGATION OF POWERS	
Powers delegated to the federal government	**Powers reserved to the states**
To tax	To regulate intrastate trade
To coin money	To establish local governments
To establish postal service	To protect public's health and welfare
To grant patents and copyrights	To ratify amendments
To regulate interstate & foreign commerce	To make state and local laws
To conduct elections	
To declare war	
To raise and support the armed forces	
To fix standards of weights and measures	
To conduct foreign affairs	

Concurrent powers

Here is a list of powers possessed by both federal and state governments:

- Both Congress and the states may tax
- Both may borrow money
- Both may charter banks and corporations
- Both may establish courts
- Both may make and enforce laws
- Both may take property for public purposes
- Both may spend money to provide for the public welfare

Implied powers of the federal government

Below is a list of federal powers that are implied by the Constitution:

- To establish banks or other corporations implied from delegated powers to tax, borrow, and regulate commerce
- To spend money for roads, schools, health, insurance, etc., implied from powers to establish post roads, to tax to provide for general welfare and defense, and to regulate commerce
- To create military academies, implied from powers to raise and support an armed force
- To locate and generate sources of power and sell surplus, implied from powers to dispose of government property, commerce, and war powers
- To assist and regulate agriculture, implied from power to tax and spend for general welfare and regulate commerce

Civil Liberties and Civil Rights in the United States

The terms civil liberties and civil rights are often used interchangeably, but there are some fine distinctions between the two terms.

The existence of **CIVIL LIBERTIES** in a society implies that the state has a positive role to play in assuring that all citizens will have equal protection and justice under the law. The term implies equal opportunities to exercise privileges of citizenship and to participate fully in the life of the nation, regardless of race, religion, sex, color or creed.

CIVIL RIGHTS refers to rights described as guarantees specified against the state authority, implying limitations on the actions of the state to interfere with citizens' liberties.

CIVIL LIBERTIES: this term implies equal opportunities to exercise privileges of citizenship and to participate fully in the life of the nation, regardless of race, religion, sex, color or creed

CIVIL RIGHTS: refers to rights described as guarantees specified against the state authority, implying limitations on the actions of the state to interfere with citizens' liberties

Although the term civil rights has been identified with the ideal of equality and the term civil liberties with the idea of freedom, the two concepts are really inseparable and interacting. Equality implies the proper ordering of liberty in a society so that one individual's freedom does not infringe on the rights of another's.

The beginning of civil liberties and the idea of civil rights in the United States goes back to ideas of the Greeks. The political philosophies of the ancient Greeks influenced the early British struggle for civil rights, and it was these philosophies that led many people to come to the New World in the first place. Religious freedom, political freedom, and the right to live one's life as one sees fit are basic to the American ideal. These ideas were embodied in the Declaration of Independence and the Constitution.

BILL OF RIGHTS: the first 10 amendments to the Constitution, designed to protect civil liberties

FIRST AMENDMENT: guarantees the basic rights of freedom of religion, speech, the press, and assembly

THIRD AMENDMENT: prevents Congress from forcing citizens to keep troops in their homes

SECOND AMENDMENT: guarantees the right to bear arms

FOURTH AMENDMENT: protection from unreasonable search and seizure

DUE PROCESS: the government must follow the same fair rules for everyone brought to trial

The Bill of Rights

All these ideas found their final expression in the Constitution's first 10 amendments, known as the **BILL OF RIGHTS**. In 1789, the first Congress passed these first amendments. By December 1791, three-fourths of the states had ratified them. **James Madison**, who wrote the amendments, said that the Bill of Rights does not "give" Americans these rights. Rather, he claimed that people already have these rights, as they are natural rights that belong to all human beings. The Bill of Rights simply prevents the government from taking away these rights.

Summary of Bill of Rights

The **FIRST AMENDMENT** guarantees the basic rights of freedom of religion, freedom of speech, freedom of the press, and freedom of assembly.

The next three amendments came out of the colonists' struggle with Great Britain. For example, the **THIRD AMENDMENT** prevents Congress from forcing citizens to keep troops in their homes. Before the Revolution, Great Britain tried to coerce the colonists to house soldiers. The **SECOND AMENDMENT** guarantees the right to bear arms. The **FOURTH AMENDMENT** is protection from unreasonable search and seizure.

Amendments five through eight protect citizens who are accused of crimes and are brought to trial. Every citizen has the right to **DUE PROCESS** of law, which means that the government must follow the same fair rules for everyone brought to trial. These rules include:

- The right to a trial by an impartial jury
- The right to be defended by a lawyer
- The right to a speedy trial

The last two amendments limit the powers of the federal government to those expressly stated in the Constitution. Any rights not expressly mentioned in the Constitution belong to the states or to the people.

The First Amendment (Detailed)

Freedom of Religion

Religious freedom has not been seriously threatened in the United States historically. The steadfast policy of the government has been guided by the premise that church and state should be separate. In the rare times that religious practices have been at cross-purposes with prevailing attitudes at particular times, restrictions have been placed on these practices.

Some of the most notable restrictions on religious practices are:

- Polygamy
- Animal sacrifice
- The use of mind-altering, illegal substances sometimes used in religious rituals

All recognized religious institutions are tax-exempt and, therefore, many quasi-religious groups have tried to take advantage of tax-exemption.

Freedom of Speech, Press, and Assembly

Though these rights historically have been given wide latitude, there have been occasions when they have been limited. The classic limitation on freedom of speech is the famous precept that an individual is prohibited from yelling "Fire!" in a crowded theatre. This prohibition is an example of the state saying that freedom of speech does not extend to speech that might endanger other people. There is also a prohibition against **SLANDER**, or knowingly stating a deliberate falsehood against someone.

SLANDER: knowingly stating a deliberate falsehood against someone

Perhaps the most heavily regulated of these freedoms is that of the press. There are many laws pertaining to printed material. For example, there are laws against **LIBEL**, the printing of a known falsehood.

LIBEL: the printing of a known falsehood

Times of national emergency may also contribute to various restrictions on the rights of press, speech, and assembly. Speech that would incite people to overthrow the government or resist lawful authority has, at times, been restricted.

Criticism

The legal system has also undergone a number of serious changes with the interpretation of some constitutional guarantees. A number of organizations are champions for civil liberties and civil rights in this country. The main criticism of these groups, however, is whether they are really protecting rights or are attempting to create new rights. Rights come with responsibility and respect for the public order.

The future of civil rights and civil liberties

How best to move forward with ensuring civil liberties and civil rights for all continues to dominate the national debate. Recently, issues seem to revolve not around individual rights but group rights. At the forefront of the debate is whether some specific remedies like **affirmative action**, **quotas**, or **gerrymandering** are fair or unfair.

It is a testament to the American system that it has been able to enter into these debates and to find solutions to come out stronger.

It is a testament to the American system that it has been able to enter into these debates, find solutions, and come out stronger. That the United States has the longest single constitutional history in the modern era is just one reason to be optimistic about the future of American liberty.

Voting

The terms **suffrage** and **franchise** refer to voting or the right to vote. Although elections are associated with democratic practices, various limitations have been placed on the right to vote throughout history. These have included property qualifications, poll taxes, residency requirements, race, and gender.

History of voting

In 1787, the Constitution of the United States provided for the election of the chief executive in Article II, Section I, and members of the national legislature in Article I, Sections II and III. A number of election abuses, however, led to the adoption of what was known as the Australian or **secret ballot** and the practice of registering voters prior to the election.

Voting machines were first used in the United States in 1892. During the nineteenth century, the electorate in the United States grew considerably. Most of the states enfranchised all white male adults, although the so-called poll tax was retained. The Twenty-fourth Amendment (ratified in 1964) to the Constitution abolished the poll tax. The Fifteenth Amendment, ratified in 1870, extended the vote to former slaves. In the period after the Civil War known as Reconstruction, many African Americans were elected to high office for the first time in American history.

Citizens and voting

Average citizens can participate in the political process by voting. Since the ratification of the Twenty-sixth Amendment in 1971, U.S. citizens who are at least 18 years old are eligible to vote. Elections are held at regular intervals at all levels of government, allowing citizens to weigh in on both national and local matters.

Elections are held at regular intervals at all levels of government, allowing citizens to weigh in on both national and local matters.

Citizens wishing to engage in the political process to a greater degree have several paths open to them, such as participating in local government or a **caucus**. Counties, states, cities, and towns are governed by locally elected boards or councils that meet publicly. At these meetings, citizens are usually able to bring their concerns and express their opinions. Citizens may also run for local elections, join a governing board, or seek support for higher office.

Political Parties and Elections

POLITICAL PARTIES endorse certain platforms that express social and political goals, and support member candidates in election campaigns. Political parties use volunteer labor, and these supporters make telephone calls, distribute printed material, and campaign for the causes and candidates. Political parties also solicit donations; contributing money to a political party is another form of participation citizens can undertake.

POLITICAL PARTIES: endorse certain platforms that express social and political goals, and support member candidates in election campaigns

Another form of political activity is to support an **issue-related political group**. Several political groups work actively to sway public opinion on various issues or on behalf of a segment of American society. These groups may have representatives who meet with state and federal legislators to **LOBBY** them—to provide them with information on an issue and persuade them to take favorable action.

LOBBY: the act of providing state or federal legislators with information on an issue and attempting to persuade them to take favorable action

Campaigning

Campaigning can be expensive. While volunteers on a **political campaign** are plentiful, campaigns also need to pay campaign specialists. They also need money to buy or rent all of the tangible and intangible things that are needed to power a political campaign, including:

- Office supplies
- Meeting places
- Transportation vehicles
- Advertising

Advertising campaigns

Television is the most expensive kind of advertising, but it also has the potential to reach the widest audience. Television commercials have the potential to reach millions of viewers. Other forms of advertising include:

- Radio and Web advertisements
- Signs

- Billboards
- Good, old-fashioned flyers

Financing campaigns

A candidate might have a significant amount of money in his or her own personal coffers. In rare cases, the candidate finances the entire campaign. However, the most prevalent source of money is **outside donations.**

The largest source of campaign finance money comes from so-called special interests.

The largest source of campaign finance money, however, comes from so-called **special interests.** For example, a large company, such as an oil company or a manufacturer of electronic goods, will want to keep prices or tariffs down and therefore will want to make sure that laws raising those prices or tariffs are not passed. To this end, the company will contribute money to the campaigns of candidates who are likely to vote to keep those prices or tariffs down. A candidate is not obligated to accept such a donation, of course, and is not obligated to vote in favor of the interests of the special interest.

Political action committees and campaigns

Social groups have many dedicated individuals who organize themselves into **political action committees**, attend meetings and rallies, and work to make sure that their message gets out to a wide audience. They will also use methods of spreading the word such as media advertising on behalf of their chosen candidates. The candidates, who will get the benefit of the exposure, no doubt welcome this kind of expenditure.

The Media

A free press is essential to maintaining responsibility and civic-mindedness in government and in the rest of society.

A free press is essential to maintaining responsibility and civic-mindedness in government and in the rest of society. The broadcast, print, and electronic media serve as social and government watchdogs.

First and foremost, the media reports on the actions taken and encouraged by leaders of the government. In many cases, these actions are common knowledge. Policy debates, discussions on controversial issues, struggles against foreign powers in economic and wartime endeavors—all are fodder for media reports. The First Amendment guarantees media in America the right to report.

Lawmakers are responsible for public legislative policy. At the same time, many company owners are responsible for public economic policy. If a corporation is stealing money from its employees or shareholders, then those employees, shareholders, and the American public at large need to know about it. Such reporting is not only informative but also usually leads to indictments, prosecutions, and jail terms for the perpetrators of such economic crimes.

Media relations

Public officials will hire one person, a department of employees, or perhaps an entire business to conduct **PUBLIC RELATIONS** efforts. The firm will write press releases, arrange media events, and do everything else to keep the politician's name in front of the public for name recognition.

PUBLIC RELATIONS: the business of using various media to keep a politician's name in front of the public to increase recognition

Evaluating Internet Sources

Internet opportunities include news Web sites as well as personal Web sites. Some sites, however, may not have undergone the same sort of scrutiny as comparable efforts released by major media outlets to newspapers, radio, and television. Those media processes have editors and fact checkers that will verify information before it is released. In contrast, more informal Web publishers, such as **bloggers**, seldom use editors or fact checkers before publishing. One way to evaluate Internet sources is by looking for scholarly sites to verify information.

One way to evaluate Internet sources is by looking for scholarly sites to verify information.

SKILL 3.3 Comparative government and politics: forms of government *(e.g., parliamentary, federal)*; **major regime types** *(e.g., democracy, autocracy)*; **major types of electoral systems; foreign policy**

Forms of Government

Autocracy and Oligarchy

Autocracies and oligarchies are systems of government where a single person (**AUTOCRACY**) or a small group of people (**OLIGARCHY**) holds the power of the state. Types of autocracies/oligarchies includes:

AUTOCRACY: a system of government in which power is held by a single person

OLIGARCHY: a system of government in which power is held by a small group of people

- **Dictatorship:** This is the rule by an individual (autocrat) or small group of individuals (oligarchs) that centralizes all political control in itself and enforces its will, often with a terrorist police force.
- **Monarchy:** This system is the rule of a nation by a monarch (a nonelected and usually hereditary leader), most often a king or queen. It may or may not be accompanied by some measure of democratic open institutions and elections at various levels. A modern example is Great Britain, where it is called a **constitutional monarchy**.
- **Totalitarianism:** This system doesn't recognize the right for any aspect of society to be outside the influence of the state. Such a government sees itself as having a legitimate concern with and authority in all levels of human existence. This applies not only to freedom of speech or press but even to social

and religious institutions. This type of regime tries to achieve a complete social conformity to its ideals. Thus, those ideologies that presume to speak to all of society's ills, such as Communism and Fascism, look to this model for what they attempt to create in society. As Benito Mussolini said, "Nothing outside of the state; nothing instead of the state." A totalitarian government is authoritarian, but an authoritarian system does not have to be totalitarian.

- **Authoritarianism:** This system may leave some autonomous institutions alone, such as the church, so long as they do not interfere with the state authority. This model can be seen in the history of Central and South America, where regimes (usually representing the interests of the upper classes) came to power and instituted dictatorships that sought to concentrate all political power in a few hands.
- **Fascism:** This is a belief as well as a political system, consisting of a one party state, centralized political control, and a repressive police system. It does tolerate private ownership of the means of production, though it maintains tight overall control. Central to its belief is the idolization of the leader, a "Cult of Personality," and most often an expansionist ideology. Some examples are German Nazism and Italian Fascism.

Democracy

DIRECT DEMOCRACY: involves all the people in a given area coming together to vote and decide on issues that will affect them

INDIRECT DEMOCRACY: involves much larger areas and populations and involves the sending of representatives to a legislative body to vote on issues affecting the people

The name for this form of government comes from the Greek for "the rule of the people." The two most prevalent types are direct and indirect democracy. **DIRECT DEMOCRACY** usually involves all the people in a given area coming together to vote and decide on issues that will affect them. It is used only when the population involved is relatively small, for instance a local town meeting. An **INDIRECT DEMOCRACY** involves much larger areas and populations and involves the sending of representatives to a legislative body to vote on issues affecting the people. Such a system can be composed of a parliamentary or presidential system. The United States follows an indirect or representative democracy.

- **Parliamentary System**: This is a system of government that has a legislature and usually involves a multiplicity of political parties and often coalitions. There is division between the head of state and head of government. The head of government is usually known as a Prime Minister; he or she is also usually the head of the largest party. The head of government and cabinet usually both sit and vote in the parliament. The head of state is most often an elected president, though in the case of a constitutional monarchy like Great Britain, the sovereign may take the place of a president as head of state. This type of government may fall when a majority in parliament votes "no confidence" in the government.

- **Presidential System**: This is a system of government with a legislature that may have a few or many political parties; there is no division between head of state and head of government, as the president serves in both capacities. The president is elected either by direct or indirect election. A president and cabinet usually do not sit or vote in the legislature, and the president may or may not be the head of the largest political party. A president can thus rule even without a majority in the legislature and can only be removed from office as the result of an election or for major infractions of the law.

SKILL 3.4 International relations: theories of international relations *(e.g., realism, liberalism)*; international relations in practice *(e.g., conflict, cooperation, diplomacy)*; powers and problems of international organizations and international law

International Relations

There are many theories of **international relations**, all of which seek to describe how sovereign countries interact, or should interact, with one another.

Primary schools of thought

There are four of the primary schools of thought in international theory:

1. **Realism** is an international relations theory that holds the nation-state as the basic unit and recognizes no international authority above individual nations. Realism is based on the assumption that nations act only in their own self-interest to preserve their own security. Realists also contend that international relations are based on the relative military and economic power between nations.
2. **Liberalism** allows for the cooperation of several states working in common interest. Instead of the Realist belief that states act based on their capabilities, Liberalism holds that states act based on their preferences.
3. **Institutionalism** is a theory of international relations that holds that there is a structure to the interactions of nations that determine how they will act. The rules that nations follow in making international decisions are called institutions. Institutions can give structure, distribute power, and provide incentives for international cooperation.
4. **Constructivism** recognizes the role that ideas and perceptions play in international relations. Constructivism makes note of traditional relations

between countries and their relative goals, identities, and perceived threats. Constructivism recognizes, for instance, that a country building up its military is likely to be taken as more of a threat by that country's traditional antagonists than by its allies.

Diplomacy

DIPLOMACY: when nations formally recognize each other and station a group of officials in one another's countries to provide formal representation on international matters

Countries sometimes engage in informal diplomacy between private individuals when they wish to discuss common issues without taking official positions.

In practice, international relations are often conducted through **DIPLOMACY**. Nations that formally recognize one another station a group of **diplomats**, led by an **ambassador**, in one another's countries to provide formal representation on international matters.

Diplomats convey official information on the policies and positions of their home countries to the host countries where they are stationed. Diplomats are also involved in negotiating international agreements on issues such as trade and the environment, as well as resolving conflicts. Countries sometimes engage in informal diplomacy between private individuals when they wish to discuss common issues without taking official positions.

Examples of diplomacy

Diplomacy also takes place within international organizations such as the United Nations. Member nations send diplomatic representatives to the U.N. and have input into forming international policy. While member countries agree to abide by U.N. resolutions as a condition of membership, there is often dissent over these resolutions in practice.

The U.N. has the ability to impose economic and other sanctions on its members for failing to follow its decisions. Though they have other types of enforcement at their disposal, these have proven to be problematic. The U.N. also has the ability to raise military forces from its member countries, and these forces have historically been limited to peacekeeping missions and not active military campaigns.

DOMAIN IV
GEOGRAPHY

PERSONALIZED STUDY PLAN

SKILL		KNOWN MATERIAL/ SKIP IT
4.1:	The world in spatial terms	☐
4.2:	Places and regions	☐
4.3:	Physical systems	☐
4.4:	Human systems	☐
4.5:	Environment and society	☐
4.6:	The uses of geography	☐

SKILL 4.1 The world in spatial terms: use of maps to acquire, process, and report information from a spatial perspective; longitude and latitude and their purposes; map projection, map type, and scale

Geography

GEOGRAPHY is the study of people, places, and environments. It involves studying location and how living things and Earth's features are distributed throughout the Earth. This area of study includes where animals, people, and plants live and the effects of their relationship with Earth's physical features. Geographers also explore the locations of Earth's features and how they came to be.

GEOGRAPHY: the study of people, places, and environments

Notable geographers and organizations

Some of the more important geographers include:

- **Eratosthenes**, an ancient Greek mathematician who calculated the size of the Earth
- **Strabo**, who wrote Geographica, a 17-volume description of the ancient world
- **Ptolemy**, who contributed his skills in mapping and theories from studies in astronomy to geographic knowledge

Explorers have contributed to the study of geography as well. **Christopher Columbus** was known for his famous first voyage, when he intended to sail west to find the riches of the east but found the Western Hemisphere instead. **Marco Polo**, **Vasco da Gama**, and **Magellan** were three of many explorers and colonizers who contributed to geographic knowledge.

The **NATIONAL GEOGRAPHIC SOCIETY** is publisher of the National Geographic magazine and funds expeditions and other activities furthering geographic education.

NATIONAL GEOGRAPHIC SOCIETY: publisher of the National Geographic magazine and funds expeditions and other activities furthering geographic education

Breaking down geographical studies

What geographers study can be broken down into four parts:

- **Location:** The exact site of anything on the Earth
- **Spatial relations:** Relationships of Earth's features, places, and groups of people with one another due to their location
- **Regional characteristics:** Characteristics of a place such as landform and climate, types of plants and animals, kinds of people who live there, and how people use the land
- **Forces that change the Earth:** Human activities and natural forces

Geographical studies are also divided into four categories:

- **Regional:** Elements and characteristics of a place or region
- **Topical:** One Earth feature or one human activity occurring throughout the entire world
- **Physical:** Earth's physical features, what creates and changes them, their relationships to each other as well as human activities
- **Human:** Human activity patterns and how they relate to the environment including political, cultural, historical, urban, and social geographical fields of study

Geography and the world

Geography is the study of the Earth, its people, and how these people adapt to life on Earth and use its resources. It is connected to history, economics, political science, sociology, anthropology, and even archaeology. Geography not only deals with people and the Earth today but also questions such as:

- How did it all begin?
- What is the background of the people of an area?
- What kind of government or political system do they have?
- How does that affect their ways of producing goods and the distribution of them?
- What kind of relationships do these people have with other groups?
- How is the way they live their lives affected by their physical environment?
- In what ways do they effect change in their way of living?

The examination of the spatial organization of the places where people live is likewise important to geography. For example, in a city, where are the factories and heavy industry buildings? Are they near airports or train stations? Are they on the edge of town, near major roads? What about housing developments? Are they near these industries, or are they far away? Where are the other industry buildings? Where are the schools and hospitals and parks? What about the police and fire stations? How close are homes to each of these things? Towns and especially cities are routinely organized into neighborhoods so that each house or home is near to most things that its residents might need on a regular basis. This means that large cities have multiple schools, hospitals, grocery stores, and fire stations.

Also related to this study of spatial relation is the distance between cities, towns, villages, or settlements. Population settlement patterns achieve **megalopolis** standards, with no clear boundaries from one town to the next. Other, more sparsely populated areas have towns that are few and far between and have relatively few people in them.

The importance of spatial relationships has changed somewhat with the advent of flight. The ability to fly has brought global commerce and goods exchange to a level never before seen. Foods can be flown around the world and, with the aid of refrigeration techniques, be kept fresh enough to sell in markets nearly everywhere. The same is true of medicine and weapons. This has totally changed the dynamics of spatial relationships.

The Use of Maps

Illustrations are used because it is often easier to demonstrate a given idea visually instead of orally. Among the more common illustrations used are various types of **maps**, **graphs**, and **charts**; photographs and **globes** are useful as well.

Map design

The disadvantage of a map is that maps are flat and the Earth is a sphere. It is impossible to reproduce an object shaped like a sphere exactly on a flat surface. In order to put the Earth's features onto a map, they must be stretched in some way. This stretching is called **DISTORTION**.

DISTORTION: when features of the Earth's surface are stretched and changed to fit on a map

Cartographers, or mapmakers, understand the problems of distortion, and they design maps so that there is as little distortion as possible.

Projections

The process of putting the features of the Earth onto a flat surface is called **PROJECTION**. Map projections are made in a number of ways, most notably by projecting an image onto a cylinder, cone, or plane.

PROJECTION: process of putting the features of the Earth onto a flat surface

- **Cylindrical Projections:** These projections are made by taking a cylinder of paper and wrapping it around a globe. A light is then used to project the globe's features onto the paper. The distortion is minimized the most where the paper touches the globe. For example, if the paper is wrapped so that it touches the globe at the equator, the map from this projection would have just a little distortion near the equator. In moving north or south of the equator, the distortion would increase. The best-known and most widely used cylindrical projection is the **Mercator Projection**. Gerardus Mercator, a Flemish mapmaker, first developed it in 1569.
- **Conical Projections:** This projection is utilizes a cone of paper. The cone is made so that it touches a globe at the base of the cone only. It can also be made so that it cuts through part of the globe in two different places. As with

a cylindrical projection, the least amount of distortion occurs where the paper touches the globe. If the cone touches at two different points, there is some distortion at both of them. Conical projections are most often used to map areas in the **middle latitudes**. Maps of the United States are most often made in this way because most of the country lies within middle latitudes.

- **Flat-Plane Projections:** These are made with a flat piece of paper that touches the globe at one point only, and the areas near this point show little distortion. Flat-plane projections are often used to show the areas of the north and south poles. One such flat projection is called a **Gnomonic Projection**. On this kind of map, all meridians appear as straight lines. Gnomonic projections are useful because any straight line drawn between points on it forms a **Great-Circle Route**.

Great-Circle Routes

GREAT-CIRCLE ROUTES: find the shortest route between two points by simply stretching a string from one point to the other

GREAT-CIRCLE ROUTES find the shortest route between two points by simply stretching a string from one point to the other. However, if the string was extended in reality, so that it took into effect the globe's curvature, it would then make a **great circle**. A great circle is any circle that cuts a sphere, such as the globe, into two equal parts. Because of distortion, most maps do not show great-circle routes as straight lines. Gnomonic projections, however, do show the shortest distance between the two places as a straight line, and because of this, they are valuable for navigation. They are also called **Great-Circle Sailing Maps**.

Parts of a map

To properly analyze a given map, one must be familiar with the various parts and symbols that most modern maps use. For the most part, this is standardized with different maps using similar parts and symbols. These can include:

- **The Title:** All maps should have a title. The title describes what information can be found on the map.
- **The Legend:** Most maps have a legend. A legend (also called a *map key*) tells the reader about the various symbols that are used on that particular map and what the symbols represent.
- **The Grid:** A grid is a series of horizontal and vertical lines that are used to find exact places and locations on the map. There are several different kinds of grid systems in use. However, most maps do use the longitude and latitude system, also known as the **Geographic Grid System**.
- **Compass Rose:** Most maps have some directional system to show which way the map is being presented. Often on a map, a small compass will be present with arrows showing the four basic directions: north, south, east, and west.

- **The Scale:** This is used to show the relationship between a unit of measurement on the map versus the real world measure on the Earth. Maps are drawn to many different scales. Some maps will show a lot of detail for a small area, while others show a greater span of distance. Whichever is being used, one should always be aware of the scale. For instance, the scale could be 1 inch = 10 miles for a small area or, for a map showing the whole world, it might have a scale where 1 inch = 1,000 miles.

Properties of maps

Maps have four main properties:

1. Size of the areas shown on the map
2. Shapes of the areas
3. Consistent scales
4. Straight line directions

A map can be drawn so that it is correct in one or more of these properties. No map can be correct in all of them.

Equal areas

In an **EQUAL AREA MAP**, the meridians and parallels are drawn so that the areas shown have the same proportions as they do on the Earth. For example, Greenland is about 118th the size of South America; thus, it will be shown as 118th the size on an equal area map. The Mercator projection is an example of a map that does not have equal areas. Greenland would appear to be about the same size of South America because Greenland lies near the North Pole.

EQUAL AREA MAP: a map whose meridians and parallels are drawn so that the areas shown have the same proportions as they do on the Earth

Conformality (correct shapes)

CONFORMAL MAPS are as close as possible to true shapes. The United States is often shown by a **Lambert Conformal Conic Projection Map**.

CONFORMAL MAPS: maps that are as close as possible to true shapes

Consistent scales

Many maps attempt to use the same scale on all parts of the map. Generally, this is easier when maps show a relatively small part of the Earth's surface. For example, a map of Florida might be a **CONSISTENT SCALE MAP**. Generally, maps showing large areas are not consistent-scale maps; this is because of distortion. Often such maps will have two scales noted in the key. One scale, for example, might be accurate to measure distances between points along the Equator. Another might be then used to measure distances between the North Pole and the South Pole.

CONSISTENT SCALE MAP: maps that attempt to use the same scale on all parts of the map

Types of maps

Maps showing physical features often try to show information about the elevation, or **relief**, of the land. **ELEVATION** is the distance above or below the sea level. The elevation is usually shown with colors. For instance, all areas on a map that are at a certain level will be shown in the same color.

ELEVATION: the distance above or below the sea level

RELIEF MAPS show the shape of the land surface as flat, rugged, or steep. Relief maps usually give more detail than simply showing the overall elevation of the land's surface. Relief can be shown with colors or **contour lines**. These lines connect all points of a land surface which are the same height surrounding the particular area of land.

RELIEF MAPS: show the shape of the land surface as flat, rugged, or steep

THEMATIC MAPS are used to show more specific information, often on a single theme, or topic. Thematic maps show the distribution or amount of something over a certain given area. Population density, climate, economic information, cultural, election or political information, are common examples of information shown on a thematic map.

THEMATIC MAPS: used to show more specific information, often on a single theme, or topic

SKILL 4.2 **Places and regions: location of major regions, countries and cities of the world; formal, functional, and perceptual characteristics of places; cultural diffusion and spatial patterns of economic activities**

Settlements and Communities

Determination and placement of settlements

SETTLEMENTS are the cradles of culture, political structure, education, and resource management. The relative placement of these settlements or communities are shaped by:

SETTLEMENTS: the cradles of culture, political structure, education, and resource management

- Proximity to natural resources
- Movement of raw materials
- Production of finished products
- Availability of a work force
- Delivery of finished products

The composition of communities, at least to some extent, will be determined by:

- Shared values
- Language

- Culture
- Religion
- Subsistence

Settlements begin in areas that offer the natural resources to support life: food and water. When an ability to manage the environment develops, one will develop a concentration of population. With the ability to transport raw materials and finished products comes mobility; with increasing technology and the rise of industrial centers comes a migration of the workforce.

Cities

Cities are the major hubs of human settlement. Almost half of the world population now lives in cities, and these percentages are much higher in developed regions. Established cities continue to grow, with the fastest growth occurring in developing areas. Metropolitan regions are made up of urban and suburban areas. In some places, cities and urban locales have become interconnected into megalopoli (e.g., Tokyo-Kawasaki-Yokohama). **Megalopolis** is a Greek word for great city.

In North America, the wealthiest economic groups tend to live outside the cities; the opposite is true in Latin America.

In North America, the wealthiest economic groups tend to live outside the cities; the opposite is true in Latin America.

There are also significant differences among the cities of the world in terms of connectedness to other cities. While European and North American cities tend to be well linked both by transportation and communication connections, these connections are limited in other places of the world. With the advent of the cell phone, communications have increased. This is significant, as rural areas must be connected via communication and transportation in order to provide food and raw materials to urban areas.

SKILL 4.3 Physical systems: processes that shape the pattern of the Earth's surface including plate tectonics, geomorphic processes, erosion, transportation, and deposition; characteristics and spatial distribution of ecosystems on Earth's surface; weather systems; climate patterns

The Earth's Surface

The Earth's surface is made up of 70 percent water and 30 percent land. Physical features of the land surface include mountains, hills, plateaus, valleys, and plains. Other minor landforms include deserts, deltas, canyons, mesas, basins, foothills, marshes and swamps. Earth's water features include oceans, seas, lakes, rivers, and canals.

Physical land features

Some major physical land features are described below:

- **Mountains** are landforms with rather steep slopes at least 2,000 feet or more above sea level. Mountains are found in groups called chains or ranges. At least one range can be found on six of the Earth's seven continents. North America has the Appalachian and Rocky Mountains; South America, the Andes; Asia, the Himalayas; Australia, the Great Dividing Range; Europe, the Alps; and Africa, the Atlas, Ahaggar, and Drakensburg Mountains.
- **Hills** are elevated landforms that are not as high as mountains. They are found everywhere on Earth including Antarctica, where they are covered by ice.
- **Plateaus** are elevated landforms usually level on top. Depending on location, they range from being an area that is very cold to one that is cool and healthful. Some plateaus are dry because mountains that keep out any moisture surround them. The Kenya Plateau in East Africa is a notable example of a plateau that is very cool. The plateau extending north from the Himalayas is extremely dry, while those in Antarctica and Greenland are covered with ice and snow. Sometimes plateaus are also called **mesas**.
- **Plains** are described as areas of flat or slightly rolling land, usually lower than the landforms next to them. Sometimes called lowlands (and sometimes located along seacoasts), they support the majority of the world's people. Some are found inland, and large rivers have formed many. This resulted in extremely fertile soil for successful cultivation of crops and numerous large settlements of people. In North America, the vast plains areas extend from the Gulf of Mexico north to the Arctic Ocean and between the Appalachian and Rocky Mountains. In Europe, rich plains extend east from Great Britain into central Europe on into the Siberian region of Russia. Plains in river valleys are found in China (the Yangtze River valley), India (the Ganges River valley), and Southeast Asia (the Mekong River valley).
- **Valleys** are land areas that are found between hills and mountains. Some have gentle slopes containing trees and plants. An example of a valley is the fertile Central Valley in California. Other valleys have very steep walls; these are referred to as canyons. One famous example is Arizona's Grand Canyon of the Colorado River.
- **Deltas** are areas of lowlands formed by soil and sediment deposited at the mouths of rivers. The soil is generally very fertile and most of these fertile river

deltas are important crop-growing areas. One well-known example is the delta of Egypt's Nile River, known for its production of cotton.

- **Basins** are low areas drained by rivers or low spots in mountains.
- **Foothills** are generally considered a low series of hills found between a plain and a mountain range.
- **Marshes and swamps** are wet lowlands providing growth of rushes and reeds.

Water features

OCEANS are the largest bodies of water on the planet. The five oceans of the Earth are:

OCEANS: the largest bodies of water on the planet

1. **Atlantic Ocean**, separating North and South America from Africa and Europe
2. **Pacific Ocean**, covering almost one-third of the entire surface of the Earth and separating North and South America from Asia and Australia
3. **Indian Ocean**, touching Africa, Asia, and Australia
4. **Arctic Ocean**, ice-filled and extending from North America and Europe to the North Pole
5. **Southern Ocean**, also known as the Antarctic Ocean

The waters of the Atlantic, Pacific, and Indian Oceans also touch the shores of Antarctica. Included in the features of the oceans are coral reefs; **atolls**, which are formed by corals around the edge of volcanic craters; and volcanic islands.

SEAS are usually saline and are smaller than oceans. They are surrounded by land. Some examples include the Mediterranean Sea, found between Europe, Asia, and Africa, and the Caribbean Sea, touching the West Indies and South and Central America. The Caspian Sea is the largest sea.

SEAS: bodies of water that are usually saline and are smaller than oceans; they are surrounded by land

A **LAKE** is a body of freshwater (usually) surrounded by land. Over 60 percent of lakes are located in Canada. There are more than a dozen types of lakes. Lake Superior in the U.S. is an example of a rift lake.

LAKE: a body of freshwater (usually) surrounded by land

RIVERS, considered a nation's lifeblood, usually begin as very small streams, formed by melting snow and rainfall, flowing from higher to lower land, emptying into a larger body of water, usually a sea or an ocean. Examples of important rivers for the people and countries affected by and/or dependent on them include: the

RIVERS: begin as very small streams, formed by melting snow and rainfall, flowing from higher to lower land, emptying into a larger body of water, usually a sea or an ocean

- Nile, Niger, and Zaire Rivers of Africa

- Rhine, Danube, and Thames Rivers of Europe
- Yangtze, Ganges, Mekong, Hwang He, and Irrawaddy Rivers of Asia
- Murray-Darling in Australia
- Orinoco in South America

River systems are made up of large rivers and numerous smaller rivers, or **tributaries**, that flow into them. Some examples include the vast **Amazon River** system in South America and the **Mississippi River** system in the United States.

CANALS: manmade water passages constructed to connect two larger bodies of water

CANALS are manmade water passages constructed to connect two larger bodies of water. Two famous examples include the **Panama Canal** across Panama's isthmus, connecting the Atlantic and Pacific Oceans, and the Suez Canal in the Middle East between Africa and the Arabian Peninsula, connecting the Red and Mediterranean Seas.

Climate and Weather

WEATHER: refers to the atmosphere, including temperature, air pressure, wind, and moisture (precipitation)

WEATHER refers to the atmosphere, including temperature, air pressure, wind, and moisture (precipitation). Precipitation can be rain, snow, hail, or sleet.

CLIMATE: average weather or daily weather conditions for a specific region or location over a long or extended period of time

CLIMATE is average weather or daily weather conditions for a specific region or location over a long or extended period of time. Studying the climate of an area includes gathering information about the area's monthly and yearly temperatures and its monthly and yearly amounts of precipitation. In addition, a characteristic of an area's climate is the length of its growing season. Different climates relate to variations in:

- Latitude
- Amount of moisture
- Temperatures in land and water
- Land surface

The regions of climates are divided according to latitudes:

- 0–23½ degrees are the **low latitudes**
- 23½–66½ degrees are the **middle latitudes**
- 66½ degrees to the Poles are the **high latitudes**

Low latitudes

Low latitudes are composed of the **tropical rainforest**, **savanna**, and **desert** climates.

Tropical rainforest

The tropical rainforest climate is found in equatorial lowlands and is hot and wet. There is sun, extreme heat, and rain every day. Although daily temperatures rarely rise above 90 degrees F, the daily humidity is always high.

Savannas

North and south of the tropical rainforests are the tropical grasslands called savannas, or—the "lands of two seasons." They have a dry winter season and a wet summer season.

Deserts

Further north and south of the savannas are the deserts. These areas are the hottest and driest parts of the Earth, receiving less than 10 inches of rain a year. These areas have extreme temperatures between night and day. After the sun sets, temperatures drop by 50 degrees or more. Among the better-known deserts are Africa's large Sahara Desert, the Arabian Desert on the Arabian Peninsula, and the Australian Outback, which covers roughly one-third of the continent.

Middle latitudes

The middle latitudes contain the **Mediterranean climate**, **humid-sub-tropical**, **humid-continental**, **marine**, **steppe**, and **desert** climates.

Mediterranean

The Mediterranean climate is the climate of the lands bordering the Mediterranean Sea; a small portion of southwestern Africa; areas in southern and southwestern Australia; a small part of the Ukraine near the Black Sea; central Chile; and Southern California. The summers are hot and dry, the winters are mild. The growing season usually lasts all year, and the small amount of rain that this climate does receive comes during the winter months. The Mediterranean climate occurs between 30 and 40 degrees north and south latitude on the western coasts of countries.

Humid subtropical

The humid subtropical climate is found north and south of the tropics and is moist. The areas with this type of climate are found on the southeastern coastal area of continents and can be found in Japan, mainland China, Australia, Africa, South America, and the United States. Warm ocean currents are found there, and the winds that blow across these currents bring in warm moist air all year round. Long, warm summers; short, mild winters; and a long growing season allow for different crops to be grown several times a year. All contribute to the productivity of this climate type, which supports more people than any of the other climates.

Marine

The marine climate is found in Western Europe, the British Isles, the Pacific Northwest, the western coast of Canada, southern Chile, southern New Zealand, and southeastern Australia. The lands are either near water or surrounded by it. The ocean winds are wet and warm, bringing a mild, rainy climate to these areas. In the summer, the daily temperatures average at or below 70 degrees F. During the winter, because of the warming effect of the ocean waters, the temperatures rarely fall below freezing.

Humid continental

In northern and central United States, northern China, south-central and southeastern Canada, and the western and southeastern parts of the former Soviet Union is the "climate of four seasons," the humid continental climate. Cold winters, hot summers, and enough rainfall to grow a variety of crops are the major characteristics of this climate. In areas where this climate type is found are some of the world's best farmlands, as well as important activities such as trading and mining. The amount of distance a place is inland, away from the coasts, determines differences in temperatures throughout the year.

Steppes

The steppe or prairie climate is located in the interiors of Asia and North America. These dry flatlands are located far from ocean breezes. Although the summers are hot and the winters are cold as in the humid continental climate, the big difference is rainfall. In the steppe climate, rainfall is light and uncertain. Totals of around 10–20 inches a year, mainly in spring and summer, are normal.

In areas of less rain, the steppes or prairies become deserts. These climates exist in the Gobi Desert of Asia, central and western Australia, southwestern United States, and in Pakistan, Argentina, and Africa, south of the Equator.

High latitudes

The two major climates found in the high latitudes are **tundra** and **taiga**.

Tundra

The word tundra, meaning "marshy plain," is a Russian word and aptly describes the climatic conditions in the northern areas of Russia, Europe, and Canada. The winters are extremely cold and very long. Most of the year, the ground is frozen, but it becomes rather mushy during the very short summer months. Less snow falls in the area of the tundra than in the eastern part of the United States. Because of extreme cold, very few people live there and no crops can be raised. Nonetheless, many plants and animals are still found in this climate.

Taiga

The taiga is the northern forest region and is located south of the tundra. The Russian word taiga means "forest." The world's largest forestlands are found here along with vast mineral wealth, fur-bearing animals, and marshes and swamps. The climate is extreme, and few people live here because raising crops is almost impossible due to the extremely short growing season. The winter temperatures are colder and the summer temperatures are hotter than those in the tundra because the taiga climate region is farther from the waters of the Arctic Ocean. The taiga is found in the northern parts of Russia, Sweden, Norway, Finland, Canada, and Alaska.

Vertical climates

A climate unique to areas with high mountains is called a **VERTICAL CLIMATE**. Temperatures, crops, vegetation, and human activities change with the elevation. An extreme example is Azerbaijan, where the diversity of 9 of the 11 types of climates can be experienced. Azerbaijan is located at the crossroads of eastern Europe and western Asia.

VERTICAL CLIMATE: a climate unique to areas with high mountains

Movement and Shifting of the Earth

Plate tectonics

PLATE TECTONICS describe the geological theory that explains the large movements of the solid portions of the Earth's crust floating on the molten mantle. There are 10 major tectonic plates with several smaller plates. The surface of the Earth can be drastically affected at the boundaries of these plates.

PLATE TECTONICS: describe the geological theory that explains the large movements of the solid portions of the Earth's crust floating on the molten mantle

Plate boundaries

There are three types of plate boundaries:

1. **Convergent boundaries** occur when plates are moving toward one another. When this happens, the two plates collide and push up against one another; this is called a **continental collision**. When one plate slides under the other, it is called **subduction**. Continental collisions can create high mountain ranges, such as the Andes and Himalayas. Subduction often results in volcanic activity along the boundary, as in the Ring of Fire along the northern coasts of the Pacific Ocean.

2. **Divergent boundaries** occur where plates are moving away from one another creating **rifts** in the surface. The Mid-Atlantic Ridge on the floor of the Atlantic Ocean and the Great Rift Valley in east Africa are examples of rifts at divergent plate boundaries.

3. **Transform boundaries** occur when plates are moving in opposite directions along their boundary, grinding against one another. The tremendous pressures that build along these boundaries often lead to earthquake activity when this pressure is released. The San Andreas Fault along the West Coast of North America is an example of a transform boundary.

Smaller scale Earth movement

Not all movement of the Earth takes place in the large-scale tectonic plates. Some examples of the smaller types of movement include erosion, weathering, transportation, and deposition:

- **Erosion** is the displacement of Earth solids. Erosion is often a result of wind, water, or ice acting on surfaces with loose particles, such as sand, loose soils, or decomposing rock. Gravity can also cause erosion on loose surfaces. Factors such as slope, soil and rock composition, plant cover, and human activity all affect erosion.
- **Weathering** is the natural decomposition of the Earth's surface from contact with the atmosphere. It is not the same as erosion but can be a part of erosion. Heat, water, ice, and pressure are all factors that can lead to weathering. Chemicals in the atmosphere can also contribute to weathering.
- **Transportation** is the movement of eroded material from one place to another by wind, water or ice. Examples of transportation include pebbles rolling down a stream bed and boulders carried by moving glaciers.
- **Deposition** is when sediments or other geological materials build up. Sand dunes and moraines are formed by transportation and deposition.

SKILL 4.4 Human systems: population topics such as demographic transition, settlement patterns and migration; spatial patterns of ethnicity, language, and religion; political aspects including frontiers and boundaries; cooperation and conflict among people and nations; globalization of economies

The Origins of Human Settlements

The **AGRICULTURAL REVOLUTION**, initiated by the invention of the plow, led to a thorough transformation of human society by making large-scale agricultural production possible and facilitating the development of agrarian societies. During the period, along with the invention of the plow, humans began to use the wheel, numbers, and writing. Coinciding with the shift from hunting wild game to the domestication of animals, this period was one of dramatic social and economic change.

AGRICULTURAL REVOLUTION: led to a thorough transformation of human society by making large-scale agricultural production possible and facilitating the development of agrarian societies

Transition to agriculture

Numerous changes in lifestyle and thinking accompanied the development of stable agricultural communities. Rather than gathering a wide variety of plants as hunter-gatherers, agricultural communities became dependent on a limited number of plants or crops that are harvested. **Subsistence** became vulnerable to the weather and was dependent upon planting and harvesting times.

In the beginning of the transition to agriculture, the tools that were used for hunting and gathering were adequate to the tasks of agriculture—the initial challenge was in adapting to a new way of life. Once that challenge was met, attention turned to the development of more advanced tools and sources of energy. Some 6,000 years ago, the first plow was invented in Mesopotamia. This plow was pulled by animals, and because of its presence, agricultural possibilities grew. Soon tools were developed that made such basic tasks as gathering seeds, planting, and cutting grain faster and easier.

Agriculture also required a great deal of physical labor and the development of a sense of discipline. Agricultural communities become stable in terms of location, and the construction of more permanent dwellings made sense. These dwellings tended to be built relatively close together, creating villages or towns.

Agriculture also required a great deal of physical labor and the development of a sense of discipline.

Settlements to Stable Communities

Settled communities that produce the necessities of life are referred to as **self-supporting**. Advances in agricultural technology soon resulted in the ability to not only be self-supporting but to produce a surplus of produce as well. This creates two opportunities:

- Trade of the surplus goods for other desired goods
- Vulnerability to others who steal to take those goods

Protecting this surplus of domesticated livestock and stored crops became an issue for the community. This led to the construction of walls and fortifications to achieve this end.

Stable communities freed people from the need to carry everything with them and move from hunting ground to hunting ground. This facilitated the invention of larger, more complex tools. As new tools were envisioned and developed, it began to make sense to have some specialization within the society. Skills began to have greater value, and people began to do work on behalf of the community that utilized their particular skills and abilities. Settled community life also gave rise to the notion of wealth, as it became feasible to keep possessions.

Managing settled communities

Due to these developments, it became necessary to maintain social and political stability to ensure that planting and harvesting times were not interrupted by internal discord or a war with a neighboring community. It also became necessary to develop ways to store the harvest to prevent its destruction by the elements and animals and be protect it from thieves.

The ability to produce surplus crops created the opportunity to trade or barter with other communities in exchange for desired goods.

The ability to produce surplus crops also created the opportunity to trade or barter with other communities in exchange for desired goods. Traders and trade routes began to develop between villages and cities. The domestication of animals expanded the range of trade and facilitated an exchange of ideas and knowledge.

Conflict and Cooperation on Earth

Competition for control of areas of the Earth's surface is a common trait of human interaction throughout history. This competition has resulted in both conflict and cooperation. Individuals and societies have divided the Earth's surface through conflict for a number of reasons:

- The domination of people or societies (colonialism)
- The control of valuable resources (oil)
- The control of strategic routes (Panama Canal)

Conflicts can be spurred by:

- Religion
- Political ideology
- National origin
- Language
- Race

Conflicts can also result from disagreement over how land, ocean, or natural resources will be developed, shared, and used. Conflicts have resulted from trade, migration, and settlement rights. They can also occur between small groups of people, between cities, between nations, between religious groups, and between multinational alliances.

Modern solutions to competition and conflict

Today, the world is primarily divided by political and administrative interests into **STATE SOVEREIGNTIES.** A particular government is recognized to control a particular region, including its territory, population, and natural resources. The only area of the Earth's surface that today is not defined by state or national sovereignty is Antarctica.

STATE SOVEREIGNTIES: the concept that a particular region is controlled by a particular government, including its territory, population, and natural resources

Nations develop **alliances** based on political philosophy, economic concerns, cultural similarities, religious interests, and/or for military defense. Some of the most notable alliances today are:

- United Nations
- North Atlantic Treaty Organization
- Caribbean Community
- Council of Arab Economic Unity
- European Union

Large companies and **multinational corporations** also compete for control of natural resources for manufacturing, development, and distribution.

SKILL 4.5 Environment and society: environmental perceptions, environmental impacts and the modification of the environment by human populations, renewable and nonrenewable resources

Humans and the Environment

Nonrenewable resources

Humans have always turned to nature for resources, from wood for the first cooking fires, to iron ore for the first metal tools, to crude oil to refine into fuel for automobiles and airplanes. Some of these resources, such as oil and metal ores, have a large but limited supply. This kind of resource is considered nonrenewable; once a **NONRENEWABLE RESOURCE** has been completely used up, more cannot be made.

NONRENEWABLE RESOURCE: a natural resource that is limited

Renewable resources

Natural resources that are virtually unlimited in supply, or which can be grown, are considered **RENEWABLE RESOURCES.** Trees that supply wood for construction and paper are considered renewable resources if managed correctly. Solar and wind energy are renewable resources because their supply is practically

RENEWABLE RESOURCES: a natural resource that is virtually unlimited

infinite. Hydrogen is a potential renewable resource that is receiving increasing attention because it can be derived from water, which is virtually unlimited.

Modifying the environment

Since the dawn of agriculture, humans have modified their environment to suit their needs and to provide food and shelter. Agriculture, for instance, often involves loosening topsoil by plowing before planting. This in turn affects how water and wind interact with the soil and can lead to erosion. In extreme cases, erosion can leave a plot of land unsuitable for agricultural use. Modern methods of farming rely less on plowing the soil before planting, but more on chemical fertilizers, pesticides, and herbicides. However, these chemicals can find their way into groundwater, affecting the environment.

Cities show how humans modify their environment to suit their needs and have a major impact on the environment. Concentrated consumption of fuels by automobiles and home heating systems affect the quality of the air in and around cities. The lack of exposed ground means that rainwater runs off roads and rooftops into sewer systems instead of seeping into the ground, often making its way into nearby streams or rivers, carrying urban debris with it.

Most countries recognize the importance of limiting the impact human populations have on the environment and have laws in place toward this goal.

Limiting human impact

Most countries recognize the importance of limiting the impact human populations have on the environment and have laws in place toward this goal. Emissions of certain compounds by factories, power plants, automobiles, and other sources are regulated. Cities collect sewage water into plants where it is treated before returning to rivers and streams. Incentives have been put in place in some areas to encourage people to use cleaner, alternative fuel sources, and many governments are supporting research into new sources of fuel that will reduce the reliance on nonrenewable resources.

ECOLOGY: the study of how living organisms interact with the physical aspects of their surroundings (their environment) including soil, water, air, and other living things

BIOGEOGRAPHY: the study of how the surface features of the Earth—form, movement, and climate—affect living things

Ecology

ECOLOGY is the study of how living organisms interact with the physical aspects of their surroundings (their environment) including soil, water, air, and other living things. **BIOGEOGRAPHY** is the study of how the surface features of the Earth—form, movement, and climate—affect living things.

Three levels of environmental understanding are critical.

1. An **ecosystem** is a community consisting of a physical environment and the organisms that live within it.

2. A **biome** is a large area of land with characteristic climate, soil, and a mixture of plants and animals. Biomes are made up of groups of ecosystems. Major biomes include deserts, chaparrals, savannas, tropical rain forests, temperate grasslands, temperate deciduous forests, taigas, and tundras.

3. A **habitat** is the set of surroundings within which members of a species normally live. Elements of the habitat include soil, water, predators, and competitors.

Species interactions

Within habitats, interactions between members of the species occur. These interactions occur between members of the same species and between members of different species. Interactions tend to be of three types:

1. **Competition** occurs between members of the same species or between members of different species for resources required to continue life, to grow, or to reproduce. For example, competition for acorns can occur between squirrels or it can occur between squirrels and woodpeckers. One species can either push out or cause the demise of another species if it is better adapted to obtain the resource. When a new species is introduced into a habitat, the result can be a loss of the native species and/or significant change to the habitat. For example, the introduction of the Asian plant Kudzu into the American South has resulted in the destruction of several native species because Kudzu grows and spreads very quickly and smothers everything in its path.

2. **Predation** occurs when organisms live by hunting and eating other organisms. The species best suited for hunting other species in the habitat will be the species that survives. Larger, predator species with better hunting skills reduce the amount of prey available for smaller and/or weaker species. This affects both the amount of available prey and the diversity of species that are able to survive in the habitat.

3. **Symbiosis** is a condition in which two organisms of different species are able to live in the same environment with both species benefiting.

By nature, different organisms are best suited for existence in particular environments. When an organism is displaced to a different environment or when the environment changes for some reason, its ability to survive is determined by its ability to **adapt** to the new environment. Adaptation can take the form of structural change, physiological change, or behavioral modification.

Biodiversity and environmental change

BIODIVERSITY: refers to the variety of species and organisms, as well as the variety of habitats, available on the Earth

BIODIVERSITY refers to the variety of species and organisms, as well as the variety of habitats, available on the Earth. Biodiversity provides the life-support system for the various habitats and species. The greater the degree of biodiversity, the more species and habitats will continue to survive.

Natural changes occur that can alter habitats (floods, volcanoes, storms, earthquakes). These changes can affect the species that exist within the habitat either by causing extinction or by changing the environment in a way that will no longer support the life systems. Climate changes can have similar effects. Inhabiting species, however, can also alter habitats particularly through migration. Human civilization, population growth, and efforts to control the environment can have many negative effects on various habitats.

Humans have often changed their environments to suit their particular needs and interests. This can result in changes that result in the extinction of species or changes to the habitat itself. For example, deforestation damages the stability of mountain surfaces. One particularly devastating example was the removal of the grasses of the Great Plains for agriculture. Tilling the ground and planting crops left the soil unprotected. Sustained drought in the 1930s dried the soil into dust. When windstorms occurred, the topsoil was stripped away and blown all the way to the Atlantic Ocean.

SKILL 4.6 The uses of geography: application of geographic concepts to interpret the past, the present, and to plan for the future

Types of Geography

PHYSICAL GEOGRAPHY: is concerned with the locations of such Earth features as climate, water, and land; how these relate to and affect each other and human activities; and what forces shaped and changed them

PHYSICAL GEOGRAPHY is concerned with the locations of such Earth features as climate, water, and land; how these relate to and affect each other and human activities; and what forces shaped and changed them. All three of these features affect the lives of all humans by having a direct influence on what is made and produced, where it occurs, how it occurs, and what makes it possible. The combination of different climate conditions, types of landforms, and other surface features all work together around the Earth to give the many varied cultures their unique characteristics and distinctions.

HUMAN GEOGRAPHY looks at human activity patterns and how they relate to the environment including political, cultural, historical, urban, and social geographical fields of study.

CULTURAL GEOGRAPHY is part of human geography. It studies the location, characteristics, and influence of the physical environment on different cultures around the Earth. Also included in these studies are comparisons and influences of the many varied cultures. Ease of travel and up-to-the-minute, state-of-the-art communication techniques ease the difficulties of understanding cultural differences making it easier to come in contact with them.

HUMAN GEOGRAPHY: looks at human activity patterns and how they relate to the environment including political, cultural, historical, urban, and social geographical fields of study

CULTURAL GEOGRAPHY: studies the location, characteristics, and influence of the physical environment on different cultures around the Earth

Humans and Geography

Canal building, ski areas, slash and burn operations, fisheries, agriculture . . . the list goes on when considering how humans relate to geography.

Geography as a benefit

Often, humans are able to use their environment to their benefit. Cancun in Mexico has become a mecca for tourists looking for an exotic beach, and Vail in Colorado is a popular skiing destination. The climates of these two areas have directly influenced their respective industries. Singapore and Abu Dhabi glitter with skyscrapers. Geography has provided natural ports, a desirable climate, and valuable oil, all of which have contributed to the success of these areas.

Geography as a threat

On the other hand, the environment can provide a distinct threat to human settlements. For example, in 1946, an earthquake struck the Aleutian Islands near Alaska. As a result, a 14-foot tsunami swept Hilo, Hawaii. The waves destroyed the waterfront and killed 159 people. Every house facing the bay was demolished and struck the buildings across the street.

The Reno-Sparks area grows in population and needs water, but the high water levels in the reservoir are destroying the cui-ui fish of the Paiute tribe.

Population impact

World human population is over 6 billion. One hundred years ago, population was less than 2 billion. Some 500 years ago, there were an estimated 10 million Indians living in the Amazonian rainforest. Today there are fewer than 200,000. Logging, mining, industrial development, and large dams cause more than an acre-and-a half of rain forest to be lost every second of every day. That rate means that every year, an area of rainforest the size of Florida disappears. More than 20 percent of the world's oxygen is produced in the Amazon rainforest. It has taken only a century for humans to significantly impact a geographical system that has been in place for a million years. And rainforests, once destroyed, cannot be regenerated the way that temperate forests can.

Environmental Policy

Because humans rely upon the environment to sustain life, social and environmental policy must be mutually supportable. Because humans draw on the natural resources of the Earth and affect the environment in many ways, environmental and social policy must be mutually supportive.

Unprecedented demand on natural resources requires that social and environmental policies become increasingly interdependent if the planet is to continue to support life and human civilization.

ENVIRONMENTAL POLICY: is concerned with the sustainability of the Earth, the region under the administration of the governing group or individual or a local habitat

ENVIRONMENTAL POLICY is concerned with the sustainability of the Earth, the region under the administration of the governing group or individual or a local habitat. The concern of environmental policy is the preservation of region, habitat, or ecosystem.

DOMAIN V
ECONOMICS

PERSONALIZED STUDY PLAN

SKILL	KNOWN MATERIAL/ SKIP IT
5.1: Microeconomics I	☐
5.2: Microeconomics II	☐
5.3: Macroeconomics I	☐
5.4: Macroeconomics II	☐

SKILL 5.1 Microeconomics I: scarcity, choice and opportunity costs, economic systems, comparative advantage and trade, supply and demand, elasticity, market efficiency and the role of government

Economics

ECONOMICS is the study of how a society allocates its scarce resources to satisfy what are basically unlimited and competing wants. A fundamental fact of economics is that resources are scarce and that wants are infinite. The fact that scarce resources have to satisfy unlimited wants means that choices have to be made. If society uses its resources to produce good A, then it does not have those resources to produce good B. More of good A means less of good B. This trade-off is referred to as the opportunity cost or the **value of the sacrificed alternative**.

ECONOMICS: the study of how a society allocates its scarce resources to satisfy what are basically unlimited and competing wants

Economics is divided into two broad categories: **macroeconomics** and **microeconomics**.

Economic questions

Economic systems refer to the arrangements a society has devised to answer what are known as the three questions:

1. What goods to produce
2. How to produce the goods
3. Whom the goods are being produced for

The "What" question: supply and demand

Different economic systems answer these questions in different ways. These are the different "isms" that define the method of resource and output allocation. A **market economy** answers these questions in terms of demand and supply and the use of markets:

- **Demand** is based on consumer preferences and satisfaction and refers to the quantities of a good or service that buyers are willing and able to buy at different prices during a given period of time.
- **Supply** is based on costs of production and refers to the quantities that sellers are willing and able to sell at different prices during a given period of time.

MARKET EQUILIBRIUM PRICE: where the decisions of buyers coincide with the decisions of sellers

The determination of **MARKET EQUILIBRIUM PRICE** is where the decisions of buyers coincide with the decisions of sellers.

ELASTICITY: a measure of the responsiveness of quantity to changes in price

Demand curves and supply curves have different shapes. The term **ELASTICITY** can be defined as a measure of the responsiveness of quantity to changes in price. If quantity is very responsive to changes in price, then supply/demand is said to be elastic; if quantity is not very responsive to changes in price, then supply/demand is inelastic.

In a market economy, consumers vote for the products they want with their dollar spending. Goods acquiring enough dollar votes are profitable, signaling to the producers that society wants their scarce resources used in this way. This is how the "What" question is answered.

The "How" question

The producer looks for the most efficient or lowest cost method of production. The lower the firm's costs for any given level of revenue, the higher the firm's profits. This is the way in which the "How" question is answered in a market economy.

The "For Whom" question

The "For Whom" question is answered in the marketplace by the determination of the equilibrium price. Price serves to ration the good to those who can and will transact at the market price. Those who cannot or will not are excluded from the market.

MARKET EFFICIENCY: obtaining the most output consistent with the preferences of consumers

This mechanism results in **MARKET EFFICIENCY** or obtaining the most output consistent with the preferences of consumers. Society's scarce resources are being used the way society wants them to be used.

International economics

COMPARATIVE ADVANTAGE: says that a nation should specialize in the production of the good it can produce at a relatively lower opportunity cost than any other nation and trade for goods that it cannot produce as cheaply

COMPARATIVE ADVANTAGE refers to international trade. This idea says that a nation should specialize in the production of the good it can produce at a relatively lower **opportunity cost** than any other nation and trade for goods that it cannot produce as cheaply. Trade on this basis results in higher levels of output, income, and employment for the trading nations. This is the reasoning behind free trade agreements such as NAFTA.

Government and the economy

Even in a capitalist economy, many believe that there is a role for government. Government is required to provide the framework for the functioning of the economy. This requires a legal system, a monetary system, and a watchdog authority to protect consumers from bad or dangerous products and practices. Some also argue that there is a need for government to correct for the misallocation of resources when the market does not function properly, as in the case of externalities, such as pollution. Government functions to provide public goods, such as national defense, and to correct for macro instability, such as inflation and unemployment.

Free enterprise, **individual entrepreneurship**, **competitive markets**, and **consumer sovereignty** are all parts of a market economy.

In a **PLANNED OR COMMAND ECONOMY**, the means of production are publicly owned and there is little, if any, private ownership. Instead of the three questions being solved by markets, a planning authority makes the decisions in place of markets. The planning authority decides what will be produced and how.

PLANNED OR COMMAND ECONOMY: a system in which the means of production are publicly owned and there is little, if any, private ownership

Between the two extremes is **MARKET SOCIALISM**. This is a mixed economic system that uses both markets and planning. Planning is usually used to direct resources in the production phase, with markets being used to determine distribution and the prices of consumer goods and wages.

MARKET SOCIALISM: a mixed economic system that uses both markets and planning

SKILL 5.2 Microeconomics II: production and cost, product markets and behavior of firms, factor markets and distribution of income

Micoreconomics

MICROECONOMICS is a study of the economy at the individual and industry, or firm, level. Microeconomics is concerned with things like consumer behavior, output and input markets, and the distribution of income.

MICROECONOMICS: a study of the economy at the individual and industry, or firm, level

A firm's production decisions are based on its costs. Every product is produced using inputs or resources. These are called **factors of production**. The four factors used in the production of every good and service are:

1. Labor
2. Land
3. Capital
4. Entrepreneurship

Costs and income

The costs for fixed factors of production, such as land, plant, and equipment, are called **fixed costs**. The costs that change with the amount of output, such as labor, are called **variable costs**. **COSTS OF PRODUCTION**, then, are the total of fixed and variable costs.

COSTS OF PRODUCTION: the total of fixed and variable costs

Each factor of production earns its **factor income** in the resource market. Labor earns **wages**; capital earns **interest**; land earns **rent**; and the entrepreneur earns **profit**. The size of the factor income depends on the scarcity of the factor and the significance of its contribution to the production process. Note that a market economy does not result in the equality of income. Each factor earns an income based on its contribution.

Kinds of market structure

There are four kinds of market structures in the output market:

1. **Perfect competition** is most closely exemplified by agriculture. Numerous firms sell a product identical to that sold by all other firms in the industry and have no control over the price. Buyers and sellers have full market information, and there are no barriers to entry. A **barrier to entry** is anything that makes it difficult for firms to enter or leave the industry. The opposite of a perfectly competitive firm is a monopoly.

2. **Monopoly** is a market structure in which there is only one seller who controls price. A monopolist becomes and remains a monopolist because of barriers to entry, which are very high. These barriers to entry include a very high fixed cost structure, which keeps new firms from entering the industry. Monopoly is illegal in the U.S. economy.

3. **Monopolistic competition** is the situation seen in shopping centers. Numerous firms each sell products that are similar but not identical, such as brand name shoes or clothing. Barriers to entry are not as high as in an oligopoly, which is why there are more firms.

4. **Oligopoly** is a market structure in which there are a few sellers of products that may be either homogeneous such as steel, or heterogeneous such as automobiles. There are high barriers to entry, which is why there are only a few firms in each industry.

Consumer behavior

Marginal propensity to consume refers to the proportion of an increase in disposable income that is used to consume goods and services, instead of being saved.

UTILITY: the measurement of happiness or satisfaction a person receives from consuming a good or service

UTILITY is the measurement of happiness or satisfaction a person receives from consuming a good or service.

SKILL 5.3 Macroeconomics I: measures of economic performance, national income accounting, unemployment, inflation, and business cycle

Macroeconomics

MACROECONOMICS is a study of the aggregates that comprise the economy on the national level:

- Output
- Consumption
- Investment
- Government spending
- Net exports

MACROECONOMICS: a study of the aggregates that comprise the economy on the national level: output, consumption, investment, government spending, and net exports

Macroeconomics is concerned with a study of the economy's overall economic performance or what is called the **GROSS DOMESTIC PRODUCT (GDP)**. The GDP is a measure of the economy's output during a specified time period.

Calculating GDP

GROSS DOMESTIC PRODUCT (GDP): a measure of the economy's output during a specified time period

A economy's output can be tabulated in two ways, both of which give the same result: the expenditures approach and the incomes approach. What is spent on national output by each sector of the economy is equal to what is earned producing national output by each of the factors of production.

The Expenditures Approach

The macroeconomy consists of four broad sectors:

1. Consumers
2. Investments by businesses
3. Government
4. The foreign sector

In the **EXPENDITURES APPROACH**, GDP is determined by the amount of spending in each sector. GDP is equal to the consumption expenditures (C) of consumers *plus* the investment expenditures (I) of businesses *plus* spending of all three levels of government (G) *plus* the net export spending (exports minus imports, X − M) in the foreign sector.

EXPENDITURES APPROACH: in this method, GDP is determined by the amount of spending in each sector

The equation is:

$$GDP = C + I + G + (X - M)$$

What is spent **buying** the national output has to equal what is **earned** in producing the national output.

The Incomes Approach

There are three precepts in this approach:

1. Labor earns wages, called **Compensation of Employees**
2. Land earns **Rental Income**
3. Capital earns **Interest Income**

Since entrepreneurial ability can be in the form of individual effort or corporations, there are two different categories: return to the individual entrepreneur, which is called **proprietor's income**, and return to the corporation, which is called **corporate profit.**

Corporate profit is a little different than proprietor's profit. Corporations do three things with their profits:

1. Pay **corporate profits tax**
2. Pay **dividends**
3. Keep the rest as **retained earnings**

INCOMES APPROACH: in this method, GDP is calculated by adding up all forms of income and then subtracting depreciation and indirect business taxes

To complete the tabulation of GDP from the **INCOMES APPROACH**, one must to adjust for two nonincome charges, and both are subtracted:

- **Indirect business taxes**, such as property taxes and sales taxes
- **Depreciation** (the amount of capital that is worn out producing the current term's output)

Phases of a nation's economy

AGGREGATE SUPPLY: the amount of national output produced

AGGREGATE DEMAND: the amount of national output purchased

When the economy is functioning smoothly, **AGGREGATE SUPPLY**, the amount of national output produced, is just equal to the **AGGREGATE DEMAND**, the amount of national output purchased. In this case, there is an economy in a period of prosperity without economic instability.

But market economies experience the fluctuations of the business cycle, the ups and downs in the level of economic activity. There are four phases:

1. **Boom:** a period of prosperity
2. **Recession:** a period of declining GDP and rising unemployment

3. **Trough:** the low point of the recession
4. **Recovery:** a period of lessening unemployment and rising prices

There are no rules pertaining to the duration or severity of any of the phases.

Inflation and unemployment

The phases result in periods of unemployment and periods of inflation.

- **Inflation** results from too much spending in the economy—buyers want to buy more than sellers can produce and bid up prices for the available output
- **Unemployment** occurs when there is not enough spending in the economy—sellers have produced more output than buyers are buying and the result is a surplus situation; firms, faced with surplus merchandise, lower their production levels and lay off workers, which leads to unemployment

These are situations that require government policy actions.

SKILL 5.4 Macroeconomics II: national income determination, fiscal policy, money and banking, monetary policy, international finance and investment, and economic growth

Measuring Economic Performance

GDP, computed by either the expenditures approach or the incomes approach, is a measure of the overall performance of the national economy. From GDP, government policymakers can:

- Determine what is happening in the economy and identify problem areas
- Measure economic growth
- Devise policies to help those problem areas

Macroeconomic instability problems of inflation and unemployment are mostly caused by inequality of aggregate demand and aggregate supply.

Maintaining a delicate balance

An economy that is growing too rapidly and has too high a level of spending has inflation, a period of increases in the price level. Inflation results in a dollar with less purchasing power and represents a situation where the appropriate government action is to slow down the economy. The government will implement policies that result in less spending in the economy to end inflation.

When there is not enough spending in the economy, producers who have surplus merchandise lower production levels and lay off workers causing unemployment. The appropriate action for government is to stimulate the economy and to take actions that result in higher levels of spending. The increase in demand leads to higher levels of employment.

Fiscal policy

FISCAL POLICY: refers to the level of government spending and/or taxes

Government can implement **contractionary** policies for inflation or **expansionary** policies for unemployment in two ways. **FISCAL POLICY** refers to the level of government spending and/or taxes.

- Expansionary fiscal policy raises government spending and/or lowers taxes to increase spending in the economy, thus eliminating unemployment
- Contractionary policies to stop inflation consist of a decrease in government spending and/or an increase in taxes, both of which lower the levels of spending in the economy

Fiscal policy requires legislative action, and laws have to be enacted.

Monetary policy

MONETARY POLICY: refers to the government's policy about the level of money in the banking system

RESERVE RATIO: refers to the government's policy regarding the level of money in the banking system; the ratio of the amount of deposit money reserved by banks to the amount of money lent out in loans

DISCOUNT RATE: the rate of interest charged by the Fed to banks that borrow from it

The other policy tool open to the government is **MONETARY POLICY**. The **Federal Reserve System** (the Fed) implements monetary policy in the United States through changing the level of money in the banking system. Simply put, banks earn income by making loans. People and businesses borrow from banks and spend the borrowed funds. If the Fed changes the amount of funds that banks have available to loan out, they change the level of spending in the economy. There are three ways that the Fed can do this.

Reserve ratio

First of all, banks cannot loan out all of their deposits. They are required to hold a certain percentage as reserves. This percentage is called the **RESERVE RATIO**. Raising the reserve ratio leaves banks with fewer reserves to loan out, and it is therefore an aspect of contractionary monetary policy (used during recessions). Lowering the reserve ratio increases lending ability and spending and is an aspect of expansionary monetary policy.

Discount rate

A second mechanism for implementing monetary policy is called the **DISCOUNT RATE**, which is the rate of interest charged by the Fed to banks that borrow from it. Lowering the discount rate encourages banks to borrow and make loans, thus leading to higher levels of spending. This is a form of expansionary monetary policy. Contractionary monetary policy would be indicated by an increase in the discount rate.

Open market operations

The third means of influencing the money supply is through **OPEN MARKET OPERATIONS**. This is when the Fed buys or sells government securities in the open market. When the Fed buys these securities, such as federal bonds from the public or banks, the Fed pays with dollars that are put into circulation. Thus, the purchase of bonds by the Fed represents a form of expansionary monetary policy, as there are more dollars in the system for loans and spending. The Fed selling bonds is a form of contractionary monetary policy.

OPEN MARKET OPERATIONS: when the Fed buys or sells government securities in the open market

An international lending system

Since today's financial markets are international, banks can borrow and lend in foreign markets. They are not constrained by the domestic market. Financial capital goes where it can earn the highest rate of return, regardless of national boundaries. This means that if the Fed is trying to implement contractionary monetary policy, banks and businesses can borrow in international markets and avoid the Fed's contractionary policies, at least in the short-run.

DOMAIN VI
BEHAVIORAL SCIENCES

PERSONALIZED STUDY PLAN

SKILL	KNOWN MATERIAL/ SKIP IT
6.1: Sociology	☐
6.2: Anthropology	☐
6.3: Psychology	☐

SKILL 6.1 Sociology: socialization, social organization, social institutions, the study of populations, multicultural diversity, social problems

Sociology

SOCIOLOGY is the study of human society through the individuals, groups, and institutions that comprise it. Sociology includes the study of every feature of human social conditions. It deals with the predominant behaviors, attitudes, and types of relationships within a society as defined by a group of people with a similar cultural background living in a specific geographical area. Sociology is divided into five major areas of study:

SOCIOLOGY: the study of human society through the individuals, groups, and institutions that comprise it

1. **Population studies:** The study of general social patterns of groups of people living in a certain geographical area
2. **Social behaviors:** The study of changes in attitudes, morale, leadership, conformity, and others
3. **Social institutions:** The study of the organization of groups of people that perform specific functions within a society; these institutions include churches, schools, hospitals, business organizations, and governments
4. **Cultural influences:** The study of customs, knowledge, arts, religious beliefs, and language
5. **Social change:** The study of wars, revolutions, inventions, fashions, and other events or activities

Methods of testing sociology theories

Sociologists use three major methods to test and verify theories:

1. **Surveys**
2. **Controlled experiments**
3. **Field observations**

Sociology and other disciplines

With its focus on human society with its attitudes, behaviors, conditions, and relationships with others, sociology is closely related to several other disciplines:

- **Anthropology,** especially when applied to groups outside of one's region, nation, or hemisphere
- **Political Science,** with regard to the impact of political and governmental regulation of activities

- **Geography**, as related to the social awareness, influence, and use of the physical environment
- **Economics**
- **Psychology**

Notable figures in sociology

Some important figures in the field of sociology are:

POSITIVISM: states that social behavior and events can be scientifically measured

- **Auguste Comte**, a French philosopher, who coined the term "sociology" and developed the theory called **POSITIVISM**, which states that social behavior and events can be scientifically measured. Positivism relies on sensory information for evaluating human experience. Comte is generally regarded as the first Western sociologist.
- **Emile Durkheim**, considered the father of sociology because he inspired universities to consider sociology as a discipline. Comte and positivism influenced Durkheim, and he essentially viewed the world as influenced by large factors such as group attitudes and cultural norms versus simply being influenced by individuals. Sociologists determine the "social facts." Durkheim is especially famous for his work on social cause of rates of suicide. He brought into this the word **anomie**, which refers to a situation in which the weakening of social structures causes deviant behavior.
- **Karl Marx** and **Friedrich Engels**, who sociologically saw the world as a socio-economic struggle between classes. The main thesis in their book *The Communist Manifesto* is that work is a social activity and that the working class will ultimately have a revolution.
- **Herbert Spencer**, who related the biology of Darwin's *Origin of Species* to sociology by viewing the development of society the same way. He coined the phrase "the survival of the fittest." Despite being a rival of Darwin, he is credited with Social Darwinism, in which competition is understood as the driving force in society.
- **Max Weber**, who said that Protestantism spurred capitalism. He also distinguished between fact and value and argued that sociology should be objective.

SKILL 6.2 Anthropology: human culture and cultural change

Anthropology

ANTHROPOLOGY is the study of culture and humanity and the relationship between the two. Anthropologists study similarities and differences among diverse groups, their relationships to other cultures, and patterns of behavior. Their research is twofold: cross-cultural and comparative. A major method of study is referred to as **participant observation**. The anthropologist studies the people of a culture by living among them and participating with them in their daily lives. Other methods may be used, but this is the most characteristic.

ANTHROPOLOGY: the study of culture and humanity and the relationship between the two

Type of anthropology

There are four types of anthropology:

1. **Archaeology:** Study of material remains of humans
2. **Social-cultural:** Study of norms, values, standards
3. **Biological:** Study of genetic characteristics
4. **Linguistics:** Study of the historical development of language

Margaret Mead popularized the discipline of anthropology by her studies of sex in the cultures of the South Pacific and Southeast Asia. Unusual for women of those times, Mead earned her Ph.D. from Columbia University in 1929. Her studies also involved breastfeeding and treatment of children in various cultures. One of her well-known works was *Coming of Age in Samoa.*

Mary Leakey and **Louis Leakey** found tools and fossils at an archeological site called **Olduvai Gorge**. Mary discovered Laetoli footprints and developed a classification system. Louis was a Kenyan who discovered prehistoric African human remains. After he was drafted into the Kenyan intelligence service when the Italians had invaded Ethiopia, Mary continued with the archaeological investigation at Olduvai Gorge.

SKILL 6.3 Psychology: basic concepts, such as learning and perception, human growth and development, personality and adjustment, social psychology

PSYCHOLOGY: the study of mental processes and behavior

Check out the Encyclopedia of Psychology here:

www.psychology.org/links/

Psychology

PSYCHOLOGY is the study of mental processes and behavior. Psychology is divided into **scientific psychology** and **applied psychology**.

Psychologists observe and record specific patterns. This observation enables psychologists to discern and predict certain behaviors. Scientific methods help verify their ideas. Psychologists help people fulfill their individual potential and strengthen understanding between individuals, groups, nations, and cultures. There is also consumer psychology, which studies how people relate to various products and services.

Methods used in psychological research

Methods used in psychological research include:

- Naturalistic observation
- Survey method
- Case study
- Experimental method
- Correlational design

For more information on psychological research check out this site:

www.psych.hanover.edu/Research/exponnet.html

Psychological researchers choose the method based up what they are trying to learn.

For **naturalistic observation**, the researcher watches people in their natural environment, making sure not to influence the outcome. In the **survey method**, researchers write and distribute a survey and then tabulate the answers it provides. **Case studies** tend to take a lot of time because they involve studying individuals or groups in depth. The **experimental method** involves designing the variables for an experimental group and a control group. **Correlational design** measures a positive or negative relationship between two variables. An example of this would be to measure the correlation between teachers' attitudes and students' attendance.

Notable figures in psychology

Some historical figures who have made significant contributions to the field of psychology include:

- **Aristotle,** the Greek philosopher, who has often been credited with the beginnings of psychology. He was interested in the human mind. He believed that the mind was a feature of the body and that the psyche was a receiver of knowledge. In his view, the point of psychology was uncovering essence of the soul.
- **Rene Descartes,** a French philosopher who described the strong influence of the body and mind on each other because of their being separate; he suggested that the pineal gland in the brain was where this interaction took place. He developed the doctrine of **NATIVISM**, the belief that humans are born with certain knowledge that is not dependent on individual experience.
- **Thomas Hobbes, John Locke, David Hume,** and **George Berkeley.** Rejecting Descartes' view of nativism, these four men believed in **EMPIRICISM**, the belief that a person's mind is empty at birth and that people gain knowledge through their senses and ideas from life experience.
- **Johannes P. Muller** and **Hermann L.F. von Hemholtz,** two German scientists who pioneered the first organized studies of perception and sensation, showing the feasibility of the scientific study of the physical processes that support mental activity.
- **William James,** who began one of the first psychology laboratories in the United States, and **Wilhelm Wundt,** a German philosopher, trained in physiology and medicine and who published the first journal dealing with experimental psychology. Wundt and James put psychology in a field by itself, separate from philosophy. Their works, along with others, led to the method of research called **INTROSPECTION**, training their subjects to observe and record feelings, experiences, and mental processes.
- **Sigmund Freud,** an Austrian physician whose theorized that humans repress inner forces in the subconscious and that these repressed feelings caused personality disorders. He developed **PSYCHOANALYSIS** to bring out the repressed thoughts and feelings. Sexual desire, in his view, is a primary human motivator.
- **Carl Jung,** a theoretical psychologist who worked with Freud between 1907 and 1912. His exploration involved Eastern and Western philosophy, including astrology. Defining **introversion** and **extroversion** was a development of his work, along with the **collective unconscious** and **synchronicity.**

For more information on Aristotle, check out this site:

www.indiana.edu/~intell/aristotle.shtml

NATIVISM: the psychological doctrine which maintains that humans are born with certain knowledge and this is not dependent on individual experience

EMPIRICISM: the belief that a person's mind is empty at birth and that people gain knowledge through their senses and ideas from life experience

INTROSPECTION: the psychological practice in which the psychologist trains his subjects to observe and record feelings, experiences, and mental processes

For more information on Sigmund Freud, check out this site:

www.iep.utm.edu/f/freud.htm

PSYCHOANALYSIS: a method of psychological study that brings out repressed thoughts and feelings through analysis

- **John B. Watson**, an American psychologist who introduced **behaviorism** and believed in nurture over nature. He said: "Give me a dozen healthy infants, well-formed, and my own specified world to bring them up in and I'll guarantee to take any one at random and train him to become any type of specialist I might select—doctor, lawyer, artist, merchant-chief and, yes, even beggar-man and thief, regardless of his talents, penchants, tendencies, abilities, vocations, and race of his ancestors."
- **Ivan Pavlov** and **B. F. Skinner**, who made significant contributions to the school of **BEHAVIORISM**, which was a reaction to the emphasis on introspection. Behaviorists believe that the environment is the most important influence on one's behavior and they look for any correlation between environmental stimuli and observable behavior. Pavlov is most noted for his experiments proving **conditioned response**, in which he was able to link a bell to salivating in a dog. Skinner built on Pavlov's work to become a strong proponent of behaviorism and is most noted for his experimental device, the "Skinner Box."
- **Max Wertheimer**, who developed **GESTALT PSYCHOLOGY**. The word Gestalt means a pattern—a whole rather than separate incidents.

BEHAVIORISM: theory that the environment is the most important influence on one's behavior

GESTALT PSYCHOLOGY: a field of psychology that considers the whole of a psychological experience rather than separate parts

For more information on Gestalt therapy, check out this site:

www.gestalttherapy.net/

Modern and social psychology

Modern psychology includes the teachings of the earlier schools as well as stimulus-response, cognitive, and humanistic psychology.

SOCIAL PSYCHOLOGY studies how social conditions affect human beings.

SOCIAL PSYCHOLOGY: studies how social conditions affect human beings

Bibliography

Adams, James Truslow. (2006). *The March of Democracy*, Vol. 1. "The Rise of the Union." New York: Charles Scribner's Sons.

Barbini, John & Warshaw, Steven. (2006). *The World Past and Present.* New York: Harcourt, Brace, Jovanovich.

Berthon, Simon & Robinson, Andrew. (2006). *The Shape of the World.* Chicago: Rand McNally.

Bice, David A. (2006). *A Panorama of Florida II.* 2nd ed. Marceline, Missouri: Walsworth Publishing Co., Inc.

Bram, Leon (Vice-President and Editorial Director). (2006). *Funk and Wagnalls New Encyclopedia.* Oxford.

Burns, Edward McNall & Ralph, Philip Lee. (2006). *World Civilizations: Their History and Culture.* 5th ed. New York: W.W. Norton & Company, Inc.

Dauben, Joseph W. (2006). *The World Book Encyclopedia.* Chicago: World Book Inc. A Scott Fetzer Company.

De Blij, H.J. & Muller, Peter O. (2006). *Geography Regions and Concepts.* 6th ed. New York: John Wiley & Sons, Inc.

Encyclopedia Americana. (2006). Danbury, Connecticut: Grolier Incorporated.

Heigh, Christopher (Editor). (2006). *The Cambridge Historical Encyclopedia of Great Britain and Ireland.* Cambridge: Cambridge University Press.

Hunkins, Francis P. & Armstrong, David G. (2006). *World Geography People and Places.* Columbus, Ohio: Charles E. Merrill Publishing Co. A Bell & Howell Company.

Jarolimek, John; Anderson, J. Hubert & Durand, Loyal, Jr. (2006). *World Neighbors.* New York: Macmillan Publishing Company. London: Collier Macmillan.

McConnell, Campbell R. (2006). *Economics-Principles, Problems, and Policies.* 10th ed. New York: McGraw-Hill Book Company.

Millard, Dr. Anne & Vanags, Patricia. (2006). *The Usborne Book of World History.* London: Usborne Publishing Ltd.

Novosad, Charles (Executive Editor). (2006). *The Nystrom Desk Atlas.* Chicago: Nystrom Division of Herff Jones, Inc.

Patton, Clyde P.; Rengert, Arlene C.; Saveland, Robert N.; Cooper, Kenneth S. & Cam, Patricia T. (2006). *A World View.* Morristown, N.J.: Silver Burdette Companion.

Schwartz, Melvin & O'Connor, John R. (2006). *Exploring A Changing World.* New York: Globe Book Company.

The Annals of America: Selected Readings on Great Issues in American History 1620-1968. (2006). United States of America: William Benton.

Tindall, George Brown & Shi, David E. (2006). *America—A Narrative History.* 4th ed. New York: W.W. Norton & Company.

Todd, Lewis Paul & Curti, Merle. (2006). *Rise of the American Nation.* 3rd ed. New York: Harcourt, Brace, Jovanovich, Inc.

Tyler, Jenny; Watts, Lisa; Bowyer, Carol; Trundle, Roma & Warrender, Annabelle (2006). *The Usbome Book of World Geography.* London: Usbome Publishing Ltd.

Willson, David H. (2006). *A History of England.* Hinsdale, Illinois: The Dryder Press, Inc.

SAMPLE TEST

SAMPLE TEST

United States History

(Average) (Skill 1.2)

1. **Which of the following best describes how the Native American nations lived in North America before Europeans arrived?**

   A. Subsistence

   B. Mercantile

   C. Capitalist

   D. Literate

(Easy) (Skill 1.2)

2. **Apartments built out of cliff faces; shared government by adult citizens; absence of aggression toward other groups. These factors characterize the Native American group known as:**

   A. Pueblo

   B. Comanche

   C. Seminole

   D. Sioux

(Easy) (Skill 1.3)

3. **Bartholomew Diaz, in seeking a route around the tip of Africa, was forced to turn back. Nevertheless, the cape he discovered near the southern tip of Africa became known as:**

   A. Cape Horn

   B. Cabo Bojador

   C. Cape of Good Hope

   D. Cape Hatteras

(Rigorous) (Skill 1.3)

4. **Which one of the following is NOT a reason why Europeans came to the New World?**

   A. To find resources in order to increase wealth

   B. To befriend the Natives who lived there

   C. To increase a ruler's power and importance

   D. To spread Christianity

(Easy) (Skill 1.3)

5. **The Middle Colonies of the Americas were:**

   A. Maryland, Virginia, North Carolina

   B. New York, New Jersey, Pennsylvania, Delaware

   C. Rhode Island, Connecticut, New York, New Jersey

   D. Vermont and New Hampshire

(Rigorous) (Skills 1.3, 2.5)

6. **The ideas and innovations of the period of the Renaissance were spread throughout Europe mainly because of:**

   A. Extensive exploration

   B. Craft workers and their guilds

   C. The invention of the printing press

   D. Increased travel and trade

(Rigorous) (Skill 1.3)

7. **The only colony NOT founded and settled for religious, political, or business reasons was:**

A. Delaware

B. Virginia

C. Georgia

D. New York

(Rigorous) (Skill 1.4)

8. **France decided in 1777 to help the American colonies in their war against Britain. This decision was based on:**

A. The naval victory of John Paul Jones over the British ship Serapis

B. The survival of the terrible winter at Valley Forge

C. The success of colonial guerilla fighters in the South

D. The defeat of the British at Saratoga

(Rigorous) (Skill 1.4)

9. **Which of the following was an important result of the French and Indian Wars?**

A. France strengthened their position in North America

B. Spain lost all its North American territories except Florida

C. Native Americans were largely unaffected by the war

D. Britain enacted and enforced taxes on the colonists

(Rigorous) (Skill 1.4)

10. **Which of the following happened first?**

A. The Boston Massacre

B. The Albany Plan of Union

C. The First Continental Congress

D. The "Shot Heard Round the World"

(Easy) (Skill 1.4)

11. **A major quarrel between colonial Americans and the British concerned a series of British Acts of Parliament dealing with:**

A. Taxes

B. Slavery

C. Native Americans

D. Shipbuilding

(Rigorous) (Skill 1.5)

12. **After ratification of the new Constitution, the most urgent of the many problems facing the new federal government was that of:**

A. Maintaining a strong army and navy

B. Establishing a strong foreign policy

C. Raising money to pay salaries and war debts

D. Setting up courts and passing laws

(Rigorous) (Skill 1.5)

13. **Which of the following was a result of the Great Compromise?**

A. A bicameral legislature

B. An independent judiciary

C. Commerce between the states

D. The Bill of Rights

(Easy) (Skill 1.5)

14. **Which concept is NOT embodied as a right in the First Amendment to the U.S. Constitution?**

    A. Peaceful assembly

    B. Protection against unreasonable search and seizure

    C. Freedom of speech

    D. Petition for redress of grievances

(Easy) (Skill 1.6)

15. **The "Trail of Tears" refers to:**

    A. The removal of the Cherokees from their native lands to Oklahoma Territory (1838–1839)

    B. The revolt and subsequent migration of the Massachusetts Pilgrims under pressure from the Iroquois

    C. The journey of the Nez Perce under Chief Joseph before their capture by the U.S. Army

    D. The 1973 standoff between federal marshals and Native Americans at Wounded Knee, South Dakota

(Average) (Skill 1.6)

16. **Which of the following cases established the precedent of judicial review?**

    A. *Brown v. Board of Education*

    B. *Marbury v. Madison*

    C. *McCulloch v. Maryland*

    D. *Plessy v. Ferguson*

(Easy) (Skill 1.6)

17. **The U.S. Constitution, adopted in 1789, provided for:**

    A. Direct election of the president by all citizens

    B. Direct election of the president by citizens who owned property

    C. Indirect election of the president by electors

    D. Indirect election of the president by the U.S. Senate

(Rigorous) (Skill 1.7)

18. **Which of the following contributed most to westward expansion by colonial Americans?**

    A. Development of large ships capable of sailing upstream in rivers such as the Hudson, Susquehanna, and Delaware

    B. The development of industry in the Northeast

    C. Improved relations with Native Americans who invited colonial Americans to travel west to settle

    D. Improved roads, mail service, and communications

(Average) (Skill 1.7)

19. **It can be reasonably stated that the change in the United States from primarily an agricultural country into an industrial power was due to all of the following EXCEPT:**

    A. Tariffs on foreign imports

    B. Millions of hardworking immigrants

    C. An increase in technological developments

    D. The change from steam to electricity for powering industrial machinery

(Average) (Skill 1.7)

20. Which of the following sets of inventors is correctly matched with the area in which they primarily worked?

A. Thomas Edison and George Westinghouse: transportation

B. Cyrus McCormick and George Washington Carver: household appliances

C. Alexander Graham Bell and Samuel F. B. Morse: communications

D. Isaac Singer and John Gorrie: agriculture

(Easy) (Skill 1.7)

21. The area of the United States was effectively doubled through purchase of the Louisiana Territory under which president?

A. John Adams

B. Thomas Jefferson

C. James Madison

D. James Monroe

(Average) (Skill 1.7)

22. Which one of the following was NOT a reason why the United States went to war with Great Britain in 1812?

A. Resentment by Spain over the sale, exploration, and settlement of the Louisiana Territory

B. The westward movement of farmers because of the need for more land

C. Canadian fur traders were agitating the northwestern Indians to fight American expansion

D. Britain continued to seize American ships on the high seas and force American seamen to serve aboard British ships

(Rigorous) (Skill 1.7)

23. What was a major source of contention between American settlers in Texas and the Mexican government in the 1830s and 1840s?

A. The Americans wished to retain slavery, which had been outlawed in Mexico

B. The Americans had agreed to learn Spanish and become Roman Catholic, but failed to do so

C. The Americans retained ties to the United States, and Santa Anna feared the power of the United States

D. All of the above were contentious issues between American settlers and the Mexican government

(Easy) (Skill 1.7)

24. With which president is the Era of the Common Man associated?

A. George Washington

B. Thomas Jefferson

C. Andrew Jackson

D. John F. Kennedy

(Rigorous) (Skill 1.7)

25. Slavery arose in the southern colonies partly as a perceived economical way to:

A. Increase the owner's wealth through human beings used as a source of exchange

B. Cultivate large plantations of cotton, tobacco, rice, indigo, and other crops

C. Provide Africans with humanitarian aid, such as health care, Christianity, and literacy

D. Keep ships' holds full of cargo on two out of three legs of the "triangular trade" voyage

(Easy) (Skill 1.8)

26. **The Compromise of 1850 came about as a result of which state's entry into the Union?**

    A. Texas

    B. Missouri

    C. California

    D. Kansas

(Average) (Skill 1.8)

27. **Which of the following groups were slave states?**

    A. Delaware, Maryland, Missouri

    B. California, Texas, Florida

    C. Kansas, Missouri, Kentucky

    D. Virginia, West Virginia, Indiana

(Average) (Skill 1.8)

28. **What was one of the results of the Lincoln-Douglas Debates?**

    A. Lincoln voiced his support for the Kansas-Nebraska Act

    B. Douglas voiced his support for expanding slavery

    C. Lincoln got the 1860 Republican nomination for president

    D. Douglas got the 1860 Constitutional Union Party nomination for president

(Easy) (Skill 1.8)

29. **Who was famous for burning Atlanta and marching to the sea?**

    A. Ulysses S. Grant

    B. Robert E. Lee

    C. William T. Sherman

    D. George Meade

(Average) (Skill 1.8)

30. **Which of the following most immediately followed the end of the Civil War?**

    A. Radical Republicans won the Senate

    B. The Civil Rights Act passed

    C. The slaves were emancipated

    D. President Lincoln was assassinated

(Rigorous) (Skill 1.8)

31. **The principle of "popular sovereignty," allowing people in any Territory to make their own decision concerning slavery, was stated by:**

    A. Henry Clay

    B. Daniel Webster

    C. John C. Calhoun

    D. Stephen A. Douglas

(Rigorous) (Skill 1.8)

32. **Who proposed the following plan for Reconstruction?**

    > It would be best for the South to remain ten years longer under military rule, and...during this time we would have Territorial Governors, with Territorial Legislatures, and the government at Washington would pay our general expenses as territories, and educate our children, white and colored?

    A. Abraham Lincoln

    B. Thaddeus Stevens

    C. John Calhoun

    D. Andrew Johnson

(Rigorous) (Skill 1.8)

33. **The Radical Republicans who pushed the harsh Reconstruction measures through Congress after Lincoln's death lost public and moderate Republican support when they went too far:**

    A. In their efforts to impeach the President

    B. By dividing ten southern states into military-controlled districts

    C. By making the ten southern states give freed African Americans the right to vote

    D. By sending carpetbaggers into the South to build up support for Congressional legislation

(Easy) (Skill 1.9)

34. **From what region did large numbers of immigrants came to the United States in the late 1800s and early 1900s?**

    A. Southern Europe

    B. The Middle East

    C. Northern Europe

    D. South Asia

(Easy) (Skill 1.9)

35. **What was one of the major transformations that the United States underwent in the last half of the nineteenth century?**

    A. Urbanization

    B. The Dust Bowl

    C. Ongoing prosperity

    D. Cattle ranching

(Average) (Skill 1.9)

36. **Which of the following was one of the planks of the Populist Party?**

    A. Private ownership of railroads

    B. Silver-based currency

    C. Subsidies to corporations

    D. Limits to public school funding

(Rigorous) (Skill 1.10)

37. **In the 1920s, the United States almost completely stopped all immigration. One of the reasons was:**

    A. A growing sense of isolationism after World War I

    B. War debts from World War I made it difficult to render financial assistance

    C. European nations were reluctant to allow people to leave since there was a need to rebuild populations and economic stability

    D. The United States did not become a member of the League of Nations

(Easy) (Skill 1.10)

38. **What do Jacob Riis, Lincoln Steffans, and Ida Tarbell have in common?**

    A. They were all powerful in party politics during the Progressive Era

    B. They were all industrial magnates who opposed Progressive reforms

    C. They were all muckrakers writing during the Progressive Era

    D. They were all African American anti-lynching activists

(Average) (Skill 1.10)

39. **The Teapot Dome scandal related to:**

A. The improper taxing of tea surpluses in Boston

B. The improper awarding of building contracts in Washington, D.C.

C. The improper sale of policy decisions by various Harding administration officials

D. The improper sale of oil reserves in Wyoming

(Rigorous) (Skill 1.10)

40. **Which of the following was NOT a factor in the United Statess' entry into World War I?**

A. The closeness of the presidential election of 1916

B. The German threat to sink all allied ships, including merchant ships

C. The desire to preserve democracy as practiced in Britain and France

D. The sinking of the Lusitania and the Sussex

(Average) (Skill 1.10)

41. **What 1924 Act of Congress severely restricted immigration in the United States?**

A. Taft-Hartley Act

B. Smoot-Hawley Act

C. Fordney-McCumber Act

D. Johnson-Reed Act

(Rigorous) (Skill 1.10, 1.11)

42. **Of all the major causes of both World War I and II, the most significant one is considered to be:**

A. Extreme nationalism

B. Military buildup and aggression

C. Political unrest

D. Agreements and alliances

(Average) (Skill 1.10)

43. **Which of the following contributed to the severity of the Great Depression in California?**

A. An influx of Chinese immigrants

B. An influx of people from the cities

C. An influx of Mexican immigrants

D. An influx of Okies

(Average) (Skill 1.11)

44. **Before the end of 1941, how did a majority of Americans feel about going to war?**

A. They wanted to make the world safe for democracy

B. They wanted to stay out of European wars

C. They wanted to invade the Philippines

D. They wanted to expel Japanese Americans

(Average) (Skill 1.12)

45. **In issuing an ultimatum for Soviet ships not to enter Cuban waters in October 1962, President John F. Kennedy, as part of his decision, used the provisions of the:**

    A. Monroe Doctrine

    B. Declaration of the Rights of Man

    C. Geneva Conventions

    D. Truman Doctrine

(Average) (Skill 1.12)

46. **The Marshall Plan called for:**

    A. Punishing Germany

    B. Rebuilding Europe

    C. Establishing NATO

    D. Disarming Japan

(Rigorous) (Skill 1.12)

47. **Which of the following most closely characterizes the Supreme Court's decision in *Brown v. Board of Education*?**

    A. Chief Justice Warren had to cast the deciding vote in a sharply divided the Supreme Court

    B. The decision was rendered along sectional lines with Northerners voting for integration and Southerners voting for segregation

    C. The decision was 7-2 with dissenting justices not even preparing a written dissent

    D. Chief Justice Warren was able to persuade the Supreme Court to render a unanimous decision

(Average) (Skill 1.13)

48. **What was an important element of Ronald Reagan's presidency?**

    A. Tearing down the Berlin Wall

    B. Increasing unemployment

    C. Favorable laws for unions

    D. Trickle-down economics

Answer Key

1. A	11. A	21. B	31. D	41. D
2. A	12. C	22. A	32. B	42. A
3. C	13. A	23. D	33. A	43. D
4. B	14. B	24. C	34. A	44. B
5. B	15. A	25. B	35. A	45. A
6. C	16. B	26. C	36. B	46. B
7. C	17. C	27. A	37. A	47. D
8. D	18. D	28. C	38. C	48. D
9. D	19. A	29. C	39. D	
10. B	20. C	30. D	40. A	

Rigor Table

RIGOR TABLE		
Rigor level	**Questions**	**TOTALS**
Easy 22%	2, 3, 5, 11, 14, 15, 17, 21, 24, 26, 29, 34, 35, 38	
Average 43%	1, 16, 19, 20, 22, 27, 28, 30, 36, 39, 41, 43, 44, 45, 46, 48	
Rigorous 35%	4, 6, 7, 8, 9, 10, 12, 13, 18, 23, 25, 31, 32, 33, 37, 40, 42, 47	

Sample Test with Rationales: United States History

(Average) (Skill 1.2)

1. **Which of the following best describes how the Native American nations lived in North America before Europeans arrived?**

   A. Subsistence

   B. Mercantile

   C. Capitalist

   D. Literate

   Answer: A: Subsistence

   Native Americans hunted, gathered, and grew only what they needed to survive. This is referred to as subsistence living. Mercantile describes the merchant economy of England and its colonies. Capitalism evolved out of mercantilism and is the economic system of most modern democracies. Most Native Americans had an oral rather than written tradition and were therefore not literate societies.

(Easy) (Skill 1.2)

2. **Apartments built out of cliff faces; shared government by adult citizens; absence of aggression toward other groups. These factors characterize the Native American group known as:**

   A. Pueblo

   B. Comanche

   C. Seminole

   D. Sioux

   Answer: A. Pueblo

   The Comanches were a nomadic Native American group that emerged around 1700 CE in the North American Plains and were decidedly aggressive toward their neighbors. The Seminoles are a Native American group that originally emerged in Florida in the mid-18th century and was made up of refugees from other Native tribes and escaped slaves. The Sioux were a Native American people who originally lived in the Dakotas, Nebraska, and Minnesota and clashed extensively with white settlers.

(Easy) (Skill 1.3)

3. **Bartholomew Diaz, in seeking a route around the tip of Africa, was forced to turn back. Nevertheless, the cape he discovered near the southern tip of Africa became known as:**

   A. Cape Horn

   B. Cabo Bojador

   C. Cape of Good Hope

   D. Cape Hatteras

   Answer: C. Cape of Good Hope

   Sir Francis Drake discovered Cape Horn as he sailed around the globe in 1578, and it is located at the southern tip of Chile. A European, Portuguese Gil Eanes, first successfully navigated Cajo Bojador on the western coast of northern Africa in 1434. Cape Hatteras is located on the U.S. Atlantic coast at North Carolina.

(Rigorous) (Skill 1.3)

4. **Which one of the following is NOT a reason why Europeans came to the New World?**

   A. To find resources in order to increase wealth

   B. To befriend the Natives who lived there

   C. To increase a ruler's power and importance

   D. To spread Christianity

   Answer: B. To befriend the Natives who lived there

   The Europeans came to the New World for a number of reasons. Often, they came to find new natural resources to extract for manufacturing. The Portuguese, Spanish, and English were sent to increase the monarch's power and spread influences such as religion (Christianity) and culture. While some Europeans did establish good relationships with the natives—e.g., the French traded with them—that was not their purpose in coming to the New World.

(Easy) (Skill 1.3)

5. **The Middle Colonies of the Americas were:**

   A. Maryland, Virginia, North Carolina

   B. New York, New Jersey, Pennsylvania, Delaware

   C. Rhode Island, Connecticut, New York, New Jersey

   D. Vermont and New Hampshire

   Answer: B. New York, New Jersey, Pennsylvania, Delaware

   Maryland, Virginia, and North Carolina were southern colonies. Rhode Island, Connecticut and New Hampshire were New England colonies, and Vermont was not one of the 13 original colonies.

(Rigorous) (Skills 1.3, 2.5)

6. **The ideas and innovations of the period of the Renaissance were spread throughout Europe mainly because of:**

   A. Extensive exploration

   B. Craft workers and their guilds

   C. The invention of the printing press

   D. Increased travel and trade

   Answer: C. The invention of the printing press

   The ideas and innovations of the Renaissance were spread throughout Europe for a number of reasons. While exploration increased travel and spread of craft may have aided the spread of the Renaissance to small degrees, nothing was as important to the spread of ideas as Gutenberg's invention of the printing press in Germany.

(Rigorous) (Skill 1.3)

7. **The only colony NOT founded and settled for religious, political, or business reasons was:**

   A. Delaware

   B. Virginia

   C. Georgia

   D. New York

Answer: C. Georgia

The Swedish and the Dutch established Delaware and New York as Middle Colonies. They were established with the intention of growth by economic prosperity from farming across the countryside. The English, with the intention of generating a strong farming economy settled Virginia, a Southern colony. Georgia was the only one of these colonies not settled for religious, political, or business reasons, as it was started as a place for debtors from English prisons.

(Rigorous) (Skill 1.4)

8. **France decided in 1777 to help the American colonies in their war against Britain. This decision was based on:**

   A. The naval victory of John Paul Jones over the British ship Serapis

   B. The survival of the terrible winter at Valley Forge

   C. The success of colonial guerilla fighters in the South

   D. The defeat of the British at Saratoga

Answer: D. The defeat of the British at Saratoga

The defeat of the British at Saratoga was the overwhelming factor in the Franco-American alliance of 1777 that helped the American colonies defeat the British. Some historians believe that without the Franco-American alliance, the American colonies would not have been able to defeat the British, and America would have remained a British colony.

(Rigorous) (Skill 1.4)

9. **Which of the following was an important result of the French and Indian Wars?**

   A. France strengthened their position in North America

   B. Spain lost all its North American territories except Florida

   C. Native Americans were largely unaffected by the war

   D. Britain enacted and enforced taxes on the colonists

Answer: D. Britain enacted and enforced taxes on the colonists

France lost most of their North American possessions as a result of the wars. Spain lost Florida as a result of the war but kept its lands in the Southwest. Native Americans ended up losing much of their land after the war. Britain taxed the colonists to raise money to pay for the war.

(Rigorous) (Skill 1.4)

10. **Which of the following happened first?**

    A. The Boston Massacre

    B. The Albany Plan of Union

    C. The First Continental Congress

    D. The "Shot Heard Round the World"

Answer: B. The Albany Plan of Union

The Boston Massacre happened in 1770. The Albany Plan of Union happened in 1754. The First Continental Congress happened in 1774. The Shot Heard Round the World happened in 1775.

(Easy) (Skill 1.4)

11. **A major quarrel between colonial Americans and the British concerned a series of British Acts of Parliament dealing with:**

    A. Taxes

    B. Slavery

    C. Native Americans

    D. Shipbuilding

    Answer: A. Taxes

    Acts of Parliament imposing taxes on the colonists always provoked resentment. Because the colonies had no direct representation in Parliament, they felt it unjust that that body should impose taxes on them with so little knowledge of their very different situation in America and no real concern for the consequences of such taxes. While slavery continued to exist in the colonies long after it had been completely abolished in Britain, it never was a source of serious debate between Britain and the colonies. By the time Britain outlawed slavery in its colonies in 1833, the American Revolution had already taken place, and the United States was free of British control. There was no series of British Acts of Parliament passed concerning Native Americans and Colonial shipbuilding was an industry that received little interference from the British.

(Rigorous) (Skill 1.5)

12. **After ratification of the new Constitution, the most urgent of the many problems facing the new federal government was that of:**

    A. Maintaining a strong army and navy

    B. Establishing a strong foreign policy

    C. Raising money to pay salaries and war debts

    D. Setting up courts and passing laws

    Answer: C. Raising money to pay salaries and war debts

    Maintaining strong military forces, establishing a strong foreign policy, and setting up a justice system were important problems facing the United States under the newly ratified Constitution. However, the most important and pressing issue was how to raise money to pay salaries and war debts from the Revolutionary War. Alexander Hamilton (1755–1804), then Secretary of the Treasury, proposed increased tariffs and taxes on products such as liquor. This money would be used to pay off war debts and to pay for internal programs. Hamilton also proposed the idea of a National Bank.

(Rigorous) (Skill 1.5)

13. **Which of the following was a result of the Great Compromise?**

    A. A bicameral legislature

    B. An independent judiciary

    C. Commerce between the states

    D. The Bill of Rights

Answer: A. A bicameral legislature

The Great Compromise determined that states would have equal representation in the Senate, while representation in the other legislative body would be based on population. The Great Compromise did not address the three branches of government. The Commerce Compromise addressed commerce between the states. The Bill of Rights emerged as a way to satisfy anti-Federalists who feared that the federal government might take away individuals' rights.

(Easy) (Skill 1.5)

14. **Which concept is NOT embodied as a right in the First Amendment to the U.S. Constitution?**

   A. Peaceful assembly

   B. Protection against unreasonable search and seizure

   C. Freedom of speech

   D. Petition for redress of grievances

Answer: B. Protection against unreasonable search and seizure

The first amendment to the Constitution reads, "Congress shall make no law respecting [...] abridging the freedom of speech, or of the press; or the right of the people peaceably to assemble, and to petition the government for a redress of grievances." The protection against unreasonable search and seizure is a constitutional right found in the fourth amendment, not the first.

(Easy) (Skill 1.6)

15. **The "Trail of Tears" refers to:**

   A. The removal of the Cherokees from their native lands to Oklahoma Territory (1838–1839)

   B. The revolt and subsequent migration of the Massachusetts Pilgrims under pressure from the Iroquois

   C. The journey of the Nez Perce under Chief Joseph before their capture by the U.S. Army

   D. The 1973 standoff between federal marshals and Native Americans at Wounded Knee, South Dakota

Answer: A. The removal of the Cherokees from their native lands to Oklahoma Territory (1838–1839)

There never was a revolt and migration of the Massachusetts Pilgrims under pressure from the Iroquois. The 1877 journey of the Nez Perce under Chief Joseph was a strategically impressive attempt to retreat from an oncoming U.S. Army into Canada. The 1973 Wounded Knee incident was the occupation of the town of Wounded Knee, South Dakota, by the American Indian Movement to call attention to issues of Native American civil rights.

(Average) (Skill 1.6)

16. **Which of the following cases established the precedent of judicial review?**

   A. *Brown v. Board of Education*

   B. *Marbury v. Madison*

   C. *McCulloch v. Maryland*

   D. *Plessy v. Ferguson*

Answer: B. *Marbury v. Madison*

Brown v. Board of Education ended the policy of "separate but equal" and was delivered in 1954. *Marbury v. Madison* established the precedent of judicial review. *McCulloch v. Maryland* ruled that the federal government had ultimate authority when its laws conflicted with state governments'. *Plessy v. Ferguson* established "separate but equal" in 1896.

(Easy) (Skill 1.6)

17. **The U.S. Constitution, adopted in 1789, provided for:**

    A. Direct election of the president by all citizens

    B. Direct election of the president by citizens who owned property

    C. Indirect election of the president by electors

    D. Indirect election of the president by the U.S. Senate

Answer: C. Indirect election of the president by electors

The United States Constitution has always arranged for the indirect election of the president by electors. The question, by mentioning the original date of adoption, might mislead someone to choose B. While standards of citizenship have been changed by amendment, the president has never been directly elected, nor does the Senate have anything to do with presidential elections. The House of Representatives, not the Senate, settles cases where neither candidate wins in the Electoral College.

(Rigorous) (Skill 1.7)

18. **Which of the following contributed most to westward expansion by colonial Americans?**

    A. Development of large ships capable of sailing upstream in rivers such as the Hudson, Susquehanna, and Delaware

    B. The development of industry in the Northeast

    C. Improved relations with Native Americans who invited colonial Americans to travel west to settle

    D. Improved roads, mail service, and communications

Answer: D. Improved roads, mail service, and communications

As the Susquehanna, Delaware, and Hudson are limited to the Northeast, they would not have helped the colonists penetrate any further west. Industry did develop in the Northeast, but it was not the biggest contributor to westward expansion. In general, colonist-Native American relations worsened as colonists moved west, so colonists were unlikely to have been invited yet further west. Improved roads, mail service, and communications made traveling west easier and more attractive as that meant not being completely cut off from news and family in the east.

(Average) (Skill 1.7)

19. **It can be reasonably stated that the change in the United States from primarily an agricultural country into an industrial power was due to all of the following EXCEPT:**

    A. Tariffs on foreign imports

    B. Millions of hardworking immigrants

    C. An increase in technological developments

    D. The change from steam to electricity for powering industrial machinery

    Answer: A. Tariffs on foreign imports

    The change in the United States from primarily an agricultural country into an industrial power was a combination of millions of hard-working immigrants, an increase in technological developments, and the change from steam to electricity for powering industrial machinery. The only reason given that really had little effect is the tariffs on foreign imports.

(Average) (Skill 1.7)

20. **Which of the following sets of inventors is correctly matched with the area in which they primarily worked?**

    A. Thomas Edison and George Westinghouse: transportation

    B. Cyrus McCormick and George Washington Carver: household appliances

    C. Alexander Graham Bell and Samuel F. B. Morse: communications

    D. Isaac Singer and John Gorrie: agriculture

    Answer: C. Alexander Graham Bell and Samuel F. B. Morse: communications

    Bell, inventor of the telephone, and Morse, inventor of the telegraph and Morse code, were both working in the area of communications. While Westinghouse did invent various technologies crucial to the railroads and thus transportation, Edison did not; rather, both are strongly linked to electrical inventions. McCormick and Carver specialized in agricultural inventions, while Singer, an inventor of the sewing machine, and Gorrie, the inventor of air conditioning and refrigeration, were best known for their household appliances.

(Easy) (Skill 1.7)

21. **The area of the United States was effectively doubled through purchase of the Louisiana Territory under which president?**

    A. John Adams

    B. Thomas Jefferson

    C. James Madison

    D. James Monroe

    Answer: B. Thomas Jefferson

    John Adams (1735–1826) was president from 1797 to 1801, before the purchase. The Louisiana Purchase, an acquisition of territory from France in 1803, occurred under Thomas Jefferson. James Madison (1751–1836) was president after the Purchase (1809–1817). James Monroe (1758–1831) was actually a signatory on the Purchase but did not become president until 1817.

(Average) (Skill 1.7)

22. Which one of the following was NOT a reason why the United States went to war with Great Britain in 1812?

A. Resentment by Spain over the sale, exploration, and settlement of the Louisiana Territory

B. The westward movement of farmers because of the need for more land

C. Canadian fur traders were agitating the northwestern Indians to fight American expansion

D. Britain continued to seize American ships on the high seas and force American seamen to serve aboard British ships

Answer: A. Resentment by Spain over the sale, exploration, and settlement of the Louisiana Territory

The United States went to war with Great Britain in 1812 for a number of reasons, including the expansion of settlers westward and the need for more land, the agitation of Native Americans by Canadian fur traders in eastern Canada, and the continued seizures of American ships by the British on the high seas. Therefore, the only statement given that was not a reason for the War of 1812 was the resentment by Spain over the sale, exploration, and settlement of the Louisiana Territory. In fact, the Spanish continually held more hostility towards the British than towards the United States. The War of 1812 is often considered to be the second American war for independence.

(Rigorous) (Skill 1.7)

23. What was a major source of contention between American settlers in Texas and the Mexican government in the 1830s and 1840s?

A. The Americans wished to retain slavery, which had been outlawed in Mexico

B. The Americans had agreed to learn Spanish and become Roman Catholic, but failed to do so

C. The Americans retained ties to the United States, and Santa Anna feared the power of the United States

D. All of the above were contentious issues between American settlers and the Mexican government

Answer: D. All of the above were contentious issues between American settlers and the Mexican government

The American settlers simply were not willing to assimilate into Mexican society but maintained their prior commitments to slave holding, the English language, Protestantism, and the U.S. government.

(Easy) (Skill 1.7)

24. With which president is the Era of the Common Man associated?

A. George Washington

B. Thomas Jefferson

C. Andrew Jackson

D. John F. Kennedy

Answer: C. Andrew Jackson

George Washington was the first president but was not associated with the common man. Thomas Jefferson favored a small federal government and allied himself with the yeoman farmer but was not associated with the common man. Andrew Jackson expanded rights to more men and so was known as the leader during the Era of the Common Man. John F. Kennedy presided over the nation at the start of a major change in attitude but not during the Era of the Common Man.

(Rigorous) (Skill 1.7)

25. **Slavery arose in the southern colonies partly as a perceived economical way to:**

A. Increase the owner's wealth through human beings used as a source of exchange

B. Cultivate large plantations of cotton, tobacco, rice, indigo, and other crops

C. Provide Africans with humanitarian aid, such as health care, Christianity, and literacy

D. Keep ships' holds full of cargo on two out of three legs of the "triangular trade" voyage

Answer: B. Cultivate large plantations of cotton, tobacco, rice, indigo, and other crops

The southern states, with their smaller populations, were heavily dependent on slave labor as a means of being able to fulfill their role and remain competitive in the greater U.S. economy. When slaves arrived in the South, the vast majority would become permanent fixtures on plantations, intended for work, not as a source of exchange. While some slave owners instructed their slaves in Christianity, provided health care, and some level of education, such attention was not their primary reason for owning slave—a cheap and ready labor force was. Whether or not ships' holds were full on two or three legs of the triangular journey was not the concern of southerner plantation owners as the final purchasers of slaves. Such details would have concerned the slave traders.

(Easy) (Skill 1.8)

26. **The Compromise of 1850 came about as a result of which state's entry into the Union?**

A. Texas

B. Missouri

C. California

D. Kansas

Answer: C. California

Texas entered the Union in 1845. Missouri was the subject of the Missouri Compromise of 1824, which would be the first such compromise between slave and free states. California entered the union after the Compromise of 1850 was drafted to avoid the issue of secession by the slave states. Kansas became a violent battleground between pro-slavery and anti-slavery forces when it was organized as a territory in 1854, before achieving statehood in 1861 as a free state.

(Average) (Skill 1.8)

27. **Which of the following groups were slave states?**

 A. Delaware, Maryland, Missouri

 B. California, Texas, Florida

 C. Kansas, Missouri, Kentucky

 D. Virginia, West Virginia, Indiana

Answer: A. Delaware, Maryland, Missouri

Delaware, Maryland, and Missouri were all slave states at the time of the Civil War. Florida and Texas were slave states, while California was a free state. Kansas, Missouri, and Kentucky were all originally slave territories, and Missouri and Kentucky were admitted to the Union as such. However, Kansas's petition to join the union in 1858 was blocked in order to preserve the balance between slave and free states. Kansas was admitted as a free state in 1861. Virginia and West Virginia were both slave states, but Indiana was a free state.

(Average) (Skill 1.8)

28. **What was one of the results of the Lincoln-Douglas Debates?**

 A. Lincoln voiced his support for the Kansas-Nebraska Act

 B. Douglas voiced his support for expanding slavery

 C. Lincoln got the 1860 Republican nomination for president

 D. Douglas got the 1860 Constitutional Union Party nomination for president

Answer: C. Lincoln got the 1860 Republican nomination for president

Lincoln did not want slavery to extend further. Douglas voiced his support for popular sovereignty but not for the expansion of slavery. Although Lincoln lost the 1858 senatorial election to Douglas, he won the 1860 Republican nomination for the presidency. Douglas got the 1860 Northern Democratic nomination for president.

(Easy) (Skill 1.8)

29. **Who was famous for burning Atlanta and marching to the sea?**

 A. Ulysses S. Grant

 B. Robert E. Lee

 C. William T. Sherman

 D. George Meade

Answer: C. William T. Sherman

Gen. Ulysses S. Grant was the final commander of the Union army during the Civil War but did not burn Atlanta. Gen. Robert E. Lee was the commander of the Confederate army. William T. Sherman burned Atlanta and continued on to Savannah. Gen. George Meade was the Union commander at the Battle of Gettysburg in 1863.

(Average) (Skill 1.8)

30. **Which of the following most immediately followed the end of the Civil War?**

 A. Radical Republicans won the Senate

 B. The Civil Rights Act passed

 C. The slaves were emancipated

 D. President Lincoln was assassinated

Answer: D. President Lincoln was assassinated

Radical Republicans won the Senate in the 1866 election. The Civil Rights Act passed in 1866. The slaves were emancipated before the war ended. Lincoln was assassinated just days after the Confederacy surrendered.

(Rigorous) (Skill 1.8)

31. **The principle of "popular sovereignty," allowing people in any Territory to make their own decision concerning slavery was stated by:**

A. Henry Clay

B. Daniel Webster

C. John C. Calhoun

D. Stephen A. Douglas

Answer: D. Stephen A. Douglas

Henry Clay (1777–1852) and Daniel Webster (1782–1852) were prominent Whigs whose main concern was keeping the United States one nation. They opposed Andrew Jackson and his Democratic party in the 1830s in favor of promoting what Clay called the American System. John C. Calhoun (1782–1850) served as Vice President under John Quincy Adams and Andrew Jackson, and then as a state senator from South Carolina. He was very pro-slavery and a champion of states' rights. The principle of popular sovereignty, in which people in each territory could make their own decisions concerning slavery, was the doctrine of Stephen A. Douglas (1813–1861). Douglas was looking for a middle ground between the abolitionists of the North and the pro-slavery Democrats of the South. However, as the polarization of pro- and anti-slavery sentiments grew, he lost the presidential election to Republican Abraham Lincoln, who later abolished slavery.

(Rigorous) (Skill 1.8)

32. **Who proposed the following plan for Reconstruction?**

> It would be best for the South to remain ten years longer under military rule, and...during this time we would have Territorial Governors, with Territorial Legislatures, and the government at Washington would pay our general expenses as territories, and educate our children, white and colored?

A. Abraham Lincoln

B. Thaddeus Stevens

C. John Calhoun

D. Andrew Johnson

Answer: B. Thaddeus Stevens

Lincoln favored lenient measures to readmit the southern states into the union. Radical Republicans, such as Stevens, wanted very strict readmission standards. John Calhoun died in 1850. Andrew Johnson favored more lenient requirements for readmission.

(Rigorous) (Skill 1.8)

33. **The Radical Republicans who pushed the harsh Reconstruction measures through Congress after Lincoln's death lost public and moderate Republican support when they went too far:**

    A. In their efforts to impeach the President

    B. By dividing ten southern states into military-controlled districts

    C. By making the ten southern states give freed African Americans the right to vote

    D. By sending carpetbaggers into the South to build up support for Congressional legislation

Answer: A. In their efforts to impeach the President

Immediately after Lincoln's death, moderate Republicans—and the public in general—supported the more radical end of the Republican spectrum. Many felt as though Andrew Johnson's policies toward the South were too soft and would allow the rebuilding of the old system of white power and slavery. The radical Republicans were so concerned that the President would make concessions to the old Southerners that they attempted to impeach him. This turned back the support that they had received from the public and from moderates.

(Easy) (Skill 1.9)

34. **From what region did large numbers of immigrants came to the United States in the late 1800s and early 1900s?**

    A. Southern Europe

    B. The Middle East

    C. Northern Europe

    D. South Asia

Answer: A. Southern Europe

Between 1891 and 1910, 12 million immigrants came to the United States, particularly from southern and eastern Europe. There were not large numbers of Middle Eastern immigrants at the time. Northern European immigrants came to the United States in large numbers earlier than the late 1800s. South Asian immigrants came to the United States in large numbers in the last half of the twentieth century.

(Easy) (Skill 1.9)

35. **What was one of the major transformations that the United States underwent in the last half of the nineteenth century?**

    A. Urbanization

    B. The Dust Bowl

    C. Ongoing prosperity

    D. Cattle ranching

Answer: A. Urbanization

In 1790, 90 percent of Americans lived on farms; by 1890, 43 percent lived on farms; and by 1930, 21 percent lived on farms. The Dust Bowl was in the 1930s. There were several economic downturns in the last half of the nineteenth century, and prosperity was not evenly distributed even in the good times. Cattle-ranching does not qualify as a major transformation.

(Average) (Skill 1.9)

36. **Which of the following was one of the planks of the Populist Party?**

A. Private ownership of railroads

B. Silver-based currency

C. Subsidies to corporations

D. Limits to public school funding

Answer: B: Silver-based currency

Populists advocated government ownership of railroads, the silver standard, and an end to corporate subsidies. The Populists did not have a plank about public schools.

(Rigorous) (Skill 1.10)

37. **In the 1920s, the United States almost completely stopped all immigration. One of the reasons was:**

A. A growing sense of isolationism after World War I

B. War debts from World War I made it difficult to render financial assistance

C. European nations were reluctant to allow people to leave since there was a need to rebuild populations and economic stability

D. The United States did not become a member of the League of Nations

Answer: A. A growing sense of isolationism after World War I

After the war, many Americans wanted to close the borders and remain isolated. The United States was owed money after World War I, rather than being in debt. There is no evidence for European reluctance to emigrate at this time and the United States not becoming a member of the League of Nations had no affect on immigration.

(Easy) (Skill 1.10)

38. **What do Jacob Riis, Lincoln Steffans, and Ida Tarbell have in common?**

A. They were all powerful in party politics during the Progressive Era

B. They were all industrial magnates who opposed Progressive reforms

C. They were all muckrakers writing during the Progressive Era

D. They were all African American anti-lynching activists

Answer: C. They were all muckrakers writing during the Progressive Era

All three were muckrakers. Jacob Riis exposed the terrible conditions of tenement dwellers; Lincoln Steffans reported on political corruption; and Ida Tarbell wrote about Standard Oil.

(Average) (Skill 1.10)

39. **The Teapot Dome scandal related to:**

A. The improper taxing of tea surpluses in Boston

B. The improper awarding of building contracts in Washington, D.C.

C. The improper sale of policy decisions by various Harding administration officials

D. The improper sale of oil reserves in Wyoming

Answer: D. The improper sale of oil reserves in Wyoming

This scandal refers to the improper sale of federal oil reserves in Teapot Dome, Wyoming, an infamous event during the Harding Administration (1921–1925). Choice C would be tempting, especially since the Secretary of the Interior personally benefited from the sale, but no significant policy decisions were involved. No building of a dome or taxing of tea were involved in the scandal.

(Rigorous) (Skill 1.10)

40. **Which of the following was NOT a factor in the United Statess' entry into World War I?**

A. The closeness of the presidential election of 1916

B. The German threat to sink all allied ships, including merchant ships

C. The desire to preserve democracy as practiced in Britain and France

D. The sinking of the Lusitania and the Sussex

Answer: A. The closeness of the presidential election of 1916

Since there was no presidential election of 1916, this could not have been a factor the United States' entry into the war; the last election had been in 1914. All the other answers were indeed factors.

(Average) (Skill 1.10)

41. **What 1924 Act of Congress severely restricted immigration in the United States?**

A. Taft-Hartley Act

B. Smoot-Hawley Act

C. Fordney-McCumber Act

D. Johnson-Reed Act

Answer: D. Johnson-Reed Act

The Taft-Harley Act (1947) prohibited unfair labor practices by labor unions. The Smoot-Hawley Act (1930) raised U.S. tariffs on imported goods to negative effect on the U.S. economy and world trade as the Fordney-McCumber Act (1922) had done before it.

(Rigorous) (Skill 1.10, 1.11)

42. **Of all the major causes of both World War I and II, the most significant one is considered to be:**

A. Extreme nationalism

B. Military buildup and aggression

C. Political unrest

D. Agreements and alliances

Answer: A. Extreme nationalism

Although military buildup and aggression, political unrest, and agreements and alliances were all characteristic of the world climate before and during World War I and World War II, the most significant cause of both wars was extreme nationalism. Nationalism is the idea that the interests and needs of a particular nation are of the utmost and primary importance above all else. The nationalism that sparked WWI included a rejection of German, Austro-Hungarian, and Ottoman imperialism by Serbs, Slavs, and others culminating in the assassination of Archduke Ferdinand by a Serb nationalist in 1914. Following WWI and the Treaty of Versailles, many Germans and others in the Central Powers, discontented with the concessions and reparations of the treaty, started a new form of nationalism. Adolf Hitler and the Nazi regime led this extreme nationalism. Hitler's ideas, an example of extreme, oppressive nationalism combined with political, social and economic scapegoating, were the primary cause of WWII.

(Average) (Skill 1.10)

43. **Which of the following contributed to the severity of the Great Depression in California?**

A. An influx of Chinese immigrants

B. An influx of people from the cities

C. An influx of Mexican immigrants

D. An influx of Okies

Answer: D. An influx of Okies

The Dust Bowl of the Great Plains destroyed agriculture in the plains areas, resulting in a large influx of Okies into California. People living in these areas lost their livelihood, and many lost their homes and possessions in the great dust storms that resulted from a period of extended drought. People from all of the states affected by the Dust Bowl made their way to California in search of a better life.

(Average) (Skill 1.11)

44. **Before the end of 1941, how did a majority of Americans feel about going to war?**

A. They wanted to make the world safe for democracy

B. They wanted to stay out of European wars

C. They wanted to invade the Philippines

D. They wanted to expel Japanese Americans

Answer: B. They wanted to stay out of European wars

Making the world safe for democracy was a rallying cry for World War I but not World War II. Many Americans were actually isolationists at the time. Liberating the Philippines happened much later in the war. Large-scale discrimination against Japanese-Americans happened after Japan bombed Pearl Harbor.

(Average) (Skill 1.12)

45. **In issuing an ultimatum for Soviet ships not to enter Cuban waters in October 1962, President John F. Kennedy, as part of his decision, used the provisions of the:**

    A. Monroe Doctrine

    B. Declaration of the Rights of Man

    C. Geneva Conventions

    D. Truman Doctrine

    Answer: A. Monroe Doctrine

    The Monroe Doctrine, initially formulated by Presidents James Monroe (1758–1831) and John Quincy Adams (1767–1848) and later enhanced by President Theodore Roosevelt (1858–1915), opposed European interference in the Americas and perceived any such attempts as a threat to U.S. security. The Declaration of the Rights of Man, widely adapted in future declarations about international human rights, was formulated in France during the French Revolution and adopted by the National Constituent Assembly in 1789 as the premise of any future French constitution. The Geneva Conventions (1864, 1929 and 1949, with later additions and amendments) established humanitarian and ethical standards for conduct during times of war and has been widely accepted as international law. The Truman Doctrine (1947) provided for the support of Greece and Turkey as a means of protecting them from Soviet influence. It thereby began the Cold War (1947–1991), a period in which the United States sought to contain the Soviet Union by limiting its influence in other countries.

(Average) (Skill 1.12)

46. **The Marshall Plan called for:**

    A. Punishing Germany

    B. Rebuilding Europe

    C. Establishing NATO

    D. Disarming Japan

    Answer: B. Rebuilding Europe

    The Treaty of Versaille punished Germany after WWI, not WWII. NATO was part of the Cold War plan for protecting Western Europe from Soviet aggression. Disarming Japan was a condition of Japan's surrender, but was separate from the Marshall Plan.

(Rigorous) (Skill 1.12)

47. **Which of the following most closely characterizes the Supreme Court's decision in *Brown v. Board of Education*?**

    A. Chief Justice Warren had to cast the deciding vote in a sharply divided the Supreme Court

    B. The decision was rendered along sectional lines with Northerners voting for integration and Southerners voting for segregation

    C. The decision was 7-2 with dissenting justices not even preparing a written dissent

    D. Chief Justice Warren was able to persuade the Supreme Court to render a unanimous decision

    Answer: D. Chief Justice Warren was able to persuade the Court to render a unanimous decision

    The Supreme Court decided 9-0 against segregated educational facilities.

(Average) (Skill 1.13)

48. **What was an important element of Ronald Reagan's presidency?**

A. Tearing down the Berlin Wall

B. Increasing unemployment

C. Favorable laws for unions

D. Trickle-down economics

Answer: D. Trickle-down economics

Although Reagan challenged Gorbachev to tear the wall down, the wall did not come down until 1989 when George H. W. Bush was president. Unemployment declined starting in 1983. Reagan was known for breaking the Air Traffic Controllers strike, not favoring unions. Reaganomics was supply-side, or trickle-down, economics.

SAMPLE TEST

World History

(Average) (Skill 2.1)

49. **Which of the following developments is most closely associated with the Neolithic Age?**

  A. Human use of fire

  B. First use of stone chipping instruments

  C. Domestication of plants

  D. Development of metallurgical alloys

(Average) (Skill 2.1)

50. **The end to hunting, gathering, and fishing of prehistoric people was due to:**

  A. Domestication of animals

  B. Building crude huts and houses

  C. Development of agriculture

  D. Organized government in villages

(Easy) (Skill 2.2)

51. **The Tigris-Euphrates Valley was the site of which two primary ancient civilizations?**

  A. Babylonian and Assyrian

  B. Sumerian and Egyptian

  C. Hyksos and Hurrian

  D. Persian and Phoenician

(Easy) (Skill 2.2)

52. **The first ancient civilization to introduce and practice monotheism was the:**

  A. Sumerians

  B. Minoans

  C. Phoenicians

  D. Hebrews

(Rigorous) (Skill 2.2)

53. **For the historian studying ancient Egypt, which of the following would be least useful?**

  A. The record of an ancient Greek historian on Greek-Egyptian interaction

  B. Letters from an Egyptian ruler to his/her regional governors

  C. Inscriptions of the Fourteenth Egyptian Dynasty

  D. Letters from a nineteenth-century Egyptologist to his wife

(Average) (Skill 2.2)

54. **Indo-European languages are native languages to each of the following EXCEPT:**

  A. Germany

  B. India

  C. Italy

  D. Finland

(Average) (Skill 2.3)

55. Chinese civilization is generally credited with the original development of which of the following sets of technologies:

A. Movable type and mass production of goods

B. Wool processing and domestication of the horse

C. Paper and gunpowder manufacture

D. Leather processing and modern timekeeping

(Average) (Skill 2.3)

56. The ____________ were fought between the Roman Empire and Carthage.

A. Civil Wars

B. Punic Wars

C. Caesarian Wars

D. Persian Wars

(Rigorous) (Skills 2.3, 2.4)

57. Of the legacies of the Roman Empire listed below, the most influential, effective, and lasting is:

A. The language of Latin

B. Roman law, justice, and political system

C. Engineering and building

D. The writings of its poets and historians

(Easy) (Skill 2.4)

58. The principle of zero in mathematics is the discovery of the ancient civilization found in:

A. Egypt

B. Persia

C. India

D. Babylon

(Easy) (Skill 2.4)

59. The native metaphysical outlook of Japan, usually characterized as a religion, is:

A. Tao

B. Shinto

C. Hindu

D. Sunni

(Rigorous) (Skill 2.4)

60. Which one of the following is NOT an important legacy of the Byzantine Empire?

A. It protected Western Europe from various attacks from the East by such groups as the Persians, Ottoman Turks, and Barbarians

B. It played a part in preserving the literature, philosophy, and language of ancient Greece

C. Its military organization was the foundation for modern armies

D. It kept the legal traditions of Roman government, collecting and organizing many ancient Roman laws

(Rigorous) (Skill 2.4)

61. Which one of the following did NOT contribute to the early medieval European civilization?

A. The heritage from the classical cultures

B. The Christian religion

C. The influence of the German Barbarians

D. The spread of ideas through trade and commerce

(Average) (Skill 2.4)

62. What Holy Roman Emperor was forced to do public penance because of his conflict with Pope Gregory VII over lay investiture of the clergy?

A. Charlemagne

B. Henry IV

C. Charles V

D. Henry VIII

(Average) (Skill 2.4)

63. At which meeting was the Trinity affirmed?

A. Council of Nicea

B. Diet of Worms

C. Council of Trent

D. Council of Chalcedon

(Rigorous) (Skill 2.4)

64. Which of the following areas would NOT be a primary area of hog production?

A. Midland England

B. The Mekong delta of Vietnam

C. Central Syria

D. Northeast Iowa

(Average) (Skill 2.4)

65. Which of the following is NOT one of the Pillars of Faith of Islam?

A. Almsgiving (zakah)

B. Pilgrimage (hajj)

C. Membership in a school of law (al-madhahib)

D. Fasting (sawm)

(Easy) (Skill 2.5)

66. Luther issued strong objection to:

A. Abuses of the Roman Catholic church

B. The prohibition of divorce

C. The Council of Trent

D. The use of the printing press for religious texts

(Rigorous) (Skills 2.5, 2.6)

67. The results of the Renaissance, Enlightenment, and the Commercial and Industrial Revolutions were most unfortunate for the people of:

A. Asia

B. Latin America

C. Africa

D. Middle East

(Rigorous) (Skill 2.6)

68. Colonial expansion by Western European powers in the eithteenth and nineteenth centuries was due primarily to:

A. Building and opening the Suez Canal

B. The Industrial Revolution

C. Marked improvements in transportation

D. Complete independence of all the Americas and loss of European domination and influence

(Rigorous) (Skill 2.6)

69. **Great Britain became the center of technological and industrial development during the nineteenth century chiefly on the basis of:**

    A. Central location relative to the population centers of Europe

    B. Colonial conquests and military victories over European powers

    C. Reliance on exterior sources of financing

    D. Resources of coal and production of steel

(Average) (Skill 2.6)

70. **The years 1793–1794 in France, characterized by numerous trials and executions of supposed enemies of the Revolutionary Convention, were known as the:**

    A. Reign of Terror

    B. Dark Ages

    C. French Inquisition

    D. Glorious Revolution

(Average) (Skill 2.8)

71. **Slobodan Milosevic rose to power after what country broke apart?**

    A. Rwanda

    B. Serbia

    C. Croatia

    D. Yugoslavia

(Rigorous) (Skill 2.8)

72. **Better transportation and advanced methods of communication are two forces that have contributed to:**

    A. Nationalism

    B. Genocide

    C. Globalism

    D. Sustainability

Answer Key

49. C	57. B	65. C
50. C	58. C	66. A
51. A	59. B	67. C
52. D	60. C	68. B
53. D	61. D	69. D
54. D	62. B	70. A
55. C	63. A	71. D
56. B	64. C	72. C

Rigor Table

RIGOR TABLE		
Rigor level	**Questions**	**TOTALS**
Easy 22%	51, 52, 58, 59, 66	
Average 43%	49, 50, 54, 55, 56, 62, 63, 65, 70, 71	
Rigorous 35%	53, 57, 60, 61, 64, 67, 68, 69, 72	

Sample Test with Rationales: World History

(Average) (Skill 2.1)

49. **Which of the following developments is most closely associated with the Neolithic Age?**

    A. Human use of fire

    B. First use of stone chipping instruments

    C. Domestication of plants

    D. Development of metallurgical alloys

    Answer: C. Domestication of plants

    The Neolithic, or "New Stone" Age as its name implies, is characterized by the use of stone implements, but the first use of stone chipping instruments appears in the Paleolithic period. Human use of fire may go back still farther and certainly predates the Neolithic era. The Neolithic period is distinguished by the domestication of plants. The development of metallurgical alloys marks the conclusion of the Neolithic Age.

(Average) (Skill 2.1)

50. **The end to hunting, gathering, and fishing of prehistoric people was due to:**

    A. Domestication of animals

    B. Building crude huts and houses

    C. Development of agriculture

    D. Organized government in villages

    Answer: C. Development of agriculture

    Although the domestication of animals, the building of huts and houses, and the first organized governments were all very important steps made by early civilizations, it was the development of agriculture that ended the once dominant practices of hunting, gathering, and fishing among prehistoric people. The development of agriculture provided a more efficient use of time and, for the first time, a surplus of food. This greatly improved the quality of life and contributed to early population growth.

(Easy) (Skill 2.2)

51. **The Tigris-Euphrates Valley was the site of which two primary ancient civilizations?**

    A. Babylonian and Assyrian

    B. Sumerian and Egyptian

    C. Hyksos and Hurrian

    D. Persian and Phoenician

    Answer: A. Babylonian and Assyrian

    While the Sumerians also lived in the southern Tigris-Euphrates valley, Egyptian civilization grew up in the Nile delta (3500 BCE–30 BCE). The Hyksos were an Asiatic people who controlled the Nile Delta during the 15th and 16th Dynasties (1674 BCE–1548 BCE). The Hurrians (2500 BCE–1000 BCE) came from the Khabur River Valley in northern Mesopotamia where they spread out to establish various small kingdoms in the region. The Persians (648 BCE to early 19th century CE) had a succession of empires based in the area today known as Iran. The Phoenicians were a seafaring people who dominated the Mediterranean during the first century BCE.

(Easy) (Skill 2.2)

52. **The first ancient civilization to introduce and practice monotheism was the:**

    A. Sumerians

    B. Minoans

    C. Phoenicians

    D. Hebrews

    Answer: D. Hebrews

    The Sumerians and Phoenicians both practiced religions in which many gods and goddesses were worshipped. Often these gods/goddesses were based on a feature of nature such as the Sun, Moon, weather, rocks, water, etc. The Minoan culture shared many religious practices with the ancient Egyptians. It seems that the king was somewhat of a god figure and the queen, a goddess. Much of the Minoan art points to worship of multiple gods. Therefore, only the Hebrews introduced and fully practiced monotheism, or the belief in one god.

(Rigorous) (Skill 2.2)

53. **For the historian studying ancient Egypt, which of the following would be least useful?**

    A. The record of an ancient Greek historian on Greek-Egyptian interaction

    B. Letters from an Egyptian ruler to his/her regional governors

    C. Inscriptions of the Fourteenth Egyptian Dynasty

    D. Letters from a nineteenth-century Egyptologist to his wife

    Answer: D. Letters from a nineteenth-century Egyptologist to his wife

    Historians use primary sources from the actual time they are studying whenever possible. Ancient Greek records of interaction with Egypt, letters from an Egyptian ruler to regional governors, and inscriptions from the Fourteenth Egyptian Dynasty are all primary sources created at or near the actual time being studied. Letters from a nineteenth-century Egyptologist would not be considered a primary source, as they were created thousands of years after the fact and may not actually be about the subject being studied.

(Average) (Skill 2.2)

54. **Indo-European languages are native languages to each of the following EXCEPT:**

    A. Germany

    B. India

    C. Italy

    D. Finland

    Answer: D. Finland

    German, the native language of Germany, Hindi, the official language of India, and Italian, spoken in Italy, are three of the hundreds of languages that are part of the Indo-European family, which also includes French, Greek, and Russian. Finnish, the language of Finland, is part of the Uralic family of languages, which also includes Estonian. It developed independently of the Indo-European family.

(Average) (Skill 2.3)

55. **Chinese civilization is generally credited with the original development of which of the following sets of technologies:**

A. Movable type and mass production of goods

B. Wool processing and domestication of the horse

C. Paper and gunpowder manufacture

D. Leather processing and modern timekeeping

Answer: C. Paper and gunpowder manufacture

While China's Bi Sheng (d. 1052) is credited with the earliest forms of moveable type (1041–1048), mass production was spearheaded by America's Henry Ford (1863–1947) in his campaign to create the first truly affordable automobile, the Model T Ford. While wool has been processed in many ways in many cultures, production on a scale beyond cottage industries was not possible without the many advances made in England during the Industrial Revolution (eighteenth century). Various theories exist about the time of domestication of the horse, with estimates ranging from 4600 BCE to 2000 BCE in Eurasia. Recent DNA evidence suggests that the horse may actually have been domesticated in different cultures at independent points. The earliest mention of gunpowder appears in ninth-century Chinese documents. The earliest examples of paper made of wood pulp come from China and have been dated as early as the second century BCE. Leather processing and timekeeping have likewise seen different developments in different places at different times.

(Average) (Skill 2.3)

56. **The ____________ were fought between the Roman Empire and Carthage.**

A. Civil Wars

B. Punic Wars

C. Caesarian Wars

D. Persian Wars

Answer: B. Punic Wars

The Punic Wars (264–146 BCE) were fought between Rome and Carthage. All the other answers are not proper names of wars.

(Rigorous) (Skills 2.3, 2.4)

57. **Of the legacies of the Roman Empire listed below, the most influential, effective, and lasting is:**

A. The language of Latin

B. Roman law, justice, and political system

C. Engineering and building

D. The writings of its poets and historians

Answer: B. Roman law, justice, and political system

Of the lasting legacies of the Roman Empire, it is its law, justice, and political system that has been the most effective and influential on the Western world today. English, Spanish, Italian, French, and others are all based on Latin, although that Roman language has itself has died out. The Roman engineering and building and their writings and poetry have also been influential but not nearly to the degree that their governmental and justice systems have been.

(Easy) (Skill 2.4)

58. The principle of zero in mathematics is the discovery of the ancient civilization found in:

A. Egypt

B. Persia

C. India

D. Babylon

Answer: C. India

Although the Egyptians practiced algebra and geometry, the Persians developed an alphabet, and the Babylonians developed Hammurabi's Code, which would come to be considered among the most important contributions of the Mesopotamian civilization, it was the Indians that created the idea of zero in mathematics, drastically changing ideas about numbers.

(Easy) (Skill 2.4)

59. The native metaphysical outlook of Japan, usually characterized as a religion, is:

A. Tao

B. Shinto

C. Hindu

D. Sunni

Answer: B. Shinto

Tao is the Chinese philosophical work that inspired Taoism, the religious tradition sourced in China. Shinto is the system of rituals and beliefs honoring the deities and spirits believed to be native to the landscape and inhabitants of Japan. Hindu is the primary religion of India, with a pantheon of deities and a caste system. Sunni is a branch of Islam, along with Shiite.

(Rigorous) (Skill 2.4)

60. Which one of the following is NOT an important legacy of the Byzantine Empire?

A. It protected Western Europe from various attacks from the East by such groups as the Persians, Ottoman Turks, and Barbarians

B. It played a part in preserving the literature, philosophy, and language of ancient Greece

C. Its military organization was the foundation for modern armies

D. It kept the legal traditions of Roman government, collecting and organizing many ancient Roman laws

Answer: C. Its military organization was the foundation for modern armies

The Byzantine Empire (1353–1453) was the successor to the Roman Empire in the East and protected Western Europe from invaders such as the Persians and Ottomans. The Byzantine Empire was a Christian incorporation of Greek philosophy, language, and literature along with Roman government and law. Therefore, although regarded as having a strong infantry, cavalry, and engineering corps, along with excellent morale among its soldiers, the Byzantine Empire is not particularly considered a foundation for modern armies.

(Rigorous) (Skill 2.4)

61. **Which one of the following did NOT contribute to the early medieval European civilization?**

    A. The heritage from the classical cultures

    B. The Christian religion

    C. The influence of the German Barbarians

    D. The spread of ideas through trade and commerce

Answer: D. The spread of ideas through trade and commerce

The heritage of the classical cultures such as Greece, the Christian religion that became dominant, and the influence of the Germanic Barbarians (Visigoths, Saxons, Ostrogoths, Vandals, and Franks) were all contributions to early medieval Europe and its plunge into feudalism. During this period, lives were often difficult and lived out on one single manor, with very little travel or spread of ideas through trade or commerce. Civilization seems to have halted progress during these years.

(Average) (Skill 2.4)

62. **What Holy Roman Emperor was forced to do public penance because of his conflict with Pope Gregory VII over lay investiture of the clergy?**

    A. Charlemagne

    B. Henry IV

    C. Charles V

    D. Henry VIII

Answer: B. Henry IV

Henry IV (1050–1106) clashed with Pope Gregory VII by insisting upon the right of a ruler to appoint members of the clergy to their offices, but he repented in 1077. Charlemagne and Charles V were also Holy Roman Emperors but in the ninth and sixteenth centuries, respectively. Henry VIII, King of England, broke with the Roman Church over his right to divorce and remarry in 1534.

(Average) (Skill 2.4)

63. **At which meeting was the Trinity affirmed?**

    A. Council of Nicea

    B. Diet of Worms

    C. Council of Trent

    D. Council of Chalcedon

Answer: A. Council of Nicea

The Nicene Creed was a result of the Council of Nicea (325 CE) and asserted Christian belief in the Trinity. At the Diet of Worms (1521), the Holy Roman Empire tried and condemned Martin Luther and his writings. The Council of Trent (1545–1563), an ecumenical council of the Roman Catholic Church, clarified many aspects of Catholic doctrine and liturgical life in an attempt to counter the Protestant Reformation. The Council of Chalcedon (451) confirmed the humanity of Christ by affirming that the Virgin Mary was indeed his human mother and therefore worthy of the Greek title Theotokos ("God-bearer").

(Rigorous) (Skill 2.4)

64. Which of the following areas would NOT be a primary area of hog production?

A. Midland England

B. The Mekong delta of Vietnam

C. Central Syria

D. Northeast Iowa

Answer: C. Central Syria

Pork is a common ingredient in the American, English, and Vietnamese cuisine, so one would reasonably expect to find hog production in Midland England, the Mekong Delta of Vietnam, and Northeast Iowa. The population of Syria is predominantly Islamic, and Islam prohibits the eating of pork. Therefore, one would be unlikely to find extensive hog production in Central Syria.

(Average) (Skill 2.4)

65. Which of the following is NOT one of the Pillars of Faith of Islam?

A. Almsgiving (zakah)

B. Pilgrimage (hajj)

C. Membership in a school of law (al-madhahib)

D. Fasting (sawm)

Answer: C. Membership in a school of law (al-madhahib)

The Five Pillars of Islam are the faith profession that there is no God but Allah and that Muhammad is his prophet. Prayer (salah), pilgrimage to Mecca (hajj), almsgiving (zakah), and fasting during the holy month of Ramadan (sawm) are all Pillars of Faith.

(Easy) (Skill 2.5)

66. Luther issued strong objection to:

A. Abuses of the Roman Catholic church

B. The prohibition of divorce

C. The Council of Trent

D. The use of the printing press for religious texts

Answer: A. Abuses of the Roman Catholic Church

Henry VIII differed with the Catholic Church on the subject of divorce. The Council of Trent is where the Catholic Church instituted reforms. Protestantism spread because of the printing press.

(Rigorous) (Skills 2.5, 2.6)

67. The results of the Renaissance, Enlightenment, and the Commercial and Industrial Revolutions were most unfortunate for the people of:

A. Asia

B. Latin America

C. Africa

D. Middle East

Answer: C. Africa

The results of the Renaissance, Enlightenment, and the Commercial and Industrial Revolutions were quite beneficial for many people in much of the world. New ideas of humanism, religious tolerance, and secularism were spreading. Increased trade and manufacturing were expanding economies in much of the world. The people of Africa, however, suffered during these times as they were largely left out of the developments. Also, the people of Africa were stolen, traded, and sold into slavery to provide a cheap labor force for the growing industries of Europe and the New World.

(Rigorous) (Skill 2.6)

68. **Colonial expansion by Western European powers in the eigthteenth and nineteenth centuries was due primarily to:**

A. Building and opening the Suez Canal

B. The Industrial Revolution

C. Marked improvements in transportation

D. Complete independence of all the Americas and loss of European domination and influence

Answer: B. The Industrial Revolution

Colonial expansion by Western European powers in the late eighteenth and nineteenth centuries was due primarily to the Industrial Revolution in Great Britain that spread across Europe and the need for new natural resources and, therefore, new locations from which to extract the raw materials needed to feed the new industries.

(Rigorous) (Skill 2.6)

69. **Great Britain became the center of technological and industrial development during the nineteenth century chiefly on the basis of:**

A. Central location relative to the population centers of Europe

B. Colonial conquests and military victories over European powers

C. Reliance on exterior sources of financing

D. Resources of coal and production of steel

Answer: D. Resources of coal and production of steel

Great Britain possessed a unique set of advantages in the eighteenth and nineteenth centuries, making it the perfect candidate for the technological advances of the Industrial Revolution. Relative isolation from the population centers in Europe meant little to Great Britain, which benefited from its own relatively unified and large domestic market and enabled it avoid the tariffs and inefficiencies of trading on the diverse (and complicated) continent. Colonial conquests and military victories over European powers were fueled by Great Britain's industrial advances in transportation and weaponry, rather than being causes of them. While Great Britain would enjoy an increasing influx of goods and capital from its colonies, the efficiency of its own domestic market consistently generated an impressive amount of capital for investment in the new technologies and industries of the age. Great Britain's rich natural resources of coal and ore enabled steel production and, set alongside new factories in a Britain's landscape, allowed the production of goods quickly and efficiently.

(Average) (Skill 2.6)

70. **The years 1793–1794 in France, characterized by numerous trials and executions of supposed enemies of the Revolutionary Convention, were known as the:**

A. Reign of Terror

B. Dark Ages

C. French Inquisition

D. Glorious Revolution

Answer: A. Reign of Terror

The period of the French Revolution known as the Reign of Terror (1793–1794) is estimated to have led to the deaths of up to 40,000 people: aristocrats, clergy, political activists, and anyone else denounced as an enemy of the Revolutionary Convention, many falsely so. The Dark Ages is the term commonly used for the Early Middle Ages in Europe, from the fall of Rome in 476 to 1000 CE. The French Inquisition was the Roman Catholic Church's attempts to codify into ecclesiastical and secular law the prosecution of heretics, most notably at the time, the Albigensians, in the thirteenth century. The Glorious Revolution (1688–1689) is the title given to the overthrow of the last Catholic British monarch, James II, in favor of his Protestant daughter, Mary, and her husband, the Dutch Prince William of Orange.

(Average) (Skill 2.8)

71. **Slobodan Milosevic rose to power after what country broke apart?**

A. Rwanda

B. Serbia

C. Croatia

D. Yugoslavia

Answer: D. Yugoslavia

Rwanda was the site of genocide, but it had nothing to do with Milosevic; Serbia and Croatia were parts of Yugoslavia that broke off when that country disintegrated. Yugoslavia disintegrated after the Cold War ended, giving rise to ethnic tensions and Mislosevic's "ethnic cleansing."

(Rigorous) (Skill 2.8)

72. **Better transportation and advanced methods of communication are two forces that have contributed to:**

A. Nationalism

B. Genocide

C. Globalism

D. Sustainability

Answer: C. Globalism

Nationalism was a major force of the twentieth century, but globalism has changed the international political landscape. There is no evidence to suggest that improved transportation and communication have contributed to more genocide (although they may contribute to more people knowing about it). Better transportation and computer-based communication have facilitated globalization. There is no clear correlation between sustainability and improved transportation and communication, although one could argue that these two forces have actually worked against sustainability.

SAMPLE TEST

Government/Civics/Political Science

(Easy) (Skill 3.1)

73. **A political scientist might use all of the following except:**

    A. Government documents

    B. A geological time-line

    C. Voting patterns

    D. Polling data

(Rigorous) (Skill 3.1)

74. **Political science is primarily concerned with:**

    A. Candidates

    B. Economic systems

    C. Boundaries

    D. Public policy

(Rigorous) (Skill 3.1)

75. **A political philosophy favoring or supporting social changes in order to correct social and economic inequalities is called:**

    A. Nationalism

    B. Liberalism

    C. Conservatism

    D. Federalism

(Average) (Skill 3.1)

76. **A map that shows where minority populations live in a given region is an example of:**

    A. A relief map

    B. A climate map

    C. A thematic map

    D. A highway map

(Average) (Skill 3.1)

77. **Which political thinker believed that the state of nature was chaotic and that the natural state of events was a war of all against all?**

    A. Hobbes

    B. Hume

    C. Locke

    D. Mill

(Average) (Skill 3.2)

78. **Which of the following documents lays out the system of government for the United States?**

    A. The Articles of Confederation

    B. The Declaration of Independence

    C. The Constitution

    D. The Bill of Rights

(Average) (Skill 3.2)

79. **Which of the following are usually considered responsibilities of citizenship under the American system of government?**

    A. Serving in public office, voluntary government service, military duty

    B. Paying taxes, jury duty, upholding the Constitution

    C. Maintaining a job, giving to charity, turning in fugitives

    D. Quartering of soldiers, bearing arms, government service

(Rigorous) (Skill 3.2)

80. **Why is the system of government in the United States referred to as a federal system?**

    A. There are different levels of government

    B. There is one central authority in which all governmental power is vested

    C. The national government cannot operate except with the consent of the governed

    D. Elections are held at stated periodic times, rather than as called by the head of the government

(Rigorous) (Skill 3.2)

81. **In the presidential election of 1888, Grover Cleveland lost to Benjamin Harrison, although Cleveland received more popular votes. How is this possible?**

    A. The votes of certain states (New York, Indiana) were thrown out because of voting irregularities

    B. Harrison received more electoral votes that Cleveland

    C. None of the party candidates received a majority of votes, and the House of Representatives elected Harrison according to Constitutional procedures

    D. Because of accusations of election law violations, Cleveland withdrew his name and Harrison became president

(Average) (Skill 3.2)

82. **Which of the following powers is delegated only to the federal government?**

    A. Taxing

    B. Chartering banks

    C. Conducting foreign affairs

    D. Making laws

(Average) (Skill 3.2)

83. **Which of the following is NOT guaranteed by the Bill of Rights?**

    A. Free speech

    B. Due process of law

    C. Assembly

    D. The supremacy of the federal government

(Easy) (Skill 3.2)

84. **Which of the following are NOT local governments in the United States?**

  A. Cities

  B. Townships

  C. School boards

  D. All of these are forms of local government

(Average) (Skill 3.2)

85. **Which of the following was added to the Constitution as an amendment?**

  A. The right of 18-year-olds to vote

  B. The use of voting machines in elections

  C. The right of the president to appoint judges

  D. The use of marijuana for medical purposes

(Average) (Skill 3.2)

86. **In the Constitutional system of checks and balances, one of the "checking" powers of the President is:**

  A. Executive privilege

  B. Approval of judges nominated by the Senate

  C. Veto of congressional legislation

  D. Approval of judged nominated by the House of Representatives

(Easy) (Skill 3.2)

87. **Which of the following was granted the right to vote in the original, unamended Constitution?**

  A. White male property owners

  B. White female property owners

  C. African-American male property owners

  D. African-American female property owners

(Average) (Skill 3.3)

88. **Which of the following is an example of a country with an oligarchic government?**

  A. The United States

  B. China

  C. Sweden

  D. Israel

(Average) (Skill 3.3)

89. **Democracy and Totalitarianism are alike in that they are both:**

  A. Organic systems

  B. Political systems

  C. Centrally planned systems

  D. Economic systems

(Easy) (Skill 3.4)

90. **Which of the following are likely to be part of the role of a diplomat?**

  A. Help to resolve international conflicts

  B. Convey official information on the policies and positions of their home countries to the host countries where they are stationed

  C. Negotiate international agreements on issues such as trade and the environment

  D. All of the above

Answer Key

73. B	82. C
74. D	83. D
75. B	84. D
76. C	85. A
77. A	86. C
78. C	87. A
79. B	88. B
80. A	89. B
81. B	90. D

Rigor Table

RIGOR TABLE		
Rigor level	**Questions**	**TOTALS**
Easy 22%	73, 84, 87, 90	
Average 43%	76, 77, 78, 79, 82, 83, 85, 86, 88, 89	
Rigorous 35%	74, 75, 80, 81	

Sample Test with Rationales: Government/Civics/Political Science

(Easy) (Skill 3.1)

73. **A political scientist might use all of the following except:**

    A. Government documents

    B. A geological time-line

    C. Voting patterns

    D. Polling data

    Answer: B. A geological time-line

    Political science is primarily concerned with the political and governmental activities of societies. Government documents can provide information about the organization and activities of a government. Voting patterns reveal the political behavior of individuals and groups. Polling data can provide insight into the predominant political views of a group of people. A geological timeline describes the changes in the physical features of the Earth over time, and would not be useful to a political scientist.

(Rigorous) (Skill 3.1)

74. **Political science is primarily concerned with:**

    A. Candidates

    B. Economic systems

    C. Boundaries

    D. Public policy

    Answer: D. Public policy

    Political science studies the actions and policies of the government of a society. Public policy is the official stance of a government on an issue, and it is a primary source for studying a society's dominant political beliefs. Candidates are an interest of political scientists but are not a primary field of study. Economic systems are of interest to an economist, and boundaries are of interest to a geographer.

(Rigorous) (Skill 3.1)

75. **A political philosophy favoring or supporting social changes in order to correct social and economic inequalities is called:**

    A. Nationalism

    B. Liberalism

    C. Conservatism

    D. Federalism

    Answer: B. Liberalism

    A political philosophy favoring rapid social changes in order to correct social and economic inequalities are called Liberalism. Liberalism was a theory that could be said to have started with the great French philosophers Montesquieu (1689–1755) and Rousseau (1712–1778). It is important to understand the difference between political, economic, and social liberalism—as they are different—and how they sometimes contrast one another in the modern world.

(Average) (Skill 3.1)

76. **A map that shows where minority populations live in a given region is an example of:**

A. A relief map

B. A climate map

C. A thematic map

D. A highway map

Answer: C. A thematic map

A relief map shows physical elevation. A climate map shows climate patterns, not human settlement patterns. A map showing where minority populations live is an example of a thematic map. Highways might be included in a map showing where minority populations live, but a highway map would not show the composition of residential neighborhoods.

(Average) (Skill 3.1)

77. **Which political thinker believed that the state of nature was chaotic and that the natural state of events was a war of all against all?**

A. Hobbes

B. Hume

C. Locke

D. Mill

Answer: A. Hobbes

Hobbes believed that people could only live in harmony with each other if they submitted to the state. Hume emphasized that the greatest happiness for the greatest number was the aim of politics. Locke argued that sovereignty resided in the people. Mill advocated for political and social reforms.

(Average) (Skill 3.2)

78. **Which of the following documents lays out the system of government for the United States?**

A. The Articles of Confederation

B. The Declaration of Independence

C. The Constitution

D. The Bill of Rights

Answer: C. The Constitution

The Articles of Confederation were superseded by the Constitution. The Declaration of Independence was a statement of principles and freedom but not an outline for governance. The Constitution describes how the American government will function. The Bill of Rights is the first ten amendments to the Constitution.

(Average) (Skill 3.2)

79. **Which of the following are usually considered responsibilities of citizenship under the American system of government?**

A. Serving in public office, voluntary government service, military duty

B. Paying taxes, jury duty, upholding the Constitution

C. Maintaining a job, giving to charity, turning in fugitives

D. Quartering of soldiers, bearing arms, government service

Answer: B. Paying taxes, jury duty, upholding the Constitution

Only paying taxes, jury duty, and upholding the Constitution are responsibilities of citizens as a result of rights and commitments outlined in the Constitution. For example, the right of citizens to a jury trial in the Sixth and Seventh Amendments and the right of the federal government to collect taxes in Article 1, Section 8. Serving in public office, voluntary government service, military duty, maintaining a job, giving to charity, and turning in fugitives are all highly admirable actions undertaken by many exemplary citizens, but they are considered purely voluntary actions, even when officially recognized and compensated. The United States has none of the compulsory military or civil service requirements of many other countries. The quartering of soldiers is an act, which, according to the Third Amendment of the Bill of Rights, requires a citizen's consent. Bearing arms is a right guaranteed under the Second Amendment of the Bill of Rights.

(Rigorous) (Skill 3.2)

80. **Why is the system of government in the United States referred to as a federal system?**

    A. There are different levels of government

    B. There is one central authority in which all governmental power is vested

    C. The national government cannot operate except with the consent of the governed

    D. Elections are held at stated periodic times, rather than as called by the head of the government

Answer: A. There are different levels of government

The United States is composed of 50 states, each responsible for its own affairs but united under a federal government. A centralized system is the opposite of a federal system. That national government cannot operate except with the consent of the governed is a founding principle of American politics. It is not a political system. A centralized democracy could still be consensual but would not be federal. Choice D is a description of electoral procedure, not a political system.

(Rigorous) (Skill 3.2)

81. **In the presidential election of 1888, Grover Cleveland lost to Benjamin Harrison, although Cleveland received more popular votes. How is this possible?**

    A. The votes of certain states (New York, Indiana) were thrown out because of voting irregularities

    B. Harrison received more electoral votes that Cleveland

    C. None of the party candidates received a majority of votes, and the House of Representatives elected Harrison according to Constitutional procedures

    D. Because of accusations of election law violations, Cleveland withdrew his name and Harrison became president

Answer: B. Harrison received more electoral votes that Cleveland

Presidential elections, according to the United States Constitution, are decided in the Electoral College. This college mirrors the composition of the House of Representatives. The popular vote for each presidential candidate determines which slate of electors in each state is selected. Thus, while Cleveland won enough support in certain states to win a majority of the national popular vote, he did not win enough states to carry the Electoral College. If neither candidate had won the necessary majority, the House of Representatives would have made the final decision, but this did not occur in 1888. The other two answers are not envisioned by the Constitution and did not occur.

(Average) (Skill 3.2)

82. **Which of the following powers is delegated only to the federal government?**

    A. Taxing

    B. Chartering banks

    C. Conducting foreign affairs

    D. Making laws

Answer: C. Conducting foreign affairs

Both state and federal governments can tax, charter banks, and make laws. Only the federal government can conduct foreign affairs.

(Average) (Skill 3.2)

83. **Which of the following is NOT guaranteed by the Bill of Rights?**

    A. Free speech

    B. Due process of law

    C. Assembly

    D. The supremacy of the federal government

Answer: D. The supremacy of the federal government

Free speech, due process, and freedom of assembly are all guaranteed by the Bill of Rights. The Bill of Rights guarantees that all authority not specifically mentioned in the Constitution reside with the people.

(Easy) (Skill 3.2)

84. **Which of the following are NOT local governments in the United States?**

    A. Cities

    B. Townships

    C. School boards

    D. All of these are forms of local government

Answer: D. All of these are forms of local government

A local government is a body with the authority to make policy and enforce decisions on behalf of a local community. Cities and townships are by definition local, not statewide or federal, governments. A more central authority might make school policy in other countries, but, in the United States, school boards are local authorities. However, according to the 2002 Census, several states run certain school districts themselves without a local school board.

(Average) (Skill 3.2)

85. **Which of the following was added to the Constitution as an amendment?**

A. The right of 18-year-olds to vote

B. The use of voting machines in elections

C. The right of the president to appoint judges

D. The use of marijuana for medical purposes

Answer: A. The right of 18-year-olds to vote

The Twenty-sixth Amendment granted 18-year-olds the right to vote. Voting machines are not addressed in the Constitution. The right of the president to appoint judges in identified in Article II. The use of medical marijuana is not addressed in the Constitution.

(Average) (Skill 3.2)

86. **In the Constitutional system of checks and balances, one of the "checking" powers of the President is:**

A. Executive privilege

B. Approval of judges nominated by the Senate

C. Veto of congressional legislation

D. Approval of judged nominated by the House of Representatives

Answer: C. Veto of congressional legislation

The power to veto congressional legislation is granted to the U.S. President in Article I of the Constitution, which states that all legislation passed by both houses of Congress must be given to the President for approval. This is a primary check on the power of Congress by the President. Congress may override a presidential veto by a two-thirds majority vote of both houses, however. Executive privilege refers to the privilege of the President to keep certain documents private. Choices B and D are incorrect, as Congress does not nominate judges. This is a presidential power.

(Easy) (Skill 3.2)

87. **Which of the following was granted the right to vote in the original, unamended Constitution?**

A. White male property owners

B. White female property owners

C. African-American male property owners

D. African-American female property owners

Answer: A. White male property owners

Of the choices, only white male property owners had the right to vote according to the Constitution. Other voters were added through amendments later.

(Average) (Skill 3.3)

88. **Which of the following is an example of a country with an oligarchic government?**

A. The United States

B. China

C. Sweden

D. Israel

Answer: B. China

The United States, Sweden, and Israel are all forms of democracy.

(Average) (Skill 3.3)

89. **Democracy and Totalitarianism are alike in that they are both:**

A. Organic systems

B. Political systems

C. Centrally planned systems

D. Economic systems

Answer: B. Political systems

While economic and political systems are often closely connected, capitalism and communism are primarily economic systems. Capitalism is a system of economics that allows the open market to determine the relative value of goods and services. Communism is an economic system where the market is planned by a central state. While Communism is a centrally planned system, this is not true of capitalism. Organic systems are studied in biology, a natural science.

(Easy) (Skill 3.4)

90. **Which of the following are likely to be part of the role of a diplomat?**

A. Help to resolve international conflicts

B. Convey official information on the policies and positions of their home countries to the host countries where they are stationed

C. Negotiate international agreements on issues such as trade and the environment

D. All of the above

Answer: D. All of the above

Nations that formally recognize one another station a group of diplomats, led by an ambassador, in one another's countries to provide formal representation on international matters, negotiate agreements, and help to resolve international agreements.

SAMPLE TEST

Geography

(Easy) (Skill 4.1)

91. Which of the following is the best example of what a physical geographer would study?

A. Tectonic plates

B. Wine country in Northern California

C. Census data

D. Urban migration

(Easy) (Skill 4.1)

92. Which of the following is NOT included in a map's key?

A. The scale

B. A compass rose

C. The grid

D. A river delta

(Average) (Skill 4.1)

93. A Mercatur Map is an example of:

A. Cylindrical projection

B. Conical projection

C. Flat-plane projection

D. Equilateral projection

(Average) (Skill 4.3)

94. A coral island, or series of islands, which consists of a reef that surrounds a lagoon describes a(n):

A. Needle

B. Key

C. Atoll

D. Mauna

(Easy) (Skill 4.3)

95. Which represents the make-up of the Earth's surface?

A. 75 percent water and 25 percent land

B. 80 percent water and 20 percent land

C. 90 percent water and 10 percent land

D. 70 percent water and 30 percent land

(Easy) (Skill 4.3)

96. Another name for a plateau is:

A. A plain

B. A mesa

C. A hill

D. A delta

(Average) (Skill 4.3)

97. The Mediterranean-type climate is characterized by:

A. Hot, dry summers and mild, relatively wet winters

B. Cool, relatively wet summers and cold winters

C. Mild summers and winters, with moisture throughout the year

D. Hot, wet summers and cool, dry winters

(Average) (Skill 4.3)

98. The climate of Southern Florida is the ____________________ type.

A. humid subtropical

B. marine west coast

C. humid continental

D. tropical wet-dry

(Average) (Skill 4.3)

99. _____ refers to the day-to-day conditions in the atmosphere.

A. Climate

B. Temperature

C. Humidity

D. Weather

(Average) (Skill 4.3)

100. A physical geographer would be concerned with which of the following groups of terms?

A. Landform, biome, precipitation

B. Scarcity, goods, services

C. Nation, state, administrative subdivision

D. Cause and effect, innovation, exploration

(Rigorous) (Skill 4.3)

101. Which of the following is an example of convergent boundaries of tectonic plates?

A. The Mid-Atlantic Range

B. The Great Rift Valley

C. The San Andreas Fault

D. The Andes Mountains

(Rigorous) (Skills 4.3, 4.5)

102. If geography is the study of how human beings live in relationship to the Earth on which they live, why do geographers include physical geography within the discipline?

A. The physical environment serves as the location for the activities of human beings

B. No other branch of the natural or social sciences studies the same topics

C. The physical environment is more important than the activities carried out by human beings

D. It is important to be able to subdue natural processes for the advancement of humankind

(Average) (Skill 4.6)

103. Which is not a concern of the study of geography?

A. The locations of such Earth features as climate, water, and land

B. The most efficient methods for extracting resources from the Earth

C. How the locations of Earth features relate to and affect each other and human activities

D. What forces have shaped and changed Earth features

Answer Key

91. A	100. A
92. D	101. D
93. A	102. A
94. C	103. B
95. D	
96. B	
97. A	
98. A	
99. D	

Rigor Table

RIGOR TABLE		
Rigor level	**Questions**	**TOTALS**
Easy 22%	91, 92, 95, 96	
Average 43%	93, 94, 97, 98, 99, 100, 103	
Rigorous 35%	101, 102	

Sample Test with Rationales: Geography

(Easy) (Skill 4.1)

91. **Which of the following is the best example of what a physical geographer would study?**

    A. Tectonic plates

    B. Wine country in Northern California

    C. Census data

    D. Urban migration

    Answer: A. Tectonic plates

    Physical geography studies Earth's physical features, such as tectonic plates. Wine country in Northern California could include physical elements, but as stated, it is a better example of regional studies. Census data and urban data are examples of human geography.

(Easy) (Skill 4.1)

92. **Which of the following is NOT included in a map's key?**

    A. The scale

    B. A compass rose

    C. The grid

    D. A river delta

    Answer: D. A river delta

    Scale, a compass rose, and a grid are all elements of the key. A river delta is a physical feature that would appear on the map itself.

(Average) (Skill 4.1)

93. **A Mercatur Map is an example of:**

    A. Cylindrical projection

    B. Conical projection

    C. Flat-plane projection

    D. Equilateral projection

    Answer: A. Cylindrical projection

    A Mercatur Map is a cylindrical projection. A Mercatur Map is not a conical or flat-plane projection. There is no such thing as an equilateral projection map.

(Average) (Skill 4.3)

94. **A coral island, or series of islands, which consists of a reef that surrounds a lagoon describes a(n):**

    A. Needle

    B. Key

    C. Atoll

    D. Mauna

    Answer: C. Atoll

    An atoll is a formation that occurs when a coral reef builds up around the top of a submerged volcanic peak, forming a ring or horseshoe of islands with a seawater lagoon in the center.

(Easy) (Skill 4.3)

95. **Which represents the make-up of the Earth's surface?**

    A. 75 percent water and 25 percent land

    B. 80 percent water and 20 percent land

    C. 90 percent water and 10 percent land

    D. 70 percent water and 30 percent land

Answer: D. 70 percent water and 30 percent land

The Earth's surface is made up of 70 percent water and 30 percent land.

(Easy) (Skill 4.3)

96. **Another name for a plateau is:**

A. A plain

B. A mesa

C. A hill

D. A delta

Answer: B. A mesa

Plateaus are elevated landforms that are usually flat on top. Plains are flat or rolling lands. A mesa is another name for a plateau. A hill is an elevated landform that is not as high as a mountain. A delta is a lowland area formed by soil and sediment deposited at the mouths of rivers.

(Average) (Skill 4.3)

97. **The Mediterranean-type climate is characterized by:**

A. Hot, dry summers and mild, relatively wet winters

B. Cool, relatively wet summers and cold winters

C. Mild summers and winters, with moisture throughout the year

D. Hot, wet summers and cool, dry winters

Answer: A. Hot, dry summers and mild, relatively wet winters

Westerly winds and nearby bodies of water create stable weather patterns along the west coasts of several continents and the coast of the Mediterranean Sea (after which this type of climate is named). Temperatures rarely fall below the freezing point and have a mean between 70 and 80 degrees Fahrenheit in the summer. Stable conditions make for little rain during the summer months.

(Average) (Skill 4.3)

98. **The climate of Southern Florida is the ____________________ type.**

A. humid subtropical

B. marine west coast

C. humid continental

D. tropical wet-dry

Answer: A. humid subtropical

The marine west coast climate is found on the western coasts of continents. Florida is on the eastern side of North America. The humid continental climate is found over large landmasses, such as Europe and the American Midwest, not along coasts such as where Florida is situated. The tropical wet-dry climate occurs in the tropics within about 15 degrees of the equator. Florida is subtropical. Florida is in a humid subtropical climate, which extends along the East Coast of the United States to about Maryland, and along the Gulf Coast to northeastern Texas.

(Average) (Skill 4.3)

99. **_____ refers to the day-to-day conditions in the atmosphere.**

A. Climate

B. Temperature

C. Humidity

D. Weather

Answer: D. Weather

Climate is the average of weather conditions over an extended period of time. Temperature and humidity are elements of weather.

(Average) (Skill 4.3)

100. A physical geographer would be concerned with which of the following groups of terms?

A. Landform, biome, precipitation

B. Scarcity, goods, services

C. Nation, state, administrative subdivision

D. Cause and effect, innovation, exploration

Answer: A. Landform, biome, precipitation

Landform, biome, and precipitation are all terms used in the study of geography. A landform is a physical feature of the Earth, such as a hill or valley. A biome is a large community of plants or animals, such as a forest. Precipitation is the moisture that falls to Earth as rain or snow. Scarcity, goods, and services are terms encountered in economics. Nation, state, and administrative subdivision are terms used in political science. Cause and effect, innovation, and exploration are terms in developmental psychology.

(Rigorous) (Skill 4.3)

101. Which of the following is an example of convergent boundaries of tectonic plates?

A. The Mid-Atlantic Range

B. The Great Rift Valley

C. The San Andreas Fault

D. The Andes Mountains

Answer: D. The Andes Mountains

The Mid-Atlantic Range and the Great Valley Rift are examples of divergent boundaries. The San Andreas Fault is an example of a transform boundary.

(Rigorous) (Skills 4.3, 4.5)

102. If geography is the study of how human beings live in relationship to the Earth on which they live, why do geographers include physical geography within the discipline?

A. The physical environment serves as the location for the activities of human beings

B. No other branch of the natural or social sciences studies the same topics

C. The physical environment is more important than the activities carried out by human beings

D. It is important to be able to subdue natural processes for the advancement of humankind

Answer: A. The physical environment serves as the location for the activities of human beings

Cultures will develop different practices depending on the predominant geographical features of the area in which they live. For instance, cultures that live along a river will have a different kind of relationship to the surrounding land than those who live in the mountains. Choice A best describes why physical geography is included in the social science of geography. Choice B is false, as physical geography is also studied under other natural sciences (such as geology). Choices C and D are matters of opinion and do not pertain to the definition of geography as a social science.

(Average) (Skill 4.6)

103. **Which is not a concern of the study of geography?**

A. The locations of such Earth features as climate, water, and land

B. The most efficient methods for extracting resources from the Earth

C. How the locations of Earth features relate to and affect each other and human activities

D. What forces have shaped and changed Earth features

Answer: B. The most efficient methods for extracting resources from the Earth

Geography is the study of the features of the Earth and how these features affect and are affected by humans. The combinations of different climate conditions, types of landforms, and other surface features all work together around the Earth to give many varied cultures their unique characteristics and distinctions.

SAMPLE TEST

Economics

(Average) (Skill 5.1)

104. An economist might engage in which of the following activities?

A. An observation of the historical effects of a nation's banking practices

B. The application of a statistical test to a series of data

C. Introduction of an experimental factor into a specified population to measure the effect of the factor

D. An economist might engage in all of these

(Average) (Skill 5.1)

105. Economics is best described as:

A. The study of how money is used in different societies

B. The study of how different political systems produce goods and services

C. The study of how human beings use limited resources to supply their needs and wants

D. The study of how human beings have developed trading practices through the years

(Rigorous) (Skill 5.1)

106. An economist investigates the spending patterns of low-income individuals. Which of the following would yield the most pertinent information?

A. Prime lending rates of neighborhood banks

B. The federal discount rate

C. Citywide wholesale distribution figures

D. Census data and retail sales figures

(Rigorous) (Skill 5.1)

107. Which of the following is one of the three questions of economics?

A. How much do goods cost?

B. How do people make choices?

C. What goods should be produced?

D. What is scarcity?

(Rigorous) (Skill 5.1)

108. A command economy is considered the opposite of an open economy. Therefore, in a command economy:

A. The open market determines how much of a good is produced and distributed

B. The government determines how much of a good is produced and distributed

C. Individuals produce and consume a specified good as commanded by their needs

D. The open market determines the demand for a good, and then the government produces and distributes the good

(Rigorous) (Skill 5.1)

109. If the price of Good G increases, what is likely to happen with regard to comparable Good H?

A. The demand for Good G will stay the same

B. The demand for Good G will increase

C. The demand for Good H will increase

D. The demand for Good H will decrease

(Rigorous) (Skill 5.2)

110. As your income rises, you tend to spend more money on entertainment. This is an expression of the:

A. Marginal propensity to consume

B. Allocative efficiency

C. Compensating differential

D. Marginal propensity to save

(Rigorous) (Skill 5.2)

111. A student buys a candy bar at lunch. The decision to buy a second candy bar relates to the concept of:

A. Equilibrium pricing

B. Surplus

C. Utility

D. Substitutability

(Average) (Skill 5.2)

112. Of the following, the best example of an oligopoly in the United States is:

A. Automobile industry

B. Electric power provision

C. Telephone service

D. Clothing manufacturer

(Average) (Skill 5.2)

113. Which of the following is NOT one of the factors of production?

A. Labor

B. Capital

C. Profits

D. Entrepreneurship

(Rigorous) (Skill 5.2)

114. What is a major difference between monopolistic competition and perfect competition?

A. Perfect competition has many consumers and suppliers while monopolistic competition does not

B. Perfect competition provides identical products while monopolistic competition provides similar, but not identical, products

C. Entry to perfect competition is difficult while entry to monopolistic competition is relatively easy

D. Monopolistic competition has many consumers and suppliers while perfect competition does not

(Rigorous) (Skill 5.3)

115. The macroeconomy consists of all but which of the following sectors?

A. Consumers

B. Investments by businesses

C. The foreign sector

D. Private

(Average) (Skill 5.4)

116. **Which best describes the economic system of the United States?**

A. Most decisions are the result of open markets with little or no government modification or regulation

B. Government makes most decisions, but there is some input by open market forces

C. Most decisions are made by open market factors with important regulatory functions and other market modifications the result of government activity

D. There is joint decision making by government and private forces with final decisions resting with the government

Answer Key

104. D	113. C
105. C	114. B
106. D	115. D
107. C	116. C
108. B	
109. C	
110. A	
111. C	
112. A	

Rigor Table

RIGOR TABLE		
Rigor level	Questions	TOTALS
Easy 22%		
Average 43%	104, 105, 112, 113, 116	
Rigorous 35%	106, 107, 108, 109, 110, 111, 114, 115	

Sample Test with Rationales: Economics

(Average) (Skill 5.1)

104. An economist might engage in which of the following activities?

A. An observation of the historical effects of a nation's banking practices

B. The application of a statistical test to a series of data

C. Introduction of an experimental factor into a specified population to measure the effect of the factor

D. An economist might engage in all of these

Answer: D. An economist might engage in all of these

Economists use statistical analysis of economic data, controlled experimentation, and historical research in their field of social science.

(Average) (Skill 5.1)

105. Economics is best described as:

A. The study of how money is used in different societies

B. The study of how different political systems produce goods and services

C. The study of how human beings use limited resources to supply their needs and wants

D. The study of how human beings have developed trading practices through the years

Answer: C. The study of how human beings use limited resources to supply their needs and wants

How money is used in different societies might be of interest to a sociologist or anthropologist. The study of how different political systems produce goods and services is a topic of study that could be included under the field of political science. The study of historical trading practices could fall under the study of history. Choice C is the best general description of the social science of economics as a whole.

(Rigorous) (Skill 5.1)

106. An economist investigates the spending patterns of low-income individuals. Which of the following would yield the most pertinent information?

A. Prime lending rates of neighborhood banks

B. The federal discount rate

C. Citywide wholesale distribution figures

D. Census data and retail sales figures

Answer: D. Census data and retail sales figures

Local lending rates and the federal discount rate might provide information on borrowing habits but not necessarily spending habits, and it gives no information on income levels. Citywide wholesale distribution figures would provide information on the business activity of a city but tell nothing about consumer activities. Census data records the income levels of households within a certain area, and retail sales figures for that area would give an economist data on spending which can be compared to income levels.

(Rigorous) (Skill 5.1)

107. Which of the following is one of the three questions of economics?

A. How much do goods cost?

B. How do people make choices?

C. What goods should be produced?

D. What is scarcity?

Answer: C. What goods should be produced?

The three questions are: What goods should be produced? How should the goods be produced? For whom are the goods being produced? The other choices are all related to economics, but are not among the three questions.

(Rigorous) (Skill 5.1)

108. A command economy is considered the opposite of an open economy. Therefore, in a command economy:

A. The open market determines how much of a good is produced and distributed

B. The government determines how much of a good is produced and distributed

C. Individuals produce and consume a specified good as commanded by their needs

D. The open market determines the demand for a good, and then the government produces and distributes the good

Answer: B. The government determines how much of a good is produced and distributed

A command economy is one in which the government determines how much of a good is produced and distributed, as was the case in the Soviet Union and is still the case in Cuba and North Korea. A command economy is the opposite of a market economy, in which the open market determines how much of a good is produced and distributed.

(Rigorous) (Skill 5.1)

109. If the price of Good G increases, what is likely to happen with regard to comparable Good H?

A. The demand for Good G will stay the same

B. The demand for Good G will increase

C. The demand for Good H will increase

D. The demand for Good H will decrease

Answer: C. The demand for Good H will increase

If consumers view Good G and Good H as equal in value but the cost of Good G increases, it follows that more consumers will now choose Good H at a lower price, increasing the demand for that good.

(Rigorous) (Skill 5.2)

110. As your income rises, you tend to spend more money on entertainment. This is an expression of the:

A. Marginal propensity to consume

B. Allocative efficiency

C. Compensating differential

D. Marginal propensity to save

Answer: A. Marginal propensity to consume

The marginal propensity to consume is a measurement of how much consumption changes compared to how much disposable income changes. Entertainment expenses are an example of disposable income. Dividing your change in entertainment spending by your total change in disposable income will give you your marginal propensity to consume.

(Rigorous) (Skill 5.2)

111. **A student buys a candy bar at lunch. The decision to buy a second candy bar relates to the concept of:**

A. Equilibrium pricing

B. Surplus

C. Utility

D. Substitutability

Answer: C. Utility

As used in the social science of economics, utility is the measurement of happiness or satisfaction a person receives from consuming a good or service. The decision of the student to increase his satisfaction by buying a second candy bar relates to this concept because he is spending money to increase his happiness.

(Average) (Skill 5.2)

112. **Of the following, the best example of an oligopoly in the United States is:**

A. Automobile industry

B. Electric power provision

C. Telephone service

D. Clothing manufacturer

Answer: A. Automobile industry

An oligopoly exists when a small group of companies controls an industry. In the United States at present, there are hundreds of electric power providers, telephone service providers, and clothing manufacturers. There are currently still just three major automobile manufacturers, however, making the automobile industry an oligopoly.

(Average) (Skill 5.2)

113. **Which of the following is NOT one of the factors of production?**

A. Labor

B. Capital

C. Profits

D. Entrepreneurship

Answer: C. Profits

Labor, capital, entrepreneurship, and also land are the four factors of production. Profits are not.

(Rigorous) (Skill 5.2)

114. **What is a major difference between monopolistic competition and perfect competition?**

A. Perfect competition has many consumers and suppliers while monopolistic competition does not

B. Perfect competition provides identical products while monopolistic competition provides similar, but not identical, products

C. Entry to perfect competition is difficult while entry to monopolistic competition is relatively easy

D. Monopolistic competition has many consumers and suppliers while perfect competition does not

Answer: B. Perfect competition provides identical products while monopolistic competition provides similar, but not identical, products

A perfect market is a hypothetical market used in economics to discuss the underlying effects of supply and demand. To control for the differences between products, it is assumed in perfect competition that all products are identical, with no differences, and the prices for these products will rise and fall based on a small number of factors. Monopolistic competition takes place in a market where each producer can act monopolistically and raise or lower the cost of its product or change its product to make different from similar products. This is the primary difference between these two models: perfect competition provides identical products, while monopolistic competition provides similar, but not identical, products.

(Rigorous) (Skill 5.3)

115. The macroeconomy consists of all but which of the following sectors?

A. Consumers

B. Investments by businesses

C. The foreign sector

D. Private

Answer: D. Private

The private sector refers to that area of politics and society not controlled by the public (i.e., the government). While it may include businesses and individual consumers, it is not considered part of the macroeconomy.

(Average) (Skill 5.4)

116. Which best describes the economic system of the United States?

A. Most decisions are the result of open markets with little or no government modification or regulation

B. Government makes most decisions, but there is some input by open market forces

C. Most decisions are made by open market factors with important regulatory functions and other market modifications the result of government activity

D. There is joint decision making by government and private forces with final decisions resting with the government

Answer: C. Most decisions are made by open market factors with important regulatory functions and other market modifications the result of government activity

The United States does not have a planned economy, as described in choices B and D. Neither is the U.S. market completely free of regulation. Products are regulated for safety and many services are regulated by certification requirements, for example. The best description of the U.S. economic system is, therefore, choice C.

SAMPLE TEST

Behavioral Sciences

(Rigorous) (Skill 6.1)

117. The advancement of understanding in dealing with human beings has led to a number of interdisciplinary areas. Which of the following interdisciplinary studies would NOT be considered under the social sciences?

A. Molecular biophysics

B. Peace studies

C. African-American studies

D. Cartographic information systems

(Average) (Skill 6.1)

118. Which of the following is most reasonably studied under the social sciences?

A. Political science

B. Geometry

C. Physics

D. Grammar

(Rigorous) (Skill 6.1)

119. Which of the following best describes current thinking on the major purpose of social science?

A. Social science is designed primarily for students to acquire facts

B. Social science should not be taught earlier than the middle school years

C. A primary purpose of social sciences is the development of good citizens

D. Social science should be taught as an elective

(Rigorous) (Skill 6.1)

120. As a sociologist, you would be most likely to observe:

A. The effects of an earthquake on farmland

B. The behavior of rats in sensory-deprivation experiments

C. The change over time in Babylonian obelisk styles

D. The behavior of human beings in television focus groups

(Average) (Skill 6.1)

121. The study of the social behavior of minority groups would be in the area of:

A. Anthropology

B. Psychology

C. Sociology

D. Cultural geography

(Average) (Skill 6.2)

122. Margaret Mead may be credited with major advances in the study of:

A. The marginal propensity to consume

B. The thinking of the Anti-Federalists

C. The anxiety levels of non-human primates

D. Interpersonal relationships in non-technical societies

(Rigorous) (Skill 6.2)

123. "Participant observation" is a method of study most closely associated with and used in:

A. Anthropology

B. Archaeology

C. Sociology

D. Political science

(Average) (Skill 6.2)

124. **A teacher and a group of students take a field trip to a Native American mound to examine artifacts. This activity most closely fits under which branch of the social sciences?**

A. Anthropology

B. Sociology

C. Psychology

D. Political Science

(Rigorous) (Skill 6.2)

125. **Which of the following demonstrates evidence of the interaction between physical and cultural anthropology?**

A. Tall Nilotic herdsmen are often expert warriors

B. Until recent years, the diet of most Asian peoples caused them to be shorter in stature than most other peoples

C. Native South American peoples adopted potato production after invasion by Europeans

D. Polynesians exhibit different skin coloration than Melanesians

(Average) (Skill 6.3)

126. **Psychology is a social science because:**

A. It focuses on the biological development of individuals

B. It focuses on the behavior of individuals and small groups of people

C. It bridges the gap between the natural and the social sciences

D. It studies the behavioral habits of lower animals

Answer: B. It focuses on the behavior of individuals and small groups of people

While it is true that psychology draws from natural sciences, it is the study of the behavior of individuals and small groups that defines psychology as a social science. The biological development of human beings and the behavioral habits of lower animals are studied in the developmental and behavioral branches of psychology.

(Average) (Skill 6.3)

127. **A social scientist studies the behavior of four people in a carpool. This is an example of:**

A. Developmental psychology

B. Experimental psychology

C. Social psychology

D. Macroeconomics

(Average) (Skill 6.3)

128. **A social scientist observes how individuals react to the presence or absence of noise. This scientist is most likely a:**

A. Geographer

B. Political scientist

C. Economist

D. Psychologist

(Easy) (Skill 6.3)

129. **Cognitive, developmental, and behavioral are three types of:**

A. Economists

B. Political scientists

C. Psychologists

D. Historians

(Average) (Skill 6.3)

130. Of the following lists, which includes individuals who have made major advances in the understanding of psychology?

A. Herodotus, Thucydides, Ptolemy

B. Adam Smith, Milton Friedman, John Kenneth Galbraith

C. Max Wertheimer, Ivan Pavlov, B. F. Skinner

D. Thomas Jefferson, Karl Marx, Henry Kissinger

Answer Key

117. A	126. B
118. A	127. C
119. C	128. D
120. D	129. C
121. C	130. C
122. D	
123. A	
124. A	
125. B	

Rigor Table

RIGOR TABLE		
Rigor level	**Questions**	**TOTALS**
Easy 22%	129	
Average 43%	118, 121, 122, 124, 126, 127, 128, 130	
Rigorous 35%	117, 119, 120, 123, 125	

Sample Test with Rationales: Behavioral Sciences

(Rigorous) (Skill 6.1)

117. **The advancement of understanding in dealing with human beings has led to a number of interdisciplinary areas. Which of the following interdisciplinary studies would NOT be considered under the social sciences?**

   A. Molecular biophysics

   B. Peace studies

   C. African-American studies

   D. Cartographic information systems

   Answer: A. Molecular biophysics

   Molecular biophysics is an interdisciplinary field combining the fields of biology, chemistry, and physics. These are all natural sciences and not social sciences

(Average) (Skill 6.1)

118. **Which of the following is most reasonably studied under the social sciences?**

   A. Political science

   B. Geometry

   C. Physics

   D. Grammar

   Answer: A. Political science

   Social sciences deal with the social interactions of people. Geometry is a branch of mathematics. Physics is a natural science that studies the physical world. Although it may be studied as part of linguistics, grammar is not recognized as a scientific field of study in itself. Only political science is considered a general field of the social sciences.

(Rigorous) (Skill 6.1)

119. **Which of the following best describes current thinking on the major purpose of social science?**

   A. Social science is designed primarily for students to acquire facts

   B. Social science should not be taught earlier than the middle school years

   C. A primary purpose of social sciences is the development of good citizens

   D. Social science should be taught as an elective

   Answer: C. A primary purpose of social sciences is the development of good citizens

   By making students aware of the importance of their place in society, how their society and others are governed, how societies develop and advance, and how cultural behaviors arise, the social sciences are currently thought to be of primary importance in developing good citizens.

(Rigorous) (Skill 6.1)

120. **As a sociologist, you would be most likely to observe:**

   A. The effects of an earthquake on farmland

   B. The behavior of rats in sensory-deprivation experiments

   C. The change over time in Babylonian obelisk styles

   D. The behavior of human beings in television focus groups

Answer: D. The behavior of human beings in television focus groups

Predominant beliefs and attitudes within human society are studied in the field of sociology. A geographer might study the effects of an earthquake on farmland. The behavior of rats in an experiment falls under the field of behavioral psychology. Changes in Babylonian obelisk styles might interest a historian. None of these answers fit easily within the definition of sociology. A focus group, where people are asked to discuss their reactions to a certain product or topic, would be the most likely method for a sociologist of observing and discovering attitudes among a selected group.

(Average) (Skill 6.1)

121. **The study of the social behavior of minority groups would be in the area of:**

A. Anthropology

B. Psychology

C. Sociology

D. Cultural geography

Answer: C. Sociology

The study of social behavior in minority groups would be primarily in the area of sociology, as it is the discipline most concerned with social interaction and being. However, it could be argued that anthropology, psychology, and cultural geography could have some interest in the study as well.

(Average) (Skill 6.2)

122. **Margaret Mead may be credited with major advances in the study of:**

A. The marginal propensity to consume

B. The thinking of the Anti-Federalists

C. The anxiety levels of non-human primates

D. Interpersonal relationships in non-technical societies

Answer: D. Interpersonal relationships in non-technical societies

Margaret Mead (1901–1978) was a pioneer in the field of anthropology, living among the people of Samoa while observing and writing about their culture in the book *Coming of Age in Samoa* in 1928. The marginal propensity to consume is an economic subject. The thinking of the Anti-Federalists is a topic in American history. The anxiety level of non-human primates is a subject studied in behavioral psychology.

(Rigorous) (Skill 6.2)

123. **"Participant observation" is a method of study most closely associated with and used in:**

A. Anthropology

B. Archaeology

C. Sociology

D. Political science

Answer: A. Anthropology

"Participant observation" is a method of study most closely associated with and used in anthropology or the study of current human cultures. Archaeologists typically study of the remains of people, animals, or other physical things. Sociology is the study of human society and usually consists of surveys, controlled experiments, and field studies. Political science is the study of political life including justice, freedom, power, and equality in a variety of methods.

(Average) (Skill 6.2)

124. **A teacher and a group of students take a field trip to a Native American mound to examine artifacts. This activity most closely fits under which branch of the social sciences?**

A. Anthropology

B. Sociology

C. Psychology

D. Political Science

Answer: A. Anthropology

Anthropology is the study of human culture and the way in which people of different cultures live. The artifacts created by people of a certain culture can provide information about the behaviors and beliefs of that culture, making anthropology the best fitting field of study for this field trip. Sociology, psychology, and political science are more likely to study behaviors and institutions directly than through individual artifacts created by a specific culture.

(Rigorous) (Skill 6.2)

125. **Which of the following demonstrates evidence of the interaction between physical and cultural anthropology?**

A. Tall Nilotic herdsmen are often expert warriors

B. Until recent years, the diet of most Asian peoples caused them to be shorter in stature than most other peoples

C. Native South American peoples adopted potato production after invasion by Europeans

D. Polynesians exhibit different skin coloration than Melanesians

Answer: B. Until recent years, the diet of most Asian peoples caused them to be shorter in stature than most other peoples

Cultural anthropology is the study of culture. Physical anthropology studies human evolution and other biologically related aspects of human culture. Choices A and D describe physical attributes of members of different cultures, but they make no connection between these attributes and the behaviors of these cultures. Choice C describes a cultural behavior of Native Americans but makes no connection to any physical attributes of the people of this culture. Choice B draws a connection between a cultural behavior (diet) and a physical attribute (height), and it is the best example demonstrating the interaction between cultural and physical anthropology.

(Average) (Skill 6.3)

126. **Psychology is a social science because:**

A. It focuses on the biological development of individuals

B. It focuses on the behavior of individuals and small groups of people

C. It bridges the gap between the natural and the social sciences

D. It studies the behavioral habits of lower animals

Answer: B. It focuses on the behavior of individuals and small groups of people

While it is true that psychology draws from natural sciences, it is the study of the behavior of individuals and small groups that defines psychology as a social science. The biological development of human beings and the behavioral habits of lower animals are studied in the developmental and behavioral branches of psychology.

(Average) (Skill 6.3)

127. **A social scientist studies the behavior of four people in a carpool. This is an example of:**

A. Developmental psychology

B. Experimental psychology

C. Social psychology

D. Macroeconomics

Answer: C. Social psychology

Developmental psychology studies the mental development of humans as they mature. Experimental psychology uses formal experimentation with control groups to examine human behavior. Social psychology is a branch of the field that investigates people's behavior as they interact within society, and it is the type of project described in the question. Macroeconomics is a field within economics and would not apply to this project.

(Average) (Skill 6.3)

128. **A social scientist observes how individuals react to the presence or absence of noise. This scientist is most likely a:**

A. Geographer

B. Political scientist

C. Economist

D. Psychologist

Answer: D. Psychologist

Psychologists scientifically study the behavior and mental processes of individuals. Studying how individuals react to changes in their environment falls under this social science. Geographers, political scientists, and economists are more likely to study the reactions of groups rather than individual reactions.

(Easy) (Skill 6.3)

129. **Cognitive, developmental, and behavioral are three types of:**

A. Economists

B. Political scientists

C. Psychologists

D. Historians

Answer: C. Psychologists

Psychologists study mental processes (cognitive psychology), the mental development of children (developmental psychology), and observe human and animal behavior in controlled circumstances (behavioral psychology).

(Average) (Skill 6.3)

130. **Of the following lists, which includes individuals who have made major advances in the understanding of psychology?**

A. Herodotus, Thucydides, Ptolemy

B. Adam Smith, Milton Friedman, John Kenneth Galbraith

C. Max Wertheimer, Ivan Pavlov, B. F. Skinner

D. Thomas Jefferson, Karl Marx, Henry Kissinger

Answer: C. Max Wertheimer, Ivan Pavlov, B. F. Skinner

Max Wertheimer developed Gestalt psychology. Ivan Pavlov contributed to behaviorism. B. F. Skinner (1904–1990) was a pioneer in behavioral psychology. Herodotus and Thucydides were early historians, and Ptolemy contributed to geography and astronomy. Smith, Friedman, and Galbraith made significant contributions to the field of economics. Jefferson, Marx, and Kissinger are figures in political science.